PENGU
DELHI

Born in Kasauli, Himachal Pradesh, in 1934, Ruskin Bond grew up in Jamnagar (Gujarat), Dehradun and Simla. His first novel, *Room on the Roof*, written when he was seventeen, received the John Llewellyn Rhys Memorial Prize in 1957. Since then he has written over three hundred short stories, essays and novellas (including *Vagrants in the Valley* and *A Flight of Pigeons*) and more than thirty books for children. He has also published two volumes of autobiography, *Scenes from a Writer's Life*, which describes his formative years growing up in Anglo-India, and *The Lamp is Lit*, a collection of essays and episodes from his journal. In 1992 he received the Sahitya Akademi award for English writing in India. He was awarded the Padma Shree in 1999.

Ruskin Bond lives with his adopted family in Mussoorie.

Books by the same author

FICTION

The Room on the Roof and Vagrants in the Valley
Night Train at Deoli & Other Stories
Time Stops at Shamli & Other Stories
Our Trees Still Grow in Dehra (Stories)
The Penguin Book of Indian Ghost Stories (Edited)
The Penguin Book of Indian Railway Stories (Edited)

NON-FICTION

Rain in the Mountains

CHILDREN'S BOOKS

Panther's Moon & Other Stories
The Room on the Roof

THE BEST OF RUSKIN BOND

DELHI IS NOT FAR

PENGUIN BOOKS

PENGUIN BOOKS

Published by the Penguin Group

Penguin Books India Pvt. Ltd, 7th Floor, Infinity Tower C, DLF Cyber City, Gurgaon 122 002, Haryana, India

Penguin Group (USA) Inc., 375 Hudson Street, New York, New York 10014, USA

Penguin Group (Canada), 90 Eglinton Avenue East, Suite 700, Toronto, Ontario, M4P 2Y3, Canada

Penguin Books Ltd, 80 Strand, London WC2R 0RL, England

Penguin Ireland, 25 St Stephen's Green, Dublin 2, Ireland (a division of Penguin Books Ltd)

Penguin Group (Australia), 707 Collins Street, Melbourne, Victoria 3008, Australia

Penguin Group (NZ), 67 Apollo Drive, Rosedale, Auckland 0632, New Zealand

Penguin Books (South Africa) (Pty) Ltd, Block D, Rosebank Office Park, 181 Jan Smuts Avenue, Parktown North, Johannesburg 2193, South Africa

Penguin Books Ltd, Registered Offices: 80 Strand, London WC2R 0RL, England

First published by Penguin Books India 1994

Copyright © Ruskin Bond 1994

All rights reserved

40 39 38 37 36 35 34

ISBN 9780140246063

This is a work of fiction. Names, characters, places and incidents are either the product of the author's imagination or are used fictitiously, and any resemblance to any actual person, living or dead, events or locales is entirely coincidental.

Typeset in Palatino by ADDS NOIDA, New Delhi
Printed at Repro India Ltd, Navi Mumbai

A PENGUIN RANDOM HOUSE COMPANY

For Siddharth—
Good luck, little one

ACKNOWLEDGEMENTS

While every effort has been made to acknowledge the publications in which the stories and essays included in this collection first appeared, in the event of any inadvertent omission, the publishers should be notified and formal acknowledgements will be included in all future editions of this book.

'My First Love' first appeared in *Sun*, 1994; 'Tribute to a Dead Friend' first appeared in *Orient/West* (Tokyo), 1963; 'The Trouble with Jinns' first appeared in *Sun*, 1994; 'Life At My Own Pace' first appeared in *The Heritage*, 1986; 'The Old Gramophone' first appeared as 'The Sound of Boyhood Days' in *Miscellany*, 1993; 'Adventures of a Book Lover' first appeared in *The Statesman* and *Books for Keeps* (UK); 'A Golden Voice Remembered' first appeared in *Span*, 1991; 'At Home in India' first appeared in *Miscellany*, 1993; 'Getting the Juices Flowing' first appeared in *The Sunday Observer*, 1981; 'Home is Under the Big Top' first appeared in *The Christian Science Monitor*, 1993; 'Adventures in a Banyan Tree' first appeared in *Lokmat Times*, 1994; 'From My Notebook' first appeared in *Writers Workshop Miscellany* (*Twenty Seven*); 'Beautiful Mandakini' first appeared in *The Pioneer*, 1991; 'Flowers on the Ganga' first appeared in *Sunday World*, 1971; 'Footloose in Agra' first appeared in *India Perspectives*, 1993.

CONTENTS

INTRODUCTION

And when all the wars are done, a butterfly will still be
beautiful.

*

And here I am again, in my little room overlooking the winding
road to Tehri, writing another Introduction.

No one has ever offered to write an Introduction for any of
my books, and so, perforce, I must do my own.

Back in the 1950's, when I wrote my first novel, unknown
authors went around trying to get their more famous counterparts
to write introductions for their books. Ever ready to oblige were
men of the stature of Graham Greene, George Orwell, E. M.
Forster and V. S. Pritchett. But I was far too shy to approach
any or the 'greats'. Moreover, I thought I was quite capable
of standing up without any support. And although at times I
have tottered, or come down with a loud thump, I think I have
managed to maintain my independence, both as a writer and as
an individual. Like the Jolly Miller of Dee, I care for nobody, no,
not I—and nobody cares for me! I refer, of course, to introducers,
celebrities, and the purveyors of literary criticism. A lot of other
people have cared for me. Indeed, the stories and selected
writings in this volume are testimonies to the many loving and
caring people I have known over the years.

*

With the help of Anubha Doyle of Penguin India, I have made a
fairly representative selection of my best writing, excluding my
work for children which is well represented elsewhere. I have not

made any selections from my non-fiction work, *Rain in the Mountains* (Viking, 1994), as this was published only recently.

The selection includes many of my early stories. Some are old favourites. Others (like the stories set in London) would be unfamiliar to most of my readers. I haven't written much about the years I spent in London (in the 1950's) but I hope to rectify this omission before long. The essays are fairly recent. I have always enjoyed writing essays. An essay is built around a particular mood in the mind of the writer. 'Give the mood, and the essay, from the first sentence to the last, grows around it as the cocoon grows around the silkworm.' (Alexander Smith, 1863)

What is the difference between an essay and a short story? It depends, I suppose, upon whose personality comes through more strongly, the author's or the characters he describes. If it is the author's, then it is really an essay. If it is the characters, then it is a story. Or is that too much of a simplification? In my own case, I have often found my stories becoming essays and vice-versa! One merges into the other. To communicate and be readable is, in the last resort, a matter of style.

People often ask me why my style is so simple. It is, in fact, deceptively simple, for no two sentences are really alike. It is clarity that I am striving to attain, not simplicity.

'When you talk you sound quite complicated,' said a friend. And I had to explain that I've spent forty years trying to simplify my style and clarify my thoughts!

Of course some people *want* literature to be difficult. And there are writers who like to make their readers toil and sweat. They hope to be taken more seriously that way. I have always tried to achieve a prose that is easy and conversational. And those who think this is simple should try it for themselves.

*

Also included here, on the suggestion of my publisher, is a complete short novel, *Delhi Is Not Far*, which is seeing the light of day for the first time.

In 1960, when I wrote it, there were no takers for short novels. Indian publishers would not touch fiction; and a novel had to be fairly long and substantial (or sensational) to find a publisher in Britain or America. *Delhi* was very low key. Another factor that went against it was the bisexual nature of its central character. After several rejections, the typescript went into a packing-case full of old papers and files and was forgotten for many years. Last winter, when I was emptying the box of its mildewed contents, I found the typescript and was about to toss it into the fire when my eye fell on the name of one of the characters for whom I'd had a particular affection. I'll keep it for old time's sake, I said to myself. And browsing through its yellowed pages again, I decided that it had improved a bit with age. When I showed the novel to David Davidar, he suggested that I include it in this collection. So here it is, along with extracts from some of my other novels (*The Room on the Roof, Vagrants in the Valley, A Flight of Pigeons*), the opening chapters of one that has yet to be written (*Rosebud*), and some of my verse, including the long autobiographical poem, *A Song For Lost Friends*.

*

When I made the notes for this Introduction (I am still old-fashioned enough to make notes), it was just another misty September morning, the hillsides lush with monsoon foliage. By evening Mussoorie was under curfew.

Today, as I type this out, it is the fifth day of curfew, and the town has yet to recover from the tragedy that overtook it last week, on September 2, Mussoorie's Black Friday. Six citizens were shot dead and a police officer was lynched by a section of the crowd. For weeks the agitation had been allowed to continue unchecked. When the crackdown came, it was devastating.

Confrontations between demonstrators and the authorities are fairly commonplace throughout the country, the causes varying from one region to another. But it was the first time the hill-station had experienced this sort of thing. The middle of a fashionable Mall is the last place you'd expect to find the dead, the dying and the wounded. The children's park wore the look of a battlefield, and the fountain, dry for months, was splashed with blood.

A curfew was the natural consequence, but no one expected it to last quite so long. On Sunday, the Jaunpuris—hill people from the outlying villages, largely unconcerned with politics and urban affairs—could not hold their annual Janmashtami fair, during which they take the image of Krishna in procession through the town. God Krishna could not bless Mussoorie this year. Perhaps he did not want to. The previous week, on Krishna's birthday, when it always rains heavily, there was no rain at all—a bad omen.

As for this hill-station, it can never be the same again. It had been going downhill for some time—a very shabby 'queen of the hills', *sans* character, *sans* charm—and now, finally, she has lost all her pretensions to royalty.

But there are compensations, even during a curfew. Confined to the house, we must finally spend more time with our families, our children; try to reassure them that the world is not such a bad place after all. Forage for food and make do with less of everything. Be friendlier with previously unsympathetic neighbours, because for once we are sharing the same hardships, the same uncertainty.

Since I live outside the main bazaar and the hillside is just above me, I can scramble up the slopes and discover anew the rich September flora.

The wild ginger is in flower. So is agrimony, lady's lace, wild geranium. The ferns are turning yellow. The fruit of the snake lily has turned red, signifying an end to the rains. A thrush whistles cheerfully on the branch of a dead walnut tree.

Yes, and when all the wars are done, a butterfly will still be beautiful.

Ruskin Bond
7 September 1994

LOVE AND FRIENDSHIP

SHORT STORIES

THE EYES HAVE IT

I had the train compartment to myself up to Rohana, then a girl got in. The couple who saw her off were probably her parents; they seemed very anxious about her comfort, and the woman gave the girl detailed instructions as to where to keep her things, when not to lean out of windows, and how to avoid speaking to strangers.

They called their goodbyes and the train pulled out of the station. As I was totally blind at the time, my eyes sensitive only to light and darkness, I was unable to tell what the girl looked like; but I knew she wore slippers from the way they slapped against her heels.

It would take me some time to discover something about her looks, and perhaps I never would. But I liked the sound of her voice, and even the sound of her slippers.

'Are you going all the way to Dehra?' I asked.

I must have been sitting in a dark corner, because my voice startled her. She gave a little exclamation and said, 'I didn't know anyone else was here.'

Well, it often happens that people with good eyesight fail to see what is right in front of them. They have too much to take in, I suppose. Whereas people who cannot see (or see very little) have to take in only the essentials, whatever registers most tellingly on their remaining senses.

'I didn't see you either,' I said. 'But I heard you come in.'

I wondered if I would be able to prevent her from discovering that I was blind. Provided I keep to my seat, I thought, it shouldn't be too difficult.

The girl said, 'I'm getting off at Saharanpur. My aunt is meeting me there.'

'Then I had better not get too familiar,' I replied. 'Aunts are

3

usually formidable creatures.'

'Where are you going?' she asked.

'To Dehra, and then to Mussoorie.'

'Oh, how lucky you are. I wish I were going to Mussoorie. I love the hills. Especially in October.'

'Yes, this is the best time,' I said, calling on my memories. 'The hills are covered with wild dahlias, the sun is delicious, and at night you can sit in front of a log fire and drink a little brandy. Most of the tourists have gone, and the roads are quiet and almost deserted. Yes, October is the best time.'

She was silent. I wondered if my words had touched her, or whether she thought me a romantic fool. Then I made a mistake.

'What is it like outside?' I asked.

She seemed to find nothing strange in the question. Had she noticed already that I could not see? But her next question removed my doubts.

'Why don't you look out of the window?' she asked.

I moved easily along the berth and felt for the window ledge. The window was open, and I faced it, making a pretence of studying the landscape. I heard the panting of the engine, the rumble of the wheels, and, in my mind's eye, I could see telegraph posts flashing by.

'Have you noticed,' I ventured, 'that the trees seem to be moving while we seem to be standing still?'

'That always happens,' she said. 'Do you see any animals?'

'No,' I answered quite confidently. I knew that there were hardly any animals left in the forests near Dehra.

I turned from the window and faced the girl, and for a while we sat in silence.

'You have an interesting face,' I remarked. I was becoming quite daring, but it was a safe remark. Few girls can resist flattery. She laughed pleasantly—a clear, ringing laugh.

'It's nice to be told I have an interesting face. I'm tired of people telling me I have a pretty face.'

Oh, so you do have a pretty face, thought I: and aloud I said: 'Well, an interesting face can also be pretty.'

'You are a very gallant young man,' she said, 'but why are you so serious?'

I thought, then, I would try to laugh for her, but the thought of laughter only made me feel troubled and lonely.

'We'll soon be at your station,' I said.

'Thank goodness it's a short journey. I can't bear to sit in a train for more than two-or-three hours.'

Yet, I was prepared to sit there for almost any length of time, just to listen to her talking. Her voice had the sparkle of a mountain stream. As soon as she left the train, she would forget our brief encounter; but it would stay with me for the rest of the journey, and for some time after.

The engine's whistle shrieked, the carriage wheels changed their sound and rhythm, the girl got up and began to collect her things. I wondered if she wore her hair in a bun, or if it was plaited; perhaps it was hanging loose over her shoulders, or was it cut very short?

The train drew slowly into the station. Outside, there was the shouting of porters and vendors and a high-pitched female voice near the carriage door; that voice must have belonged to the girl's aunt.

'Goodbye,' the girl said.

She was standing very close to me, so close that the perfume from her hair was tantalizing. I wanted to raise my hand and touch her hair but she moved away. Only the scent of perfume still lingered where she had stood.

There was some confusion in the doorway. A man, getting into the compartment, stammered an apology. Then the door banged, and the world was shut out again. I returned to my berth. The guard blew his whistle and we moved off. Once again, I had a game to play and a new fellow-traveller.

The train gathered speed, the wheels took up their song, the carriage groaned and shook. I found the window and sat in front of it, staring into the daylight that was darkness for me.

So many things were happening outside the window: it could be a fascinating game, guessing what went on out there.

The man who had entered the compartment broke into my reverie.

'You must be disappointed,' he said. 'I'm not nearly as attractive a travelling companion as the one who just left.'

'She was an interesting girl,' I said. 'Can you tell me—did she keep her hair long or short?'

'I don't remember,' he said, sounding puzzled. 'It was her eyes I noticed, not her hair. She had beautiful eyes—but they were of no use to her. She was completely blind. Didn't you notice?'

THE THIEF

I was still a thief when I met Arun, and though I was only fifteen, I was an experienced and fairly successful hand.

Arun was watching the wrestlers when I approached him. He was about twenty, a tall, lean fellow, and he looked kind and simple enough for my purpose. I hadn't had much luck of late, and thought I might be able to get into this young person's confidence. He seemed quite fascinated by the wrestling. Two well-oiled men slid about in the soft mud, grunting and slapping their thighs. When I got Arun into conversation he didn't seem to realize I was a stranger.

'You look like a wrestler yourself,' I said.

'So do you,' he replied, which put me out of my stride for a moment, because at the time I was rather thin and bony and not very impressive physically.

'Yes,' I said. 'I wrestle sometimes.'

'What's your name?'

'Deepak,' I lied.

Deepak was about my fifth name. I had earlier called myself Ranbir, Sudhir, Trilok and Surinder.

After this preliminary exchange, Arun confined himself to comments on the match, and I didn't have much to say. After a while he walked away from the crowd of spectators. I followed him.

'Hello,' he said. 'Enjoying yourself?'

I gave him my most appealing smile. 'I want to work for you,' I said.

He didn't stop walking. 'And what makes you think I want someone to work for me?'

'Well,' I said, 'I've been wandering about all day, looking for the best person to work for. When I saw you, I knew that no one else had a chance.'

7

'You flatter me,' he said.

'That's all right.'

'But you can't work for me.'

'Why not?'

'Because I can't pay you.'

I thought that over for a minute. Perhaps I had misjudged my man.

'Can you feed me?' I asked.

'Can you cook?' he countered.

'I can cook,' I lied.

'If you can cook,' he said, 'I'll feed you.'

He took me to his room and told me I could sleep in the veranda. But I was nearly back on the street that night. The meal I cooked must have been pretty awful, because Arun gave it to the neighbour's cat and told me to be off. But I just hung around smiling in my most appealing way; and then he couldn't help laughing. He sat down on the bed and laughed for a full five minutes, and later patted me on the head and said, never mind, he'd teach me to cook in the morning.

Not only did he teach me to cook, but he taught me to write my name and his, and said he would soon teach me to write whole sentences, and add money on paper when you didn't have any in your pocket!

It was quite pleasant working for Arun. I made the tea in the morning and later went out shopping. I would take my time buying the day's supplies and made a profit of about twenty-five paise a day. I would tell Arun that rice was fifty-six paise a pound (it generally was), but I would get it at fifty paise a pound. I think he knew I made a little this way, but he didn't mind, he wasn't giving me a regular wage.

I was really grateful to Arun for teaching me to write. I knew that once I could write like an educated man there would be no limit to what I could achieve. It might even be an incentive to be honest.

Arun made money by fits and starts. He would be borrowing one week, lending the next. He would keep worrying about his next cheque but, as soon as it arrived, he would go out and celebrate lavishly.

One evening he came home with a wad of notes, and at night I saw him tuck the bundles under his mattress, at the head of the bed.

I had been working for Arun for nearly a fortnight and, apart from the shopping, hadn't done much to exploit him. I had every opportunity for doing so. I had a key to the front door, which meant I had access to the room whenever Arun was out. He was the most trusting person I had ever met. And that was why I couldn't make up my mind to rob him.

It's easy to rob a greedy man, because he deserves to be robbed; it's easy to rob a rich man, because he can afford to be robbed; but it's difficult to rob a poor man, even one who really doesn't care if he's robbed. A rich man or a greedy man or a careful man wouldn't keep his money under a pillow or mattress, he'd lock it up in a safe place. Arun had put his money where it would be child's play for me to remove it without his knowledge.

It's time I did some real work, I told myself; I'm getting out of practice. . . . If I don't take the money, he'll only waste it on his friends. . . . He doesn't even pay me. . . .

Arun was asleep. Moonlight came in from the veranda and fell across the bed. I sat up on the floor, my blanket wrapped round me, considering the situation. There was quite a lot of money in that wad, and if I took it I would have to leave town—I might make the 10.30 express to Amritsar. . . .

Slipping out of the blanket, I crept on all fours through the door and up to the bed, and peeped at Arun. He was sleeping peacefully with a soft and easy breathing. His face was clear and unlined; even I had more markings on my face, though mine were mostly scars.

My hand took on an identity of its own as it slid around under the mattress, the fingers searching for the notes. They found them, and I drew them out without a crackle.

Arun sighed in his sleep and turned on his side, towards me. My free hand was resting on the bed, and his hair touched my fingers.

I was frightened when his hair touched my fingers, and crawled quickly and quietly out of the room.

When I was in the street, I began to run. I ran down the bazaar road to the station. The shops were all closed, but a few lights came from upper windows. I had the notes at my waist, held there by the string of my pyjamas. I felt I had to stop and count the notes though I knew it might make me late for the train. It was already 10.20 by the clock tower. I slowed down to a walk, and my fingers flicked through the notes. There were about a hundred rupees in fives. A good haul. I could live like a prince for a month or two.

When I reached the station I did not stop at the ticket-office (I had never bought a ticket in my life) but dashed straight onto the platform. The Amritsar Express was just moving out. It was moving slowly enough for me to be able to jump on the footboard of one of the carriages, but I hesitated for some urgent, unexplainable reason.

I hesitated long enough for the train to leave without me.

When it had gone, and the noise and busy confusion of the platform had subsided, I found myself standing alone on the deserted platform. The knowledge that I had a hundred stolen rupees in my pyjamas only increased my feeling of isolation and loneliness. I had no idea where to spend the night; I had never kept any friends, because sometimes friends can be one's undoing; I didn't want to make myself conspicuous by staying at a hotel. And the only person I knew really well in town was the person I had robbed!

Leaving the station, I walked slowly through the bazaar keeping to dark, deserted alleys. I kept thinking of Arun. He would still be asleep, blissfully unaware of his loss.

I have made a study of men's faces when they have lost something of material value. The greedy man shows panic, the rich man shows anger, the poor man shows fear; but I knew that neither panic nor anger nor fear would show on Arun's face when he discovered the theft; only a terrible sadness not for the loss of the money but for my having betrayed his trust.

I found myself on the maidan and sat down on a bench with my feet tucked up under my haunches. The night was a little cold, and I regretted not having brought Arun's blanket along. A light drizzle added to my discomfort. Soon it was raining heavily. My shirt and pyjamas stuck to my skin and a cold wind brought the rain whipping across my face. I told myself that sleeping on a bench was something I should have been used to by now, but the veranda had softened me.

I walked back to the bazaar and sat down on the step of a closed shop. A few vagrants lay beside me, rolled up tight in thin blankets. The clock showed midnight, I felt for the notes; they were still with me, but had lost their crispness and were damp with rainwater.

Arun's money. In the morning he would probably have given me a rupee to go to the pictures but now I had it all. No more cooking his meals, running to the bazaar, or learning to write whole sentences. Whole sentences. . . .

They were something I had forgotten in the excitement of a hundred rupees. Whole sentences, I knew, could one day bring me more than a hundred rupees. It was a simple matter to steal (and sometimes just as simple to be caught) but to be a really big man, a wise and successful man, that was something. I should go back to Arun, I told myself, if only to learn how to write.

Perhaps it was also concern for Arun that drew me back; a sense of sympathy is one of my weaknesses, and through hesitation over a theft I had often been caught. A successful thief must be pitiless. I was fond of Arun. My affection for him, my sense of sympathy, but most of all my desire to write whole sentences, drew me back to the room.

I hurried back to the room extremely nervous, for it is easier to steal something than to return it undetected. If I was caught beside the bed now, with the money in my hand, or with my hand under the mattress there could be only one explanation: that I was actually stealing. If Arun woke up, I would be lost.

I opened the door clumsily, then stood in the doorway in clouded moonlight. Gradually my eyes became accustomed to the darkness of the room. Arun was still asleep. I went on all fours again and crept noiselessly to the head of the bed. My hand came up with the notes. I felt his breath on my fingers. I was fascinated by his tranquil features and easy breathing and remained motionless for a minute. Then my hand explored the mattress, found the edge, slipped under it with the notes.

I awoke late next morning to find that Arun had already made the tea. I found it difficult to face him in the harsh light of day. His hand was stretched out towards me. There was a five-rupee note between his fingers. My heart sank.

'I made some money yesterday,' he said. 'Now you'll get paid regularly.' My spirit rose as rapidly as it had fallen. I congratulated myself on having returned the money.

But when I took the note, I realized that he knew everything. The note was still wet from last night's rain.

'Today I'll teach you to write a little more than your name,' he said.

He knew; but neither his lips nor his eyes said anything about their knowing.

I smiled at Arun in my most appealing way; and the smile came by itself, without my knowing it.

THE NIGHT TRAIN AT DEOLI

When I was at college I used to spend my summer vacations in Dehra, at my grandmother's place. I would leave the plains early in May and return late in July. Deoli was a small station about thirty miles from Dehra; it marked the beginning of the heavy jungles of the Indian Terai.

The train would reach Deoli at about five in the morning, when the station would be dimly lit with electric bulbs and oil lamps, and the jungle across the railway tracks would just be visible in the faint light of dawn. Deoli had only one platform, an office for the Stationmaster and a waiting room. The platform boasted a tea-stall, a fruit vendor, and a few stray dogs; not much else, because the train stopped there for only ten minutes before rushing on into the forests.

Why it stopped at Deoli, I don't know. Nothing ever happened there. Nobody got off the train and nobody got in. There were never any coolies on the platform. But the train would halt there a full ten minutes, and then a bell would sound, the guard would blow his whistle, and presently Deoli would be left behind and forgotten.

I used to wonder what happened in Deoli, behind the station walls. I always felt sorry for that lonely little platform, and for the place that nobody wanted to visit. I decided that one day I would get off the train at Deoli, and spend the day there, just to please the town.

I was eighteen, visiting my grandmother, and the night train stopped at Deoli. A girl came down the platform, selling baskets.

It was a cold morning and the girl had a shawl thrown across her shoulders. Her feet were bare and her clothes were old, but she was a young girl, walking gracefully and with dignity.

When she came to my window, she stopped. She saw that I was looking at her intently, but at first she pretended not to notice.

13

She had a pale skin, set off by shiny black hair, and dark, troubled eyes. And then those eyes, searching and eloquent, met mine.

She stood by my window for some time and neither of us said anything. But when she moved on, I found myself leaving my seat and going to the carriage door, and stood waiting on the platform, looking the other way. I walked across to the tea-stall. A kettle was boiling over on a small fire, but the owner of the stall was busy serving tea somewhere on the train. The girl followed me behind the stall.

'Do you want to buy a basket?' she asked. 'They are very strong, made of the finest cane. . . .'

'No,' I said, 'I don't want a basket.'

We stood looking at each other for what seemed a very long time, and she said, 'Are you sure you don't want a basket?'

'All right, give me one,' I said, and I took the one on top and gave her a rupee, hardly daring to touch her fingers.

As she was about to speak, the guard blew his whistle; she said something, but it was lost in the clanging of the bell and the hissing of the engine. I had to run back to my compartment. The carriage shuddered and jolted forward.

I watched her as the platform slipped away. She was alone on the platform and she did not move, but she was looking at me and smiling. I watched her until the signal-box came in the way, and then the jungle hid the station, but I could still see her standing there alone. . . .

I sat up awake for the rest of the journey. I could not rid my mind of the picture of the girl's face and her dark, smouldering eyes.

But when I reached Dehra the incident became blurred and distant, for there were other things to occupy my mind. It was only when I was making the return journey, two months later, that I remembered the girl.

I was looking out for her as the train drew into the station, and I felt an unexpected thrill when I saw her walking up the platform. I sprang off the footboard and waved to her.

When she saw me, she smiled. She was pleased that I

remembered her. I was pleased that she remembered me. We were both pleased, and it was almost like a meeting of old friends.

She did not go down the length of the train selling baskets, but came straight to the tea-stall; her dark eyes were suddenly filled with light. We said nothing for some time but we couldn't have been more eloquent.

I felt the impulse to put her on the train there and then, and take her away with me; I could not bear the thought of having to watch her recede into the distance of Deoli station. I took the baskets from her hand and put them down on the ground. She put out her hand for one of them, but I caught her hand and held it.

'I have to go to Delhi,' I said.

She nodded, 'I do not have to go anywhere.'

The guard blew his whistle for the train to leave and how I hated the guard for doing that.

'I will come again,' I said. 'Will you be here?'

She nodded again, and, as she nodded, the bell clanged and the train slid forward. I had to wrench my hand away from the girl and run for the moving train.

This time I did not forget her. She was with me for the remainder of the journey, and for long after. All that year she was a bright, living thing. And when the college term finished I packed in haste and left for Dehra earlier than usual. My grandmother would be pleased at my eagerness to see her.

I was nervous and anxious as the train drew into Deoli, because I was wondering what I should say to the girl and what I should do. I was determined that I wouldn't stand helplessly before her, hardly able to speak or do anything about my feelings.

The train came to Deoli, and I looked up and down the platform, but I could not see the girl anywhere.

I opened the door and stepped off the footboard. I was deeply disappointed, and overcome by a sense of foreboding. I felt I had to do something, and so I ran up to the Stationmaster and said, 'Do you know the girl who used to sell baskets here?'

'No, I don't,' said the Stationmaster. 'And you'd better get on the train if you don't want to be left behind.'

But I paced up and down the platform, and stared over the railings at the station yard; all I saw was a mango tree and a dusty road leading into the jungle. Where did the road go? The train was moving out of the station, and I had to run up the platform and jump for the door of my compartment. Then, as the train gathered speed and rushed through the forests, I sat brooding in front of the window.

What could I do about finding a girl I had seen only twice, who had hardly spoken to me, and about whom I knew nothing—absolutely nothing—but for whom I felt a tenderness and responsibility that I had never felt before?

My grandmother was not pleased with my visit after all, because I didn't stay at her place more than a couple of weeks. I felt restless and ill at ease. So I took the train back to the plains, meaning to ask further questions of the Stationmaster at Deoli.

But at Deoli there was a new Stationmaster. The previous man had been transferred to another post within the past week. The new man didn't know anything about the girl who sold baskets. I found the owner of the tea-stall, a small, shrivelled-up man, wearing greasy clothes, and asked him if he knew anything about the girl with the baskets.

'Yes, there was such a girl here, I remember quite well,' he said. 'But she has stopped coming now.'

'Why?' I asked. 'What happened to her?'

'How should I know?' said the man. 'She was nothing to me.'

And once again I had to run for the train.

As Deoli platform receded, I decided that one day I would have to break journey there, spend a day in the town, make enquiries, and find the girl who had stolen my heart with nothing but a look from her dark, impatient eyes.

With this thought I consoled myself throughout my last term in college. I went to Dehra again in the summer and when, in the early hours of the morning, the night train drew into Deoli station, I looked up and down the platform for signs of the girl, knowing I wouldn't find her but hoping just the same.

Somehow, I couldn't bring myself to break journey at Deoli

and spend a day there. (If it was all fiction or a film, I reflected, I would have got down and cleaned up the mystery and reached a suitable ending for the whole thing). I think I was afraid to do this. I was afraid of discovering what really happened to the girl. Perhaps she was no longer in Deoli, perhaps she was married, perhaps she had fallen ill. . . .

In the last few years I have passed through Deoli many times, and I always look out of the carriage window, half expecting to see the same unchanged face smiling up at me. I wonder what happens in Deoli, behind the station walls. But I will never break my journey there. It may spoil my game. I prefer to keep hoping and dreaming, and looking out of the window up and down that lonely platform, waiting for the girl with the baskets.

I never break my journey at Deoli, but I pass through as often as I can.

THE PHOTOGRAPH

I was ten years old. My grandmother sat on the string bed, under the mango tree. It was late summer and there were sunflowers in the garden and a warm wind in the trees. My grandmother was knitting a woollen scarf for the winter months. She was very old, dressed in a plain white sari; her eyes were not very strong now, but her fingers moved quickly with the needles, and the needles kept clicking all afternoon. Grandmother had white hair, but there were very few wrinkles on her skin.

I had come home after playing cricket on the maidan. I had taken my meal, and now I was rummaging in a box of old books and family heirlooms that had just that day been brought out of the attic by my mother. Nothing in the box interested me very much, except for a book with colourful pictures of birds and butterflies. I was going through the book, looking at the pictures, when I found a small photograph between the pages. It was a faded picture, a little yellow and foggy; it was a picture of a girl standing against a wall, and behind the wall there was nothing but sky; but from the other side a pair of hands reached up, as though someone was going to climb the wall. There were flowers growing near the girl, but I couldn't tell what they were; there was a creeper too, but it was just a creeper.

I ran out into the garden. 'Granny!' I shouted. 'Look at this picture! I found it in the box of old things. Whose picture is it?'

I jumped on the bed beside my grandmother, and she walloped me on the bottom and said, 'Now I've lost count of my stitches, and the next time you do that I'll make you finish the scarf yourself.'

Granny was always threatening to teach me how to knit, which I thought was a disgraceful thing for a boy to do; it was a good deterrent for keeping me out of mischief. Once I had torn the drawing room curtains, and Granny had put a needle and thread in

18

my hand and made me stitch the curtain together, even though I make long, two-inch stitches, which had to be taken out by my mother and done again.

She took the photograph from my hand, and we both stared at it for quite a long time. The girl had long, loose hair, and she wore a long dress that nearly covered her ankles, and sleeves that reached her wrists, and there were a lot of bangles on her hands; but, despite all this drapery, the girl appeared to be full of freedom and movement; she stood with her legs apart and her hands on her hips, and she had a wide, almost devilish smile on her face.

'Whose picture is it?' I asked.

'A little girl's, of course,' said Grandmother. 'Can't you tell?'

'Yes, but did you know the girl?'

'Yes, I knew her,' said Granny, 'but she was a very wicked girl and I shouldn't tell you about her. But I'll tell you about the photograph. It was taken in your grandfather's house, about sixty years ago and that's the garden wall, and over the wall there was a road going to town.'

'Whose hands are they,' I asked, 'coming up from the other side?'

Grandmother squinted and looked closely at the picture, and shook her head. 'It's the first time I've noticed,' she said. 'That must have been the sweeper boy's. Or maybe they were your grandfather's.'

'They don't look like grandfather's hands,' I said. 'His hands are all bony.'

'Yes, but this was sixty years ago.'

'Didn't he climb up the wall, after the photo?'

'No, nobody climbed up. At least, I don't remember.'

'And you remember well, Granny.'

'Yes, I remember.... I remember what is not in the photograph. It was a spring day, and there was a cool breeze blowing, nothing like this. Those flowers at the girl's feet, they were marigolds, and the bougainvillaea creeper, it was a mass of purple. You cannot see these colours in the photo, and even if you could, as nowadays, you wouldn't be able to smell the flowers or feel the breeze.'

19

'And what about the girl?' I said. 'Tell me about the girl.'

'Well, she was a wicked girl,' said Granny. 'You don't know the trouble they had getting her into those fine clothes she's wearing.'

'I think they are terrible clothes,' I said.

'So did she. Most of the time, she hardly wore a thing. She used to go swimming in a muddy pool with a lot of ruffianly boys, and ride on the backs of buffaloes. No boy ever teased her, though, because she could kick and scratch and pull his hair out!'

'She looks like it too,' I said. 'You can tell by the way she's smiling. At any moment something's going to happen.'

'Something did happen,' said Granny. 'Her mother wouldn't let her take off the clothes afterwards, so she went swimming in them, and lay for half an hour in the mud.'

I laughed heartily and Grandmother laughed too.

'Who was the girl?' I said. 'You must tell me who she was.'

'No, that wouldn't do,' said Grandmother, but I pretended I didn't know. I knew, because Grandmother still smiled in the same way, even though she didn't have as many teeth.

'Come on, Granny,' I said, 'tell me, tell me.'

But Grandmother shook her head and carried on with the knitting; and I held the photograph in my hand looking from it to my grandmother and back again, trying to find points in common between the old lady and the little pig-tailed girl. A lemon-coloured butterfly settled on the end of Grandmother's knitting needle, and stayed there while the needles clicked away. I made a grab at the butterfly, and it flew off in a dipping flight and settled on a sunflower.

'I wonder whose hands they were,' whispered Grandmother to herself, with her head bowed, and her needles clicking away in the soft warm silence of that summer afternoon.

MY FIRST LOVE

A yah, my childhood governess, was my first love. She was thirty and I was six. She was a tall, broad-limbed woman, and in my view extremely handsome. The west-coast fishing community to which she belonged, and the Arab and African blood she had inherited, were partly responsible for her magnificent build and colourful personality. Occasionally when one of my parents' guests called her ugly without really taking a proper look at her, I would exclaim, 'No she is beautiful!' The vehemence of my reply would disconcert the guests and embarrass my parents.

We lived in a small Indian State on the Kathiawar coast, where my father had a job as guardian-tutor for the Maharaja's children. He conducted a small school in a corner of the palace, and was fully occupied most of the day. My mother would frequently be visiting other Anglo-Indian families. And I, being considered too much of a menace to be taken to other people's houses, was left in the charge of Ayah.

Most children who saw Ayah drew away from her in fright. Her size, her wrestler's arms, her broad quivering hips, were at first disconcerting to a child. She had thick, crinkly hair and teeth stained red with the juice of innumerable paan-leaves. Her hands were rough and heavy, as I knew from the number of times she had brought them down on my bottom. When she was angry, her face resembled a menacing thundercloud; but when she smiled with pleasure it was as though the sun had just emerged, lighting up her features with a great dazzle. Ayah frequently beat me, but soon afterwards she would be overcome by remorse, and then she would take me in her strong arms and plant heavy wet kisses on my eyes and cheeks and mouth. She was in love with my soft white skin, and often made believe that I was her own child, pressing my face to her

21

great breasts, bathing and dressing me with infinite tenderness, and defending me against everyone, including my parents.

Sometimes, when my parents were out, I would insist that she bathe with me. We would wallow together in the long marble tub; I, small, pink and podgy; and Ayah, like a benevolent hippopotamus, causing the bath-tub to overflow. She scrubbed and soaped me, while I relaxed and enjoyed the sensation of her rough hands moving over my back and tummy. And then, before she could heave herself out of the tub, I would leap from the water and charge out of the bathroom without my clothes. Ayah would come flapping after me, a sheet tied hurriedly about her waist; and we would race through the rooms until finally she caught up with me, gave me several resounding slaps, watched me burst into tears, and then break down herself and take me to her comfortable bosom.

Ayah taught me many things. One of these was the eating of paan—a betel leaf containing lime, finely-cut areca nut, and some cardamom.

It was the scarlet tinge in the mouth which came from eating paan that appealed most to me. I did not care much for the taste, which was bitter, but I was fascinated by the red juice which Ayah was able to spit so accurately about the garden. When my parents were out, she would share her paan with me, and we would sit in the kitchen and gossip with the cook. Before my parents came home, Ayah would make me rinse my mouth with warm water, and with her rough fingers she would scrub my teeth clean.

A number of snakes lived in the old walls surrounding both our bungalow and the palace grounds. They seldom ventured into the house, but when they did, Ayah was against killing them. She always maintained that they would not harm us provided we left them alone.

She once told me the story of a snake who married a poor but beautiful girl. At first the girl very naturally did not wish to marry the snake, whom she had met in a forest. But the snake insisted, saying, 'I will kill you if you refuse,' which of course left her with no alternative. Then the snake led his bride away, and took her to a great treasure. 'I was a prince in my former life,' explained the snake, 'and this is my treasure. Now it is all yours.' And then he very gallantly disappeared.

'Which goes to show that even snakes are good at heart,' said Ayah.

Sometimes she would leave a saucer of milk beneath an old peepul tree, and once I saw a young cobra glide up to the saucer and finish the milk. When I told Ayah about this, she was a little perturbed, and said she had actually left the milk out for the spirits who lived in the peepul tree.

'I haven't seen any spirits in the tree,' I told her.

'And I hope you never will, my son,' said Ayah. 'But they are there all the same. If you happen to be standing beneath the tree after dark, and feel like yawning don't forget to snap your fingers in front of your mouth, otherwise the spirit will jump down your throat.'

'And what if it does?' I asked.

For a moment Ayah was at a loss for an answer; then she brightened and said, 'It will probably upset your tummy.'

The peepul was a cool tree to sit beneath. Its heart-shaped leaves spun round in the faintest breeze, sending currents of cool air down from its branches. The leaf itself was likened by Ayah to the perfect male torso—a broad chest tapering down to a very slim waist—and she told me I ought to be built that way when I grew up.

One day we strayed into the ruined palace, which had turrets and towers and winding passageways. And there we found a room with many small windows, each window-pane set with coloured glass. I was often to spend hours in this room, gazing out at the palace and lake and gardens through the coloured window-panes. When the sun came through the windows, the entire room was suffused with beams of red and gold and green and purple light, playing on the walls and on my face and clothes.

The State had a busy little port, and Arab dhows sailed to and fro across the Gulf of Kutch. My father was friendly with the captain of a steamer making trips to Aden and back. The captain was a jovial, whisky-drinking Scotsman, who stuffed me with chocolates and suggested that I join the crew of his ship. The idea appealed to me, and I made elaborate plans for the voyage, only to discover one day when I went down to the docks that the ship had sailed away forever.

Ayah was more dependable. She hated seeing me disappointed. When I told her about the treachery of Captain MacWhir she consoled me with the promise of a ride in a tonga—a two-wheeled horse-drawn buggy. Apparently she had a friend who plied a tonga in the bazaar.

He came the next day, a young man sporting an orange waistcoat and a magnificent moustache. His name was Bansi Lal. Ayah put me on the front seat beside him, while she sat at the back to try and maintain some sort of equilibrium. We went out of the gate at a brisk trot, but as soon as we were on the open road circling the lake, Bansi Lal lashed his horse into a gallop, and we went tearing along the road at a furious and exhilarating pace. Ayah shouted to her friend to slow down, and I shouted to him to go faster. He grinned at both of us while a devil danced in his eyes, and he cracked his whip and called endearments to both Ayah and his horse.

When finally we reached open country, he slowed down and brought the tonga to rest in a mango-grove. Ayah struggled out and, after berating Bansi Lal, sank down on the grass while I went off to explore the mango-grove. The fruit on the trees was as yet unripe, but the crows and mynahs had already begun to feast on the mangoes. I wandered about for some time, returning to the clearing by a different route to find Ayah and Bansi Lal embracing each other. Ayah had her back to me, but the tonga-driver had a rapt, rather funny expression on his face. This changed to a look of confusion when he saw me watching them with undisguised curiosity, and he got up hurriedly, fumbling with his pyjama-strings. I threw myself gaily upon Ayah and asked her what she had been doing; but for once she gave me an evasive reply. I don't think the incident had any immediate effect on my innocence, but as I grew older I found myself looking back on it with a certain amount of awe.

Both Ayah and I—for different reasons, as it turned out—

24

began looking forward to our weekly tonga rides. Bansi Lal took us to some very lonely places—scrub-jungle or ruins or abandoned brick-kilns—and he and Ayah were extraordinarily tolerant of where I wandered during these excursions.

But the tonga-rides really meant the end of my affair with Ayah. One day she informed my parents that she intended marrying Bansi Lal and going away with him. While my parents considered this a perfectly natural desire on Ayah's part, I looked upon it as an act of base treachery. For several days I went about the house in a rebellious and sulky mood, refusing to speak to Ayah no matter how much she coaxed and petted me.

On Ayah's last day with us, Bansi Lal arrived in his tonga to take her away. He had painted the woodwork, scrubbed his horse down, and changed his orange waistcoat for a green one. He gave me a cheerful salaam, but I scowled darkly at him from the veranda steps, and he looked guiltily away.

Ayah tossed her bedding and few belongings into the tonga, and then came to say goodbye to me. But I had hidden myself in the jasmine bushes, and though she called and looked for me, I would not emerge. Sadly, she climbed into the tonga, weighing it down at the back. Bansi Lal cracked his whip, shouted to his horse, and the tonga went rattling away down the gravel path. Ayah still looked to left and right, hoping to see me; and at last, unable to bear my misery any longer, I came out from the bushes and ran after the tonga, waving to her. Bansi reined in his horse, and Ayah got down and gathered me up in her great arms; and when the tonga finally took her away, there was a dazzling smile on her sweet and gentle face—the face of the lover whom I was never to see again. . . .

A GUARDIAN ANGEL

I can still picture the little Dilaram bazaar as I first saw it twenty years ago. Hanging on the hem of Aunt Mariam's sari, I had followed her along the sunlit length of the dusty road and up the wooden staircase to her rooms above the barber's shop.

There were a number of children playing on the road, and they all stared at me. They must have wondered what my dark, black-haired aunt was doing with a strange child who was fairer than most. She did not bother to explain my presence, and it was several weeks before the bazaar people learned something of my origins.

Aunt Mariam, my mother's younger sister, was at that time about thirty. She came from a family of Christian converts, originally Muslims of Rampur. My mother had married an Englishman, who died while I was still a baby; she herself was not a strong woman, and fought a losing battle with tuberculosis while bringing me up.

My sixth birthday was approaching when she died, in the middle of the night, without my being aware of it, and I woke up to experience, for a day, all the terrors of abandonment.

But that same evening Aunt Mariam arrived. Her warmth, worldliness and carefree chatter gave me the reassurance I needed so badly. She slept beside me that night and next morning, after the funeral, took me with her to her rooms in the bazaar. This small flat was to be my home for the next year-and-a-half.

Before my mother's death I had seen very little of my aunt. From the remarks I occasionally overheard, it appeared that Aunt Mariam had, in some indefinable way, disgraced the family. My mother was cold towards her, and I could not help wondering why because a more friendly and cheerful extrovert than Aunt Mariam could hardly be encountered.

There were other relatives, but they did not come to my rescue with the same readiness. It was only later, when the financial issues became clearer, that innumerable uncles and aunts appeared on the scene.

The age of six is the beginning of an interesting period in the life of a boy, and the months I spent with Aunt Mariam are not difficult to recall. She was a joyous, bubbling creature—a force of nature rather than a woman—and every time I think of her I am tempted to put down on paper some aspect of her conversation, or her gestures, or her magnificent physique.

She was a strong woman, taller than most men in the bazaar, but this did not detract from her charms. Her voice was warm and deep, her face was a happy one, broad and unlined, and her teeth gleamed white in the dark brilliance of her complexion.

She had large soft breasts, long arms and broad thighs. She was majestic, and at the same time she was graceful. Above all, she was warm and full of understanding, and it was this tenderness of hers that overcame resentment and jealousy in other women.

She called me Ladla, her darling, and told me she had always wanted to look after me. She had never married. I did not, at that age, ponder the reasons for her single state. At six, I took all things for granted and accepted Mariam for what she was—my benefactress and guardian angel.

Her rooms were untidy compared with the neatness of my mother's house. Mariam revelled in untidiness. I soon grew accustomed to the topsy-turviness of her rooms and found them comfortable. Beds (hers a very large and soft one) were usually left unmade, while clothes lay draped over chairs and tables.

A large water-colour hung on a wall, but Mariam's bodice and knickers were usually suspended from it, and I cannot recall the subject of the painting. The dressing table was a fascinating place, crowded with all kinds of lotions, mascaras, paints, oils and ointments.

Mariam would spend much time sitting in front of the mirror running a comb through her long black hair, or preferably having young Mulia, a servant girl, comb it for her. Though a Christian, my aunt retained several Muslim superstitions, and never went into the open with her hair falling loose.

Once Mulia came into the rooms with her own hair open. 'You ought not to leave your hair open. Better knot it,' said Aunt Mariam.

'But I have not yet oiled it, Aunty,' replied Mulia. 'How can I put it up?'

'You are too young to understand. There are jinns—aerial spirits—who are easily attracted by long hair and pretty black eyes like yours.'

'Do jinns visit human beings, Aunty?'

'Learned people say so. Though I have never seen a jinn myself, I have seen the effect they can have on one.'

'Oh, do tell about them,' said Mulia.

'Well, there was once a lovely girl like you, who had a wealth of black hair,' said Mariam. 'Quite unaccountably she fell ill, and in spite of every attention and the best medicines, she kept getting worse. She grew as thin as a whipping post, her beauty decayed, and all that remained of it till her dying day was her wonderful head of hair.'

It did not take me long to make friends in the Dilaram bazaar. At first I was an object of curiosity, and when I came down to play in the street both women and children would examine me as though I was a strange marine creature.

'How fair he is,' observed Mulia.

'And how black his aunt,' commented the washerman's wife, whose face was riddled with the marks of smallpox.

'His skin is very smooth,' pointed out Mulia, who took considerable pride in having been the first to see me at close quarters. She pinched my cheeks with obvious pleasure.

'His hair and eyes are black,' remarked Mulia's ageing mother.

'Is it true that his father was an Englishman?'

'Mariam-bi says so,' said Mulia. 'She never lies.'

'True,' said the washerman's wife. 'Whatever her faults—and there are many—she has never been known to lie.'

My aunt's other 'faults' were a deep mystery to me; nor did

anyone try to enlighten me about them.

Some nights she had me sleep with her, other nights (I often wondered why) she gave me a bed in an adjoining room, although I much preferred remaining with her—especially since, on cold January nights, she provided me with considerable warmth.

I would curl up into a ball just below her soft tummy. On the other side, behind her knees, slept Leila, an enchanting Siamese cat given to her by an American businessman whose house she would sometimes visit. Every night, before I fell asleep, Mariam would kiss me, very softly, on my closed eyelids. I never fell asleep until I had received this phantom kiss.

At first I resented the nocturnal visitors that Aunt Mariam frequently received: their arrival meant that I had to sleep in the spare room with Leila. But when I found that these people were impermanent creatures, mere ships that passed in the night, I learned to put up with them.

I seldom saw those men, though occasionally I caught a glimpse of a beard or an expensive waistcoat or white pyjamas. They did not interest me very much, though I did have a vague idea that they provided Aunt Mariam with some sort of income, thus enabling her to look after me.

Once, when one particular visitor was very drunk, Mariam had to force him out of the flat. I glimpsed this episode through a crack in the door. The man was big, but no match for Aunt Mariam.

She thrust him out onto the landing, and then he lost his footing and went tumbling downstairs. No damage was done, and the man called on Mariam again a few days later, very sober and contrite, and was re-admitted to my aunt's favours.

Aunt Mariam must have begun to worry about the effect these comings and goings might have on me, because after a few months she began to make arrangements for sending me to a boarding-school in the hills.

I had not the slightest desire to go to school and raised many objections. We had long arguments in which she tried vainly to impress upon me the desirability of receiving an education.

'To make a living, my Ladla,' she said, 'you must have an education.

'But you have no education,' I said, 'and you have no difficulty in making a living!'

Mariam threw up her arms in mock despair. 'Ten years from now I will not be able to make such a living. Then who will support and help me? An illiterate young fellow, or an educated gentleman? When I am old, my son, when I am old

Finally, I succumbed to her arguments and agreed to go to a boarding-school. And when the time came for me to leave, both Aunt Mariam and I broke down and wept at the railway station.

I hung out of the window as the train moved away from the platform, and saw Mariam, her bosom heaving, being helped from the platform by Mulia and some of our neighbours.

My incarceration in a boarding-school was made more unbearable by the absence of any letters from Aunt Mariam. She could write little more than her name.

I was looking forward to my winter holidays and my return to Aunt Mariam and the Dilaram bazaar, but this was not to be. During my absence there had been some litigation over my custody, and my father's relatives claimed that Aunt Mariam was not a fit person to be a child's guardian.

And so when I left school, it was not to Aunt Mariam's place that I was sent, but to a strange family living in a railway colony near Moradabad. I remained with these relatives until I finished school, but that is a different story.

I did not see Aunt Mariam again. The Dilaram bazaar and my beautiful aunt and the Siamese cat all became part of the receding world of my childhood.

I would often think of Mariam, but as time passed she became more remote and inaccessible in my memory. It was not until many years later, when I was a young man, that I visited the Dilaram bazaar again. I knew from my foster parents that Aunt Mariam was dead. Her heart, it seemed, had always been weak.

I was anxious to see the Dilaram bazaar and its residents again, but my visit was a disappointment. The place had disappeared; or rather, it had been swallowed up by a growing city.

It was lost in the complex of a much larger market which had sprung up to serve a new government colony. The older people had died, and the young ones had gone to colleges or factories or offices in different towns. Aunt Mariam's rooms had been pulled down.

I found her grave in the little cemetery on the town's outskirts. One of her more devoted admirers had provided a handsome gravestone, surmounted by a sculptured angel. One of the wings had broken off, and the face was chipped, which gave the angel a slightly crooked smile.

But in spite of the broken wing and the smile, it was a very ordinary stone angel and could not hold a candle to my Aunt Mariam, the very special guardian angel of my childhood.

THE KITEMAKER

T here was but one tree in the street known as Gali Ram Nath—an ancient banyan that had grown through the cracks of an abandoned mosque—and little Ali's kite had caught in its branches. The boy, barefoot and clad only in a torn shirt, ran along the cobbled stones of the narrow street to where his grandfather sat nodding dreamily in the sunshine of their back courtyard.

'Grandfather,' shouted the boy. 'My kite has gone!'

The old man woke from his daydream with a start and, raising his head, displayed a beard that would have been white, had it not been dyed red with mehendi leaves.

'Did the twine break?' he asked. 'I know that kite twine is not what it used to be.'

'No, grandfather, the kite is stuck in the banyan tree.'

The old man chuckled. 'You have yet to learn how to fly a kite properly, my child. And I am too old to teach you, that's the pity of it. But you shall have another.'

He had just finished making a new kite from bamboo paper and thin silk, and it lay in the sun, firming up. It was a pale pink kite, with a small green tail. The old man handed it to Ali, and the boy raised himself on his toes and kissed his grandfather's hollowed-out cheek.

'I will not lose this one,' he said. 'This kite will fly like a bird.' And he turned on his heels and skipped out of the courtyard.

The old man remained dreaming in the sun. His kite shop was gone, the premises long since sold to a junk dealer; but he still made kites, for his own amusement and for the benefit of his grandson, Ali. Not many people bought kites these days. Adults disdained them, and children preferred to spend their money at the cinema. Moreover, there were not many open spaces left for the flying of

32

kites. The city had swallowed up the open grassland that had stretched from the old fort's walls to the river bank.

But the old man remembered a time when grown men flew kites, and great battles were fought, the kites swerving and swooping in the sky, tangling with each other until the string of one was severed. Then the defeated but liberated kite would float away into the blue unknown. There was a good deal of betting, and money frequently changed hands.

Kite-flying was then the sport of kings, and the old man remembered how the Nawab himself would come down to the riverside with his retinue to participate in this noble pastime. There was time, then, to spend an idle hour with a gay, dancing strip of paper. Now everyone hurried, in a heat of hope, and delicate things like kites and daydreams were trampled underfoot.

He, Mehmood the kitemaker, had in the prime of his life been well-known throughout the city. Some of his more elaborate kites once sold for as much as three or four rupees each.

At the request of the Nawab he had once made a very special kind of kite, unlike any that had been seen in the district. It consisted of a series of small, very light paper disks, trailing on a thin bamboo frame. To the end of each disk he fixed a sprig of grass, forming a balance on both sides.

The surface of the foremost disk was slightly convex, and a fantastic face was painted on it, having two eyes made of small mirrors. The disks, decreasing in size from head to tail, assumed an undulatory form, and gave the kite the appearance of a crawling serpent. It required great skill to raise this cumbersome device from the ground, and only Mehmood could manage it.

Everyone had heard of the 'Dragon Kite' that Mehmood had built, and word went round that it possessed supernatural powers. A large crowd assembled in the open to watch its first public launching in the presence of the Nawab.

At the first attempt it refused to leave the ground.

The disks made a plaintive, protesting sound, and the sun was trapped in the little mirrors, and made of the kite a living, complaining creature. And then the wind came from the right direction, and the Dragon Kite soared into the sky, wriggling its way higher and higher, with the sun still glinting in its devil-eyes. And when it went very high, it pulled fiercely on the twine, and Mehmood's young sons had to help him with the reel; but still the kite pulled, determined to be free, to break loose, to live a life of its own. And eventually it did so.

The twine snapped, the kite leaped away toward the sun, sailed on heavenward until it was lost to view. It was never found again, and Mehmood wondered afterwards if he made too vivid, too living a thing of the great kite. He did not make another like it, and instead he presented to the Nawab a musical kite, one that made a sound like a violin when it rose in the air.

Those were more leisurely, more spacious days. But the Nawab had died years ago, and his descendants were almost as poor as Mehmood himself. Kitemakers, like poets, once had their patrons; but no one knew Mehmood, simply because there were too many people in the Gali, and they could not be bothered with their neighbours.

When Mehmood was younger and had fallen sick, everyone in the neighbourhood had come to ask after his health; but now, when his days were drawing to a close, no one visited him. True, most of his old friends were dead and his sons had grown up: one was working in a local garage, the other had been in Pakistan at the time of Partition and had not been able to rejoin his relatives.

The children who had bought kites from him ten years ago were now grown men, struggling for a living; they did not have time for the old man and his memories. They had grown up in a swiftly changing and competitive world, and they looked at the old kitemaker and the banyan tree with the same indifference,

Both were taken for granted—permanent fixtures that were of no concern to the raucous, sweating mass of humanity that surrounded them. No longer did people gather under the banyan tree to discuss their problems and their plans: only in the summer months did a few seek shelter from the fierce sun.

But there was the boy, his grandson; it was good that Mehmood's son worked close by, for it gladdened the old man's heart to watch the small boy at play in the winter sunshine, growing under his eyes like a young and well-nourished sapling putting forth new leaves each day. There is a great affinity between trees and men. We grow at much the same pace, if we are not hurt or starved or cut down. In our youth we are resplendent creatures, and in our declining years we stoop a little, we remember, we stretch our brittle limbs in the sun, and then, with a sigh, we shed our last leaves.

Mehmood was like the banyan, his hands gnarled and twisted like the roots of the ancient tree. Ali was like the young mimosa planted at the end of the courtyard. In two years both he and the tree would acquire the strength and confidence of their early youth.

The voices in the street grew fainter, and Mehmood wondered if he was going to fall asleep and dream, as he so often did, of a kite so beautiful and powerful that it would resemble the great white bird of the Hindus, Garuda, God Vishnu's famous steed. He would like to make a wonderful new kite for little Ali. He had nothing else to leave the boy.

He heard Ali's voice in the distance, but did not realize that the boy was calling him. The voice seemed to come from very far away.

All was at the courtyard door, asking if his mother had as yet returned from the bazaar. When Mehmood did not answer, the boy came forward repeating his question. The sunlight was slanting across the old man's head, and a small white butterfly rested on his flowing beard. Mehmood was silent; and when Ali put his small brown hand on the old man's shoulder, he met with no response. The boy heard a faint sound, like the rubbing of marbles in his pocket.

Suddenly afraid, Ali turned and moved to the door, and then ran down the street shouting for his mother. The butterfly left the old man's beard and flew to the mimosa tree, and a sudden gust of wind caught the torn kite and lifted it in the air, carrying it far above the struggling city into the blind blue sky.

MY FATHER'S TREES IN DEHRA

Our trees still grow in Dehra. This is one part of the world where trees are a match for man. An old peepul may be cut down to make way for a new building, two peepul trees will sprout from the walls of the building. In Dehra the air is moist, the soil hospitable to seeds and probing roots. The valley of Dehra Dun lies between the first range of the Himalayas and the smaller but older Siwalik range. Dehra is an old town, but it was not in the reign of Rajput prince or Mughal king that it really grew and flourished; it acquired a certain size and importance with the coming of British and Anglo-Indian settlers. The English have an affinity with trees, and in the rolling hills of Dehra they discovered a retreat which, in spite of snakes and mosquitoes, reminded them, just a little bit, of England's green and pleasant land.

The mountains to the north are austere and inhospitable; the plains to the south are flat, dry and dusty. But Dehra is green. I look out of the train window at daybreak, to see the sal and shisham trees sweep by majestically, while trailing vines and great clumps of bamboo give the forest a darkness and density which add to its mystery. There are still a few tigers in these forests; only a few, and perhaps they will survive, to stalk the spotted deer and drink at forest pools.

I grew up in Dehra. My grandfather built a bungalow on the outskirts of the town, at the turn of the century. The house was sold a few years after independence. No one knows me now in Dehra, for it is over twenty years since I left the place, and my boyhood friends are scattered and lost; and although the India of Kim is no more, and the Grand Trunk Road is now a procession of trucks instead of a slow-moving caravan of horses and camels, India is still a country in which people are easily lost and quickly forgotten.

From the station I take either a taxi or a tonga. I can take either a taxi or a snappy little scooter-rickshaw (Dehra had neither, before 1950), but, because I am on an unashamedly sentimental pilgrimage, I take a tonga, drawn by a lean, listless pony, and driven by a tubercular old Muslim in a shabby green waistcoat. Only two or three tongas stand outside the station. There were always twenty or thirty here in the nineteen-forties, when I came home from boarding-school to be met at the stationby my grandfather; but the days of the tonga are nearly over, and in many ways this is a good thing, because most tonga ponies are overworked and underfed. Its wheels squeaking from lack of oil and its seat slipping out from under me, the tonga drags me through the bazaars of Dehra. A couple of miles at this slow, funereal pace makes me impatient to use my own legs, and I dismiss the tonga when we get to the small Dilaram Bazaar.

It is a good place from which to start walking.

The Dilaram Bazaar has not changed very much. The shops are run by a new generation of bakers, barbers and banias, but professions have not changed. The cobblers belong to the lower castes, the bakers are Muslims, the tailors are Sikhs. Boys still fly kites from the flat rooftops, and women wash clothes on the canal steps. The canal comes down from Rajpur and goes underground here, to emerge about a mile away.

I have to walk only a furlong to reach my grandfather's house. The road is lined with eucalyptus, jacaranda and laburnum trees. In the compounds there are small groves of mangoes, lichis and papayas. The poinsettia thrusts its scarlet leaves over garden walls. Every veranda has its bougainvillaea creeper, every garden its bed of marigolds. Potted palms, those symbols of Victorian snobbery, are popular with Indian housewives. There are a few houses, but most of the bungalows were built by 'old India hands', on their retirement from the army, the police or the railways. Most of the present owners are Indian businessmen or government officials.

I am standing outside my grandfather's house. The wall has been raised, and the wicket-gate has disappeared; I cannot get a clear view of the house and garden. The name-plate identifies the owner as Major General Saigal; the house has had more than one owner since my grandparents sold it in 1949.

On the other side of the road there is an orchard of lichi trees. This is not the season for fruit, and there is no one looking after the garden. By taking a little path that goes through the orchard, I reach higher ground and gain a better view of our old house.

Grandfather built the house with granite rocks taken from the foothills. It shows no sign of age. The lawn has disappeared; but the big jackfruit tree, giving shade to the side veranda, is still there. In this tree I spent my afternoons, absorbed in my Magnets, Champions and Hotspurs, while sticky mango juice trickled down my chin. (One could not eat the jackfruit unless it was cooked into a vegetable curry.) There was a hole in the bole of the tree in which I kept my pocket-knife, top, catapult and any badges or buttons that could be saved from my father's RAF tunics when he came home on leave. There was also an Iron Cross, a relic of the First World War, given to me by my grandfather. I have managed to keep the Iron Cross; but what did I do with my top and catapult? Memory fails me. Possibly they are still in the hole in the jackfruit tree; I must have forgotten to collect them when we went away after my father's death. I am seized by a whimsical urge to walk in at the gate, climb into the branches of the jackfruit tree, and recover my lost possessions. What would the present owner, the Major General (retired), have to say if I politely asked permission to look for a catapult left behind more than twenty years ago?

An old man is coming down the path through the lichi trees. He is not a Major General but a poor street vendor. He carries a small tin trunk on his head, and walks very slowly. When he sees me he stops and asks me if I will buy something. I can think of nothing I need, but the old man looks so tired, so very old, that I am afraid he will collapse if he moves any further along the path without resting. So I ask him to show me his wares. He cannot get the box off his head by himself, but together we manage to set it down in the shade, and the old man insists on spreading its entire contents on the grass; bangles, combs, shoelaces, safety-pins, cheap stationery, buttons, pomades, elastic and scores of other household necessities.

When I refuse buttons because there is no one to sew them on for me, he plies me safely-pins. I say no; but as he moves from one article to another, his querulous, persuasive voice slowly wears down my resistance, and I end up by buying envelopes, a letter pad (pink roses on bright blue paper), a one-rupee fountain pen guaranteed to leak and several yards of elastic. I have no idea what I will do with the elastic, but the old man convinces me that I cannot live without it.

Exhausted by the effort of selling me a lot of things I obviously do not want, he closes his eyes and leans back against the trunk of a lichi tree. For a moment I feel rather nervous. Is he going to die sitting here beside me? He sinks to his haunches and puts his chin on his hands. He only wants to talk.

'I am very tired, hazoor,' he says. 'Please do not mind if I sit here for a while.'

'Rest for as long as you like,' I say. 'That's a heavy load you've been carrying.'

He comes to life at the chance of a conversation, and says, 'When I was a young man, it was nothing. I could carry my box up from Rajpur to Mussoorie by the bridle-path—seven steep miles! But now I find it difficult to cover the distance from the station to the Dilaram Bazaar.'

'Naturally. You are quite old.'

'I am seventy, sahib.'

'You look very fit for your age.' I say this to please him; he looks frail and brittle. 'Isn't there someone to help you?' I ask.

'I had a servant boy last month, but he stole my earnings and ran off to Delhi. I wish my son was alive—he would not have permitted me to work like a mule for a living—but he was killed in the riots in forty-seven.'

'Have you no other relatives?'

'I have outlived them all. That is the curse of a healthy life. Your friends, your loved ones, all go before you, and at the end you are left alone. But I must go too, before long. The road to the bazaar seems to grow longer every day. The stones are harder. The sun is hotter in the summer, and the wind much colder in the winter. Even some of the trees that were there in my youth have grown old and have died. I have outlived the trees.'

He has outlived the trees. He is like an old tree himself, gnarled and twisted. I have the feeling that if he falls asleep in the orchard, he will strike root here, sending out crooked branches. I can imagine a small bent tree wearing a black waist-coat; a living scarecrow.

He closes his eyes again, but goes on talking.

'The English memsahibs would buy great quantities of elastic. Today it is ribbons and bangles for the girls, and combs for the boys. But I do not make much money. Not because I cannot walk very far. How many houses do I reach in a day? Ten, fifteen. But twenty years ago I could visit more than fifty houses. *That* makes a difference.'

'Have you always been here?'

'Most of my life, hazoor. I was here before they built the motor road to Mussoorie. I was here when the sahibs had their own carriages and ponies and the memsahibs their own rickshaws. I was here before there were any cinemas. I was here when the Prince of Wales came to Dehra Dun. . . . Oh, I have been here a long time, hazoor. I was here when that house was built,' he says, pointing with his chin towards my grandfather's house. 'Fifty, sixty years ago it must have been. I cannot remember exactly. What is ten years when you have lived seventy? But it was a tall, red-bearded sahib who built that house. He kept many creatures as pets. A kachwa, a turtle, was one of them. And there was a python, which crawled into my box one day and gave me a terrible fright. The sahib used to keep it hanging from his shoulders, like a garland. His wife, the burra-mem, always bought a lot from me—lots of elastic. And there were sons, one a teacher, another in the Air Force, and there were always children in the house. Beautiful children. But they went away many years ago. Everyone has gone away.'

I do not tell him that I am one of the 'beautiful children', I doubt if he would believe me. His memories are of another age, another place, and for him there are no strong bridges into the present.

'But others have come,' I say.

'True, and that is as it should be. That is not my complaint. My complaint—should God be listening—is that I have been left behind.'

He gets slowly to his feet and stands over his shabby tin box, gazing down at it with a mixture of disdain and affection. I help him to lift and balance it on the flattened cloth on his head. He does not have the energy to turn and make a salutation of any kind; but, setting his sights on the distant hills, he walks down the path with steps that are shaky and slow but still wonderfully straight.

I wonder how much longer he will live. Perhaps a year or two, perhaps a week, perhaps an hour. It Will be an end of living, but it will not be death. He is too old for death; he can only sleep; he can only fall gently, like an old, crumpled brown leaf.

I leave the orchard. The bend in the road hides my grandfather's house. I reach the canal again. It emerges from under a small culvert, where ferns and maidenhair grow in the shade. The water, coming from a stream in the foothills, rushes along with a familiar sound; it does not lose its momentum until the canal has left the gently sloping streets of the town.

There are new buildings on this road, but the small police station is housed in the same old limewashed bungalow. A couple of off-duty policemen, partly uniformed but with their pyjamas on, stroll hand in hand on the grass verge. Holding hands (with persons of the same sex of course) is common practice in northern India, and denotes no special relationship.

I cannot forget this little police station. Nothing very exciting ever happened in its vicinity until, in 1947, communal riots broke out in Dehra. Then, bodies were regularly fished out of the canal and dumped on a growing pile in the station compound. I was only a boy, but when I looked over the wall at that pile of corpses, there was no one who paid any attention to me. They were too busy to send me away; at the same time they knew that I was perfectly safe. While Hindu and Muslim were at each other's throats, a white boy could walk the streets in safety. No one was any longer interested in the Europeans.

The people of Dehra are not violent by nature, and the town has no history of communal discord. But when refugees from the partitioned Punjab poured into Dehra in their thousands, the atmosphere became charged with tension. These refugees, many of them Sikhs, had lost their homes and livelihoods; many had seen their loved ones butchered. They were in a fierce and vengeful frame of mind. The calm, sleepy atmosphere of Dehra was shattered during two months of looting and murder. Those Muslims who could get away, fled. The poorer members of the community remained in a refugee camp until the holocaust was over; then they returned to their former occupations, frightened and deeply mistrustful. The old boxman was one of them.

I cross the canal and take the road that will lead me to the riverbed. This was one of my father's favourite walks. He, too, was a walking man. Often, when he was home on leave, he would say, 'Ruskin, let's go for a walk,' and we would slip off together and walk down to the river-bed or into the sugar-cane fields or across the railway lines and into the jungle.

On one of these walks (this was before Independence), I remember him saying, 'After the war is over, we'll be going to England. Would you like that?'

'I don't know,' I said. 'Can't we stay in India?'

'It won't be ours any more.'

'Has it always been ours?' I asked.

'For a long time,' he said. 'Over two hundred years. But we have to give it back now.'

'Give it back to whom?' I asked. I was only nine.

'To the Indians,' said my father.

The only Indians I had known till then were my ayah and the cook and the gardener and their children, and I could not imagine them wanting to be rid of us. The only other Indian who came to the house was Dr Ghose, and it was frequently said of him that he was more English than the English. I could understand my father better when he said, 'After the war, there'll be a job for me in England. There'll be nothing for me here.'

The war had at first been a distant event; but somehow it kept coming closer. My aunt, who lived in London with her two children, was killed with them during an air-raid; then my father's younger brother died of dysentery on the long walk out from Burma. Both these tragic events depressed my father. Never in good health (he had been prone to attacks of malaria), he looked more worn and wasted every time he came home. His personal life was far from being happy, as he and my mother had separated, she to marry again. I think he looked forward a great deal to the days he spent with me; far more than I could have realized at the time. I was someone to come back to; someone for whom things could be planned; someone who could learn from him.

Dehra suited him. He was always happy when he was among trees, and this happiness communicated itself to me. I felt like drawing close to him. I remember sitting beside him on the veranda steps when I noticed the tendril of a creeping vine that was trailing near my feet. As we sat there, doing nothing in particular—in the best gardens, time has no meaning—I found that the tendril was moving almost imperceptibly away from me and towards my father. Twenty minutes later it had crossed the veranda steps and was touching his feet. This, in India, is the sweetest of salutations.

There is probably a scientific explanation for the plant's behaviour—something to do with the light and warmth on the veranda steps—but I like to think that its movements were motivated simply by an affection for my father. Sometimes, when I sat alone beneath a tree, I felt a little lonely or lost. As soon as my father rejoined me, the atmosphere lightened, the tree itself became more friendly.

Most of the fruit trees round the house were planted by Father; but he was not content with planting trees in the garden. On rainy days we would walk beyond the river-bed, armed with cuttings and saplings, and then we would amble through the jungle, planting flowering shrubs between the sal and shisham trees.

'But no one ever comes here,' I protested the first time. 'Who is going to see them?'

'Some day,' he said, '*someone* may come this way If people keep cutting trees, instead of planting them, there'll soon be no forests left at all, and the world will be just one vast desert.'

The prospect of a world without trees became a sort of

nightmare for me (and one reason why I shall never want to live on a treeless moon), and I assisted my father in his tree-planting with great enthusiasm.

'One day the trees will move again,' he said. 'They've been standing still for thousands of years. There was a time when they could walk about like people, but someone cast a spell on them and rooted them to one place. But they're always trying to move—see how they reach out with their arms!'

We found an island, a small rocky island in the middle of a dry river-bed. It was one of those river-beds, so common in the foothills, which are completely dry in the summer but flooded during the monsoon rains. The rains had just begun, and the stream could still be crossed on foot, when we set out with a number of tamarind, laburnum and coral-tree saplings and cuttings. We spent the day planting them on the island, then ate our lunch there, in the shelter of a wild plum.

My father went away soon after that tree-planting. Three months later, in Calcutta, he died.

I was sent to boarding-school. My grandparents sold the house and left Dehra. After school, I went to England. The years passed, my grandparents died, and when I returned to India I was the only member of the family in the country.

And now I am in Dehra again, on the road to the river-bed.

The houses with their trim gardens are soon behind me, and I am walking through fields of flowering mustard, which make a carpet of yellow blossom stretching away towards the jungle and the foothills.

The river-bed is dry at this time of the year. A herd of skinny cattle graze on the short brown grass at the edge of the jungle. The sal trees have been thinned out. Could our trees have survived? Will our island be there, or has some flash-flood during a heavy monsoon washed it away completely?

As I look across the dry water-course, my eye is caught by the spectacular red plumes of the coral blossom. In contrast with the dry, rocky river-bed, the little island is a green oasis. I walk across to the trees and notice that a number of parrots have come to live in

44

them. A koel-bird challenges me with a rising *who-are-you, who-are-you. . . .*

But the trees seem to know me. They whisper among themselves and beckon me nearer. And looking round, I find that other trees and wild plants and grasses have sprung up under the protection of the trees we planted.

They have multiplied. They are moving. In this small forgotten corner of the world, my father's dreams are coming true, and the trees are moving again.

THE LEOPARD

I first saw the leopard when I was crossing the small stream at the bottom of the hill.

The ravine was so deep that for most of the day it remained in shadow. This encouraged many birds and animals to emerge from cover during daylight hours. Few people ever passed that way: only milkmen and charcoal-burners from the surrounding villages.

As a result, the ravine had become a little haven of wildlife, one of the few natural sanctuaries left near Mussoorie, a hill-station in northern India.

Below my cottage was a forest of oak and maple and Himalayan rhododendron. A narrow path twisted its way down through the trees, over an open ridge where red sorrel grew wild, and then steeply down through a tangle of wild raspberries, creeping vines and slender bamboo.

At the bottom of the hill the path led on to a grassy verge, surrounded by wild dog roses. (It is surprising how closely the flora of the lower Himalayas, between 5,000 to 8,000 feet, resembles that of the English countryside.)

The stream ran close by the verge, tumbling over smooth pebbles, over rocks worn yellow with age, on its way to the plains and to the little Song River and finally to the sacred Ganges.

When I first discovered the stream it was early April and the wild roses were flowering—small white blossoms lying in clusters.

I walked down to the stream almost every day, after two or three hours of writing. I had lived in cities too long, and had returned to the hills to renew myself, both physically and mentally. Once you have lived with mountains for any length of time, you belong to them, and must return again and again.

Nearly every morning, and sometimes during the day, I heard

the cry of the barking deer. And in the evening, walking through the forest, I disturbed parties of pheasant. The birds went gliding down the ravine on open, motionless wings. I saw pine martens and a handsome red fox, and I recognized the footprints of a bear.

As I had not come to take anything from the forest, the birds and animals soon grew accustomed to my presence; or possibly they recognized my footsteps. After some time, my approach did not disturb them.

The langurs in the oak and rhododendron trees, who would at first go leaping through the branches at my approach, now watched me with some curiosity as they munched the tender green shoots of the oak.

The young ones scuffled and wrestled like boys, while their parents groomed each other's coats, stretching themselves out on the sunlit hillside. But one evening, as I passed, I heard them chattering in the trees, and I knew I was not the cause of their excitement.

As I crossed the stream and began climbing the hill, the grunting and chattering increased, as though the langurs were trying to warn me of some hidden danger. A shower of pebbles came rattling down the steep hillside, and I looked up to see a sinewy, orange-gold leopard poised on a rock about twenty feet above me.

It was not looking towards me, but had its head thrust attentively forward, in the direction of the ravine. Yet it must have sensed my presence, because it slowly turned its head and looked down at me.

It seemed a little puzzled at my presence there; and when, to give myself courage, I clapped my hands sharply, the leopard sprang away into the thickets, making absolutely no sound as it melted into the shadows.

I had disturbed the animal in its quest for food. But a little after I heard the quickening cry of a barking deer as it fled through the forest. The hunt was still on.

The leopard, like other members of the cat family, is nearing extinction in India, and I was surprised to find one so close to

Mussoorie. Probably the deforestation that had been taking place in the surrounding hills had driven the deer into this green valley; and the leopard, naturally, had followed.

It was some weeks before I saw the leopard again, although I was often made aware of its presence. A dry, rasping cough sometimes gave it away. At times I felt almost certain that I was being followed.

Once, when I was late getting home, and the brief twilight gave way to a dark, moonless night, I was startled by a family of porcupines running about in a clearing. I looked around nervously, and saw two bright eyes staring at me from a thicket. I stood still, my heart banging away against my ribs. Then the eyes danced away, and I realized that they were only fireflies.

In May and June, when the hills were brown and dry, it was always cool and green near the stream, where ferns and maidenhair and long grasses continued to thrive.

Downstream I found a small pool where I could bathe, and a cave with water dripping from the roof, the water spangled gold and silver in the shafts of sunlight that pushed through the slits in the cave roof.

'He maketh me to lie down in green pastures: he leadeth me beside the still waters.' Perhaps David had discovered a similar paradise when he wrote those words; perhaps I, too, would write good words. The hill-station's summer visitors had not discovered this haven of wild and green things. I was beginning to feel that the place belonged to me, that dominion was mine.

The stream had at least one other regular visitor, a spotted forktail, and though it did not fly away at my approach it became restless if I stayed too long, and then it would move from boulder to boulder uttering a long complaining cry.

I spent an afternoon trying to discover the bird's nest, which I was certain contained young ones, because I had seen the forktail carrying grubs in her bill. The problem was that when the bird flew upstream I had difficulty in following her rapidly enough as the rocks were sharp and slippery.

Eventually I decorated myself with bracken fronds and, after slowly making my way upstream, hid myself in the hollow stump of a tree at a spot where the forktail often disappeared. I had no intention of robbing the bird: I was simply curious to see its home.

By crouching down, I was able to command a view of a small stretch of the stream and the sides of the ravine; but I had done little to deceive the forktail, who continued to object strongly to my presence so near her home.

I summoned up my reserves of patience and sat perfectly still for about ten minutes. The forktail quietened down. Out of sight, out of mind. But where had she gone? Probably into the walls of the ravine where I felt sure, she was guarding her nest.

I decided to take her by surprise, and stood up suddenly, in time to see not the forktail on her doorstep, but the leopard bounding away with a grunt of surprise! Two urgent springs, and it had crossed the stream and plunged into the forest.

I was as astonished as the leopard, and forgot all about the forktail and her nest. Had the leopard been following me again? I decided against this possibility. Only man-eaters follow humans, and, as far as I knew, there had never been a man-eater in the vicinity of Mussoorie.

During the monsoon the stream became a rushing torrent, bushes and small trees were swept away, and the friendly murmur of the water became a threatening boom. I did not visit the place too often, as there were leeches in the long grass.

One day I found the remains of a barking deer which had only been partly eaten. I wondered why the leopard had not hidden the rest of his meal, and decided that it must have been disturbed while eating.

Then, climbing the hill, I met a party of hunters resting beneath the oaks. They asked me if I had seen a leopard. I said I had not. They said they knew there was a leopard in the forest.

Leopard skins, they told me, were selling in Delhi at over 1,000 rupees each. Of course there was a ban on the export of skins, but they gave me to understand that there were ways and means. . . . I thanked them for their information and walked on, feeling uneasy and disturbed.

The hunters had seen the carcass of the deer, and they had seen the leopard's pug-marks, and they kept coming to the forest. Almost every evening I heard their guns banging away; for they were ready to fire at almost anything.

'There's a leopard about,' they always told me. 'You should carry a gun.'

'I don't have one,' I said.

There were fewer birds to be seen, and even the langurs had moved on. The red fox did not show itself; and the pine martens, who had become quite bold, now dashed into hiding, at my approach. The smell of one human is like the smell of any other.

And then the rains were over and it was October; I could lie in the sun, on sweet-smelling grass, and gaze up through a pattern of oak leaves into a blinding blue heaven. And I would praise God for leaves and grass and the smell of things, the smell of mint and bruised clover, and the touch of things—the touch of grass and air and sky, the touch of the sky's blueness.

I thought no more of the men. My attitude towards them was similar to that of the denizens of the forest. These were men, unpredictable, and to be avoided if possible.

On the other side of the ravine rose Pari Tibba, Hill of the Fairies: a bleak, scrub-covered hill where no one lived.

It was said that in the previous century Englishmen had tried building their houses on the hill, but the area had always attracted lightning, due to either the hill's location or due to its mineral deposits; after several houses had been struck by lightning, the settlers had moved on to the next hill, where the town now stands.

To the hillmen it is Pari Tibba, haunted by the spirits of a pair of ill-fated lovers who perished there in a storm; to others it is known as Burnt Hill, because of its scarred and stunted trees.

One day, after crossing the stream, I climbed Pari Tibba—a stiff undertaking, because there was no path to the top and I had to scramble up a precipitous rock-face with the help of rocks and roots that were apt to come loose in my groping hand.

But at the top was a plateau with a few pine trees, their upper branches catching the wind and humming softly. There I found the ruins of what must have been the houses of the first settlers—just a few piles of rubble, now overgrown with weeds, sorrel, dandelions and nettles.

As I walked through the roofless ruins, I was struck by the silence that surrounded me, the absence of birds and animals, the sense of complete desolation.

The silence was so absolute that it seemed to be ringing in my ears. But there was something else of which I was becoming increasingly aware: the strong feline odour of one of the cat family.

I paused and looked about. I was alone. There was no movement of dry leaf or loose stone. The ruins were for the most part open to the sky. Their rotting rafters had collapsed, jamming together to form a low passage like the entrance to a mine; and this dark cavern seemed to lead down into the ground.

The smell was stronger when I approached this spot, so I stopped again and waited there, wondering if I had discovered the lair of the leopard, wondering if the animal was now at rest after a night's hunt.

Perhaps he was crouching there in the dark, watching me, recognizing me, knowing me as the man who walked alone in the forest without a weapon.

I like to think that he was there, that he knew me, and that he acknowledged my visit in the friendliest way: by ignoring me altogether.

Perhaps I had made him confident—too confident, too careless, too trusting of the human in his midst. I did not venture any further; I was not out of my mind. I did not seek physical contact, or even another glimpse of that beautiful sinewy body, springing from rock to rock. It was his trust I wanted, and I think he gave it to me.

But did the leopard, trusting one man, make the mistake of bestowing his trust on others? Did I, by casting out all fear—my own fear, and the leopard's protective fear—leave him defenseless?

Because next day, coming up the path from the stream, shouting and beating drums, were the hunters. They had a long bamboo pole across their shoulders; and slung from the pole, feet up, head down, was the lifeless body of the leopard, shot in the neck and in the head.

'We told you there was a leopard!' they shouted, in great good humour. 'Isn't he a fine specimen?'

'Yes,' I said. 'He was a beautiful leopard.'

I walked home through the silent forest. It was very silent, almost as though the birds and animals knew that their trust had been violated.

I remembered the lines of a poem by D. H. Lawrence; and, as I climbed the steep and lonely path to my home, the words beat out their rhythm in my mind: 'There was room in the world for a mountain lion and me.'

THE MAN WHO WAS KIPLING

I was sitting on a bench in the Indian Section of the Victoria and Albert Museum in London, when a tall, stooping, elderly gentleman sat down beside me. I gave him a quick glance, noting his swarthy features, heavy moustache, and horn-rimmed spectacles. There was something familiar and disturbing about his face, and I couldn't resist looking at him again.

I noticed that he was smiling at me.

'Do you recognize me?' he asked, in a soft pleasant v oice.

'Well, you do seem familiar,' I said. 'Haven't we met somewhere?'

'Perhaps. But if I seem familiar to you, that is at least something. The trouble these days is that people don't *know* me anymore—I'm a familiar, that's all. Just a name standing for a lot of outmoded ideas.'

A little perplexed, I asked. 'What is it you do?'

'I wrote books once. Poems and tales Tell me, whose books do you read?'

'Oh, Maugham, Priestley, Thurber. And among the older lot, Bennett and Wells—'I hesitated, groping for an important name, and I noticed a shadow, a sad shadow, pass across my companion's face.

'Oh, yes, and Kipling,' I said, 'I read a lot of Kipling.'

His face brightened up at once, and the eyes behind the thick-lensed spectacles suddenly came to life.

'I'm Kipling,' he said.

I stared at him in astonishment, and then, realizing that he might perhaps be dangerous, I smiled feebly and said, 'Oh, yes?'

'You probably don't believe me. I'm dead, of course.'

'So I thought.'

'And you don't believe in ghosts?'

'Not as a rule.'

'But you'd have no objection to talking to one, if he came along?'

'I'd have no objection. But how do I know you're Kipling? How do I know you're not an imposter?'

'Listen, then:

> When my heavens were turned to blood,
> When the dark had filled my day,
> Furthest, but most faithful, stood
> That lone star I cast away.
> I had loved myself, and I
> Have not lived and dare not die.

'Once,' he said, gripping me by the arm and looking me straight in the eye. 'Once in life I watched a star; but I whistled her to go.'

'Your star hasn't fallen yet,' I said, suddenly moved, suddenly quite certain that I sat beside Kipling. 'One day, when there is a new spirit of adventure abroad, we will discover you again.'

'Why have they heaped scorn on me for so long?'

'You were too militant, I suppose—too much of an Empire man. You were too patriotic for your own good.'

He looked a little hurt. 'I was never very political,' he said. 'I wrote over six hundred poems, and you could only call a dozen of them political, I have been abused for harping on the theme of the White Man's burden but my only aim was to show off the Empire to my audience—and I believed the Empire was a fine and noble thing. Is it wrong to believe in something? I never went deeply into political issues, that's true. You must remember, my seven years in India were very youthful years. I was in my twenties, a little immature if you like, and my interest in India was a boy's interest. Action appealed to me more than anything else. You must understand that.'

'No one has described action more vividly, or India so well. I feel at one with Kim wherever he goes along the Grand Trunk Road, in the temples at Banaras, amongst the Saharanpur fruit gardens, on the snow-covered Himalayas. *Kim* has colour and movement and poetry.'

He sighed, and a wistful look came into his eyes.

'I'm prejudiced, of course,' I continued. 'I've spent most of my life in India—not *your* India, but an India that does still have much of the colour and atmosphere that you captured. You know, Mr Kipling, you can still sit in a third-class railway carriage and meet the most wonderful assortment of people. In any village you will still find the same courtesy, dignity and courage that the Lama and Kim found on their travels.'

'And the Grand Trunk Road? Is it still a long winding procession of humanity?'

'Well, not exactly,' I said, a little ruefully. 'It's just a procession of motor vehicles now. The poor Lama would be run down by a truck if he became too dreamy on the Grand Trunk Road. Times *have* changed. There are no more Mrs Hawksbees in Simla, for instance.'

There was a far-away look in Kipling's eyes. Perhaps he was imagining himself a boy again; perhaps he could see the hills or the red dust of Rajputana; perhaps he was having a private conversation with Privates Mulvaney and Ortheris, or perhaps he was out hunting with the Seonee wolf-pack. The sound of London's traffic came to us through the glass doors, but we heard only the creaking of bullock-cart wheels and the distant music of a flute.

He was talking to himself, repeating a passage from one of his stories. 'And the last puff of the daywind brought from the unseen villages the scent of damp wood-smoke, hot cakes, dripping undergrowth, and rotting pine-cones. That is the true smell of the Himalayas, and if once it creeps into the blood of a man, that man will at the last, forgetting all else, return to the hills to die.'

A mist seemed to have risen between us—or had it come in from the streets?—and when it cleared, Kipling had gone away.

I asked the gatekeeper if he had seen a tall man with a slight stoop, wearing spectacles.

'Nope,' said the gatekeeper. 'Nobody been by for the last ten minutes.'

'Did someone like that come into the gallery a little while ago?'

'No one that I recall. What did you say the bloke's name was?'

'Kipling,' I said.

'Don't know him.'

'Didn't you ever read *The Jungle Books*?'

'Sounds familiar. Tarzan stuff, wasn't it?'

I left the museum, and wandered about the streets for a long time, but I couldn't find Kipling anywhere. Was it the boom of London's traffic that I heard, or the boom of the Sutlej river racing through the valleys?

THE LAST TIME I SAW DELHI

I'd had this old and faded negative with me for a number of years and had never bothered to make a print from it. It was a picture of my maternal grandparents. I remembered my grandmother quite well, because a large part of my childhood had been spent in her house in Dehra after she had been widowed; but although everyone said she was fond of me, I remembered her as a stern, somewhat aloof person, of whom I was a little afraid.

I hadn't kept many family pictures and this negative was yellow and spotted with damp.

Then last week, when I was visiting my mother in hospital in Delhi, while she awaited her operation, we got talking about my grandparents, and I remembered the negative and decided I'd make a print for my mother.

When I got the photograph and saw my grandmother's face for the first time in twenty-five years, I was immediately struck by my resemblance to her. I have, like her, lived a rather spartan life, happy with my one room, just as she was content to live in a room of her own while the rest of the family took over the house! And like her, I have lived tidily. But I did not know the physical resemblance was so close—the fair hair, the heavy build, the wide forehead. She looks more like me than my mother!

In the photograph she is seated on her favourite chair, at the top of the veranda steps, and Grandfather stands behind her in the shadows thrown by a large mango tree which is not in the picture. I can tell it was a mango tree because of the pattern the leaves make on the wall. Grandfather was a slim, trim man, with a drooping moustache that was fashionable in the twenties. By all accounts he had a mischievous sense of humour, although he looks unwell in the picture. He appears to have been quite swarthy. No wonder he was so successful in dressing up 'native' style and passing himself off as a street-vendor. My mother tells me he even took my grandmother in on one occasion, and sold her a basketful of bad oranges. His character was in strong contrast to my grandmother's rather forbidding personality and Victorian sense of propriety; but they made a good match.

But here's the picture, and I am taking it to show my mother who lies in the Lady Hardinge Hospital, awaiting the removal of her left breast.

It is early August and the day is hot and sultry. It rained during the night, but now the sun is out and the sweat oozes through my shirt as I sit in the back of a stuffy little taxi taking me through the suburbs of Greater New Delhi.

On either side of the road are the houses of well-to-do Punjabis, who came to Delhi as refugees in 1947 and now make up more than half the capital's population. Industrious, flashy, go-ahead people. Thirty years ago, fields extended on either side of this road, as far as the eye could see. The Ridge, an outcrop of the Aravallis, was scrub jungle, in which the black buck roamed. Feroz Shah's fourteenth century hunting lodge stood here in splendid isolation. It is still here, hidden by petrol pumps and lost within the sounds of buses, cars, trucks and scooter-rickshaws. The peacock has fled the forest, the black buck is extinct. Only the jackal remains. When, a thousand years from now, the last human has left this contaminated planet for some other star, the jackal and the crow will remain, to survive for years on all the refuse we leave behind.

It is difficult to find the right entrance to the hospital, because for about a mile along the Panchkuin Road the pavement has been obliterated by tea-shops, furniture shops, and piles of accumulated junk. A public hydrant stands near the gate, and dirty water runs across the road.

I find my mother in a small ward. It is a cool, dark room, and a ceiling fan whirrs pleasantly overhead. A nurse, a dark pretty girl from the South, is attending to my mother. She says, 'In a minute,' and proceeds to make an entry on a chart.

My mother gives me a wan smile and beckons me to come nearer. Her cheeks are slightly flushed, due possibly to fever;

otherwise she looks her normal self. I find it hard to believe that the operation she will have tomorrow will only give her, at the most, another year's lease on life.

I sit at the foot of her bed. This is my third visit, since I flew back from Jersey, using up all my savings in the process; and I will leave after the operation, not to fly away again, but to return to the hills which have always called me back.

'How do you feel?' I ask.

'All right. They say they will operate in the morning. They've stopped my smoking.'

'Can you drink? Your rum, I mean?'

'No. Not until a few days after the operation.'

She has a fair amount of grey in her hair, natural enough at fifty-four. Otherwise she hasn't changed much; the same small chin and mouth, lively brown eyes. Her father's face, not her mother's.

The nurse has left us. I produce the photograph and hand it to my mother.

'The negative was lying with me all these years. I had it printed yesterday.'

'I can't see without my glasses.'

The glasses are lying on the locker near her bed. I hand them to her. She puts them on and studies the photograph.

'Your grandmother was always very fond of you.'

'It was hard to tell. She wasn't a soft woman.'

'It was her money that got you to Jersey, when you finished school. It wasn't much, just enough for the ticket.'

'I didn't know that.'

'The only person who ever left you anything. I'm afraid I've nothing to leave you, either.'

'You know very well that I've never cared a damn about money. My father taught me to write. That was inheritance enough.'

'And what did I teach you?'

'I'm not sure. . . . Perhaps you taught me how to enjoy myself now and then.'

She looked pleased at this. 'Yes, I've enjoyed myself between troubles. But your father didn't know how to enjoy himself. That's why we quarrelled so much. And finally separated.'

'He was much older than you.'

'You've always blamed me for leaving him, haven't you?

'I was very small at the time. You left us suddenly. My father had to look after me, and it wasn't easy for him. He was very sick. Naturally I blamed you.'

'He wouldn't let me take you away.'

'Because you were going to marry someone else.'

I break off, we have been over this before. I am not there as my father's advocate, and the time for recrimination has passed.

And now it is raining outside, and the scent of wet earth comes through the open doors, overpowering the odour of medicines and disinfectants. The dark-eyed nurse comes in again and informs me that the doctor will soon be on his rounds. I can come again in the evening, or early morning before the operation.

'Come in the evening,' says my mother. 'The others will be here then.'

'I haven't come to see the others.'

'They are looking forward to seeing you.' 'They' being my stepfather and half-brothers.

'I'll be seeing them in the morning.'

'As you like.

And then I am on the road again, standing on the pavement, on the fringe of a chaotic rush of traffic, in which it appears that every vehicle is doing its best to overtake its neighbour. The blare of horns can be heard in the corridors of the hospital, but everyone is conditioned to the noise and pays no attention to it. Rather, the sick and the dying are heartened by the thought that people are still well enough to feel reckless, indifferent to each other's safety! In Delhi there is a feverish desire to be first in line, the first to get anything. . . . This is probably because no one ever gets around to dealing with second-comers.

When I hail a scooter-rickshaw and it stops a short distance away, someone elbows his way past me and gets in first. This epitomizes the philosophy and outlook of the Delhi-wallah.

So I stand on the pavement waiting for another scooter, which doesn't come. In Delhi, to be second in the race is to be last.

I walk all the way back to my small hotel, with a foreboding of having seen my mother for the last time.

FROM SMALL BEGINNINGS

And the last puff of the day-wind brought from the unseen villages, the scent of damp wood-smoke, hot cakes, dripping undergrowth, and rotting pine-cones. That is the true smell of the Himalayas, and if once it creeps into the blood of a man, that man will at the last, forgetting all else, return to the hills to die.

—Rudyard Kipling

O n the first clear September day, towards the end of the rains, I visited the pine-knoll, my place of peace and power.

It was months since I'd last been there. Trips to the plains, a crisis in my affairs, involvements with other people and their troubles, and an entire monsoon had come between me and the grassy, pine-topped slope facing the Hill of Fairies (Pari Tibba to the locals). Now I tramped through late monsoon foliage—tall ferns, bushes festooned with flowering convolvulus—crossed the stream by way of its little bridge of stones—and climbed the steep hill to the pine slope.

When the trees saw me, they made as if to turn in my direction. A puff of wind came across the valley from the distant snows. A long-tailed blue magpie took alarm and flew noisily out of an oak tree. The cicadas were suddenly silent. But the trees remembered me. They bowed gently in the breeze and beckoned me nearer, welcoming me home. Three pines, a straggling oak, and a wild cherry. I went among them, acknowledged their welcome with a touch of my hand against their trunks—the cherry's smooth and polished; the pine's patterned and whorled; the oak's rough, gnarled, full of experience. He'd been there longest, and the wind had bent his upper branches and twisted a few, so that he looked shaggy and undistinguished. But, like the philosopher who is careless about his dress and appearance, the oak has secrets, a hidden wisdom. He has learnt the art of survival!

While the oak and the pines are older than me and have been here many years, the cherry tree is exactly seven years old. I know, because I planted it.

One day I had this cherry seed in my hand, and on an impulse I thrust it into the soft earth, and then went away and forgot all about it. A few months later I found a tiny cherry tree in the long grass. I did not expect it to survive. But the following year it was two feel tall. And then some goats ate its leaves, and a grass cutter's scythe injured the stem, and I was sure it would wither away. But it renewed itself, sprang up even faster; and within three years it was a healthy, growing tree, about five feet tall.

I left the hills for two years—forced by circumstances to make a living in Delhi—but this time I did not forget the cherry tree. I thought about it fairly often, sent telepathic messages of encouragement in its direction. And when, a couple of years ago, I returned in the autumn, my heart did a somersault when I found my tree sprinkled with pale pink blossom. (The Himalayan cherry flowers in November.) And later, when the fruit was ripe, the tree was visited by finches, tits, bulbuls and other small birds, all come to feast on the sour, red cherries.

Last summer I spent a night on the pine-knoll, sleeping on the grass beneath the cherry tree. I lay awake for hours, listening to the chatter of the stream and the occasional tonk-tonk of a nightjar; and watching, through the branches overhead, the stars turning in the sky, and I felt the power of the sky and earth, and the power of a small cherry seed. . . .

And so, when the rains are over, this is where I come, that I might feel the peace and power of this place. It's a big world and momentous events are taking place all the time. But this is where I have seen it happen.

This is where I will write my stories. I can see everything from here—my cottage across the valley; behind and above me, the town and the bazaar, straddling the ridge; to the left, the high mountains and the twisting road to the source of the great river; below me, the little stream and the path to the village; ahead, the Hill of Fairies, the fields beyond; the wide valley below, and then another range of hills and then the distant plains. I can even see Prem Singh in the garden, putting the mattresses out in the sun.

From here he is just a speck on the far hill, but I know it is Prem by the way he stands. A man may have a hundred disguises, but in the end it is his posture that gives him away. Like my grandfather, who was a master of disguise and successfully roamed the bazaars as fruit-vendor or basket-maker; but we could always recognize him because of his pronounced slouch.

Prem Singh doesn't slouch, but he has this habit of looking up at the sky (regardless of whether it's cloudy or clear), and at the moment he's looking at the sky.

Eight years with Prem. He was just a sixteen-year-old boy when I first saw him, and now he has a wife and child.

I had been in the cottage for just over a year. . . . He stood on the landing outside the kitchen door. A tall boy, dark, with good teeth and brown, deep-set eyes; dressed smartly in white drill—his only change of clothes. Looking for a job. I liked the look of him. But—

'I already have someone working for me,' I said.

'Yes, sir. He is my uncle.'

In the hills, everyone is a brother or uncle.

'You don't want me to dismiss your uncle?'

'No, sir. But he says you can find a job for me.'

'I'll try. I'll make enquiries. Have you just come from your village?'

'Yes. Yesterday I walked ten miles to Pauri. There I got a bus.'

'Sit down. Your uncle will make some tea.'

He sat down on the steps, removed his white keds, wriggled his toes. His feet were both long and broad, large feet, but not ugly. He was unusually clean for a hill boy. And taller than most.

'Do you smoke?' I asked.

'No, sir.'

'It is true,' said his uncle, 'he does not smoke. All my nephews smoke, but this one, he is a little peculiar, he does not smoke—neither beedi nor hookah.'

'Do you drink?'

'It makes me vomit.'

'Do you take bhang?'

'No, sahib.'

'You have no vices. It's unnatural.'

'He is unnatural, sahib,' said his uncle.

'Does he chase girls?'

'They chase him, sahib.'

'So he left the village and came looking for a job.' I looked at him. He grinned, then looked away, began rubbing his feet.

'Your name is?'

'Prem Singh.'

'All right, Prem, I will try to do something for you.'

I did not see him for a couple of weeks. I forgot about finding him a job. But when I met him again, on the road to the bazaar, he told me that he had got a temporary job in the Survey, looking after the surveyor's tents.

'Next week we will be going to Rajasthan,' he said.

'It will be very hot. Have you been in the desert before?'

'No, sir.'

'It is not like the hills. And it is far from home.'

'I know. But I have no choice in the matter. I have to collect some money in order to get married.'

In his region there was a bride price, usually of two thousand rupees.

'Do you have to get married so soon?'

'I have only one brother and he is still very young. My mother is not well. She needs a daughter-in-law to help her in the fields and with the cows and in the house. We are a small family, so the work is greater.'

65

Every family has its few terraced fields, narrow and stony, usually perched on a hillside above a stream or river. They grow rice, barley, maize, potatoes—just enough to live on. Even if they produced sufficient for marketing, the absence of roads makes it difficult to get the produce to the market towns. There is no money to be earned in the villages, and money is needed for clothes, soap, medicines, and recovering the family jewellery from the moneylenders. So the young men leave their villages to find work, and to find work they must go to the plains. The lucky ones get into the army. Others enter domestic service or take jobs in garages, hotels, wayside tea-shops, schools. . . .

In Mussoorie the main attraction is the large number of schools, which employ cooks and bearers. But the schools were full when Prem arrived. He'd been to the recruiting centre at Roorkee, hoping to get into the army; but they found a deformity in his right foot, the result of a bone broken when a landslip carried him away one dark monsoon night; he was lucky, he said, that it was only his foot and not his head that had been broken.

He came to the house to inform his uncle about the job and to say goodbye. I thought: another nice person I probably won't see again; another ship passing in the night, the friendly twinkle of its lights soon vanishing in the darkness. I said 'come again', held his smile with mine so that I could remember him better, and returned to my study and my typewriter. The typewriter is the repository of a writer's loneliness. It stares unsympathetically back at him every day, doing its best to be discouraging. Maybe I'll go back to the old-fashioned quill pen and marble ink-stand; then I can feel like a real writer, Balzac or Dickens, scratching away into the endless reaches of the night—Of course, the days and nights are seemingly shorter than they need to be! They must be, otherwise why do we hurry so much and achieve so little, by the standards of the past. . . .

Prem goes, disappears into the vast faceless cities of the plains, and a year slips by, or rather I do, and then here he is again, thinner and darker and still smiling and still looking for a job. I should have known that hill men don't disappear for ever. The spirit-haunted rocks don't let their people wander too far, lest they lose them forever.

I was able to get him a job in the school. The Headmaster's wife needed a cook. I wasn't sure if Prem could cook very well but I sent him along and they said they'd give him a trial. Three days later the Headmaster's wife met me on the road and started gushing all over me. She was the type who gushes.

'We're so grateful to you! Thank you for sending me that lovely boy. He's so polite. And he cooks very well. A little too hot for my husband, but otherwise delicious—just delicious! He's a real treasure—a lovely boy.' And she gave me an arch look—the famous look which she used to captivate all the good-looking young prefects who became perfects, it was said, only if she approved of them.

I wasn't sure if she didn't want something more than a cook, and I only hoped that Prem would give every satisfaction.

He looked cheerful enough when he came to see me on his off day.

'How are you getting on?' I asked.

'Lovely,' he said, using his mistress's favourite expression.

'What do you mean—lovely? Do they like your work?'

'The memsahib likes it. She strokes me on the cheek whenever she enters the kitchen. The sahib says nothing. He takes medicine after every meal.'

'Did he always take medicine—or only now that you're doing the cooking?'

'I am not sure. I think he has always been sick.'

He was sleeping in the Headmaster's veranda and getting sixty rupees a month. A cook in Delhi got a hundred and sixty. And a cook in Paris or New York got ten times as much. I did not say as much to Prem. He might ask me to get him a job in New York. And that would be the last I saw of him! He, as a cook, might well get a job making curries off Broadway; I, as a writer, wouldn't get to first base. And only my Uncle Ken knew the secret of how to make a living without actually doing any work. But then, of course, he had four sisters. And each of them was married to a fairly prosperous husband. So Uncle Ken divided up his year among them. Three months with Aunt Ruby in Nainital. Three months with Aunt Susie in Kashmir. Three months with my mother (not quite so affluent) in Jamnagar. And three months in the Vet Hospital in Bareilly, where Aunt Mabel ran the hospital for her veterinary husband. In this way he never overstayed his welcome. A sister can look after a brother for just three months at a time and no more. Uncle K had it worked out to perfection.

But I had no sisters, and I couldn't live forever on the royalties of a single novel. So I had to write others. So I came to the hills.

The hill men go to the plains to make a living. I had to come to the hills to try and make mine.

'Prem,' I said, 'why don't you work for me?'

'And what about my uncle?'

'He seems ready to desert me any day. His grandfather is ill, he says, and he wants to go home.'

'His grandfather died last year.'

That's what I mean—he's getting restless. And I don't mind if he goes. These days he seems to be suffering from a form of sleeping sickness. I have to get up first and make his tea . . .'

Sitting here under the cherry tree, whose leaves are just beginning to turn yellow, I rest my chin on my knees and gaze across the valley to where Prem moves about in the garden. Looking back over the seven years he has been with me, I recall some of the nicest things about him. They come to me in no particular order—just pieces of cinema—coloured slides slipping across the screen of memory . . .

Prem rocking his infant son to sleep—crooning to him, passing his large hand gently over the child's curly head—Prem following me down to the police-station when I was arrested,* and waiting outside until I reappeared—his smile, when I found him in Delhi—his large, irrepressible laughter, most in, evidence when he was seeing an old Laurel and Hardy movie.

Of course there were times when he could be infuriating, stubborn, deliberately pig-headed, sending me little notes of

---

*On a warrant from Bombay, charging me with writing an allegedly obscene short story!

resignation—but I never found it difficult to overlook these little acts of self-indulgence. He had brought much love and laughter into my life, and what more could a lonely man ask for?

It was his stubborn streak that limited the length of his stay in the Headmaster's household. Mr Good was tolerant enough. But Mrs Good was one of those women who, when they are pleased with you, go out of their way to help, pamper and flatter; and who, when they are displeased, become vindictive, going out of their way to harm or destroy. Mrs Good sought power—over her husband, her dog, her favourite pupils, her servant. . . . She had absolute power over the husband and the dog; partial power over her slightly bewildered pupils; and none at all over Prem, who missed the subtleties of her designs upon his soul. He did not respond to her mothering; or to the way in which she tweaked him on the cheeks, brushed against him in the kitchen, or made admiring remarks about his looks and physique. Memsahibs, he knew, were not for him. So he kept a stony face and went diligently about his duties. And she felt slighted, put in her place. Her liking turned to dislike. Instead of admiring remarks, she began making disparaging remarks about his looks, his clothes, his manners. She found fault with his cooking. No longer was it 'lovely'. She even accused him of taking away the dog's meat and giving it to a poor family living on the hillside: no more heinous crime could be imagined! Mr Good threatened him with dismissal. So Prem became stubborn. The following day he withheld the dog's food altogether; threw it down the khud where it was seized upon by innumerable strays; and went off to the pictures.

It was the end of his job. 'I'll have to go home now,' he told me, 'I won't get another job in this area. The Mem will see to that.'

'Stay a few days,' I said.

'I have only enough money with which to get home.'

'Keep it for going home. You can stay with me for a few days, while you look around. Your uncle won't mind sharing his food with you.'

His uncle did mind. He did not like the idea of working for his nephew as well; it seemed to him no part of his duties. And he was apprehensive that Prem might get his job.

So Prem stayed no longer than a week.

Here on the knoll the grass is just beginning to turn October yellow. The first clouds approaching winter cover the sky. The trees are Very still. The birds are silent. Only a cricket keeps singing on the oak tree. Perhaps there will be a storm before evening. A storm like that in which Prem arrived at the cottage with his wife and child—but that's jumping too far ahead. . . .

After he had returned to his village, it was several months before I saw him again. His uncle told me he had taken a job in Delhi. There was an address. It did not seem complete, but I resolved that when I was next in Delhi, I would try to see him.

The opportunity came in May, as the hot winds of summer blew across the plains. It was the time of year when people who can afford it, try to get away to the hills. I dislike New Delhi at the best of times, and I hate it in summer. People compete with each other in being bad-tempered and mean. But I had to go down—I don't remember why, but it must have seemed very necessary at the time—and I took the opportunity to try and see Prem.

Nothing went right for me. Of course the address was all wrong, and I wandered about in a remote, dusty, treeless colony called Vasant Vihar (Spring Garden) for over two hours, asking all the domestic servants I came across if they could put me in touch with Prem Singh of Village Koli, Pauri Garhwal. There were innumerable Prem Singhs, but apparently none who belonged to Village Koli. I returned to my hotel and took two days to recover from heatstroke before returning to Mussoorie, thanking God for mountains!

And then the uncle gave me notice. He'd found a better-paid job in Dehra Dun and was anxious to be off. I didn't try to stop him.

For the next six months I lived in the cottage without any help. I did not find this difficult. I was used to living alone. It wasn't service that I needed but companionship. In the cottage it was very quiet. The ghosts of long dead residents were sympathetic but unobtrusive. The song of the whistling thrush was beautiful, but I knew he was not singing for me. Up the valley came the sound of a flute, but I never saw the flute player. My affinity was with the little red fox who roamed the hillside below the cottage. I met him one night and wrote these lines:

As I walked home last night
I saw a lone fox dancing
In the cold moonlight.
I stood and watched—then
Took the low road, knowing
The night was his by right.
Sometimes, when words ring true,
I'm like a lone fox dancing
In the morning dew.

During the rains, watching the dripping trees and the mist climbing the valley, I wrote a great deal of poetry. Loneliness is of value to poets. But poetry didn't bring me much money, and funds were low. And then, just as I was wondering if I would have to give up my freedom and take a job again, a publisher bought the paperback rights of one of my children's stories, and I was free to live and write as I pleased—for another three months!

That was in November. To celebrate, I took a long walk through the Landour Bazaar and up the Tehri road. It was a good day for walking; and it was dark by the time I returned to the outskirts of the town. Someone stood waiting for me on the road above the cottage. I hurried past him.

If I am not for myself,
Who will be for me?
And if I am not for others,
What am I?
And if not now, when?

I startled myself with the memory of these words of Hillel, the ancient Hebrew sage. I walked back to the shadows where the youth stood, and saw that it was Prem.

'Prem!' I said. 'Why are you sitting out here, in the cold? Why did you not go to the house?'

'I went, sir, but there was a lock on the door. I thought you had gone away.'

'And you were going to remain here, on the road?'

'Only for tonight. I would have gone down to Dehra in the morning.'

'Come, let's go home. I have been waiting for you. I looked for you in Delhi, but could not find the place where you were working.'

'I have left them now.'

'And your uncle has left me. So will you work for me now?'

'For as long as you wish.'

'For as long as the gods wish.'

We did not go straight home, but returned to the bazaar and took our meal in the Sindhi Sweet Shop; hot puris and strong sweet tea.

We walked home together in the bright moonlight. I felt sorry for the little fox, dancing alone.

*

That was twenty years ago, and Prem and his wife and three children are still with me. But we live in a different house now, on another hill.

WOULD ASTLEY RETURN?

The house was called 'Undercliff', because that's where it stood—under a cliff. The man who went away—the owner of the house—was Robert Astley. And the man who stayed behind—the old family retainer—was Prem Bahadur.

Astley had been gone many years. He was still a bachelor in his late thirties when he'd suddenly decided that he wanted adventure, romance, faraway places; and he'd given the keys of the house to Prem Bahadur—who'd served the family for thirty years—and had set off on his travels.

Someone saw him in Sri Lanka. He'd been heard of in Burma, around the ruby mines at Mogok. Then he turned up in Java, seeking a passage through the Sunda Straits. After that the trail petered out. Years passed. The house in the hill-station remained empty.

But Prem Bahadur was still there, living in an outhouse.

Every day he opened up Undercliff, dusted the furniture in all the rooms, made sure that the bedsheets and pillowcases were clean, and set out Astley's dressing-gown and slippers.

In the old days, whenever Astley had come home after a journey or a long tramp in the hills, he had liked to bathe and change into his gown and slippers, no matter what the hour. Prem Bahadur still kept them ready. He was convinced that Robert would return one day.

Astley himself had said so.

'Keep everything ready for me, Prem, old chap. I may be back after a year, or two years, or even longer, but I'll be back, I promise you. On the first of every month I want you to go to my lawyer, Mr Kapoor. He'll give you your salary and any money that's needed for the rates and repairs. I want you to keep the house tip-top!'

'Will you bring back a wife, Sahib?'

'Lord, no! Whatever put that idea in your head?'

'I thought, perhaps—because you wanted the house kept ready. . . .'

'Ready for me, Prem. I don't want to come home and find the old place falling down.'

And so Prem had taken care of the house—although there was no news from Astley. What had happened to him? The mystery provided a talking-point whenever local people met on the Mall. And in the bazaar the shopkeepers missed Astley because he was a man who spent freely.

His relatives still believed him to be alive. Only a few months back a brother had turned up—a brother who had a farm in Canada and could not stay in India for long. He had deposited a further sum with the lawyer and told Prem to carry on as before. The salary provided Prem with his few needs. Moreover, he was convinced that Robert would return.

Another man might have neglected the house and grounds, but not Prem Bahadur. He had a genuine regard for the absent owner. Prem was much older—now almost sixty and none too strong, suffering from pleurisy and other chest troubles—but he remembered Robert as both a boy and a young man. They had been together on numerous hunting and fishing trips in the mountains. They had slept out under the stars, bathed in icy mountain streams, and eaten from the same cooking-pot. Once, when crossing a small river, they had been swept downstream by a flash-flood, a wall of water that came thundering down the gorges without any warning during the rainy season. Together they had struggled back to safety. Back in the hill-station, Astley told everyone that Prem had saved his life; while Prem was equally insistent that he owed his life to Robert.

*

This year the monsoon had begun early and ended late. It dragged on through most of September, and Prem Bahadur's cough grew worse and his breathing more difficult.

He lay on his charpai on the veranda, staring out at the garden, which was beginning to get out of hand, a tangle of dahlias, snake-lilies and convolvulus. The sun finally came out. The wind shifted from the south-west to the north-west, and swept the clouds away.

Prem Bahadur had shifted his charpai into the garden, and was lying in the sun, puffing at his small hookah, when he saw Robert Astley at the gate.

He tried to get up but his legs would not oblige him. The hookah slipped from his hand.

Astley came walking down the garden path and stopped in front of the old retainer, smiling down at him. He did not look a day older than when Prem Bahadur had last seen him.

'So you have come at last,' said Prem.

'I told you I'd return.'

'It has been many years. But you have not changed.'

'Nor have you, old chap.'

'I have grown old and sick and feeble.'

'You'll be fine now. That's why I've come.'

'I'll open the house,' said Prem, and this time he found himself getting up quite easily.

'It isn't necessary,' said Astley.

'But all is ready for you!'

'I know. I have heard of how well you have looked after everything. Come then, let's take a last look round. We cannot stay, you know.'

Prem was a little mystified but he opened the front door and took Robert through the drawing-room and up the stairs to the bedroom. Robert saw the dressing-gown and the slippers, and he placed his hand gently on the old man's shoulder.

When they returned downstairs and emerged into the sunlight, Prem was surprised to see himself—or rather his skinny body—stretched out on the charpai. The hookah lay on the ground, where it had fallen.

Prem looked at Astley in bewilderment.

'But who is that—lying there?'

'It was you. Only the husk now, the empty shell. This is the real you, standing here beside me.'

'You came for me?'

'I couldn't come until you were ready. As for me, I left *my* shell a long time ago. But you were determined to hang on, keeping this house together. Are you ready now?'

'And the house?'

'Others will live in it. But come, it's time to go fishing. . . .'

Astley took Prem by the arm, and they walked through the dappled sunlight under the deodars and finally left that place for ever.

THE FUNERAL

'I don't think he should go,' said Aunt M.

'He's too small,' concurred Aunt B. 'He'll get upset and probably throw a tantrum. And you know Padre Lal doesn't like having children at funerals.'

The boy said nothing. He sat in the darkest corner of the darkened room, his face revealing nothing of what he thought and felt. His father's coffin lay in the next room, the lid fastened forever over the tired, wistful countenance of the man who had meant so much to the boy. Nobody else had mattered—neither uncles nor aunts nor fond grandparents; least of all the mother who was hundreds of miles away with another husband. He hadn't seen her since he was four—that was just over five years ago—and he did not remember her very well.

The house was full of people—friends, relatives, neighbours. Some had tried to fuss over him but had been discouraged by his silence, the absence of tears. The more understanding of them had kept their distance.

Scattered words of condolence passed back and forth like dragonflies on the wind. 'Such a tragedy!'. . . . 'Only forty'. . . . 'No one realized how serious it was'. . . . 'Devoted to the child'. . . .

It seemed to the boy that everyone who mattered in the hill-station was present. And for the first time they had the run of the house; for his father had not been a sociable man. Books, music, flowers and his stamp collection had been his main preoccupations, apart from the boy.

A small hearse, drawn by a hill pony, was led in at the gate, and several able-bodied men lifted the coffin and manoeuvred it into the carriage. The crowd drifted away. The cemetery was about a mile down the road, and those who did not have cars would have to walk the distance.

The boy stared through a window at the small procession passing through the gate. He'd been forgotten for the moment— left in care of the servants, who were the only ones to say behind. Outside, it was misty. The mist had crept up the valley and settled like a damp towel on the face of the mountain. Everyone was wet, although it hadn't rained.

The boy waited until everyone had gone, and then he left the room and went out on the veranda. The gardener, who had been sitting in a bed of nasturtiums, looked up and asked the boy if he needed anything; but the boy shook his head and retreated indoors. The gardener, looking aggrieved because of the damage done to the flower-beds by the mourners, shambled off to his quarters. The sahib's death meant that he would be out of job very soon. The house would pass into other hands, the boy would go to an orphanage. There weren't many people who kept gardeners these days. In the kitchen, the cook was busy preparing the only big meal ever served in the house. All those relatives, and the Padre too, would come back famished, ready for a sombre but nevertheless substantial meal. He too would be out of job soon; but cooks were always in demand.

The boy slipped out of the house by a back-door and made his way into the lane through a gap in a thicket of dog-roses. When he reached the main road, he could see the mourners wending their way round the hill to the cemetery. He followed at a distance.

It was the same road he had often taken with his father during their evening walks. The boy knew the name of almost every plant and wildflower that grew on the hillside. These, and various birds and insects, had been described and pointed out to him by his father.

Looking northwards, he could see the higher ranges of the Himalayas and the eternal snows. The graves in the cemetery were so laid out that if their incumbents did happen to rise one day, the first thing they would see would be the glint of the sun on those snow-covered peaks. Possibly the site had been chosen for the view. But to the boy it did not seem as if anyone would be able to thrust aside those massive tombstones and rise from their graves to enjoy the view. Their rest seemed as eternal as the snows. It would take an earthquake to burst those stones asunder and thrust the coffins up from the earth. The boy wondered why people hadn't made it easier for the dead to rise. They were so securely entombed that it appeared as though no one really wanted them to get out.

'God has need of your father. . . .' In those words a well-meaning missionary had tried to console him.

And had God, in the same way, laid claim to the thousands of men, women and children who had been put to rest here in these neat and serried rows? What could he have wanted them for? Of what use are we to God when we are dead, wondered the boy.

The cemetery gate stood open, but the boy leant against the old stone wall and stared down at the mourners as they shuffled about with the unease of a batsman about to face a very fast bowler. Only this bowler was invisible and would come up stealthily and from behind.

Padre Lal's voice droned on through the funeral service, and then the coffin was lowered—down, deep down—the boy was surprised at how far down it seemed to go! Was that other, better world down in the depths of the earth? How could anyone, even a Samson, push his way back to the surface again? Superman did it in comics, but his father was a gentle soul who wouldn't fight too hard against the earth and the grass and the roots of tiny trees. Or perhaps he'd grow into a tree and escape that way! 'If ever I'm put away like this,' thought the boy, 'I'll get into the root of a plant and then I'll become a flower and then maybe a bird will come and carry my seed away. . . . I'll get out somehow!'

A few more words from the Padre, and then some of those present threw handfuls of earth over the coffin before moving away.

Slowly, in twos and threes, the mourners departed. The mist swallowed them up. They did not see the boy behind the wall. They were getting hungry.

He stood there until they had all gone, then he noticed that the gardeners or caretakers were filling in the grave. He did not know whether to go forward or not. He was a little afraid. And it was too late now. The grave was almost covered.

He turned and walked away from the cemetery. The road stretched ahead of him, empty, swathed in mist. He was alone. What had his father said to him once? 'The strongest man in the world is he who stands alone.'

Well, he was alone, but at the moment he did not feel very strong.

For a moment he thought his father was beside him, that they were together on one of their long walks. Instinctively he put out his hand, expecting his father's warm, comforting touch. But there was nothing there, nothing, no one. . . .

He clenched his fists and pushed them deep down into his pockets. He lowered his head so that no one would see his tears. There were people in the mist, but he did not want to go near them, for they had put his father away.

'He'll find a way out,' the boy said fiercely to himself. 'He'll get out somehow!'

THE ROOM OF MANY COLOURS

L ast week I wrote a story, and all the time I was writing it I thought it was a good story; but when it was finished and I had read it through, I found that there was something missing, that it didn't ring true. So I tore it up. I wrote a poem, about an old man sleeping in the sun, and this was true, but it was finished quickly, and once again I was left with the problem of what to write next. And I remembered my father, who taught me to write; and I thought, why not write about my father, and about the trees we planted, and about the people I knew while growing up and about what happened on the way to growing up. . . .

And so, like Alice, I must begin at the beginning, and in the beginning there was this red insect, just like a velvet button, which I found on the front lawn of the bungalow. The grass was still wet with overnight rain.

I placed the insect on the palm of my hand and took it into the house to show my father.

'Look, Dad,' I said, 'I haven't seen an insect like this before. Where has it come from?'

'Where did you find it?' he asked.

'On the grass.'

'It must have come down from the sky,' he said. 'It must have come down with the rain.'

Later he told me how the insect really happened but I preferred his first explanation. It was more fun to have it dropping from the sky.

I was seven at the time, and my father was thirty-seven, but, right from the beginning, he made me feel that I was old enough to talk to him about everything—insects, people, trees, steam-engines, King George, comics, crocodiles, the Mahatma, the Viceroy, America, Mozambique and Timbuctoo. We took long walks together, explored

81

old ruins, chased butterflies and waved to passing trains.

My mother had gone away when I was four, and I had very dim memories of her. Most other children had their mothers with them, and I found it a bit strange that mine couldn't stay. Whenever I asked my father why she'd gone, he'd say, 'You'll understand when you grow up.' And if I asked him *where* she'd gone, he'd look troubled and say, 'I really don't know.' This was the only question of mine to which he didn't have an answer.

But I was quite happy living alone with my father; I had never known any other kind of life.

We were sitting on an old wall, looking out to sea at a couple of Arab dhows and a tramp streamer, when my father said, 'Would you like to go to sea one day?'

'Where does the sea go?' I asked.

'It goes everywhere.'

'Does it go to the end of the world?'

'It goes right round the world. It's a round world.'

'It can't be.'

'It is. But it's so big, you can't see the roundness. When a fly sits on a water-melon, it can't see right round the melon, can it? The melon must seem quite flat to the fly. Well, in comparison to the world, we're much, much smaller than the tiniest of insects.'

'Have you been around the world?' I asked.

'No, only as far as England. That's where your grandfather was born.'

'And my grandmother?'

'She came to India from Norway when she was quite small. Norway is a cold land, with mountains and snow, and the sea cutting deep into the land. I was there as a boy. It's very beautiful, and the people are good and work hard.'

'I'd like to go there.'

'You will, one day. When you are older, I'll take you to Norway.'

'Is it better than England?'

'It's quite different.'

'Is it better than India?'

'It's quite different.'

'Is India like England?'

'No, it's different.'

'Well, what does "different" mean?'

'It means things are not the same. It means people are different. It means the weather is different. It means trees and birds and insects are different.'

'Are English crocodiles different from Indian crocodiles?'

'They don't have crocodiles in England.'

'Oh, then it must be different.'

'It would be a dull world if it was the same everywhere,' said my father.

He never lost patience with my endless questioning. If he wanted a rest, he would take out his pipe and spend a long time lighting it. If this took very long I'd find something else to do. But sometimes I'd wait patiently until the pipe was drawing, and then return to the attack.

'Will we always be in India?' I asked.

'No, we'll have to go away one day. You see, it's hard to explain, but it isn't really our country.'

'Ayah says it belongs to the King of England, and the jewels in his crown were taken from India, and that when the Indians get their jewels back the King will lose India! But first they have to get the crown from the King, but this is very difficult, she says because the crown is always on his head. He even sleeps wearing his crown!'

Ayah was my nanny. She loved me deeply, and was always filling my head with strange and wonderful stories.

My father did not comment on Ayah's views. All he said was, 'We'll have to go away some day.'

'How long have we been here?' I asked.

'Two hundred years.'

'No, I mean us.'

'Well, you were born in India, so that's seven years for you.'

'Then can't I stay here?'

'Do you want to?'

'I want to go across the sea. But can we take Ayah with us?'

'I don't know, son. Let's walk along the beach.'

*

We lived in an old palace beside a lake. The palace looked like a ruin from the outside, but the rooms were cool and comfortable. We lived in one wing, and my father organized a small school in another wing. His pupils were the children of the Raja and the Raja's relatives. My father had started life in India as a tea-planter; but he had been trained as a teacher and the idea of starting a school in a small state facing the Arabian Sea had appealed to him. The pay wasn't much, but we had a palace to live in, the latest 1938-model Hillman to drive about in, and a number of servants. In those days, of course, everyone had servants (although the servants did not have any!). Ayah was our own; but the cook, the bearer, the gardener, and the bhisti were all provided by the state.

Sometimes, I sat in the schoolroom with the other children (who were all much bigger than me), sometimes I remained in the house with Ayah, sometimes I followed the gardener, Dukhi, about the spacious garden.

Dukhi means 'sad', and, though I never could discover if the gardener had anything to feel sad about, the name certainly suited him. He had grown to resemble the drooping weeds that he was always digging up with a tiny spade. I seldom saw him standing up. He always sat on the ground with his knees well up to his chin, and attacked the weeds from this position. He could spend all day on his haunches, moving about the garden simply by shuffling his feet along the grass.

I tried to imitate his posture, sitting down on my heels and putting my knees into my armpits; but could never hold the position for more than five minutes.

Time had no meaning in a large garden, and Dukhi never hurried. Life, for him, was not a matter of one year succeeding another, but of five seasons—winter, spring, hot weather, monsoon and autumn—arriving and departing. His seedbeds had always to be in readiness for the coming season, and he did not look any further than the next monsoon. It was impossible to tell his age. He may have been thirty-six or eighty-six. He was either very young for his years or very old for them.

Dukhi loved bright colours, especially reds and yellows. He liked strongly scented flowers, like jasmine and honeysuckle. He couldn't understand my father's preference for the more delicately perfumed petunias and sweetpeas. But I shared Dukhi's fondness for the common, bright orange marigold, which is offered in temples and is used to make garlands and nosegays. When the garden was bare of all colour, the marigold would still be there, gay and flashy, challenging the sun.

Dukhi was very fond of making nosegays, and I liked to watch him at work. A sunflower formed the centre-piece. It was surrounded by roses, marigolds and oleander, fringed with green leaves, and bound together with silver thread. The perfume was over-powering. The nosegays were presented to me or my father on special occasions, that is, on a birthday or to guests of my father's who were considered important.

One day I found Dukhi making a nosegay, and said, 'No one is coming today, Dukhi. It isn't even a birthday.'

'It is a birthday, chhota sahib,' he said. 'Little sahib' was the title he had given me. It wasn't much of a title compared to Raja sahib, Diwan sahib or Burra sahib but it was nice to have a title at the age of seven.

'Oh,' I said. 'And is there a party, too?'

'No party.'

'What's the use of a birthday without a party? What's the use of a birthday without presents?'

'This person doesn't like presents—just flowers.'

'Who is it?' I asked, full of curiosity.

'If you want to find out, you can take these flowers to her. She lives right at the top of that far side of the palace. There are twenty-two steps to climb. Remember that, chhota sahib you take twenty-three steps, you will go over the edge and into the lake!'

I started climbing the stairs.

It was a spiral staircase of wrought iron, and it went round and round and up and up, and it made me quite dizzy and tired.

At the top I found myself on a small balcony, which looked out over the lake and another palace, at the crowded city and the distant harbour. I heard a voice, a rather high, musical voice, saying (in English), 'Are you a ghost?' I turned to see who had spoken but found the balcony empty. The voice had come from a dark room.

I turned to the stairway, ready to flee, but the voice said, 'Oh, don't go, there's nothing to be frightened of!'

And so I stood still, peering cautiously into the darkness of the room.

'First, tell me—are you a ghost?'

'I'm a boy,' I said.

'And I'm a girl. We can be friends. I can't come out there, so you had better come in. Come along, I'm not a ghost either—not yet, anyway!'

As there was nothing very frightening about the voice, I stepped into the room. It was dark inside, and, coming in from the glare, it took me some time to make out the tiny, elderly lady seated on a cushioned, gilt chair. She wore a red sari, lots of coloured bangles on her wrists, and golden ear-rings. Her hair was streaked with white, but her skin was still quite smooth and unlined, and she had large and very beautiful eyes.

'You must be Master Bond!' she said. 'Do you know who I am?'

'You're a lady with a birthday,' I said, 'but that's all I know. Dukhi didn't tell me any more.'

'If you promise to keep it a secret, I'll tell you who I am. You see, everyone thinks I'm mad. Do you think so too?'

'I don't know.'

'Well, you must tell me if you think so,' she said with a chuckle. Her laugh was the sort of sound made by the gecko, the little wall-lizard, coming from deep down in the throat. 'I have a feeling you are a truthful boy. Do you find it very difficult to tell the truth?'

'Sometimes.'

'Sometimes. Of course, there are times when I tell lies—lots of little lies—because they're such fun! But would you call me a liar? I wouldn't, if I were you, but *would* you?'

'Are you a liar?'

'I'm asking you! If I were to tell you that I was a queen—that I am a queen—would you believe me?'

I thought deeply about this, and then said, 'I'll try to believe you.'

'Oh, but you *must* believe me. I'm a real queen. I'm a Rani! Look I've got diamonds to prove it!' And she held out her hands, and there was a ring on each finger, the stones glowing and glittering in the dim light. 'Diamonds, rubies, pearls and emeralds! Only a queen can have these!' She was most anxious that I should believe her.

'You must be a queen,' I said.

'Right!' she snapped. 'In that case, would you mind calling me "Your Highness"?'

'Your Highness,' I said.

She smiled. It was a slow, beautiful smile. Her face lit up. 'I could love you,' she said. 'But better still, I'll give you something to eat. Do you like chocolates?'

'Yes, Your Highness.'

'Well,' she said, taking a box from the table beside her, 'these have come all the way from England. Take two. Only two, mind, otherwise the box will finish before Thursday, and I don't want that to happen because I won't get any more till Saturday. That's when Captain MacWhirr's ship gets in, the *S.S.Lucy* loaded with boxes and boxes of chocolates!'

'All for you?' I asked in considerable awe.

'Yes, of course. They have to last at least three months. I get them from England. I get only the best chocolates. I like them with pink, crunchy fillings, don't you?'

'Oh, yes!' I exclaimed, full of envy.

'Never mind,' she said. 'I may give you one, now and then—if you're *very* nice to me! Here you are, help yourself. . . .' She pushed the chocolate box towards me.

I took a silver-wrapped chocolate, and then just as I was

thinking of taking a second, she quickly took the box away.

'No more!' she said. 'They have to last till Saturday.'

'But I took only *one,*' I said with some indignation.

'Did you?' She gave me a sharp look, decided I was telling the truth, and said graciously, 'Well, in that case you can have another. '

Watching the Rani carefully, in case she snatched the box away again, I selected a second chocolate, this one with a green wrapper. I don't remember what kind of a day it was outside, but I remember the bright green of the chocolate wrapper.

I thought it would be rude to eat the chocolates in front of a queen, so I put them in my pocket and said, 'I'd better go now. Ayah will be looking for me.'

'And when will you be coming to see me again?'

'I don't know,' I said.

'Your Highness.'

'Your Highness.'

'There's something I want you to do for me,' she said, placing one finger on my shoulder and giving me a conspiratorial look. 'Will you do it?'

'What is it, Your Highness?'

'What is it? Why do you ask? A real prince never asks where or why or whatever, he simply does what the princess asks of him. When I was princess—before I became a queen, that is—I asked a prince to swim across the lake and fetch me a lily growing on the other bank.'

'And did he get it for you?'

'He drowned half way across. Let *that* be a lesson to you. Never agree to do something without knowing what it is.'

'But I thought you said.

'Never mind what I *said.* It's what I *say* that matters!'

'Oh, all right,' I said, fidgeting to be gone. 'What is it you want me to do?'

'Nothing.' Her tiny rosebud lips pouted and she stared sullenly at a picture on the wall. Now that my eyes had grown used to the dim light in the room, I noticed that the walls were hung with portraits of stout Rajas and Ranis: turbaned and bedecked in fine clothes. There were also portraits of Queen Victoria and King George V of England. And, in the centre of all this distinguished company, a large picture of Mickey Mouse.

'I'll do it if it isn't too dangerous,' I said.

'Then listen.' She took my hand and drew me towards her—what a tiny hand she had!—and whispered, 'I want a red rose. From the palace garden. But be careful! Don't let Dukhi the gardener catch you. He'll know it's for me. He knows I love roses. And he hates me! I'll tell you why, one day. But if he catches you, he'll do something terrible.'

'To me?'

'No, to himself. That's much worse, isn't it? He'll tie himself into knots, or lie naked on a bed of thorns, or go on a long fast with nothing to eat but fruit, sweets and chicken! So you will be careful, won't you?'

'Oh, but he doesn't hate you,' I cried in protest, remembering the flowers he'd sent for her, and looking around, I found that I'd been sitting on them. 'Look, he sent these flowers for your birthday!'

'Well, if he sent them for my birthday, you can take them back,' she snapped. 'But if he sent them for *me*. . .' and she suddenly softened and looked coy, 'then I might keep them. Thank you, my dear, it was a very sweet thought.' And she leaned forward as though to kiss me.

'It's late, I must go!' I said in alarm, and turning on my heels, ran out of the room and down the spiral staircase.

*

Father hadn't started lunch or rather tiffin, as we called it then. He usually waited for me, if I was late. I don't suppose he enjoyed eating alone.

For tiffin we usually had rice, a mutton curry (koftas or meat balls, with plenty of gravy, was my favourite curry), fried dal and a hot lime or mango pickle. For supper we had English food—a soup, roast pork and fried potatoes, a rich gravy made by my father, and a custard or caramel pudding. My father enjoyed cooking, but it was only in the morning that he found time for it. Breakfast was his own creation. He cooked eggs in a variety of interesting ways, and favoured some Italian recipes which he had collected during a trip to Europe, long before I was born.

In deference to the feelings of our Hindu friends, we did not eat beef; but, apart from mutton and chicken, there was a plentiful supply of other meats—partridge, venison, lobster, and even porcupine!

'And where have you been?' asked my father, helping himself to the rice as soon as he saw me come in.

'To the top of the old palace,' I said.

'Did you meet anyone there?'

'Yes, I met a tiny lady who told me she was a Rani. She gave me chocolates.'

'As a rule, she doesn't like visitors.'

'Oh, she didn't mind me. But is she really a queen?'

'Well, she's the daughter of a Maharaja. That makes her a princess. She never married. There's a story that she fell in love with a commoner, one of the palace servants, and wanted to marry him, but of course they wouldn't allow that. She became very melancholic, and started living all by herself in the old palace. They give her everything she needs, but she doesn't go out or have visitors. Everyone says she's mad.'

'How do they know?' I asked.

'Because she's different from other people, I suppose.'

'Is that being mad?'

'No. Not really, I suppose madness is not *seeing* things as others see them.'

'Is that very bad?'

'No,' said Father, who for once was finding it very difficult to explain something to me. 'But people who are like that— people whose minds are so different that they don't think, step by step, as we do, whose thoughts jump all over the place—such people are very difficult to live with. . . .'

'Step by step,' I repeated. 'Step by step. . . .'

'You aren't eating,' said my father. 'Hurry up, and you can come with me to school today.'

I always looked forward to attending my father's classes. He did not take me to the schoolroom very often, because he wanted school to be a treat, to begin with; then, later, the routine wouldn't be so unwelcome.

Sitting there with older children, understanding only half of what they were learning, I felt important and part grown-up. And of course I did learn to read and write, although I first learnt to read upside-down, by means of standing in front of the others' desks and peering across at their books. Later, when I went to school, I had some difficulty in learning to read the right way up; and even today I sometimes read upside-down, for the sake of variety. I don't mean that I read standing on my head; simply that I hold the book upside-down.

I had at my command a number of rhymes and jingles, the most interesting of these being 'Solomon Grundy':

Solomon Grundy,
Born on a Monday,
Christened on Tuesday,
Married on Wednesday,
Took ill on Thursday,
Worse on Friday,
Died on Saturday,
Buried on Sunday:
This is the end of
Solomon Grundy.

Was that all that life amounted to, in the end? And were we all Solomon Grundies? These were questions that bothered me, at times.

Another puzzling rhyme was the one that went:

Hark, hark,
The dogs do bark,
The beggars are coming to town;
Some in rags,
Some in bags,
And some in velvet gowns.

This rhyme puzzled me for a long time. There were beggars aplenty in the bazaar, and sometimes they came to the house, and some of them did wear rags and bags (and some nothing at all) and the dogs did bark at them, but the beggar in the velvet gown never came our way.

'Who's this beggar in a velvet gown?' I asked my father.

'Not a beggar at all,' he said.

'Then why call him one?'

And I went to Ayah and asked her the same question, 'Who is the beggar in the velvet gown?'

'Jesus Christ,' said Ayah.

Ayah was a fervent Christian and made me say my prayers at night, even when I was very sleepy. She had, I think, Arab and Negro blood in addition to the blood of the Koli fishing community to which her mother had belonged. Her father, a sailor on an Arab dhow, had been a convert to Christianity. Ayah was a large, buxom woman, with heavy hands and feet, and a slow, swaying gait that had all the grace and majesty of a royal elephant. Elephants for all their size, are nimble creatures; and Ayah too, was nimble, sensitive, and gentle with her big hands. Her face was always sweet and childlike.

Although a Christian, she clung to many of the beliefs of her parents, and loved to tell me stories about mischievous spirits and evil spirits, humans who changed into animals, and snakes who had been princes in their former lives.

There was the story of the snake who married a princess. At first the princess did not wish to marry the snake, whom she had met in a forest, but the snake insisted, saying, 'I'll kill you if you won't marry me,' and of course that settled the question. The snake led his bride away and took her to a great treasure. 'I was a prince in my former life,' he explained. 'This treasure is yours.' And then the snake very gallantly disappeared.

'Snakes,' declared Ayah, 'were very lucky omens if seen early in the morning.'

'But what if the snake bites the lucky person?' I asked.

'He will be lucky all the same,' said Ayah with a logic that was all her own.

Snakes! There were a number of them living in the big garden, and my father had advised me to avoid the long grass. But I had seen snakes crossing the road (a lucky omen, according to Ayah) and they were never aggressive.

'A snake won't attack you,' said Father, 'provided you leave it alone. Of course, if you step on one it will probably bite.'

'Are all snakes poisonous?'

'Yes, but only a few are poisonous enough to kill a man. Others use their poison on rats and frogs. A good thing, too, otherwise during the rains the house would be taken over by the frogs.'

One afternoon, while Father was at school, Ayah found a snake in the bath-tub. It wasn't early morning and so the snake couldn't have been a lucky one. Ayah was frightened and ran into the garden calling for help. Dukhi came running. Ayah ordered me to stay outside while they went after the snake.

And it was while I was alone in the garden—an unusual circumstance, since Dukhi was nearly always there—that I remembered the Rani's request. On an impulse, I went to the nearest rose bush and plucked the largest rose, pricking my thumb in the process.

And then, without waiting to see what had happened to the snake (it finally escaped), I started up the steps to the top of the old palace.

When I got to the top, I knocked on the door of the Rani's room. Getting no reply, I walked along the balcony until I reached another doorway. There were wooden panels around the door, with elephants, camels and turbaned warriors carved into it. As the door was open, I walked boldly into the room; then stood still in astonishment. The room was filled with a strange light.

There were windows going right round the room, and each small window-pane was made of a different coloured piece of glass. The sun that came through one window flung red and green and purple colours on the figure of the little Rani who stood there with her face pressed to the glass.

She spoke to me without turning from the window. 'This is my favourite room. I have all the colours here. I can see a different world through each pane of glass. Come, join me!' And she beckoned to me, her small hand fluttering like a delicate butterfly.

I went up to the Rani. She was only a little taller than me, and we were able to share the same window-pane.

'See, it's a red world!' she said.

The garden below, the palace and the lake, were all tinted red. I watched the Rani's world for a little while and then touched her on the arm and said, 'I have brought you a rose!'

She started away from me, and her eyes looked frightened. She would not look at the rose.

'Oh, why did you bring it?' she cried, wringing her hands. 'He'll be arrested now!'

'Who'll be arrested?'

'The prince, of course!'

'But I took it,' I said. 'No one saw me. Ayah and Dukhi were inside the house, catching a snake.'

'Did they catch it?' she asked, forgetting about the rose.

'I don't know. I didn't wait to see!'

'They should follow the snake, instead of catching it. It may lead them to a treasure. All snakes have treasures to guard.'

This seemed to confirm what Ayah had been telling me, and I resolved that I would follow the next snake that I met.

'Don't you like the rose, then?' I asked.

'Did you steal it?'

'Yes.'

'Good. Flowers should always be stolen. They're more fragrant, then.'

*

Because of a man called Hitler, war had been declared in Europe, and Britain was fighting Germany.

In my comic papers, the Germans were usually shown as blundering idiots; so I didn't see how Britain could possibly lose the war, nor why it should concern India, nor why it should be necessary for my father to join up. But I remember his showing me a newspaper headline which said:

> BOMBS FALL ON BUCKINGHAM PALACE—
> KING AND QUEEN SAFE

I expect that had something to do with it.

He went to Delhi for an interview with the RAF and I was left in Ayah's charge.

It was a week I remember well, because it was the first time I had been left on my own. That first night I was afraid—afraid of the dark, afraid of the emptiness of the house, afraid of the howling of the jackals outside. The loud ticking of the clock was the only reassuring sound: clocks really made themselves heard in those days! I tried concentrating on the ticking, shutting out other sounds and the menace of the dark, but it wouldn't work. I thought I heard a faint hissing near the bed, and sat up, bathed in perspiration, certain that a snake was in the room. I shouted for Ayah and she came running, switching on all the lights.

'A snake!' I cried. 'There's a snake in the room!'

'Where, baba?'

'I don't know where, but I *heard* it.'

Ayah looked under the bed, and behind the chairs and tables, but there was no snake to be found. She persuaded me that I must have heard the breeze whispering in the mosquito curtains.

But I didn't want to be left alone.

'I'm coming to you,' I said and followed her into her small room near the kitchen.

Ayah slept on a low string cot. The mattress was thin, the blanket worn and patched up; but Ayah's warm and solid body made up for the discomfort of the bed. I snuggled up to her and was soon asleep.

I had almost forgotten the Rani in the old palace and was about to pay her a visit when, to my surprise, I found her in the garden.

I had risen early that morning, and had gone running barefoot over the dew-drenched grass. No one was about, but I startled a flock of parrots and the birds rose screeching from a banyan tree and wheeled away to some other corner of the palace grounds. I was just in time to see a mongoose scurrying across the grass with an egg in its mouth. The mongoose must have been raiding the poultry farm at the palace.

I was trying to locate the mongoose's hideout, and was on all fours in a jungle of tall cosmos plants when I heard the rustle of clothes, and turned to find the Rani staring at me.

She didn't ask me what I was doing there, but simply said: 'I don't think he could have gone in there.'

'But I saw him go this way,' I said.

'Nonsense! He doesn't live in this part of the garden. He lives in the roots of the banyan tree.'

'But that's where the snake lives,' I said.

'You mean the snake who was a prince. Well, that's who I'm looking for!'

'A snake who was a prince!' I gaped at the Rani.

She made a gesture of impatience with her butterfly hands, and said, 'Tut, you're only a child, you can't *understand*. The prince lives in the roots of the banyan tree, but he comes out early every morning. Have you seen him?'

'No. But I saw a mongoose.'

The Rani became frightened. 'Oh dear, is there a mongoose in the garden? He might kill the prince!'

'How can a mongoose kill a prince?' I asked.

'You don't understand, Master Bond. Princes, when they die, are born again as snakes.'

'*All* princes?'

'No, only those who die before they can marry.'

'Did your prince die before he could marry you?'

'Yes. And he returned to this garden in the form of a beautiful snake.'

'Well,' I said, 'I hope it wasn't the snake the water-carrier killed last week.'

'He killed a snake!' The Rani looked horrified. She was quivering all over. 'It might have been the prince!'

'It was a brown snake,' I said.

'Oh, then it wasn't him.' She looked very relieved. 'Brown snakes are only ministers and people like that. It has to be a green snake to be a prince.'

'I haven't seen any green snakes here.'

'There's one living in the roots of the banyan tree. You won't kill it, will you?'

'Not if it's really a prince.'

'And you won't let others kill it?'

'I'll tell Ayah.'

'Good. You're on my side. But be careful of the gardener. Keep him away from the banyan tree. He's always killing snakes. I don't trust him at all.'

She came nearer and, leaning forward a little, looked into my eyes.

'Blue eyes—I trust them. But don't trust green eyes. And yellow eyes are evil.'

'I've never seen yellow eyes.'

"That's because you're pure,' she said, and turned away and hurried across the lawn as though she had just remembered a very urgent appointment.

The sun was up, slanting through the branches of the banyan tree, and Ayah's voice could be heard calling me for breakfast.

'Dukhi,' I said, when I found him in the garden later that day. 'Dukhi, don't kill the snake in the banyan tree.'

'A snake in the banyan tree!' he exclaimed, seizing his hoe.

'No, no!' I said. 'I haven't seen it. But the Rani says there's one. She says it was a prince in its former life, and that we shouldn't kill it.'

'Oh,' said Dukhi, smiling to himself. 'The Rani says so. All right, you tell her we won't kill it.'

'Is it true that she was in love with a prince but that he died before she could marry him?'

'Something like that,' said Dukhi. 'It was a long time ago—before I came here.'

'My father says it wasn't a prince, but a commoner. Are you a commoner, Dukhi?'

'A commoner? What's that, chhota sahib?'

'I'm not sure. Someone very poor, I suppose.'

'Then I must be a commoner,' said Dukhi.

'Were *you* in love with the Rani?' I asked.

Dukhi was so startled that he dropped his hoe and lost his balance; the first time I'd seen him lose his poise while squatting on his haunches.

'Don't say such things, chhota sahib!'

'Why not?'

'You'll get me into trouble.'

'Then it must be true.'

Dukhi threw up his hands in mock despair and started collecting his implements.

'It's true, it's true!' I cried, dancing round him, and then I ran indoors to Ayah and said, 'Ayah, Dukhi was in love with the Rani!'

Ayah gave a shriek of laughter, then looked very serious and put her finger against my lips.

'Don't say such things,' she said. 'Dukhi is of a very low caste. People won't like it if they hear what you say. And besides, the Rani told you her prince died and turned into a snake. Well, Dukhi hasn't become a snake as yet, has he?'

True, Dukhi didn't look as though he could be anything but a gardener; but I wasn't satisfied with his denials or with Ayah's attempts to still my tongue. Hadn't Dukhi sent the Rani a nosegay?

*

When my father came home, he looked quite pleased with himself.

'What have you brought for me?' was the first question I asked.

He had brought me some new books, a dart-board, and a train set; and in my excitement over examining these gifts, I forgot to ask about the result of his trip.

It was during tiffin that he told me what had happened— and what was going to happen.

'We'll be going away soon,' he said. 'I've joined the Royal Air Force. I'll have to work in Delhi.'

'Oh! Will you be in the war, Dad? Will you fly a plane?'

'No, I'm too old to be flying planes. I'll be forty years old in July. The RAF, will be giving me what they call intelligence work—decoding secret messages and things like that and I don't suppose I'll be able to tell you much about it.'

This didn't sound as exciting as flying planes; but it sounded important and rather mysterious.

'Well, I hope it's interesting,' I said. 'Is Delhi a good place to live in?'

'I'm not sure. It will be very hot by the middle of April. And you won't be able to stay with me, Ruskin—not at first, anyway, not until I can get married quarters and then, only if your mother returns. . . . Meanwhile, you'll stay with your grandmother in Dehra.' He must have seen the disappointment in my face because he quickly added: 'Of course I'll come to see you often. Dehra isn't far from Delhi—only a night's train journey.'

But I was dismayed. It wasn't that I didn't want to stay with my grandmother, but I had grown so used to sharing my father's life and even watching him at work, that the thought of being separated from him was unbearable.

'Not as bad as going to boarding-school,' he said. 'And that's the only alternative.'

'Not boarding-school,' I said quickly, 'I'll run away from boarding-school.'

'Well, you won't want to run away from your grandmother. She's very fond of you. And if you come with me to Delhi, you'll be alone all day in a stuffy little hut, while I'm away at work. Sometimes I may have to go on tour—then what happens?'

'I don't mind being on my own.' And this was true: I had already grown accustomed to having my own room and my own trunk and my own bookshelf and I felt as though I was about to lose these things.

'Will Ayah come too?' I asked.

My father looked thoughtful. 'Would you like that?'

'Ayah must come,' I said firmly. 'Otherwise I'll run away.'

'I'll have to ask her,' said my father.

Ayah, it turned out, was quite ready to come with us: in fact, she was indignant that Father should have considered leaving her behind. She had brought me up since my mother went away, and she wasn't going to hand over charge to any upstart aunt or governess. She was pleased and excited at the prospect of the move, and this helped to raise my spirits.

'What is Dehra like?' I asked my father.

'It's a green place,' he said. 'It lies in a valley in the foothills of the Himalayas, and it's surrounded by forests. There are lots of trees in Dehra.'

'Does Grandmother's house have trees?'

'Yes. There's a big jackfruit tree in the garden. Your grandmother planted it when I was a boy. And there's an old banyan tree, which is good to climb. And there are fruit trees, lichis, mangoes, papayas.'

'Are there any books?'

'Grandmother's books won't interest you. But I'll be bringing you books from Delhi, whenever I come to see you.'

I was beginning to look forward to the move. Changing houses had always been fun. Changing towns ought to be fun, too.

A few days before we left, I went to say goodbye to the Rani. 'I'm going away,' I said.

'How lovely!' said the Rani. 'I wish I could go away!'

'Why don't you?'

'They won't let me. They're afraid to let me out of the palace.'

'What are they afraid of, Your Highness?'

'That I might run away. Run away, far far away, to the land where the leopards are learning to pray.'

Gosh, I thought, she's really quite crazy . . . But then she was silent, and started smoking a small hookah.

She drew on the hookah, looked at me, and asked: 'Where is your mother?'

'I haven't one.'

'Everyone has a mother. Did yours die?'

'No: She went away.'

She drew on her hookah again and then said, very sweetly, 'Don't go away . . .'

'I must,' I said. 'It's because of the war.'

'What war? Is there a war on? You see, no one tells me anything.'

'It's between us and Hitler,' I said.

'And who is Hitler?'

'He's a German.'

'I knew a German once, Dr Schreinherr, he had beautiful hands.'

'Was he an artist?'

'He was a dentist.'

The Rani got up from her couch and accompanied me out on to the balcony. When we looked down at the garden, we could see Dukhi weeding a flower-bed. Both of us gazed down at him in silence, and I wondered what the Rani would say if I asked her if she had ever been in love with the palace gardener. Ayah had told me it would be an insulting question; so I held my peace. But as I walked slowly down the spiral staircase, the Rani's voice came after me.

'Thank him,' she said. 'Thank him for the beautiful rose.'

THE GIRL FROM COPENHAGEN

I

This is not a love story; but it is a story about love. You will know what I mean.

When I was living and working in London I knew a Vietnamese girl called Phuong. She studied at the Polytechnic. During the summer vacations she joined a group of students—some of them English, most of them French, German, Indian and African—picking raspberries for a few pounds a week, and drinking in some real English country air. Late one summer, on her return from a farm, she introduced me to Ulla, a sixteen-year-old Danish girl who had come over to England for a similar holiday.

'Please look after Ulla for a few days,' said Phuong. 'She doesn't know anyone in London.'

'But I want to look after you,' I protested. I had been infatuated with Phuong for some time; but, though she was rather fond of me, she did not reciprocate my advances, and it was possible that she had conceived of Ulla as a device to get rid of me for a little while.

'This is Ulla,' said Phuong, thrusting a blonde child into my arms. 'Bye, and don't get up to any mischief!'

Phuong disappeared, and I was left alone with Ulla at the entrance to the Charing Cross Underground Station. She grinned at me, and I smiled back rather nervously. She had blue eyes and a smooth, tanned skin. She was small for a Scandinavian girl, reaching only to my shoulders, and her figure was slim and boyish. She was carrying a small travelling-bag. It gave me an excuse to do something.

'We'd better leave your bag somewhere,' I said, taking it from her.

And after depositing it in the left-luggage office, we were back on the pavement, grinning at each other.

'Well, Ulla,' I said. 'How many days do you have in London.'

'Only two. Then I go back to Copenhagen.'

'Good. Well, what would you like to do?'

'Eat. I'm hungry.'

I wasn't hungry; but there's nothing like a meal to help two strangers grow acquainted. We went to a small and not very expensive Indian restaurant off Fitzroy Square, and burnt our tongues on an orange-coloured Hyderabad chicken curry. We had to cool off with a Tamil Koykotay before we could talk.

'What do you do in Copenhagen?' I asked.

'I go to school. I'm joining the University next year.'

'And your parents?'

'They have a bookshop.'

'Then you must have done a lot of reading.'

'Oh, no, I don't read much. I can't sit in one place for long. I like swimming and tennis and going to the theatre.'

'But you have to sit in a theatre.'

'Yes, but that's different.'

'It's not sitting that you mind, but sitting and reading.'

'Yes, you are right. But most Danish girls like reading—they read more books than English girls.'

'You are probably right,' I said.

As I was out of a job just then, and had time on my hands, we were able to feed the pigeons in Trafalgar Square and while away the afternoon in a coffee-bar, before going on to a theatre. Ulla was wearing tight jeans and an abbreviated duffle coat, and as she had brought little else with her, she wore this outfit to the theatre. It created quite a stir in the foyer, but Ulla was completely unconscious of the stares she received. She enjoyed the play, laughed loudly in all the wrong places, and clapped her hands when no one else did.

The lunch and the theatre had lightened my wallet, and dinner consisted of baked beans on toast in a small snack-bar. After picking up Ulla's bag, I offered to take her back to Phuong's place.

'Why there?' she said. 'Phuong must have gone to bed.'

'Yes, but aren't you staying with her?'

'Oh, no. She did not ask me.'

'Then where are you staying? Where have you kept the rest of your things?'

'Nowhere. This is all I brought with me,' she said, indicating the travel-bag.

'Well, you can't sleep on a park bench,' I said. 'Shall I get you a room in a hotel?'

'I don't think so. I have only the money to return to Copenhagen.' She looked crestfallen for a few moments; then she brightened, and slipped her arm through mine. 'I know, I'll stay with you. Don't mind?'

'No, but my landlady—' I began; then stopped; it would have been a lie. My landlady, a generous, broad-minded soul, would not have minded in the least.

'All right,' I said. 'I don't mind.'

When we reached my room in Swiss Cottage, Ulla threw off her coat and opened the window wide. It was a warm summer's night, and the scent of honeysuckle came through the open window. She kicked her shoes off, and walked about the room barefooted. Her toenails were painted a bright pink. She slipped out of her blouse and jeans, and stood before the mirror in her lace pants. A lot of sunbathing had made her quite brown, but her small breasts were white.

She slipped into bed and said, 'Aren't you coming?'

I crept in beside her and lay very still, while she chattered on about the play and the friends she made in the country. I switched off the bed-lamp and she fell silent. Then she said, 'Well, I'm sleepy. Goodnight!' And turning over, she immediately fell asleep.

I lay awake beside her, conscious of the growing warmth of her body. She was breathing easily and quietly. Her long, golden hair touched my cheek. I kissed her gently on the lobe of the ear, but she was fast asleep. So I counted eight hundred and sixty-two Scandinavian sheep, and managed to fall asleep.

Ulla woke fresh and frolicsome. The sun streamed in through the window, and she stood naked in its warmth, performing calisthenics. I busied myself with the breakfast. Ulla ate three eggs and a lot of bacon, and drank two cups of coffee. I couldn't help admiring her appetite.

'And what shall we do today?' she asked, her blue eyes shining. They were the bright blue eyes of a Siamese kitten.

'I'm supposed to visit the Employment Exchange,' I said.

'But that is bad. Can't you go tomorrow—after I have left?'

'If you like.'

'I like.'

And she gave me a swift, unsettling kiss on the lips.

We climbed Primrose Hill and watched boys flying kites. We lay in the sun and chewed blades of grass, and then we visited the Zoo, where Ulla fed the monkeys. She consumed innumerable ices. We lunched at a small Greek restaurant, and I forgot to phone Phuong, and in the evening we walked all the way home through scruffy Camden Town, drank beer, ate a fine, greasy dinner of fish and chips, and went to bed early—Ulla had to catch the boat-train next morning.

'It has been a good day,' she said.

'I'd like to do it again tomorrow.'

'But I must go tomorrow.'

'But you must go.'

She turned her head on the pillow and looked wonderingly into my eyes, as though she were searching for something. I don't know if she found what she was looking for; but she smiled, and kissed me softly on the lips.

'Thanks for everything,' she said.

She was fresh and clean, like the earth after spring rain.

I took her fingers and kissed them, one by one. I kissed her breasts, her throat, her forehead; and, making her close her eyes, I kissed her eyelids.

We lay in each other's arms for a long time, savouring the warmth and texture of each other's bodies. Though we were both very young and inexperienced, we found ourselves imbued with a tender patience, as though there lay before us not just this one passing night, but all the nights of a lifetime, all eternity.

There was a great joy in our loving, and afterwards we fell

asleep in each other's arms like two children who have been playing in the open all day.

The sun woke me next morning. I opened my eyes to see Ulla's slim, bare leg dangling over the side of the bed. I smiled at her painted toes. Her hair pressed against my face, and the sunshine fell on it, making each hair a strand of burnished gold.

The station and the train were crowded, and we held hands and grinned at each other, too shy to kiss.

'Give my love to Phuong,' she said.

'I will.'

We made no promises—of writing, or of meeting again. Somehow our relationship seemed complete and whole, as though it had been destined to blossom for those two days. A courting and a marriage and a living together had been compressed, perfectly, into one summer night. . . .

I passed the day in a glow of happiness; I thought Ulla was still with me; and it was only at night, when I put my hand out for hers, and did not find it, that I knew she had gone.

But I kept the window open all through the summer, and the scent of the honeysuckle was with me every night.

TRIBUTE TO A DEAD FRIEND

Now that Thanh is dead, I suppose it is not too treacherous of me to write about him. He was only a year older than I. He died in Paris, in his twenty-second year, and Pravin wrote to me from London and told me about it. I will get more details from Pravin when he returns to India next month; just now I only know that Thanh is dead.

It is supposed to be in very bad taste to discuss a person behind his back; and to discuss a dead person behind his back is most unfair, for he cannot even retaliate. But Thanh had this very weakness of criticizing absent people, and it cannot hurt him now if I do a little to expose his colossal Ego.

Thanh was a fraud all right, but no one knew it. He had beautiful round eyes, a flashing smile, and a sweet voice, and everyone said he was a charming person. He was certainly charming, but I have found that charming people are seldom sincere. I think I was the only person who came anywhere near to being his friend, for he had cultivated a special loneliness of his own, and it was difficult to intrude on it.

I met him in London in the summer of '54. I was trying to become a writer, while I worked part-time at a number of different jobs. I had been two years in London, and was longing for the hills and rivers of India. Thanh was Vietnamese. His family was well-to-do, and though the Communists had taken their home-town of Hanoi, most of the family was in France, well-established in the restaurant business. Thanh did not suffer from the same financial distress as other students whose homes were in Northern Vietnam. He wasn't studying anything in particular, but practised assiduously on the piano, though the only thing he could play fairly well was Chopin's Funeral March.

My friend Pravin, a happy-go-lucky, very friendly Gujarati

107

boy, introduced me to Thanh. Pravin, like a good Indian, thought all Asians were superior people, but he didn't know Thanh well enough to know that Thanh didn't like being an Asian.

At first, Thanh was glad to meet me. He said he had for a long time been wanting to make friends with an Englishman, a real Englishman, not one who was a Pole or a Cockney or a Jew; he was most anxious to improve his English and talk like Mr Glendenning of the BBC. Pravin, knowing that I had been born and bred in India, that my parents had been born and bred in India, suppressed his laughter with some difficulty. But Thanh was soon disillusioned. My accent was anything but English. It was a pronounced *chi-chi* accent.

'You speak like an Indian!' exclaimed Thanh, horrified. 'Are you an Indian?'

'He's Welsh,' said Pravin with a wink.

Thanh was slightly mollified. Being Welsh was the next best thing to being English. Only he disapproved of the Welsh for speaking with an Indian accent.

Later, when Pravin had gone, and I was sitting in Thanh's room, drinking Chinese tea, he confided in me that he disliked Indians.

'Isn't Pravin your friend?' I asked.

'I don't trust him,' he said. 'I have to be friendly, but I don't trust him at all. I don't trust any Indians.'

'What's wrong with them?'

'They are too inquisitive,' complained Thanh. 'No sooner have you met one of them than he is asking you who your father is, and what your job is, and how much money have you got in the Bank?'

I laughed, and tried to explain that in India inquisitiveness is a sign of a desire for friendship, and that he should feel flattered when asked such personal questions. I protested that I was an Indian myself, and he said if that was so, he wouldn't trust me either.

But he seemed to like me, and often invited me to his rooms.

He could make some wonderful Chinese and French dishes. When we had eaten, he would sit down at his second-hand piano and play Chopin. He always complained that I didn't listen properly.

He complained of my untidiness and my unwarranted self-confidence. It was true that I appeared most confident when I was not very sure of myself. I boasted of an intimate knowledge of London's geography, but I was an expert at losing my way and then blaming it on someone else.

'You are a useless person,' said Thanh, while with chopsticks I stuffed my mouth with delicious pork and fried rice. 'You cannot find your way anywhere. You cannot speak English properly. You do not know any people except Indians. How are you going to be a writer?'

'If I am as bad as all that,' I said, 'why do you remain my friend?'

'I want to study your stupidity,' he said.

That was why he never made any real friends. He loved to work out your faults and examine your imperfections. There was no such thing as a real friend, he said. He had looked everywhere, but he could not find the perfect friend.

'What is your idea of a perfect friend?' I asked him. 'Does he have to speak perfect English?'

But sarcasm was only wasted on Thanh—he admitted that perfect English was one of the requisites of a perfect friend!

Sometimes, in moments of deep gloom, he would tell me that he did not have long to live.

'There is a pain in my chest,' he complained. 'There is something ticking there all the time. Can you hear it?'

He would bare his bony chest for me, and I would put my ear to the offending spot; but I could never hear any ticking.

'Visit the hospital,' I advised. 'They'll give you an X-ray and a proper check-up.'

'I have had X-rays,' he lied. 'They never show anything.'

Then he would talk of killing himself. This was his theme song: he had no friends, he was a failure as a musician, there was no other career open to him, he hadn't seen his family for five years, and he couldn't go back to Indo-China because of the Communists. He magnified his own troubles and minimized other people's troubles. When I was in hospital with an old acquaintance, amoebic dysentery, Pravin came to see me every day. Thanh, who was not very busy, came only once and never again. He said the hospital ward depressed him.

'You need a holiday,' I told him when I was out of hospital. 'Why don't you join the students' union and work on a farm for a week or two? That should toughen you up.'

To my surprise, the idea appealed to him, and he got ready for the trip. Suddenly, he became suffused with goodwill towards all mankind. As evidence of his trust in me, he gave me the key of his room to keep (though he would have been secretly delighted if I had stolen his piano and chopsticks, giving him the excuse to say 'never trust an Indian or an Anglo-Indian'), and introduced me to a girl called Vu-Phuong, a small, very pretty Annamite girl, who was studying at the Polytechnic. Miss Vu, Thanh told me, had to leave her lodgings next week, and would I find somewhere else for her to stay? I was an experienced hand at finding bed-sitting rooms, having changed my own abode five times in six months (that sweet, nomadic London life!). As I found Miss Vu very attractive, I told her I would get her a room, one not far from my own, in case she needed any further assistance.

Later, in confidence, Thanh asked me not to be too friendly with Vu-Phuong, as she was not to be trusted.

But as soon as he left for the farm, I went round to see Vu in her new lodgings, which were one tube-station away from my own. She seemed glad to see me, and as she too could make French and Chinese dishes, I accepted her invitation to lunch. We had chicken noodles, soya sauce, and fried rice. I did the washing-up. Vu said: 'Do you play cards, Ruskin?' She had a sweet, gentle voice, that brought out all the gallantry in a man. I began to feel protective, and hovered about her like a devoted cocker spaniel.

'I'm not much of a card-player,' I said.

'Never mind, I'll tell your fortune with them.'

She made me shuffle the cards; then scattered them about on

the bed in different patterns. I would be very rich, she said; I would travel a lot, and I would reach the age of forty. I told her I was comforted to know it.

The month was June, and Hampstead Heath was only ten minutes walk from the house. Boys flew kites from the hill, and little painted boats scurried about on the ponds. We sat down on the grass, on the slope of the hill, and I held Vu's hand.

For three days I ate with Vu, and we told each other our fortunes, and lay on the grass on Hampstead Heath, and on the fourth day I said, 'Vu, I would like to marry you.'

'I will think about it,' she said.

Thanh came back on the sixth day and said, 'You know, Ruskin, I have been doing some thinking, and Vu is not such a bad girl after all. I will ask her to marry me. That is what I need—a wife!'

'Why didn't you think of it before?' I said. 'When will you ask her?'

'Tonight,' he said. 'I will come to see you afterwards, and tell you if I have been successful.'

I shrugged my shoulders resignedly, and waited. Thanh left me at six in the evening, and I waited for him till ten o'clock, all the time feeling a little sorry for him. More disillusionment for Thanh! Poor Thanh. . . .

He came in at ten o'clock, his face beaming. He slapped me on the back and said I was his best friend.

'Did you ask her?' I said.

'Yes. She said she would think about it. That is the same as "yes".'

'It isn't,' I said, unfortunately for both of us. 'She told me the same thing.'

Thanh looked at me as though I had just stabbed him in the back. *Et tu* Ruskin, was what his expression said.

We took a taxi and sped across to Vu's rooms. The uncertain nature of her replies was too much for both of us; without a definite answer, neither of us would have been able to sleep that night.

Vu was not at home. The landlady met us at the door, and told us that Vu had gone to the theatre with an Indian gentleman.

Thanh gave me a long, contemptuous look.

'Never trust an Indian,' he said.

'Never trust a woman,' I replied.

At twelve o'clock I woke Pravin. Whenever I could not sleep, I went to Pravin. He knew the remedy for all ailments. As on previous occasions, he went to the cupboard and produced a bottle of Cognac. We got drunk. He was seventeen and I was nineteen, and we were both quite decadent.

Three weeks later I returned to India. Thanh went to Paris, to help in his sister's restaurant. I did not hear of Vu-Phuong again.

And now, a year later, there is the letter from Pravin. All he can tell me is that Thanh died of some unknown disease. I wonder if it had anything to do with the ticking in his chest, or with his vague threats of suicide. I doubt if I will ever know. And I will never know how much I hated Thanh, and how much I loved him, or if there was any difference between hating and loving him.

TALES OF THE MACABRE

A JOB WELL DONE

D huki, the gardener, was clearing up the weeds that grew in profusion around the old disused well. He was an old man, skinny and bent and spindly-legged; but he had always been like that; his strength lay in his wrists and in his long, tendril-like fingers. He looked as frail as a petunia, but he had the tenacity of a vine.

'Are you going to cover the well?' I asked. I was eight, a great favourite of Dhuki. He had been the gardener long before my birth; had worked for my father, until my father died, and now worked for my mother and stepfather.

'I must cover it, I suppose,' said Dhuki. 'That's what the Major sahib wants. He'll be back any day, and if he finds the well still uncovered he'll get into one of his raging fits and I'll be looking for another job!'

The 'Major sahib' was my stepfather, Major Summerskill. A tall, hearty, back-slapping man, who liked polo and pig-sticking. He was quite unlike my father. My father had always given me books to read. The Major said I would become a dreamer if I read too much, and took the books away. I hated him; and did not think much of my mother for marrying him.

'The boy's too soft,' I heard him tell my mother. 'I must see that he gets riding lessons.'

But, before the riding lessons could be arranged, the Major's regiment was ordered to Peshawar. Trouble was expected from some of the frontier tribes. He was away for about two months. Before leaving, he had left strict instructions for Dhuki to cover up the old well.

'Too damned dangerous having an open well in the middle of the garden,' my stepfather had said. 'Make sure that it's completely covered by the time I get back.'

115

Dhuki was loth to cover up the old well. It had been there for over fifty years long before the house had been built. In its walls lived a colony of pigeons. Their soft cooing filled the garden with a lovely sound. And during the hot, dry, summer months, when taps ran dry, the well was always a dependable source of water. The bhisti still used it, filling his goatskin bag with the cool clear water and sprinkling the paths around the house to keep the dust down.

Dhuki pleaded with my mother to let him leave the well uncovered.

'What will happen to the pigeons?' he asked.

'Oh, surely they can find another well,' said my mother. 'Do close it up soon, Dhuki. I don't want the Sahib to come back and find that you haven't done anything about it.'

My mother seemed just a little bit afraid of the Major. How can we be afraid of those we love? It was a question that puzzled me then, and puzzles me still.

The Major's absence made life pleasant again. I returned to my books, spent long hours in my favourite banyan tree, ate buckets of mangoes, and dawdled in the garden talking to Dhuki.

Neither he nor I were looking forward to the Major's return. Dhuki had stayed on after my mother's second marriage only out of loyalty to her and affection for me; he had really been my father's man. But my mother had always appeared deceptively frail and helpless, and most men, Major Summerskill included, felt protective towards her. She liked people who did things for her.

'Your father liked this well,' said Dhuki. 'He would often sit here in the evenings, with a book in which he made drawings of birds and flowers and insects.'

I remembered those drawings, and I remembered how they had all been thrown away by the Major when he had moved into the house. Dhuki knew about it too. I didn't keep much from him.

'It's a sad business closing this well,' said Dhuki again. 'Only a fool or a drunkard is likely to fall into it.'

But he had made his preparations. Planks of salwood, bricks and cement were neatly piled up around the well.

'Tomorrow,' said Dhuki. 'Tomorrow I will do it. Not today.

Let the birds remain for one more day. In the morning, baba, you can help me drive the birds from the well.'

On the day my stepfather was expected back, my mother hired a tonga and went to the bazaar to do some shopping. Only a few people had cars in those days. Even colonels went about in tongas. Now, a clerk finds it beneath his dignity to sit in one.

As the Major was not expected before evening, I decided I would make full use of my last free morning: I took all my favourite books and stored them away in an outhouse, where I could come for them from time to time. Then, my pockets bursting with mangoes, I climbed into the banyan tree. It was the darkest and coolest place on a hot day in June.

From behind the screen of leaves that concealed me, I could see Dhuki moving about near the well. He appeared to be most unwilling to get on with the job of covering it up.

'Baba!' he called, several times; but I did not feel like stirring from the banyan tree. Dhuki grasped a long plank of wood and placed it across one end of the well. He started hammering. From my vantage point in the banyan tree, he looked very bent and old.

A jingle of tonga bells and the squeak of unoiled wheels told me that a tonga was coming in at the gate. It was too early for my mother to be back. I peered through the thick, waxy leaves of the tree, and nearly fell off my branch in surprise. It was my stepfather, the Major! He had arrived earlier than expected.

I did not come down from the tree. I had no intention of confronting my stepfather until my mother returned.

The Major had climbed down from the tonga and was watching his luggage being carried onto the veranda. He was red in the face and the ends of his handlebar moustache were stiff with brilliantine. Dhuki approached with a half-hearted salaam.

'Ah, so there you are, you old scoundrel!' exclaimed the Major, trying to sound friendly and jocular. 'More jungle than garden, from what I can see. You're getting too old for this sort of work, Dhuki. Time to retire! And where's the memsahib?'

'Gone to the bazaar,' said Dhuki.

'And the boy?'

Dhuki shrugged. 'I have not seen the boy, today, Sahib.'

'Damn!' said the Major. 'A fine homecoming, this. Well, wake up the cook-boy and tell him to get some sodas.'

'Cook-boy's gone away,' said Dhuki.

'Well, I'll be double-damned,' said the Major.

The tonga went away, and the Major started pacing up and down the garden path. Then he saw Dhuki's unfinished work at the well. He grew purple in the face, strode across to the well, and started ranting at the old gardener.

Dhuki began making excuses. He said something about a shortage of bricks; the sickness of a niece; unsatisfactory cement; unfavourable weather; unfavourable gods. When none of this seemed to satisfy the Major, Dhuki began mumbling about something bubbling up from the bottom of the well, and pointed down into its depths. The Major stepped onto the low parapet and looked down. Dhuki kept pointing. The Major leant over a little.

Dhuki's hand moved swiftly, like a conjurer's making a pass. He did not actually push the Major. He appeared merely to tap him once on the bottom. I caught a glimpse of my stepfather's boots as he disappeared into the well. I couldn't help thinking of Alice in Wonderland, of Alice disappearing down the rabbit hole.

There was a tremendous splash, and the pigeons flew up, circling the well thrice before settling on the roof of the bungalow.

By lunch-time—or tiffin, as we called it then—Dhuki had the well covered over with the wooden planks.

'The Major will be pleased,' said my mother, when she came home. 'It will be quite ready by evening, won't it, Dhuki?'

By evening, the well had been completely bricked over. It was the fastest bit of work Dhuki had ever done.

Over the next few weeks, my mother's concern changed to anxiety, her anxiety to melancholy, and her melancholy to resignation. By being gay and high-spirited myself, I hope I did something to cheer her up. She had written to the Colonel of the Regiment, and had been informed that the Major had gone home on leave a fortnight previously. Somewhere, in the vastness of India, the Major had disappeared.

It was easy enough to disappear and never be found. After several months had passed without the Major turning up, it was presumed that one of two things must had happened. Either he had been murdered on the train, and his corpse flung into a river; or, he had run away with a tribal girl and was living in some remote corner of the country.

Life had to carry on for the rest of us. The rains were over, and the guava season was approaching.

My mother was receiving visits from a colonel of His Majesty's 32nd Foot. He was an elderly, easygoing, seemingly absent-minded man, who didn't get in the way at all, but left slabs of chocolate lying around the house.

'A good sahib,' observed Dhuki, as I stood beside him behind the bougainvillaea, watching the colonel saunter up the veranda steps, 'See how well he wears his sola topi! It covers his head completely.'

'He's bald underneath,' I said.

'No matter. I think he will be all right.'

'And if he isn't,' I said, 'we can always open up the well again.'

Dhuki dropped the nozzle of the hose pipe, and water gushed out over our feet: But he recovered quickly, and taking me by the hand, led me across to the old well, now surmounted by a three-tiered cement platform which looked rather like a wedding cake.

'We must not forget our old well,' he said. 'Let us make it beautiful, baba. Some flower pots, perhaps.'

And together we fetched pots, and decorated the covered well with ferns and geraniums. Everyone congratulated Dhuki on the fine job he'd done. My only regret was that the pigeons had gone away.

THE TROUBLE WITH JINNS

My friend Jimmy has only one arm. He lost the other when he was a young man of twenty-five. The story of how he lost his good right arm is a little difficult to believe, but I swear that it is absolutely true.

To begin with, Jimmy was (and presumably still is) a Jinn. Now a Jinn isn't really a human like us. A Jinn is a spirit creature from another world who has assumed, for a lifetime, the physical aspect of a human being. Jimmy was a true Jinn, and he had the Jinn's gift of being able to elongate his arm at will. Most Jinns can stretch their arm to a distance of twenty or thirty feet; Jimmy could attain forty feet. His arm would move through space or up walls or along the ground like a beautiful gliding serpent. I have seen him stretched out beneath a mango tree, helping himself to ripe mangoes from the top of the tree. He loved mangoes. He was a natural glutton, and it was probably his gluttony that first led him to misuse his peculiar gifts.

We were at school together at a hill-station in northern India. Jimmy was particularly good at basketball. He was clever enough not to lengthen his arm too much, because he did not want anyone to know that he was a Jinn. In the boxing ring he generally won his fights. His opponents never seemed to get past his amazing reach. He just kept tapping them on the nose until they retired from the ring bloody and bewildered.

It was during the half-term examinations that I stumbled on Jimmy's secret. We had been set a particularly difficult algebra paper, but I had managed to cover a couple of sheets with correct answers and was about to forge ahead on another sheet when I noticed someone's hand on my desk. At first I thought it was the invigilator's. But when I looked up, there was no one beside me. Could it be the boy sitting directly behind? No, he was engrossed in his question paper, and had his hands to himself. Meanwhile, the hand on my desk had grasped my answer-sheets and was cautiously moving off. Following its descent, I found that it was attached to an arm of amazing length and pliability. This moved stealthily down the desk and slithered across the floor, shrinking all the while, until it was restored to its normal length. Its owner was of course one who had never been any good at algebra.

I had to write out my answers a second time, but after the exam, I went straight up to Jimmy, told him I didn't like his game, and threatened to expose him. He begged me not to let anyone know, assured me that he couldn't really help himself, and offered to be of service to me whenever I wished. It was tempting to have Jimmy as my friend, for with his long reach he could obviously be useful. I agreed to overlook the matter of the pilfered papers, and we became the best of pals.

It did not take me long to discover that Jimmy's gift was more of a nuisance than a constructive aid. That was because Jimmy had a second rate mind and did not know how to make proper use of his powers. He seldom rose above the trivial. He used his long arm in the tuck-shop, in the classroom, in the dormitory. And when we were allowed out to the cinema, he used it in the dark of the hall.

Now, the trouble with all Jinns is that they have a weakness for women with long black hair. The longer and blacker the hair, the better for Jinns. And should a Jinn manage to take possession of the woman he desires, she goes into a decline and her beauty decays. Everything about her is destroyed except for the beautiful long black hair.

Jimmy was still too young to be able to take possession in this way, but he couldn't resist touching and stroking long black hair. The cinema was the best place for the indulgence of his whims. His arm would start stretching, his fingers would feel their way along the rows of seats, and his lengthening limb would slowly work its way along the aisle until it reached the back of the seat in which sat the object of his admiration. His hand would stroke the long black hair with great tenderness; and if the girl felt anything and looked round, Jimmy's hand would disappear behind the seat and lie there poised like the hood of a snake, ready to strike again.

At college two or three years later, Jimmy's first real victim succumbed to his attentions. She was a Lecturer in Economics, not very good-looking, but her hair, black and lustrous, reached almost to her knees. She usually kept it in plaits; but Jimmy saw her one morning, just after she had taken a head-bath, and her hair lay spread out on the cot on which she was reclining. Jimmy could no longer control himself. His spirit, the very essence of his personality, entered the woman's body, and the next day she was distraught, feverish and excited. She would not eat, went into a coma, and in a few days dwindled to a mere skeleton. When she died, she was nothing but skin and bone; but her hair had lost none of its loveliness.

I took pains to avoid Jimmy after this tragic event. I could not prove that he was the cause of the lady's sad demise, but in my own heart I was quite certain of it; for since meeting Jimmy I had read a good deal about Jinns, and knew their ways.

We did not see each other for a few years. And then, holidaying in the hills last year, I found we were staying at the same hotel. I could not very well ignore him, and after we had taken a few beers together I began to feel that I had perhaps misjudged Jimmy, and that he was not the irresponsible Jinn I had taken him for. Perhaps the college lecturer had died of some mysterious malady that attacks only college lecturers, and Jimmy had nothing at all to do with it.

We had decided to take our lunch and a few bottles of beer to a grassy knoll just below the main motor-road. It was late afternoon and I had been sleeping off the effects of the beer when I woke to find Jimmy looking rather agitated.

'What's wrong?' I asked.

'Up there, under the pine trees,' he said. 'Just above the road. Don't you see them?'

'I see two girls,' I said. 'So what?'

'The one on the left. Haven't you noticed her hair?'

'Yes, it is very long and beautiful and—now look, Jimmy, you'd better get a grip on yourself!' But already his hand was out of sight, his arm snaking up the hillside and across the road.

Presently I saw the hand emerge from some bushes near the girls, and then cautiously make its way to the girl with the black tresses. So absorbed was Jimmy in the pursuit of his favourite pastime that he failed to hear the blowing of a horn. Around the bend of the road came a speeding Mercedes-Benz truck.

Jimmy saw the truck, but there wasn't time for him to shrink his arm back to normal. It lay right across the entire width of the road, and when the truck had passed over it, it writhed and twisted like a mortally wounded python.

By the time the truck-driver and I could fetch a doctor, the arm (or what was left of it) had shrunk to its ordinary size. We took Jimmy to hospital, where the doctors found it necessary to amputate. The truck-driver, who kept insisting that the arm he ran over was at least thirty feet long, was arrested on a charge of drunken driving.

Some weeks later I asked Jimmy, 'Why are you so depressed? You still have one arm. Isn't it gifted in the same way?'

'I never tried to find out,' he said, 'and I'm not going to try now.'

He is of course still a Jinn at heart, and whenever he sees a girl with long black hair he must be terribly tempted to try out his one good arm and stroke her beautiful tresses. But he has learnt his lesson. It is better to be a human without any gifts than a Jinn or a genius with one too many.

HE SAID IT WITH ARSENIC

I s there such a person as a born murderer—in the sense that there are born writers and musicians, born winners and losers? One can't be sure. The urge to do away with troublesome people is common to most of us, but only a few succumb to it.

If ever there was a born murderer, he must surely have been William Jones. The thing came so naturally to him. No extreme violence, no messy shootings or hackings or throttling; just the right amount of poison, administered with skill and discretion.

A gentle, civilized sort of person was Mr Jones. He collected butterflies and arranged them systematically in glass cases. His ether bottle was quick and painless. He never stuck pins into the beautiful creatures.

Have you ever heard of the Agra Double Murder? It happened, of course, a great many years ago, when Agra was a far-flung outpost of the British Empire. In those days, William Jones was a male nurse in one of the city's hospitals. The patients—especially terminal cases—spoke highly of the care and consideration he showed them. While most nurses, both male and female, preferred to attend to the more hopeful cases, nurse William was always prepared to stand duty over a dying patient.

He felt a certain empathy for the dying; he liked to see them on their way. It was just his good nature, of course.

On a visit to nearby Meerut, he met and fell in love with Mrs Browning, the wife of the local Stationmaster. Impassioned love letters were soon putting a strain on the Agra-Meerut postal service. The envelopes grew heavier—not so much because the letters were growing longer but because they contained little packets of a powdery white substance, accompanied by detailed instructions as to its correct administration.

Mr Browning, an unassuming and trustful man—one of the

world's born losers, in fact—was not the sort to read his wife's correspondence. Even when he was seized by frequent attacks of colic, he put them down to an impure water supply. He recovered from one bout of vomiting and diarrhoea only to be racked by another.

He was hospitalized on a diagnosis of gastroenteritis; and, thus freed from his wife's ministrations, soon got better. But on returning home and drinking a glass of nimbu-pani brought to him by the solicitous Mrs Browning, he had a relapse from which he did not recover.

Those were the days when deaths from cholera and related diseases were only too common in India, and death certificates were easier to obtain than dog licences.

After a short interval of mourning (it was the hot weather and you couldn't wear black for long) Mrs Browning moved to Agra, where she rented a house next door to William Jones.

I forgot to mention that Mr Jones was also married. His wife was an insignificant creature, no match for a genius like William. Before the hot weather was over, the dreaded cholera had taken her too. The way was clear for the lovers to unite in holy matrimony.

But Dame Gossip lived in Agra too, and it was not long before tongues were wagging and anonymous letters were being received by the Superintendent of Police. Enquiries were instituted. Like most infatuated lovers, Mrs Browning had hung on to her beloved's letters and billet-doux, and these soon came to light. The silly woman had kept them in a box beneath her bed.

Exhumations were ordered in both Agra and Meerut. Arsenic keeps well, even in the hottest weather, and there was no dearth of it in the remains of both victims.

Mr Jones and Mrs Browning were arrested and charged with murder.

*

'Is Uncle Bill really a murderer?' I asked from the drawing room sofa in my grandmother's house in Dehra. (It's time that I told you that William Jones was my uncle, my mother's half-brother.)

I was eight or nine at the time. Uncle Bill had spent the previous summer with us in Dehra and had stuffed me with bazaar sweets and pastries, all of which I had consumed without suffering any ill effects.

'Who told you that about Uncle Bill?' asked Grandmother.

'I heard it in school. All the boys were asking me the same question—"Is your uncle a murderer?" They say he poisoned both his wives.'

'He had only one wife,' snapped Aunt Mabel.

'Did he poison her?'

'No, of course not. How can you say such a thing!'

'Then why is Uncle Bill in gaol?'

'Who says he's in gaol?'

'The boys at school. They heard it from their parents. Uncle Bill is to go on trial in the Agra fort.'

There was a pregnant silence in the drawing room, then Aunt Mabel burst out: 'It was all that awful woman's fault.'

'Do you mean Mrs Browning?' asked Grandmother.

'Yes, of course. She must have put him up to it. Bill couldn't have thought of anything so—so diabolical!'

'But he sent her the powders, dear. And don't forget—Mrs Browning has since. . . .'

Grandmother stopped in mid-sentence, and both she and Aunt Mabel glanced surreptitiously at me.

'Committed suicide,' I filled in. 'There were still some powders with her.'

Aunt Mabel's eyes rolled heavenwards. 'This boy is impossible. I don't know what he will be like when he grows up.'

'At least I won't be like Uncle Bill,' I said. 'Fancy poisoning people! If I kill anyone, it will be in a fair fight. I suppose they'll hang Uncle?'

'Oh, I hope not!'

Grandmother was silent. Uncle Bill was her stepson but she did have a soft spot for him. Aunt Mabel, his sister, thought he was wonderful. I had always considered him to be a bit soft but had to

126

admit that he was generous. I tried to imagine him dangling at the end of a hangman's rope, but somehow he didn't fit the picture.

As things turned out, he didn't hang. White people in India seldom got the death sentence, although the hangman was pretty busy disposing off dacoits and political terrorists. Uncle Bill was given a life-sentence and settled down to a sedentary job in the prison library at Naini, near Allahabad. His gifts as a male nurse went unappreciated; they did not trust him in the hospital.

He was released after seven or eight years, shortly after the country became an independent republic. He came out of gaol to find that the British were leaving, either for England or the remaining colonies. Grandmother was dead. Aunt Mabel and her husband had settled in South Africa. Uncle Bill realized that there was little future for him in India and followed his sister out to Johannesburg. I was in my last year at boarding-school. After my father's death, my mother had married an Indian, and now my future lay in India.

I did not see Uncle Bill after his release from prison, and no one dreamt that he would ever turn up again in India.

In fact, fifteen years were to pass before he came back, and by then I was in my early thirties, the author of a book that had become something of a best-seller. The previous fifteen years had been a struggle—the sort of struggle that every young freelance writer experiences—but at last the hard work was paying 'off and the royalties were beginning to come in.

I was living in a small cottage on the outskirts of the hill-station of Fosterganj, working on another book, when I received an unexpected visitor.

He was a thin, stooped, grey-haired man in his late fifties, with a straggling moustache and discoloured teeth. He looked feeble and harmless but for his eyes which were a pale cold blue. There was something slightly familiar about him.

'Don't you remember me?' he asked. 'Not that I really expect you to, after all these years.

'Wait a minute. Did you teach me at school?'

'No—but you're getting warm.' He put his suitcase down and I glimpsed his name on the airlines label. I looked up in astonishment. 'You're not—you couldn't be. . . .'

'Your Uncle Bill,' he said with a grin and extended his hand. 'None other!' And he sauntered into the house.

I must admit that I had mixed feelings about his arrival. While I had never felt any dislike for him, I hadn't exactly approved of what he had done. Poisoning, I felt, was a particularly reprehensible way of getting rid of inconvenient people: not that I could think of any commendable ways of getting rid of them! Still, it had happened a long time ago, he'd been punished, and presumably he was a reformed character.

'And what have you been doing all these years?' he asked me, easing himself into the only comfortable chair in the room.

'Oh just writing,' I said.

'Yes, I heard about your last book. It's quite a success, isn't it?'

'It's doing quite well. Have you read it?'

'I don't do much reading.'

'And what have you been doing all these years, Uncle Bill?'

'Oh, knocking about here and there. Worked for a soft drink company for some time. And then with a drug firm. My knowledge of chemicals was useful.'

'Weren't you with Aunt Mabel in South Africa?'

'I saw quite a lot of her, until she died a couple of years ago. Didn't you know?'

'No. I've been out of touch with relatives.' I hoped he'd take that as a hint. 'And what about her husband?'

'Died too, not long after. Not many of us left, my boy. That's why, when I saw something about you in the papers, I thought—why not go and see my only nephew again?'

'You're welcome to stay a few days,' I said quickly. 'Then I have to go to Bombay.' (This was a lie, but I did not relish the prospect of looking after Uncle Bill for the rest of his days.)

'Oh, I won't be staying long,' he said. 'I've got a bit of money put by in Johannesburg. It's just that—so far as I know—you're my only living relative, and I thought it would be nice to see you again.'

Feeling relieved, I set about trying to make Uncle Bill as comfortable as possible. I gave him my bedroom and turned the window-seat into a bed for myself. I was a hopeless cook but, using all my ingenuity, I scrambled some eggs for supper. He waved aside my apologies; he'd always been a frugal eater, he said. Eight years in gaol had given him a cast-iron stomach.

He did not get in my way but left me to my writing and my lonely walks. He seemed content to sit in the spring sunshine and smoke his pipe.

It was during our third evening together that he said, 'Oh, I almost forgot. There's a bottle of sherry, in my suitcase. I brought it especially for you.'

'That was very thoughtful of you, Uncle Bill. How did you know I was fond of sherry?'

'Just my intuition. You do like it, don't you?'

'There's nothing like a good sherry.'

He went to his bedroom and came back with an unopened bottle of South African sherry.

'Now you just relax near the fire,' he said agreeably. 'I'll open the bottle and fetch glasses.'

He went to the kitchen while I remained near the electric fire, flipping through some journals. It seemed to me that Uncle Bill was taking rather a long time. Intuition must be a family trait, because it came to me quite suddenly—the thought that Uncle Bill might be intending to poison me.

After all, I thought, here he is after nearly fifteen years, apparently for purely sentimental reasons. But I had just published a best-seller. And I was his nearest relative. If I was to die Uncle Bill could lay claim to my estate and probably live comfortably on my royalties for the next five or six years!

What had really happened to Aunt Mabel and her husband, I wondered. And where did Uncle Bill get the money for an air ticket to India?

Before I could ask myself any more questions, he reappeared with the glasses on a tray. He set the tray on a small table that stood between us. The glasses had been filled. The sherry sparkled.

I stared at the glass nearest me, trying to make out if the liquid in it was cloudier than that in the other glass. But there appeared to be no difference.

I decided I would not take any chances. It was a round tray, made of smooth Kashmiri walnut wood. I turned it round with my index finger, so that the glasses changed places.

'Why did you do that?' asked Uncle Bill.

'It's a custom in these parts. You turn the tray with the sun, a complete revolution. It brings good luck.'

Uncle Bill looked thoughtful for a few moments, then said, 'Well, let's have some more luck,' and turned the tray around again.

'Now you've spoilt it,' I said. 'You're not supposed to keep revolving it! That's bad luck. I'll have to turn it about again to cancel out the bad luck.'

The tray swung round once more, and Uncle Bill had the glass that was meant for me.

'Cheers!' I said, and drank from my glass.

It was good sherry.

Uncle Bill hesitated. Then he shrugged, said 'Cheers', and drained his glass quickly.

But he did not offer to fill the glasses again.

Early next morning he was taken violently ill. I heard him retching in his room, and I got up and went to see if there was anything I could do. He was groaning, his head hanging over the side of the bed. I brought him a basin and a jug of water.

'Would you like me to fetch a doctor?' I asked.

He shook his head. 'No I'll be all right. It must be something I ate.'

'It's probably the water. It's not too good at this time of the year. Many people come down with gastric trouble during their first few days in Fosterganj.'

'Ah, that must be it,' he said, and doubled up as a fresh spasm of pain and nausea swept over him.

He was better by evening—whatever had gone into the glass must have been by way of the preliminary dose and a day later he was well enough to pack his suitcase and announce his departure.

The climate of Fosterganj did not agree with him, he told me.

Just before he left, I said: 'Tell me, Uncle, why did you drink it?

'Drink what? The water?'

'No, the glass of sherry into which you'd slipped one of your famous powders.'

He gaped at me, then gave a nervous whinnying laugh. 'You will have your little joke, won't you?'

'No, I mean it,' I said. 'Why did you drink the stuff? It was meant for me, of course.'

He looked down at his shoes, then gave a little shrug and turned away.

'In the circumstances,' he said, 'it seemed the only decent thing to do.'

I'll say this for Uncle Bill: he was always the perfect gentleman.

HANGING AT THE MANGO-TOPE

The two captive policemen, Inspector Hukam Singh and Sub-Inspector Guler Singh, were being pushed unceremoniously along the dusty, deserted, sun-drenched road. The people of the village had made themselves scarce. They would reappear only when the dacoits went away.

The leader of the dacoit gang was Mangal Singh Bundela, great-grandson of a Pindari adventurer who had been a thorn in the side of the British. Mangal was doing his best to be a thorn in the flesh of his own govermnent. The local police force had been strengthened recently but it was still inadequate for dealing with the dacoits who knew the ravines better than any surveyor. The dacoit Mangal had made a fortune out of ransom; his chief victims were the sons of wealthy industrialists, money-lenders or landowners. But today he had captured two police officials; of no value as far as ransom went, but prestigious prisoners who could be put to other uses . . .

Mangal Singh wanted to show off in front of the police. He would kill at least one of them—his reputation demanded it but he would let the other go, in order that his legendary power and ruthlessness be given the maximum publicity. A legend is always a help!

His red and green turban was tied rakishly to one side. His dhoti extended right down to his ankles. His slippers were embroidered with gold and silver thread. His weapon was not an ancient matchlock, but a well-greased .303 rifle. Two of his men had similar rifles. Some had revolvers. Only the smaller fry carried swords or country-made pistols. Mangal Singh's gang, though traditional in many ways, was up-to-date in the matter of weapons. Right now they had the policemen's guns too.

'Come along, Inspector sahib,' said Mangal Singh, in tones of

132

police barbarity, tugging at the rope that encircled the stout Inspector's midriff. 'Had you captured me today, you would have been a hero. You would have taken all the credit, even though you could not keep up with your men in the ravines. Too bad you chose to remain sitting in your jeep with the Sub-Inspector. The jeep will be useful to us, you will not. But I would like you to be a hero all the same—and there is none better than a dead hero!'

Mangal Singh's followers doubled up with laughter. They loved their leader's cruel sense of humour.

'As for you, Guler Singh,' he continued, giving his attention to the Sub-Inspector, 'you are a man from my own village. You should have joined me long ago. But you were never to be trusted. You thought there would be better pickings in the police, didn't you?'

Guler Singh said nothing, simply hung his head and wondered what his fate would be. He felt certain that Mangal Singh would devise some diabolical and fiendish method of dealing with his captives. Guler Singh's only hope was Constable Ghanshyam, who hadn't been caught by the dacoits because, at the time of the ambush, he had been in the bushes relieving himself.

'To the mango-tope!' said Mangal Singh, prodding the policemen forward.

'Listen to me, Mangal,' said the perspiring Inspector, who was ready to try anything to get out of his predicament. 'Let me go, and I give you my word there'll be no trouble for you in this area as long as I am posted here. What could be more convenient than that?'

'Nothing,' said Mangal Singh. 'But your word isn't good. *My* word is different. I have told my men that I will hang you at the mango-tope, and I mean to keep my word. But I believe in fair-play—I like a little sport! You may yet go free if your friend here, Sub-Inspector Guler Singh, has his wits about him.'

The Inspector and his subordinate exchanged doubtful puzzled looks. They were not to remain puzzled for long. On reaching the mango-tope, the dacoits produced a good strong hempen rope, one end looped into a slip-knot. Many a garland of marigolds had the Inspector received during his mediocre career. Now, for the first time, he was being garlanded with a hangman's noose. He had seen hangings, he had rather enjoyed them; but he had no stomach for his own. The Inspector begged for mercy. Who wouldn't have in his position?

'Be quiet,' commanded Mangal Singh. 'I do not want to know about your wife and your children and the manner in which they will starve. You shot my son last year.'

'Not I!' cried the Inspector. 'It was some other.'

'You led the party. But now, just to show you that I'm a sporting fellow, I am going to have you strung up from this tree, and then I am going to give Guler Singh six shots with a rifle, and if he can sever the rope that suspends you before you are dead, well then, you can remain alive and I will let you go! For your sake, I hope the Sub-Inspector's aim is good. He will have to shoot fast. My man Phambiri, who has made this noose, was once executioner in a city jail. He guarantees that you won't last more than fifteen seconds at the end of *his* rope.'

Guler Singh was taken to a spot about forty yards away. A rifle was thrust into his hands. Two dacoits clambered into the branches of the mango tree. The Inspector, his hands tied behind, could only gaze at them in horror. His mouth opened and shut as though he already had need of more air. And then, suddenly, the rope went taut, up went the Inspector, his throat caught in a vice, while the branch of the tree shook and mango-blossoms fluttered to the ground. The Inspector dangled from the rope, his feet about three feet above the ground.

'You can shoot,' said Mangal Singh, nodding to the Sub-Inspector.

And Guler Singh, his hands trembling a little, raised the rifle to his shoulder and fired three shots in rapid succession. But the rope was swinging violently and the Inspector's body was jerking about like a fish on a hook. The bullets went wide.

Guler Singh found the magazine empty. He reloaded, wiped the stinging sweat from his eyes, raised the rifle again, took more careful aim. His hands were steadier now. He rested the sights on the upper portion of the rope, where there was less motion. Normally he was a good shot; but he had never been asked to demonstrate his skill in circumstances such as these.

The Inspector still gyrated at the end of his rope. There was life in him yet. His face was purple. The world, in those choking moments, was a medley of upside-down roofs and a red sun spinning slowly towards him.

Guler Singh's rifle cracked again. An inch or two wide this time. But the fifth shot found its mark, sending small tuffs of rope winging into the air.

The shot did not sever the rope; it was only a nick.

Guler Singh had one shot left. He was quite calm. The rifle-sight followed the rope's swing, less agitated now that the Inspector's convulsions were lessening. Guler Singh felt sure he could sever the rope this time.

And then, as his finger touched the trigger, an odd, disturbing thought slipped into his mind, hung there, throbbing. 'Whose life are you trying to save? Hukam Singh has stood in the way of your promotion more than once. He had you charge-sheeted for accepting fifty rupees from an unlicensed rickshaw-puller. He makes you do all the dirty work, blames you when things go wrong, takes the credit when there is credit to be taken. But for him, you'd be an Inspector!'

The rope swayed slightly to the right. The rifle moved just a fraction to the left. The last shot rang out, clipping a sliver of bark from the mango tree.

The Inspector was dead when they cut him down.

'Bad luck,' said Mangal Singh Bundela. 'You nearly saved him. But the next time I catch up with you, Guler Singh, it will be your turn to hang from the mango tree. So keep well away! You know that I am a man of my word. I keep it now, by giving you your freedom.'

A few minutes later the party of dacoits had melted away into the late afternoon shadows of the scrub forest. There was the sound of a jeep starting up. Then silence—a silence so profound that it seemed to be shouting in Guler Singh's ears.

As the village people began to trickle out of their houses, Constable Ghanshyam appeared as if from nowhere, swearing that he had lost his way in the jungle. Several people had seen the incident from their windows; they were unanimous in praising the Sub-Inspector for his brave attempt to save his superior's life. He had done his best.

'It is true,' thought Guler Singh. 'I did my best.'

That moment of hesitation before the last shot, the question that had suddenly reared up in the darkness of his mind, had already gone from his memory. We remember only what we want to remember.

'I did my best,' he told everyone.

And so he had.

A FACE IN THE DARK

Mr Oliver, an Anglo-Indian teacher, was returning to his school late one night, on the outskirts of the hill-station of Simla. From before Kipling's time, the school had been run on English public school lines; and the boys, most of them from wealthy Indian families, wore blazers, caps and ties. *Life* magazine, in a feature on India, had once called it the 'Eton of the East'. Mr Oliver had been teaching in the school for several years.

The Simla Bazaar, with its cinemas and restaurants, was about three miles from the school; and Mr Oliver, a bachelor, usually strolled into the town in the evening, returning after dark, when he would take a short cut through the pine forest.

When there was a strong wind, the pine trees made sad, eerie sounds that kept most people to the main road. But Mr Oliver was not a nervous or imaginative man. He carried a torch, and its gleam—the batteries were running down—moved fitfully down the narrow forest path. When its flickering light fell on the figure of a boy, who was sitting alone on a rock, Mr Oliver stopped. Boys were not supposed to be out after dark.

'What are you doing out here, boy?' asked Mr Oliver sharply, moving closer so that he could recognize the miscreant. But even as he approached the boy, Mr Oliver sensed that something was wrong. The boy appeared to be crying. His head hung down, he held his face in his hands, and his body shook convulsively. It was a strange, soundless weeping, and Mr Oliver felt distinctly uneasy.

'Well, what's the matter?' he asked, his anger giving way to concern. 'What are you crying for?' The boy would not answer or look up. His body continued to be racked with silent sobbing. 'Come on, boy, you shouldn't be out here at this hour. Tell me the trouble. Look up!' The boy looked up. He took his hands from his face and looked up at his teacher. The light from Mr Oliver's torch

137

fell on the boy's face—if you could call it a face.

It had no eyes, ears, nose or mouth. It was just a round smooth head—with a school cap on top of it! And that's where the story should end. But for Mr Oliver it did not end here.

The torch fell from his trembling hand. He turned and scrambled down the path, running blindly through the trees and calling for help. He was still running towards the school buildings when he saw a lantern swinging in the middle of the path. Mr Oliver stumbled up to the watchman, gasping for breath. 'What is it, Sahib?' asked the watchman. 'Has there been an accident? Why are you running?'

'I saw something—something horrible—a boy weeping in the forest—and he had no face!'

'No face, Sahib?'

'No eyes, nose, mouth—nothing!'

'Do you mean it was like this, Sahib?' asked the watchman, and raised the lamp to his own face. The watchman had no eyes, no ears, no features at all—not even an eyebrow! And that's when the wind blew the lamp out.

FROM A LITTLE ROOM

ESSAYS AND VIGNETTES

LIFE AT MY OWN PACE

All my life I've been a walking person. To this day I have neither owned nor driven a car, bus, tractor, aeroplane, motor-boat, scooter, truck, or steam-roller. Forced to make a choice, I would drive a steam-roller, because of its slow but solid progress and unhurried finality.

In my early teens I did for a brief period ride a bicycle, until I rode into a bullock-cart and broke my arm; the accident only serving to underline my unsuitability for wheeled conveyance that is likely to take my feet off the ground. Although dreamy and absent-minded, I have never *walked* into a bullock-cart.

Perhaps there is something to be said for Sun-signs. Mine being Taurus, I have, like the bull, always stayed close to grass, and have lived my life at my own leisurely pace only being stirred into furious activity when goaded beyond endurance. I have every sympathy for bulls and none for bull-fighters.

I was born in the Kasauli military hospital in 1934, and was baptized in the little Anglican church which still stands in the hill-station. My father had done his schooling at the Lawrence Royal Military School, at Sanawar, a few miles away, but he had gone into 'tea' and then teaching, and at the time I was born he was out of a job. In any case, the only hospital in Kasauli was the Pasteur Institute for the treatment of rabies, and as neither of my parents had been bitten by a mad dog, it was the army who took charge of my delivery.

But my earliest memories are not of Kasauli, for we left when I was two or three months old; they are of Jamnagar, a small State in coastal Kathiawar, where my father took a job as English tutor to several young princes and princesses. This was in the tradition of Forester and Ackerley, but my father did not have literary ambitions, although after his death I was to come across a notebook filled with

141

love-poems addressed to my mother, presumably written while they were courting.

This was where the walking really began, because Jamnagar was full of palaces and spacious lawns and gardens, and by the time I was three I was exploring much of this territory on my own, with the result that I encountered my first cobra, who, instead of striking me dead as the best fictional cobras are supposed to do, allowed me to pass.

Living as he did so close to the ground, and sensitive to every footfall, that intelligent snake must have known instinctively that I presented no threat, that I was just a small human discovering the use of his legs. Envious of the snake's swift gliding movements, I went indoors and tried crawling about on my belly, but I wasn't much good at it. Legs were better.

Amongst my father's pupils in one of these small States were three beautiful princesses. One of them was about my age, but the other two were older, and they were the ones at whose feet I worshipped. I think I was four or five when I had this strong crush on two 'older' girls—eight and ten respectively. At first I wasn't sure that they were girls, because they always wore jackets and trousers and kept their hair quite short. But my father told me they were girls, and he never lied to me.

My father's schoolroom and our own living quarters were located in one of the older palaces, situated in the midst of a veritable jungle of a garden. Here I could roam to my heart's content, amongst marigolds and cosmos growing rampant in the long grass, an ayah or a bearer often being sent post-haste after me, to tell me to beware of snakes and scorpions.

One of the books read to me as a child was a work called *Little Henry and His Bearer*, in which little Henry converts his servant to Christianity. I'm afraid something rather different happened to me. My ayah, bless her soul, taught me to eat paan and other forbidden delights from the bazaar, while the bearer taught me to abuse in choice Hindustani—an attribute that has stood over the years.

Neither of my parents were overly religious, and religious

tracts came my way far less frequently than they do now. (*Little Henry* was a gift from a distant aunt.) Nowadays everyone seems to feel I have a soul worth saving, whereas, when I was a boy, I was left severely alone by both preachers and adults. In fact the only time I felt threatened by religion was a few years later, when, visiting the aunt I have mentioned, I happened to fall down her steps and sprain my ankle. She gave me a triumphant look and said, 'See what happens when you don't go to church!'

My father was a good man. He taught me to read and write long before I started going to school, although it's true to say that I first learned to read *upside-down*. This happened because I would sit on a stool in front of the three princesses, watching them read and write and so the view I had of their books was an upside-down view; I still read that way occasionally, when a book gets boring.

He gave me books like *Peter Pan* and *Alice in Wonderland* (which I lapped up), but he was a fanatical stamp-collector, had dozens of albums, and corresponded and dealt regularly with Stanley Gibbons in London. After he died, the collections disappeared, otherwise I might well have been left a fortune in rare stamps!

My mother was at least twelve years younger, and liked going out to parties and dances. She was quite happy to leave me in the care of the ayah and bearer. I had no objection to the arrangement. The servants indulged me; and so did my father, bringing me books, toys, comics, chocolates, and of course stamps, when he returned from visits to Bombay.

Walking along the beach, collecting seashells, I got into the habit of staring hard at the ground, a habit which has stayed with me all my life. Apart from helping my thought-processes, it also results in my picking up odd objects—coins, keys, broken bangles, marbles, pens, bits of crockery, pretty stones, ladybirds, feathers, snail-shells. Occasionally, of course, this habit results in my walking some way past my destination (if I happen to have one), and why not? It simply means discovering a new and different destination, sights and sounds that I might not have experienced had I ended my walk exactly where it was supposed to end. And I am not looking at the ground all the time. Sensitive like the snake to approaching footfalls, I look up from time to time to examine the faces of passers-by, just in case they have something they wish to say to me.

A bird singing in a bush or tree has my immediate attention; so does any unfamiliar flower or plant, particularly if it grows in an unusual place such as a crack in a wall or rooftop, or in a yard full of junk where I once found a rose-bush blooming on the roof of an old Ford car.

There are other kinds of walks that I shall come to later, but it wasn't until I came to Dehra Dun and my grandmother's house that I really found my feet as a walker.

In 1939, when World War II broke out, my father joined the RAF, and my mother and I went to stay with her mother in Dehra Dun, while my father found himself in a tent in the outskirts of Delhi.

It took two or three days by train from Jamnagar to Dehra Dun, but trains were not quite as crowded then as they are today (the population being much smaller), and provided no one got sick, a long train journey was something of any extended picnic, with halts at quaint little stations, railway-meals in abundance brought by waiters in smart uniforms, an ever-changing landscape, bridges over mighty rivers, forest, desert, farmland, everything sundrenched, the air clear and unpolluted except when dust storms swept across the plains. Bottled drinks were a rarity then, the occasional lemonade or 'vimto' being the only aerated soft drinks, apart from soda-water. We made our own orange juice or lime juice, and took it with us.

By journey's end we were wilting and soot-covered, but Dehra's bracing winter climate brought us back to life.

Scarlet poinsettia leaves and trailing bougainvillaea as adorned the garden walls, while in the compounds grew mangoes, lichis, papayas, guavas, and lemons large and small. It was a popular place for retiring Anglo-Indians, and my maternal grandfather, after retiring from the Railways, had built a neat, compact bungalow on the Old Survey Road. There it stands today, unchanged except in ownership. Dehra was a small, quiet, garden-town, only parts of which are still recognizable, forty years after I first saw it.

I remember waking in the train early in the morning, and looking out of the window at heavy forest, trees of every description but mostly sal and shisham; here and there a forest glade, or a stream of clear water—quite different from the muddied waters of the streams and rivers we'd crossed the previous day. As we passed over a largish river (the Song) we saw a herd of elephants bathing; and leaving the forests of the Siwalik hills, we entered the Doon valley where fields of rice and flowing mustard stretched away to the foothills.

Outside the station we climbed into a tonga, or pony-trap, and rolled creakingly along quiet roads until we reached my grandfather's house. Grandfather had died a couple of years previously, and Grandmother had lived alone, except for occasional visits from her married daughters and their families, and from the unmarried but wandering son Ken, who was to turn up from time to time, especially when his funds were low. Granny also had a tenant, Miss Kellner, who occupied a portion of the bungalow.

Miss Kellner had been crippled in a carriage accident in Calcutta when she was a girl, and had been confined to a chair all her adult life. She had been left some money by her parents, and was able to afford an ayah and four stout palanquin-bearers, who carried her about when she wanted the chair moved and took her for outings in a real sedan-chair or sometimes a rickshaw—she had both. Her hands were deformed and she could scarcely hold a pen, but she managed to play cards quite dexterously and taught me a number of card-games, which I have forgotten now, as Miss Kellner was the only person with whom I *could* play cards: she allowed me to cheat. She took a fancy to me, and told Granny that I was the only one of her grandchildren with whom she could hold an intelligent conversation; Granny said that I was merely adept at flattery. It's true Miss Kellner's cook made marvellous meringues, coconut biscuits, and curry puffs, and these would be used very successfully to lure me over to her side of the garden, where she was usually to be found sitting in the shade of an old mango tree, shuffling her deck of cards. Granny's cook made a good kofta curry, but he did not go in for the exotic trifles that Miss Kellner served up.

Granny employed a full-time gardener, a wizened old character named Dukhi (sad), and I don't remember that he ever laughed or smiled. I'm not sure what deep tragedy dwelt behind those dark eyes (he never spoke about himself, even when questioned) but he was tolerant of me, and talked to me about flowers and their characteristics.

There were rows and rows of sweet-peas; beds full of phlox and sweet-smelling snapdragons; geraniums on the veranda steps, hollyhocks along the garden wall. . . . Behind the house were the fruit trees, somewhat neglected since my grandfather's death, and it was here that I liked to wander in the afternoons, for the old orchard was dark and private and full of possibilities. I made friends with an old jack-fruit tree, in whose trunk was a large hole in which I stored marbles, coins, catapults, and other treasures much as a crow stores the bright objects it picks up during its peregrinations.

I have never been a great tree-climber, having a tendency to fall off the branches, but I liked climbing walls (and still do), and it was not long before I had climbed the wall behind the orchard, to drop into unknown territory and explore the bazaars and by-lanes of Dehra.

*

'Great, grey, formless India,' as Kipling had called it, was, until I was eight or nine, unknown territory for me, and I had heard only vaguely of the freedom movement and Nehru and Gandhi; but then, a child of today's India is just as vague about them. Most domiciled Europeans and Anglo-Indians were apolitical. That the rule of the Sahib was not exactly popular in the land was made plain to me on the few occasions I ventured far from the house. Shouts of 'Red Monkey'! or 'White Pig!' were hurled at me with some enthusiasm but without any physical follow-up. I had the sense, even then, to follow the old adage, 'Sticks and stones may break my bones, but words can never hurt me.'

It was a couple of years later, when I was eleven, just a year or two before independence, that two passing cyclists, young men, swept past and struck me over the head. I was stunned but not hurt. They rode away with cries of triumph—I suppose it was a rare achievement to have successfully assaulted someone whom they associated with the ruling race—but although I could hardly (at that age) be expected to view them with Gandhian love and tolerance, I did not allow the resentment to rankle. I know I did not mention the incident to anyone—not to my mother or grandmother, or even to Mr Ballantyne, the S.P., a family friend who dropped in at the house quite frequently. Perhaps it was personal pride that prevented me from doing so; or perhaps I had already learnt to accept the paradox that India could be as cruel as it could be kind.

With my habit, already formed, of taking long walks into unfamiliar areas, I exposed myself more than did most Anglo-Indian boys of my age. Boys bigger than me rode bicycles; boys smaller than me stayed at home!

My parents' marriage had been on the verge of breaking up, and I was eight or nine when they finally separated. My mother was soon married again, to a Punjabi businessman, while I went to join my father in his air force hutment in Delhi. I would return to Dehra, not once but many times in the course of my life, for the town, even when it ceased to enchant, continued to exert a considerable influence on me, both as a writer and as a person; not a literary influence (for that came almost entirely from books) but as an area whose atmosphere was to become a part of my mind and sensuous nature.

I had a very close relationship with my father and was more than happy with him in Delhi, although he would be away almost every day, and sometimes, when he was hospitalized with malaria, he would be away almost every night too. When he was free he took me for long walks to the old tombs and monuments that dotted the wilderness that then surrounded New Delhi; or to the bookshops and cinemas of Connaught Place, the capital's smart shopping complex, then spacious and uncluttered. I shared his fondness for musicals, and wartime Delhi had a number of cinemas offering all the glitter of Hollywood.

I wasn't doing much reading then—I did not, in fact, become a great reader until after my father's death—but played gramophone records when I was alone in the house, or strolled about the quiet avenues of New Delhi, waiting for my father to return from his office. There was very little traffic in those days, and the roads were comparatively safe.

I was lonely, shy and aloof, and when other children came my way I found it difficult to relate to them. Not that they came my way very often. My father hadn't the time or the inclination to socialize, and in the evenings he would sit down to his stamp collection, while I helped to sort, categorize and mount his treasures.

I was quite happy with this life. During the day, when there was nothing else to do, I would make long lists of films or books or records; and although I have long since shed this hobby, it had the effect of turning me into an efficient cataloguer. When I became a writer, the world lost a librarian or archivist.

My father felt that this wasn't the right sort of life for a growing boy, and arranged for me to go to a boarding-school in Simla. As often happens, when the time approached for me to leave, I did make friends with some other boys who lived down the road.

Trenches had been dug all over New Delhi, in anticipation of Japanese air-raids, and there were several along the length of the road on which we lived. These were ideal places for games of cops and robbers, and I was gradually drawn into them. The heat of midsummer, with temperatures well over 100° Fahrenheit, did not keep us indoors for long, and in any case the trenches were cooler than the open road. I discovered that I was quite strong too, in comparison with most boys of my age, and in the wrestling-bouts that were often held in the trenches I invariably came out, quite literally, on top. At eight or nine I was a chubby boy; I hadn't learnt to use my fists (and never did), but I knew how to use my weight, and when I sat upon an opponent he usually remained sat upon until I decided to move.

I don't remember all their names, but there was a dark boy called Joseph, Goan I think, who was particularly nice to me, no matter how often I sat upon him. Our burgeoning friendship was cut short when my father and I set out for Simla. My father had two weeks' leave, and we would spend that time together before I was shut up in school. Ten years in a boarding-school was to convince me that such places bring about an unnatural separation between children and parents that is good for neither body nor soul.

That fortnight with my father was the only happy spell in my life for some time to come. We walked up to the Hanuman Temple on Jakke Hill; took a rickshaw-ride to Sanjauli, while my father told me the story of Kipling's phantom-rickshaw, set on that very road; ate ice creams at Davice's restaurant (and as I write this, I learn that this famous restaurant has just been destroyed in a fire); browsed in bookshops and saw more films; made plans for the future. 'We will go to England after the war.'

He was, in fact, the only friend I had as a child, and after his death I was to be a lonely boy until I reached my late teens.

School seemed a stupid and heartless place after my father had gone away. The traditions even in prep school—such as ragging and caning, compulsory games and daily chapel attendance, prefects larger than life, and Honours Boards for everything from School Captaincy to choir membership—had apparently been borrowed from *Tom Brown's Schooldays*. It was all part of the process of turning us into 'leaders of men'. Well, my leadership qualities remained exactly at zero, and in time I was to discover the sad fact that the world at large judges you according to who you are, rather than what you have done.

My father had been transferred to Calcutta and wasn't keeping well. Malaria again. And the jaundice. But his last letter sounded quite cheerful. He'd been selling his valuable stamp collection, so as to have enough money for us to settle in England.

One day my class teacher sent for me.

'I want to talk to you, Bond,' he said. 'Let's go for a walk.'

I knew it wasn't going to be a walk I would enjoy; I knew instinctively that something was wrong.

As soon as my unfortunate teacher (no doubt cursing the Headmaster for giving him such an unpleasant task) started on the theme of 'God wanting your father in a higher and better place'—

as though there could be any better place than Jakke Hill in midsummer!—I knew my father was dead, and burst into tears.

Later, the Headmaster sent for me and made me give him the pile of letters from my father that I had been keeping in my locker. He probably felt it was unmanly of me to cling to them.

'You might lose them,' he said. 'Why not keep them with me? At the end of term, before you go home, you can come and collect them.'

Reluctantly I gave him the letters. He told me he had heard from my mother and stepfather and that I would be going to them when school closed.

At the end of the year, the day before school closed, I went to the HM's office and asked him for my letters.

'What letters?' he said. His desk was piled with papers and correspondence, and he was irritated by the interruption.

'My father's letters,' I explained. 'You said you would keep them for me, sir.'

'Letters, letters. Are you sure you gave them to me?' He was growing more irritated. 'You must be mistaken, Bond. What would I want from your father's letters?'

'I don't know, sir. You said I could collect them before going home.'

'Look, I don't remember your letters and I'm very busy just now. So run along. I'm sure you're mistaken, but if I find any personal letters of yours, I'll send them on to you.'

I don't suppose his forgetfulness was anything more than the muddled indifference that grows in many of those who have charge of countless small boys, but for the first time in my life, I knew what it was like to hate someone.

And I had discovered that words could hurt too.

THE OLD GRAMOPHONE

I t was a large square mahogany box, well polished, and there was a handle you had to wind, and lids that opened top and front. You changed the steel needle every time you changed the record.

The records were kept flat in a cardboard box to prevent them from warping. If you didn't pack them flat, the heat and humidity turned them into strange shapes which would have made them eligible for an exhibition of modern sculpture.

The winding, the changing of records and needles, the selection of a record were boyhood tasks that I thoroughly enjoyed. I was very methodical in these matters. I hated records being scratched, or the turntable slowing down in the middle of a record, bringing the music of the song to a slow and mournful stop: this happened if the gramophone wasn't fully wound. I was especially careful with my favourites, such as Nelson Eddy singing 'The Mounties' and 'The Hills of Home', various numbers sung by the Ink Spots, and a medley of marches.

All this musical activity (requiring much physical exertion on the part of the listener!) took place in a little-known port called Jamnagar, on the west coast of our country, where my father taught English to the young princes and princesses of the State. The gramophone had been installed to amuse me and my mother, but my mother couldn't be bothered with all the effort that went into playing it.

I loved every aspect of the gramophone, even the cleaning of the records with a special cloth. One of my first feats of writing was to catalogue all the records in our collection—only about fifty to begin with—and this cataloguing I did with great care and devotion. My father liked 'grand opera'—Caruso, Gigli, and Galli-Curci—but I preferred the lighter ballads of Nelson Eddy, Deanna

Durbin, Gracie Fields, Richard Tauber, and 'The Street Singer' (Arthur Tracy). It may seem incongruous, to have been living within sound of the Arabian Sea and listening to Nelson sing most beautifully of the mighty Missouri river, but it was perfectly natural to me. I grew up with that music, and I love it still.

I was a lonely boy, without friends of my own age, so that the gramophone and the record collection meant a lot to me. My catalogue went into new and longer editions, taking in the names of composers, lyricists and accompanists.

When we left Jamnagar, the gramophone accompanied us on the long train journey (three days and three nights, with several changes) to Dehra Dun. Here, in the spacious grounds of my grandparents' home at the foothills of the Himalayas songs like 'The Hills of Home' and 'Shenandoah' did not seem out of place.

Grandfather had a smaller gramophone and a record collection of his own. His tastes were more 'modern' than mine. Dance music was his passion, and there were any number of fox-trots, tangos and beguines played by the leading dance bands of the 1940s. Granny preferred waltzes and taught me to waltz. I would waltz with her on the broad veranda, to the strains of *The Blue Danube* and *The Skater's Waltz*, while a soft breeze rustled in the banana fronds. I became quite good at the waltz, but then I saw Gene Kelly tap-dancing in a brash, colourful MGM musical, and—base treachery!—forsook the waltz and began tap-dancing all over the house, much to Granny's dismay.

All this is pure nostalgia, of course, but why be ashamed of it? Nostalgia is simply an attempt to try and preserve that which was good in the past. . . . The past has served us: why not serve the past in this way?

When I was sent to boarding-school and was away from home for nine long months, I really missed the gramophone. How I looked forward to coming home for the winter holidays! There were, of course, some new records waiting for me. And Grandfather had taken to the Brazilian rumba, which was all the rage just then. Yes, Grandfather did the rumba with great aplomb.

I believe he'd moved on to the samba and then the calypso, but by then I'd left India and was away for five years. A great deal had changed in my absence. My grandparents had moved on, and my mother had sold the old gramophone and replaced it with a large radiogram. But this wasn't so much fun: I wanted something I could wind!

I keep hoping our old gramophone will turn up somewhere— maybe in an antique shop or in someone's attic or store-room, or at a sale. Then I shall buy it back, whatever the cost, and instal it in my study and have the time of my life winding it up and playing the old records. I now have tapes of some of them, but that won't stop me listening to the gramophone. I have even kept a box of needles in readiness for the great day.

A LITTLE WORLD OF MUD

I had never imagined there was much to be found in the rainwater pond behind our house in north India except for large quantities of mud and sometimes a water-buffalo. It was Grandfather who introduced me to the pond's diversity of life, so beautifully arranged that each individual gained some benefit from the well-being of the mass. To the inhabitants of the pond, the pond was the world; and to the inhabitants of the world, maintained Grandfather, the world was but a muddy pond.

When Grandfather first showed me the pond world, he chose a dry place in the shade of an old peepul tree, where we sat for an hour, gazing steadily at the thin, green scum on the water. The buffaloes had not arrived for their afternoon dip, and the surface of the pond was still.

For the first ten minutes we saw nothing. Then a small black blob appeared in the middle of the pond; gradually it rose higher, until at last we could make out a frog's head, its great eyes staring hard at us. He did not know if we were friend or enemy and kept his body out of sight. A heron, his mortal enemy, might have been wading about in search of him. When he had made sure we were not herons, he informed his friends and neighbours, and soon there were several big heads and eyes just above the surface of the water. Throats swelled, and a wurk, wurk, wurk began.

In the shallow water near the tree we could see a dark shifting shadow. When touched with the end of a stick, the dark mass immediately became alive. Thousands of little black tadpoles wriggled into life, pushing and hustling each other.

'What do tadpoles eat?' I asked.

'They eat each other most of the time,' said Grandfather. 'It may seem an unpleasant custom, but when you think of the thousands of tadpoles that are hatched, you'll realize what a useful system it is. If all the young tadpoles in this pond became frogs, they'd take up every inch of ground between here and the house!'

'Their croaking would certainly drive Grandmother crazy,' I said.

All the same, I took home a number of frogs, placed them in a large glass jar, and left them on the window-sill of my bedroom.

At about four o'clock in the morning the entire household was awakened by a loud and fearful noise, and my grandparents, aunts and servants gathered on the veranda for safety. They were furious when they discovered that my frogs were the cause of the noise. Seeing the dawn breaking, the frogs had with one accord begun their morning song. Grandmother wanted to throw the frogs, bottle and all, out of the window; but Grandfather gave the bottle a good shaking and the frogs stayed quiet. Everyone went back to bed, but I was obliged to stay awake, to shake the bottle whenever the frogs showed signs of bursting into song. Long before breakfast, I had let them loose in the garden.

I was soon visiting the pond on my own, exploring its banks and shallows; and taking off my shoes, I would wade into the muddy water up to my knees, and pluck the water-lilies floating on the surface.

One day, when I reached the pond, I found it occupied by buffaloes. Their owner, a boy a little older than me, was swimming about in the middle of the pond. He pulled himself up on the back of one of his buffaloes, stretched his slim brown body out on the animal's glistening back, and started singing to himself.

When the boy saw me staring at him, he smiled, showing gleaming white teeth in his dark, sun-burnished face. He invited me into the water for a swim. I told him I couldn't swim, and he offered to teach me. I hesitated, knowing that my Grandmother held strict and rather old-fashioned views about my mixing with village children; but, deciding that Grandfather—who sometimes smoked a hookah on the sly—would get me out of any trouble that might arise, I took the bold step of accepting the boy's offer. And once taken, the step did not seem so very bold.

He dived off the back of his buffalo and swam across to me. And I, having removed my shirt and shorts, followed his instructions until I was floundering about among the water-lilies. His name was Ramu, and he promised to give me swimming lessons every afternoon; and so it was during the afternoons—especially summer afternoons when everyone was asleep—that we met.

Before long I was able to swim across the pond to sit with Ramu astride a contented buffalo standing like an island in the middle of a muddy ocean. Sometimes we would try racing the buffaloes, Ramu and I sitting on different beasts. But they were lazy creatures and would leave one comfortable spot only to look for another; or, if they were in no mood for games, would simply roll over on their backs, taking us with them into the mud and green slime of the pond. I would emerge from the pond in shades of green and khaki, slip into the house through the bathroom, and bathe under the tap before getting into my clothes.

Ramu came from a family of low-caste farmers and had received no schooling. But he was well versed in folklore and knew a great deal about birds and animals.

'Many birds are sacred,' he told me, as a bluejay swooped down from the peepul tree and carried off a grasshopper. Ramu said that both the bluejay and the god Shiva were called Nilkanth. Shiva had a blue throat, like the bird, because out of compassion for the human race he had swallowed a deadly poison which was meant to destroy the world. Keeping the poison in his throat, he had not let it go further.

'Are squirrels sacred?' I asked.

'The god Krishna loved them,' said Ramu. 'He would take them in his arms and stroke them with his long fingers. That is why they have four dark lines down their back from head to tail. Krishna was very dark, and the lines are the marks of his fingers.'

Both Ramu and my grandfather felt that we should be more gentle with birds and animals, that we should not kill them indiscriminately.

'We must acknowledge their rights on the earth,' said Grandfather. 'Everywhere, birds and animals are finding it more difficult to live, because we are destroying their forests. They have to keep moving as the trees disappear.'

Ramu and I spent many long summer afternoons at the pond. We never saw each other again after I left my grandparents' house; he could not read or write, so we were unable to keep in touch.

No one knew of our friendship. Only the buffaloes and the frogs were our confidants. They had accepted us as part of their own world, their muddy but comfortable pond. And when I went away, both they and Ramu must have assumed that I would return again like the birds.

ADVENTURES OF A BOOK LOVER

My father died when I was ten, and for the next few years books became a scare commodity in my life, for my mother and stepfather were not great readers. In my rather lonely early teens I was to discover that books could be good friends, reliable companions, and I seized upon almost any printed matter that came my way, whether it was a girl's classic like *Little Women*, or a *Hotspur* or *Champion comic*, or a detective story, or *The Naturalist on the River Amazons* by Henry Walter Bates. The only books I balked at reading were collections of sermons (amazing how often they turned up in those early years) and self-improvement books, since I hadn't the slightest desire to improve myself in any way.

I think it all began in that forest rest-house in the Siwalik Hills, a sub-tropical range cradling the Doon valley in northern India. Here my stepfather and his guntoting friends were given to hunting birds and animals that roamed those forests. He was a poor shot, so he cannot really be blamed for the absence of wild-life today; but he did his best to eliminate every creature that came within his sights.

On one of these shikar trips, we were staying in a rest-house near the Timli Pass. My stepfather and his friends were 'after tiger' (you were out of fashion if you weren't after big game) and set out every morning with an army of paid villagers to 'beat' the jungle, that is, to make enough noise with drums, whistles, tin trumpets and empty kerosene tins, to disturb the tiger and drive the unwilling beast into the open where he could conveniently be dispatched. Truly bored by this form of sport, I stayed behind in the rest-house, and in the course of a morning's exploration of the bungalow, discovered a dusty but crowded bookshelf half-hidden in a corner of the back veranda.

Who had left them there? A literary forest officer? A memsahib who had been bored by her husband's camp-fire boasting? Or someone like me who had no enthusiasm for the 'manly' sport of slaughtering wild animals, and brought his library along to pass the time?

Possibly the poor fellow had gone into the jungle one day, as a gesture towards his more blood-thirsty companions, and been trampled by an elephant or gored by a wild boar, or (more likely) accidentally shot by one of his companions—and they had taken his remains away and left his books behind. Anyway, there they were—a shelf of some fifty volumes, obviously untouched for several years. I wiped the dust off the covers and examined the titles. As my reading taste had not yet formed, I was ready to try anything. The bookshelf was varied in its contents—and my own interests have remained equally wide-ranging.

On that fateful day in the forest rest-house, I discovered two very funny books. One was P. G. Wodehouse's *Love among the Chickens*, an early Ukridge story and still one of my favourites. The other was *The Diary of a Nobody* by George and Weedon Grossmith, who spent more time on the stage than in the study but are now remembered mainly for this hilarious book. It isn't everyone's cup of tea. Recently I lent my copy to a Swiss friend, who could see nothing funny about it. I must have read it a dozen times; I pick it up whenever I'm feeling low, and on one occasion it even cured me of a peptic ulcer!

Anyway, back to the rest-house. By the time the perspiring hunters came back late in the evening, I had started on M. R. James's *Ghost Stories of an Antiquary*, which had me hooked on ghost stories for the rest of my life. It kept me awake most of the night, until the oil in the kerosene lamp had finished.

Next morning, fresh and optimistic again, the shikaris set out for a different area, where they hoped to locate their tiger. All day I could hear the beaters' drums throbbing in the distance. This did not prevent me from finishing James or a collection of stories called *The Big Karoo* by Pauline Smith—wonderfully evocative of the life of the pioneering Boers in South Africa.

My concentration was disturbed only once, when I looked up and saw a spotted deer crossing the open clearing in front of the bungalow. The deer disappeared into the forest and I returned to my book.

Dusk had fallen when I heard the party returning from the hunt. The great men were talking loudly and seemed excited. Perhaps they had got their tiger! I came out on the veranda to meet them.

'Did you shoot the tiger?' I asked.

'No, Ruskin,' said my stepfather. 'I think we'll catch up with it tomorrow. But you should have been with us—we saw a spotted deer!'

There were three days left and I knew I would never get through the entire bookshelf. So I chose *David Copperfield*—my first encounter with Dickens—and settled down in the veranda armchair to make the acquaintance of Mr Micawber and his family, along with Aunt Betsy Trotwood, Mr Dick, Peggotty, and a host of other larger-than-life characters. I think it would be true to say that Copperfield set me off on the road to literature; I identified with young David and wanted to grow up to be a writer like him.

But on my second day with the book an event occurred which interrupted my reading for a little while.

I had noticed, on the previous day, that a number of stray dogs—some of them belonging to watchmen, villagers and forest rangers—always hung about the bungalow, waiting for scraps of food to be thrown away. It was about ten in the morning (a time when wild animals seldom come into the open), when I heard a sudden yelp coming from the clearing. Looking up, I saw a large, full-grown leopard making off with one of the dogs. The other dogs, while keeping their distance, set up a furious barking, but the leopard and its victim had soon disappeared. I returned to Copperfield, and it was getting late when the shikaris returned.

They looked dirty, sweaty and disgruntled. Next day we were to return to the city, and none of them had anything to show for a week in the jungle.

'I saw a leopard this morning,' I said modestly.

No one took me seriously. 'Did you really?' said the leading shikari, glancing at the book in my hands. 'Young Master Copperfield says he saw a leopard!'

'Too imaginative for his age,' said my stepfather. 'Comes from reading so much, I expect.'

I went to bed and left them to their tales of 'good old days' when rhinos, cheetahs and possibly even unicorns were still available for slaughter. Camp broke up before I could finish Copperfield, but the forest ranger said I could keep the book. And so I became the only member of the expedition with a trophy to take home.

After that adventure, I was always looking for books in unlikely places. Although I never went to college, I think I have read as much, if not more, than most collegiates, and it would be true to say that I received a large part of my education in second-hand bookshops. London had many, and Calcutta once had a large number of them, but I think the prize must go to a small town in Wales called Hay-on-Wye, which has twenty-six bookshops and over a million books. It's in the world's quiet corners that book lovers still flourish—a far from dying species!

One of my treasures is a little novel called *Sweet Rocket* by Mary Johnston. It was a failure when it was first published in 1920. It has only the thinnest outline of a story but the author sets out her ideas in lyrical prose that seduces me at every turn of the page. Miss Johnston was a Virginian. She did not travel outside America. But her little book did. I found it buried under a pile of railway timetables at a bookstall in Simla, the old summer capital of India—almost as though it had been waiting there for me, these seventy years!

Among my souvenirs is a charming little recipe book, small enough to slip into an apron pocket. (You need to be a weightlifter to pick up some of the cookery books that are published today.) This one's charm lies not so much in its recipes for roast lamb and mint sauce (which are very good too) but in the margins of each page, enlivened with little Victorian maxims concerning good food and wise eating. Here are a few chosen at random:

- There is skill in all things, even in making porridge.
- Dry bread at home is better than curried prawns abroad.
- Eating and drinking should not keep men from thinking.
- Better a small fish than an empty dish.
- Let not your tongue cut your throat.

I have collected a number of 'little' books, like my father's *Finger Prayer Book*, which is the size of a small finger but is replete with Psalms and the complete Book of Common Prayer. Another is *The Pocket Trivet: An Anthology for Optimists*, published by *The Morning Post* newspaper in 1932 and designed to slip into the waistcoat pocket. But what is a trivet, one might well ask.

Well, it's a stand for a small pot or kettle, fixed securely over a grate. To be right as a trivet is to be perfectly and thoroughly right—just right, like the short sayings in this tiny anthology which range from Emerson's 'Hitch your wagon to a star!' to the Japanese proverb: 'In the market place there is money to be made, but under the cherry tree there is rest.'

It helps me forget the dilapidated old building in which I live and work, and to look instead at the ever-changing cloud patterns as seen from my small bedroom-cum-study window. There is no end to the shapes made by the clouds, or to the stories they set off in my head.

Most of our living has to happen in the mind. And, to quote an anonymous sage from my *Trivet*: 'The world is only the size of each man's head.'

UPON AN OLD WALL DREAMING

I t is time to confess that at least half my life has been spent in idleness. My old school would not be proud of me. Nor would my Aunt Muriel.

'You spend most of your time sitting on that wall, doing nothing,' scolded Aunt Muriel, when I was seven or eight. 'Are you *thinking* about something?'

'No, Aunt Muriel.'

'Are you *dreaming*?'

'I'm awake!'

'Then what on earth are you doing there?'

'Nothing, Aunt Muriel.'

'He'll come to no good,' she warned the world at large. 'He'll spend all his life sitting on walls, doing nothing.'

And how right she proved to be! Sometimes I bestir myself, and bang out a few sentences on my old typewriter, but most of the time I'm still sitting on that wall, preferably in the winter sunshine. Thinking? Not very deeply. Dreaming? But I've grown too old to dream. Meditation, perhaps. That's been fashionable for some time. But it isn't that either. Contemplation might come closer to the mark.

Was I born with a silver spoon in my mouth that I could afford to sit in the sun for hours, doing nothing? Far from it; I was born poor and remained poor, as far as worldly riches went. But one has to eat and pay the rent. And there have been others to feed too. So I have to admit that between long bouts of idleness there have been short bursts of creativity. My typewriter after more than thirty years of loyal service, has finally collapsed, proof enough that it has not lain idle all this time.

Sitting on walls, apparently doing nothing, has always been my favourite form of inactivity. But for these walls, and the many

163

idle hours I have spent upon them, I would not have written even a fraction of the hundreds of stories, essays and other diversions that have been banged out on the typewriter over the years. It is not the walls themselves that set me off or give me ideas, but a personal view of the world that I receive from sitting there.

Creative idleness, you could call it. A receptivity to the world around me—the breeze, the warmth of the old stone, the lizard on the rock, a raindrop on a blade of grass—these and other impressions impinge upon me as I sit in that passive, benign condition that makes people smile tolerantly at me as they pass. 'Eccentric writer,' they remark to each other, as they drive on, hurrying in a heat of hope, towards the pot of gold at the end of their personal rainbows.

It's true that I am eccentric in many ways, and old walls bring out the essence of my eccentricity.

I do not have a garden wall. This shaky tumbledown house in the hills is perched directly above a motorable road, making me both accessible and vulnerable to casual callers of all kinds—inquisitive tourists, local busybodies, schoolgirls with their poems, hawkers selling candy-floss, itinerant sadhus, scrap merchants, potential Nobel prize winners. . . .

To escape them, and to set my thoughts in order, I walk a little way up the road, cross it, and sit down on a parapet wall overlooking the Woodstock spur. Here, partially shaded by an overhanging oak, I am usually left alone. I look suitably down and out, shabbily dressed, a complete nonentity—not the sort of person you would want to be seen talking to!

Stray dogs sometimes join me here. Having been a stray dog myself at various periods of my life, I can empathize with these friendly vagabonds of the road. Far more intelligent than your inbred Pom or Peke, they let me know by their silent companionship that they are on the same wave-length. They sport about on the road, but they do not yap at all and sundry.

Left to myself on the wall, I am soon in the throes of composing a story or poem. I do not write it down—that can be done later—I just work it out in my mind, memorize my words, so to speak, and keep them stored up for my next writing session.

Occasionally a car will stop, and someone I know will stick his head out and say, 'No work today, Mr Bond? How I envy you! Not a care in the world!'

I travel back in time some fifty years to Aunt Muriel asking me the same question. The years melt away, and I am a child again, sitting on the garden wall, doing nothing.

'Don't you get bored sitting there?' asks the latest passing motorist, who has one of those half beards which are in vogue with TV news readers. 'What are you doing?'

'Nothing, aunty,' I reply.

He gives me a long hard stare.

'You must be dreaming. Don't you recognize me?'

'Yes, Aunt Muriel.'

He shakes his head sadly, steps on the gas, and goes roaring up the hill in a cloud of dust.

'Poor old Bond,' he tells his friends over evening cocktails. 'Must be going round the bend. This morning he called me Aunty.'

A GOLDEN VOICE REMEMBERED

My father was very fond of opera and operetta, but, living in India fifty or sixty years ago, he had to depend on gramophone records if he wanted to listen to his favourite arias from *La Bohème* or *Madam Butterfly*. He had an impressive collection of Caruso records, as well as Chaliapin, Gigli, Galli-Curci, and others. We travelled a great deal, and the square black wind-up gramophone went with us all over India. We had to pack the records very flat, otherwise they took on strange shapes in the heat and humidity. Changing needles and winding the gramophone were chores that I enjoyed as a small boy.

When, in 1929-30, sound came to the cinema, it ushered in a great musical era. Although grand opera did not prove very popular with cinema audiences, operettas and stage musicals went down very well, and favourites such as *Naughty Marietta* (1935), *Rose Marie* (1936), *Maytime* (1937), and *New Moon* (1940) were soon turned into very popular screen musicals. My father took me to see some of these, in small cinemas in small cantonment towns all over northern India, and I became a great fan of the American baritone, Nelson Eddy, an opera singer who made it big in Hollywood and appeared in as many as seventeen film musicals between 1935 and 1947.

Eddy's marching songs in particular appealed to me, and I sang them lustily in the garden, on the road, or on the rooftop. They still come booming forth when I set out for a walk in the hills around my Himalayan home: 'Stouthearted Men' from *New Moon*, 'Tramp, Tramp, Tramp' from *Naughty Marietta*, 'Tokay' from *Bitter Sweet* (1940), 'Ride, Cossack, Ride' from *Balalaika* (1939), and 'Soldiers of Fortune' from *The Girl of the Golden West* (1938). Sigmund Romberg, Victor Herbert, and Rudolf Friml were the stouthearted composers of most of these musicals.

166

A lesser-known but very pleasing Eddy vehicle was *Let Freedom Ring* (1939), a sort of patriotic Western in which Eddy fights small-town political corruption and discrimination. Forgotten now, it was quite a hit in its time, and featured some of his best songs, including, as a climax, his rousing rendering of 'The Star-Spangled Banner.' He was then at the height of his popularity—America's highest paid singer—and had he chosen to run for President, he might well have given his opponents a run for their money.

He is probably best remembered for the eight operettas he made with Jeanette MacDonald. Together they became known as 'America's Singing Sweethearts.' They made love in duets, such as 'Indian Love Call' (*Rose Marie*), 'Wanting You' (*New Moon*), 'Will You Remember?' (*Maytime*), and 'Ah, Sweet Mystery of Life' (*Naughty Marietta*). These were romantic, sentimental films, but the lovely ringing voices of the stars more than made up for stereotyped plots and dialogue. One exception to the formula was *Sweethearts* (1938), scripted by the acerbic Dorothy Parker of *The New Yorker*; she brought some of her acid wit to the set sugary recipe. The usually hostile critics agreed that the film was brightly acted and splendidly sung by its stars.

Another somewhat unusual operetta was *The Chocolate Soldier* (1941), in which Eddy appeared opposite Metropolitan opera star Rise Stevens. His masquerading as a flamboyant Cossack was a revelation to many who had dismissed him as a wooden actor. 'The most effective piece of acting he ever committed to film,' writes film historian Clive Hirschman in *Hollywood Musicals*. Eddy also revelled in singing Musorgsky's 'Song of the Flea'. He enjoyed singing in Russian, and his rendering of the 'Song of the Volga Boatman' in *Balalaika* was superb. Some of his old recordings have been reissued in *Russian Songs and Arias*, published by Mac/Eddy Records in 1982.

*

I have always been drawn to Nelson Eddy, the singer and the person. For one thing, I like baritones and don't see why it should always be the tenors who get the leading roles in opera. They are invariably the heroes, while the basses and baritones have to make do as villains or buffoons.

Eddy was one baritone who got to play the hero. Not once, but over and over again. And it wasn't as though he couldn't sing tenor. His marvellous range enabled him to dub for both tenor and bass in *Phantom of the Opera* (1943); and in Walt Disney's *Make Mine Music* (1946), he lent his voice to Willie, an opera-singing whale whose one ambition was to sing at the Met. The music for the entire sequence comprised 'Shortnin' Bread' (a traditional song), and operatic excerpts from Rossini's 'The Barber of Seville', Donizetti's 'Lucia de Lammermoor', Leoncavallo's 'I Pagliacci', Wagner's 'Tristan and Isolde', Boito's 'Mefistofele', and Flotow's 'Martha'. All the parts in these excerpts—soprano, tenor, baritone, bass and chorus—were sung by Eddy. They were the best items in an otherwise disappointing film.

As a youngster in his hometown of Providence, Rhode Island, where he was born on June 29, 1901, Eddy had taught himself opera by listening to phonograph records by Scotti, Werrenrath, and other great baritones of the day. He would sing along with the recording until he was satisfied with the results. After he left school, he tried his hand at a newspaper career, working for two large Philadelphia papers. Later he became a copywriter for an advertising agency, and did rather well until it became apparent that music was his first and most important love. He was fired for singing on the job. The great American baritone David Bispham heard from a newspaper friend about the 'singing reporter' and met Eddy soon afterward. Bispham was so impressed that he agreed to become Eddy's coach, thus beginning his formal vocal training.

For a time Eddy sang with the Philadelphia Civic Opera Company. While singing in *Tannhauser*, Eddy met Edouard Lippe, veteran opera singer, who suggested that the young man go to Europe for further training. When the impoverished singer protested that he was unable to afford the trip, Lippe suggested that Eddy borrow on his future, and the young baritone managed to obtain a loan from a banker friend of the family; he went to study under

William V. Vilonat, teacher of many Philadelphia students, in Dresden, Germany. After several months of study in Dresden and Paris, Eddy was about to return to the United States when he learned that he had been chosen for baritone roles with the Dresden Opera Company. 'I don't think Vilonat has ever forgiven me for turning down that chance,' he said later. 'But I wanted to see America again. I wanted to put myself in the hands of the American public, sink or swim.'

In 1924 Eddy made his debut at the Metropolitan Opera House in the role of Tonio in *Pagliacci*. He mastered some thirty-two operatic roles. 'Nelson Eddy,' wrote the music critic of the *Philadelphia Record* in 1924, 'had an electrifying effect on the audience. A young man with that indefinable gift, so seldom seen, of arresting the audience's interest and holding it continuously, Mr Eddy was a star from the moment he appeared on stage.'

Concert tours occupied Eddy for the next few years, and by 1933 he had sung in nearly every large city in the United States. It was the concert stage that brought him to the attention of Hollywood. A distinguished assembly in Los Angeles was awaiting the start of a concert by a noted opera star. The star, however, had suddenly become critically ill, and a substitute was rushed by plane from San Diego. The substitute was Nelson Eddy, practically unknown on the West Coast at the time. When he began to sing, the audience at once accepted him. It was a brilliant success, with the baritone responding to no less than fourteen encores. The next day motion picture studios began calling him. Within a week he had signed a contract with Metro-Goldwyn-Mayer (MGM), and had sung his first song on the screen—in Joan Crawford's *Dancing Lady* (1934). A year later, with *Naughty Marietta*, he catapulted to stardom.

*

Recently on a BBC request programme, I was fortunate to pick up Nelson Eddy's rendering, in Russian, of the 'Song of the Volga Boatman' (from the 1939 film *Balalaika*), and was captivated all over again by the singer's full-bodied baritone. It made me wonder why so little is heard about him today, although we are constantly being reminded of the greatness of Paul Robeson or Lawrence Tibbett. Eddy was definitely in their class, and superior to singers like Howard Keel who succeeded him in MGM musicals. Perhaps his versatility worked against him. He sang in everything from opera to musical comedy, radio shows, and nightclub acts; and music critics like to be able to pigeonhole their singers in a particular category. His popularity roused the ire of rivals and critics, who seldom missed an opportunity to snipe at him. One critic complained of his singing in *Phantom of the Opera*, and went on to praise the bass who was singing in the same operatic sequence; it turned out that the bass was Nelson Eddy dubbing for a non-singing actor.

Although none of his films was a flop, it was in the concert field that Nelson Eddy achieved his real fame. His screen personality was watered down, but his dynamic magnetism and masterful voice when heard live came across with full force. Besides, he hated the Hollywood game, he disliked L. B. Mayer (head of MGM studios), and he continued his film career mainly to boost his concert attendances. He firmly refused to discuss his personal life with the press, suing columnist Louella Parsons for implying that his on-screen romance with Jeanette MacDonald was continued off-screen. The 'singing sweethearts' of the screen were not, in fact, particularly fond of each other, but you wouldn't have guessed it; they were such good professionals.

'I love to sing and meet the people,' Eddy once said, and that was exactly what he did during the twenty years that followed his last film in 1947. His radio show ran for thirteen years, and in 1953 he made the transition to nightclubs. Many remember him from this period, including Buzz Kennedy, an Australian columnist who met him when Eddy toured Australia in the mid-1960s. 'He was one of the nicest people I've met,' recalls Kennedy today. And the hypercritical reviewer of *Variety* wrote of one of Eddy's last appearances: 'He required less than a minute to put a jam-packed audience in his hip pocket.'

It was in front of another jam-packed audience, in Miami Beach, Florida, on March 6, 1967, that Nelson Eddy collapsed on stage, having just sung 'Ah, Sweet Mystery of Life'. 'Would you bear with me a minute?' he asked his audience. 'I can't seem to get the words out.' These were his last words. Minutes later he was dead.

*

Well, my childhood record collection had long since disappeared, and I wasn't going to wait another year for the BBC to play a Nelson Eddy record. So I started making enquiries, and found, to my delight, that a number of music companies in America had reissued the old songs as well as tapes of his radio shows. The latter were fascinating, as they included songs that had never been released in his recording days. In two years of diligent collecting, I now have on tape or disk more than 200 Nelson Eddy songs, far more than I ever heard as a boy.

I open my window to look out at the Himalayas striding away into the sky, while those lovely old songs drift out over the sunwashed hillside—'While My Lady Sleeps,' 'Shenandoah,' 'The Hills of Home,' 'Song of the Open Road,' 'Neath the Southern Moon,' 'By the Waters of Minnetonka,' 'When I Have Sung My Songs to You.'

'When I have sung my songs to you, I'll sing no more,' goes the old ballad.

But for one faithful listener, Nelson Eddy is still singing.

AT HOME IN INDIA

There are many among us who, given the opportunity to leave India, are only too happy to go. But whenever I have had the chance to go away, I have held back. Or something has held me back.

What is it that has such a hold on me, but leaves others free to go where they will, sometimes never to come back?

A few years ago I was offered a well-paid job on a magazine in Hong Kong. I thought about it for weeks, worried myself to distraction, and finally, with a great sigh of relief, turned it down.

My friends thought I was crazy. They still do. Most of them would have jumped at a comparable offer, even if it had meant spending the rest of their lives far from the palm-fringed coasts or pine-clad mountains of this land. Many friends have indeed gone away, never to return, except perhaps to get married, very quickly, before they are off again! Don't they feel homesick, I wonder.

I am almost paranoid at the thought of going away and then being unable to come back. This almost happened to me when, as a boy, I went to England, longed to return to India, and did not have the money for the passage. For two years I worked and slaved like a miser (something I have never done since) until I had enough to bring me home.

And 'home' wasn't parents and brothers and sisters. They were no longer here. Home, for me, was India.

So what is it that keeps me here? My birth? I take too closely after a Nordic grandparent to pass for a typical son of the soil. Hotel receptionists often ask me for my passport.

'Must I carry a passport to travel in my own country?' I ask.

'But you don't look like an Indian,' they protest.

'I'm a Red Indian,' I say.

India is where I was born and went to school and grew to

manhood. India was where my father was born and went to school and worked and died. India is where my grandfather lived and died. Surely that entitles me to a place in the Indian sun? If it doesn't, I can revert to my mother's family And go back to the time of Timur the Lame. How far back does one have to go in order to establish one's Indianness?

It must be the land itself that holds me. But so many of my fellow Indians have been born (and reborn) here, and yet they think nothing of leaving the land. They will leave the mountains for the plains; the villages for the cities; their country for another country; and if other countries were a little more willing to open their doors, we would have no population problem—mass emigration would have solved it.

But it's more than the land that holds me. For India is more than a land. India is an atmosphere. Over thousands of years, the races and religions of the world have mingled here and produced that unique, indefinable phenomenon, the Indian: so terrifying in a crowd, so beautiful in himself.

And oddly enough, I'm one too. I know that I'm as Indian as the postman or the paanwala or your favourite MP.

Race did not make me an Indian. Religion did not make me an Indian. But history did. And in the long run, it's history that counts.

GETTING THE JUICES FLOWING

It has been said that life begins at forty. Possibly. But I have found that it begins to sag at forty-five.

The other morning, stooping to tie my shoelaces, I found myself out of breath. Nothing like that had ever happened to me before. It was due, of course, to my stomach getting in the way and pressing against my chest. I was badly out of condition. And I decided that the best solution would be a daily jog around the hill-station where I live—Mussoorie.

I bought a new pair of keds; but, unable to find a pair of shorts of the right size, I gave a gallic shrug and decided to do my jogging in my pyjamas—around the hill, past the waterworks, the rickshaw shed, and the cemetery. But I thought it would be unwise to jog on an empty stomach, so I consumed a mini-breakfast of a soft-boiled egg and toast.

At five in the morning there was no one to watch me, and it was a very slow jog. On my return, I was so famished that I ate a second breakfast—two fried eggs with several parathas—and felt as fit as an old fiddle. But after a week of slow jogs, accompanied by two breakfasts, I discovered that even my pyjamas were getting too tight.

Finally I came to the conclusion that my technique was all wrong. So I cut out the jogging and stuck to the two breakfasts.

Rai Singh, my milkman, thought it would be a good idea if I walked with him to his village, five miles from the station. I fell in with the suggestion and packed a hamper with buns, boiled eggs, fried potatoes, and two kinds of jam. As an afterthought, I added three varieties of churan digestive powder.

Rai Singh and I set out along the winding mountain path. By noon we had covered two-and-a-half miles, and I was feeling hungry. Besides, the hamper, which I had insisted on carrying as a form of yoga, was getting heavier by the minute. So we sat down in the shade of a pine tree, and I prepared an attractive spread for both of us. Rai Singh went off to wash his hands at a spring, a short distance away. As he seemed to be taking a long time, I went to see what delayed him. I found him gathering wild strawberries. We filled a shoulder-bag with wild strawberries and returned to the picnic spot.

All the food had disappeared. The hamper had gone too. Everything had been divided up equally by a band of monkeys. Several of the young ones had their faces smeared with jam. One large female had swallowed all the churan, and I couldn't help thinking that she would be an unpopular monkey by the end of the day.

Rai Singh and I sat down on the grass and ate wild strawberries. 'Never mind,' he said. 'I will prepare a meal for you as soon as we get to the village.'

He was as good as his word; and after a heavy meal of rice and beans, I slept the afternoon away in Rai Singh's hut. Towards evening he brought me a jug of home-made wine. It had been made (he assured me) from wild strawberries. After two glasses of it, I felt that all my problems were solved; I was ready to climb Everest. But Rai Singh put me to bed instead.

Next morning I breakfasted on curds, pickle and parathas, and returned to the hill-station with a milk-can full of strawberry wine. I'd got my juices flowing again.

Rai Singh had promised me a can of the wonderful tonic every time I visited him, and already I was planning a bi-weekly fitness trek to the village.

BIRD LIFE IN THE CITY

Having divided the last ten years of my life between Delhi and Mussoorie, I have come to the heretical conclusion that there is more bird life in the cities than there is in the hills and forests around our hill-stations.

For birds to survive, they must learn to live with and off humans; and those birds, like crows, sparrows and mynas, who do this to perfection, continue to thrive as our cities grow; whereas the purely wild birds, those who depend upon the forests for life, are rapidly disappearing, simply because the forests are disappearing.

Recently, I saw more birds in one week in a New Delhi colony than I had seen during a month in the hills. Here, one must be patient and alert if one is to spot just a few of the birds so beautifully described in Salim Ali's *Indian Hill Birds*. The babblers and thrushes are still around, but the flycatchers and warblers are seldom seen or heard.

But in Delhi, if you have just a bit of garden and perhaps a guava tree, you will be visited by innumerable bulbuls, tailor-birds, mynas, hoopoes, parrots and tree-pies. Or, if you own an old house, you will have to share it with pigeons and sparrows, perhaps swallows or swifts. And if you have neither garden nor rooftop, you will still be visited by the crows.

Where man goes, the crow follows. He has learnt to perfection the art of living off humans. He will, I am sure, be the first bird on the moon, scavenging among the paper-bags and cartons left behind by untidy astronauts.

Crows favour the densest areas of human population, and there must be at least one for every human. Many crows seem to have been humans in their previous lives: they possess all the cunning and sense of self-preservation of man. At the same time, there are many humans who have obviously been crows; we haven't lost their thieving instincts.

Watch a crow sidling along the garden wall with a shabby genteel air, cocking a speculative eye at the kitchen door and any attendant humans. He reminds one of a newspaper reporter, hovering in the background until his chance comes—and then pouncing! I have even known a crow to make off with an egg from the breakfast table. No other bird, except perhaps the sparrow, has been so successful in exploiting human beings.

The myna, although he too is quite at home in the city, is more of a gentleman. He prefers fruit on the tree to scraps from the kitchen, and visits the garden as much out of a sense of sociability as in expectation of hand-outs. He is quite handsome, too, with his bright orange bill and the mask around his eyes. He is equally at home on a railway platform as on the ear of a grazing buffalo, and, being omnivorous, has no trouble in coexisting with man.

The sparrow, on the other hand, is not a gentleman. Uninvited, he enters your home, followed by his friends, relatives and political hangers-on, and proceeds to quarrel, make love and leave his droppings on the sofa-cushions, with a complete disregard for the presence of humans. The party will then proceed into the garden and destroy all the flower-buds. No birds have succeeded so well in making fools of humans.

Although the bluejay, or roller, is quite capable of making his living in the forest, he seems to show a preference for the haunts of men, and would rather perch on a telegraph wire than in a tree. Probably he finds the wire a better launching-pad for his sudden rocket-flights and aerial acrobatics.

In repose he is rather shabby; but in flight, when his outspread wings reveal his brilliant blues, he takes one's breath away. As his food consists of beetles and other insect pests, he can be considered man's friend and ally.

Parrots make little or no distinction between town and country life. They are the freelancers of the bird world—sturdy, independent and noisy. With flashes of blue and green, they swoop across the road, settle for a while in a mango tree, and then, with shrill delighted cries, move on to some other field or orchard.

They will sample all the fruit they can, without finishing any. They are destructive birds but, because of their bright plumage, graceful flight and charming ways, they are popular favourites and can get away with anything. No one who has enjoyed watching a flock of parrots in swift and carefree flight could want to cage one of these virile birds. Yet so many people do cage them.

After the peacock, perhaps the most popular bird in rural India is the sarus crane—a familiar sight around the jheels and river banks of northern India and Gujarat. The sarus pairs for life and is seldom seen without his mate. When one bird dies, the other often pines away and seemingly dies of grief. It is this near-human quality of devotion that has earned the birds their popularity with the villagers of the plains.

As a result, they are well protected.

In the long run, it is the 'common man', and not the scientist or conservationist, who can best give protection to the birds and animals living around him. Religious sentiment has helped preserve the peacock and a few other birds. It is a pity that so many other equally beautiful birds do not enjoy the same protection.

But the wily crow, the cheeky sparrow, and the sensible myna, will always be with us. Quite possibly they will survive the human species.

And it is the same with other animals. While the cringing jackal has learnt the art of survival, his master, the magnificent tiger, is on his way to extinction.

HOME IS UNDER THE BIG TOP

The big circus tent looms up out of the monsoon mist, standing forlorn in a quagmire of mud and slush. It has rained ceaselessly for two days and nights. The chairs stand about in deep pools of water. One or two of them float around with their legs in the air. There will be no show for the third night running, and tomorrow there will be problems, with the ring-hands to be fed and the ground rent to be paid: a hundred odd bills to be settled, and no money at the gate.

Nina, a dark, good-looking girl—part Indian, part Romanian—who has been doing the high-wire act for several years, sits at the window of a shabby hotel room and gazes out at the heavy downpour.

At one time, she tells me, she was with a very small circus, touring the remote areas of the Konkan on India's west coast. The tent was so low that when she stood on her pedestal her head touched the ceiling-cloth. She can still hear the hiss of the Petromax lamps. The band was a shrill affair: It made your hair stand on end!

The manager of a big circus happened to be passing through, and he came in and saw Nina's act, and that was the beginning of a life of constant travel.

She remembers her first night with the new circus, and the terrible suspense she went through. Suddenly feeling like a country bumpkin, she looked about her in amazement. There were more than twenty elephants, countless horses, and a menacing array of lions and tigers. She looked at the immense proportions of the tent and wanted to turn and run. The lights were a blinding brilliance—she had never worked in a spotlight before.

As the programme ran through, she stood at the rear curtains waiting for her entrance. She peeped through the curtains and felt sure she would be lost in that wide circus ring. Though her costume was new, she suddenly felt shabby. She had spangled her crimson velvet costume with scarlet sequins so that the whole thing was a red blaze. Her feet were sweating in white kid boots.

She cannot recall how she entered the ring. But she remembers standing on her pedestal and looking over her shoulder to see if the supporting wires were pulled taut. Her attention was caught by the sea of faces behind her. All the artists, the ring-hands, and the stable boys were there, eager to look over the new act.

Her most critical audience was the group of foreign artists who stood to one side in a tight, curious knot. There were two Italian brothers, a family of Belgians, and a half-Russian, half-English aerial ballet artist, a tiny woman who did a beautiful act on the single trapeze.

Nina has no recollection of how she got through her act. She did get through it somehow and was almost in tears when she reached the exit gate. She hurried to the seclusion of her dressing room tent, and there she laid her head upon her arms and sobbed. She did not hear the tent flaps open and was surprised at the sudden appearance of the tiny woman at her side.

'Ah, no!' exclaimed the little trapeze-artist, laying a hand on the girl's head. 'Never tears on your first night! It was a lovely act, my child. Why do you cry? You are sensitive and beautiful in the ring.'

Nina sobbed all the more and would not be comforted by the kind woman's words. Yet it was the beginning of a friendship that lasted for several years. The woman's name was Isabella. She took the young girl under her wing with deep maternal care.

She showed Nina how to use ring makeup and what colours looked best at night. She was nimble-fingered and made costumes and coronets for the girl, and taught her grace in the ring. Once she made a blue and silver outfit. The first night Nina wore it, she performed solely for her friend, although the circus tent was crowded and appreciative.

The circus was kind to Nina, and she grew used to its ways. It was the outside world that puzzled her sometimes. What did her audiences think, she wondered. Did they see more than a winged stranger, green and gold and blue, hovering above them? Did they know that once she returned to the solitary square of her small dressing-room, she often crept outside the tent to hear the wind singing in the trees? Did they know that she wrote poetry?

Whenever she glanced at a map of India, the towns were not merely dots with names. They were familiar to her because the circus had been there, and she called each name softly. They sprang alive, clothed in the mood in which she had committed them to her memory. She loved the smaller towns and villages, she liked the dusty roads and the damp smell of the fields, the tall swaying stalks of sugar cane, the bright yellow carpets of mustard.

As the rain streams down outside, she sits at the window of her small hotel room, remembering all these things, bringing them to life for me. The room has bright green walls and cobwebs in the corners. The open window frames the sky and solitary peepul tree, and she is grateful for both. At twilight the birds come to roost.

There is an old bedraggled crow that comes faithfully to perch on the parapet opposite the window. He has seen a good deal of life, this crow, for his feathers have long since lost their gloss. He cocks his head to one side and regards the girl intently.

'Hello, old crow,' she says. At the sound of her voice he grows uneasy, spreads his wings and dives into the rain with his scrawny neck stretched taut. Nina, too, is restless. She is longing for the high, bright, private world above the circus ring.

The ring, she tells me, has a way of welcoming its people back. And the tent, faded and old, drenched as it is at present, is a better home than a lonely room in a shabby hotel.

PEDESTRIAN IN PERIL

I think it was really my love of walking that first took me to the hills, and then kept me there for two decades. It had become increasingly difficult for me to walk about in Delhi, and I resented this, because I had been walking about Delhi before most of my readers were born. As a youth I walked from Connaught Place to Humayun's tomb, and from Paharganj to Pusa, and although as the years passed I still covered these distances occasionally, it was so longer a pleasurable activity. Rather it became an obstacle race, an exercise in survival.

Now whenever I visit Delhi, I do not even try covering long distances. Even crossing a road is something of a feat for me. Usually I wedge myself between two well-built women—and cross over in their company. No Maruti owner would risk damage to his car by colliding with us.

But being a compulsive walker, I stay out of Delhi as much as possible and do most of my walking in the hills. Even hill-stations are congested these days, but as I live on the outskirts of one, I have no difficulty in marching off for a few miles with only myself and a circling eagle for company. Here too, motor roads have multiplied. But it is possible to leave them at will, taking any old path that leads through fields of maize or mustard, or through oak and rhododendron forest, until a village is reached.

Here there is always hospitality if you are not the arrogant or fastidious sort. And occasionally you might come across a mountain stream where you can rest on a bed of ferns. And if there is no stream, you will eventually find a spring, perhaps a mere trickle of water but welcome all the same. Some springs dried up last year when the rains failed. Let us hope for the sake of bird and beast and thirsty trekker that it rains this winter.

Although I have given up walking in Delhi, it is still possible to do so in some of the smaller towns in the plains. But only just. When growing up in Dehra Dun, I walked all over that town, and all around it, and I tried again last week but it wasn't the same.

My maternal grandfather once taught me the art of zigzagging. If you take a zigzag walk, he said, you will see more of a place and also have some interesting encounters. Distrust the straight and narrow, that was his philosophy.

In those days one zigzagged from choice; now one does so out of necessity. One zigzags between scooters, tempos, buses, trucks, cars, bicycles, bullock-cacts and various forms of locomotion. When a town of forty thousand people has, over a period of forty years, become a city of over a hundred thousand, the resultant traffic congestion may well be imagined. And even as you struggle to make your way along one of those overburdened roads, you are helped along by the stench from overflowing drains and piles of refuse that seems never to shrink or go away.

One cannot really blame anyone. It must happen when a small town acquires the population of a large city. And no one seems to mind. Perhaps it was all part of what Swami Vivekananda once called our 'kitchen mentality', the attitude that as long as the kitchen is clean, what happens on the road is none of our business.

Anyway, I need to walk in order to live, and although I have been defeated by Delhi, I am not going to let Dehra do the same. If I walk to the old cemetery, I might enjoy a reasonably quiet stroll. My maternal grandfather, he who taught me to zigzag, is buried there, and it would be nice to locate his grave. But it is thirty years since I last visited the cemetery. Will I find it without difficulty?

It took me the better part of the morning. Two of the busiest roads had to be crossed, and there were no Amazons to get between. As I stood on the kerb, wondering how I was going to get across, a partially blind man carrying a stick tapped me on the arm and asked me if I could take him across. This put me in a quandary. It would have been churlish of me to refuse, but I was hardly the best choice for the task.

'I don't see too well myself,' I said, which was perfectly true. 'But I will see what I can do.' A frail old lady now approached us, I

183

knew she was going to ask me to take her across the road, so I got in first. 'Could you lead two blind men across the road, madam?' I asked. Well, she got us safely across, and then looked back and asked me, 'Where is the second blind man?'

'Don't worry,' I said, 'he probably changed his mind.'

When I did get to the cemetery, I found it was no longer the quiet place of yore. A line of motor workshops had sprung up in front, while a slum colony had spread along one of the boundary walls. Once reputed to be the most beautiful cemetery in northern India, it still had its trees, but of the garden only traces remained. Quite obviously, funds were lacking.

I did not think I would find my grandfather's grave in the wilderness of worn and weathered tombs. Many had lost their inscriptions. They represented the presence in the Doon Valley of well over a thousand Europeans, from the first soldiers and settlers of the early nineteenth century to the more recent few who 'stayed on'—and passed on. Strangely enough, I had barely begun my search when I found myself before my grandfather's grave. The inscription, placed there by my grandmother, stood out more clearly than most. 'In memory of my beloved husband, William Dudley Clerke, died 9th January 1935'.

And this was the 9th of January, too. It was becoming a day of coincidences. Or had something more than coincidence led me here on the anniversary of my grandfather's death? And if so, why? Perhaps the coming months will give me the answer.

ESCAPE TO NOWHERE

By the end of August, the hill-dweller has got the monsoon blues. Heartily sick of cloud and fog, drizzle and downpour, he longs for a little sunshine, some dryness in the air.

Forsaking my jammed typewriter, and mildewed books and files, I set out for Dehradun in the valley. It was damp there too, and sultry, but at least there were occasional bursts of sunshine. I took a room in a small hotel and lay beneath a whirring fan, waiting for the cool of the evening.

Evening walks in Dehra are not what they used to be. Speeding vehicles stop for no one, and you take your life in your hands every time you cross a road. Most of the roads came into existence over a hundred years ago, and were originally meant for pedestrians and pony-drawn tongas. Now, neither pedestrians nor ponies have any rights.

Wait until dark and the hazards are even greater, for street lights do not exist on the smaller roads, while open ditches and other obstacles are there in abundance, just waiting to trap you. Returning to my room muddied and dishevelled, I was consoled by the old man who brought me a cup of tea. Things were much worse in Agra, he told me.

'And what were you doing in Agra?' I asked.

'I was in the madhouse, the pagalkhana, for ten years. Then one day, when no one was looking, I slipped away.'

He burst into laughter, and naturally I had to join in.

'Inside or outside, there's no difference,' he added. 'The roads are full of pagals these days.'

*

185

Next day, going out in search of a little sanity, I decided I'd call on Nergis Dalai, a fellow writer whom I hadn't seen for some years.

As I approached the Dilawar Bazaar, the area where she lived, I noticed that the traffic on the main road had come to a standstill and that smoke was issuing from a couple of small shops. A crowd had gathered and now, as a police van arrived, people began to scatter, most of them running in my direction. I always seem to be standing in the way of advancing hordes.

Looking for some avenue of escape, I found a gap in a wall, leading into an old orchard of lichi trees. I sat beneath a lichi tree, recalling the days when Dehra was famous for its lichis. Now only a few gardens remain, for owners find it more profitable to sell their land for buildings. Will lichis vanish forever? They don't grow anywhere else.

When the main road seemed normal again, I left the protection of the trees and took another chance with my fellow humans. Two boys were discussing the recent incident. One said the shop had been burnt down because it had been selling brown sugar. The other said it had been burnt down because it had *refused* to sell brown sugar.

My own blood-sugar level was by now distinctly low, so I hurried along to Nergis Dalal's flat, knowing she would give me sustenance. Hadn't she written half-a-dozen cookery books?

Nor was I disappointed. Pullau rice, kofta curry, and a chocolate soufflé awaited me. I was on the right track again!

*

When I got back to my hotel, I found Mr Arora of the Green Bookshop waiting for me in the veranda. He had a surprise for me, he said. He wouldn't tell me what it was until I got into his car.

Ten minutes later we drove in at the gates of Welhem Girls' School. And within minutes I found myself trapped in a classroom, surrounded by some two hundred girls, their ages ranging from fourteen to eighteen. And I was expected to talk to them! Usually tongue-tied in front of one girl, how was I to converse with two hundred? Jules Verne had a similar problem, I believe. No wonder he preferred to be 20,000 leagues under the sea—which was where I wanted to be just then!

Bright-eyed and eager they were, waiting for words of wisdom to flow from my lips. I had none to impart! I looked around the sea of faces. Here was beauty and intelligence combined! I was struck dumb.

Their principal, Mrs Verma, came to my rescue and said nice things about my writing. I answered a few questions, trying to be witty if not wise. The girls were kind and indulgent.

When it was all over, I found myself back in my hotel room. A smart young Gurkha brought me a cup of tea.

'Where's the old man?' I asked.

'One of his sons came for him,' he said. 'They've taken him back to Agra.'

So that was the end of *his* great escape. Was it the end of mine?

IN THE GARDEN OF MY DREAMS

The cosmos has all the genius of simplicity. The plant stands tall and erect; its foliage is uncomplicated; its inflorescences are bold, fresh, cheerful. Any flower, from a rose to a rhododendron, can be complicated. The cosmos is splendidly simple.

No wonder it takes its name from the Greek cosmos, meaning the universe as an ordered whole—the sum total of experience! For this unpretentious flower does seem to sum it all up: perfection without apparent striving for it, the artistry of the South American footballer! Needless to say, it came from tropical America.

And growing it is no trouble. A handful of seed thrown in a waste patch or on a grassy hill slope, and a few months later there they are, *en masse*, doing their samba in the sunshine. They are almost wild, but not quite. They need very little attention, but if you take them too much for granted they will go away the following year. Simple they may be, but not insensitive. They need plenty of space. And as my own small apartment cannot accommodate them, they definitely belong to my dream garden.

My respect for the cosmos goes back to my childhood when I wandered into what seemed like a forest of these flowers, all twice my height (I must have been five at the time) but looking down on me in the friendliest way, their fine feathery foliage giving off a faint aroma. Now when I find them flowering on the hillsides in mellow October sunshine, they are like old friends and I greet them accordingly, pressing my face to their petals.

Not everyone likes the cosmos. I have met some upper-class ladies (golf club members) who complain that it gives them hay fever, and they use this as an excuse to root out all cosmos from their gardens. I expect they are just being snobbish. There are other flowers which give off just as much pollen dust.

I have noticed the same snobbishness in regard to marigolds, especially the smaller Indian variety. 'Cultivated' people won't cultivate these humble but attractive flowers. Is it because they are used for making garlands? Or because they are not delicately scented? Or because they are so easily grown in the backyards of humble homes?

My grandparents once went to war with each other over the marigold. Grandfather had grown a few in one corner of the garden. Just as they began flowering, they vanished—Granny had removed them overnight! There was a row, and my grandparents did not speak to each other for several days. Then, by calling them 'French' marigolds, Grandfather managed to reintroduce them to the garden. Granny liked the idea of having something 'French' in her garden. Such is human nature!

Sometimes a wildflower can put its more spectacular garden cousins to shame. I am thinking now of the commelina, which I discover in secret places after the rains have passed. Its bright sky-blue flowers take my breath away. It has a sort of unguarded innocence that is beyond corruption.

Wild roses give me more pleasure than the sophisticated domestic variety. On a walk in the Himalayan foothills I have encountered a number of these shrubs and climbers—the ineptly named dog rose, sparkling white in summer; the sweet briar with its deep pink petals and bright red rose-hips; the trailing rose, found in shady places; and the wild raspberry (the fruit more attractive than the flower) which belongs to the same family.

A sun-lover, I like plenty of yellow on the hillsides and in gardens—sunflowers, Californian poppies, winter jasmine, St. John's Wort, buttercups, wild strawberries, mustard in bloom.... But if you live in a hot place, you might prefer cooling blues and soft purples—forget-me-nots, bluebells, cornflowers, lavender.

I'd go far for a sprig of sweetly-scented lavender. To many older people the word lavender is as good as a charm; it seems to recall the plaintive strain of once familiar music—

> Lavender's blue, dilly dilly,
> Lavender's green,
> When I am king, dilly dilly,
> You'll be my queen.

This tame-looking, blue-green, stiff, sticky, and immovable shrub holds as much poetry and romance in its wiry arms as would fill a large book. Most cultivated flowers were originally wild and many take their names from the botanists who first 'tamed' them. Thus, the dahlia is named after Mr Dahl, a Swede; the rudbeckia after Rudbeck, a Dutchman; the zinnia after Dr Zinn, a German; and the lobelia after Monsieur Lobel, a Flemish physician. They and others brought to Europe many of the flowers they found growing wild in tropical America, Asia and Africa.

But I am no botanist. I prefer to be the butterfly, perfectly happy in going from flower to flower in search of nectar.

OWLS IN THE FAMILY

One winter morning, my grandfather and I found a baby spotted owlet by the veranda steps of our home in Dehradun. When Grandfather picked it up the owlet hissed and clacked its bill but then, after a meal of raw meat and water, settled down under my bed.

Spotted owlets are small birds. A fully grown one is no larger than a thrush and they have none of the sinister appearance of large owls. I had once found a pair of them in our mango tree and by tapping on the tree trunk had persuaded one to show an enquiring face at the entrance to its hole. The owlet is not normally afraid of man nor is it strictly a night bird. But it prefers to stay at home during the day as it is sometimes attacked by other birds who consider all owls their enemies.

The little owlet was quite happy under my bed. The following day we found a second baby owlet in almost the same spot on the veranda and only then did we realize that where the rainwater pipe emerged through the roof, there was a rough sort of nest from which the birds had fallen. We took the second young owl to join the first and fed them both.

When I went to bed, they were on the window ledge just inside the mosquito netting and later in the night, their mother found them there. From outside, she crooned and gurgled for a long time and in the morning, I found she had left a mouse with its tail tucked through the netting. Obviously she put no great trust in me as a foster parent.

The young birds thrived and ten days later, Grandfather and I took them into the garden to release them. I had placed one on a branch of the mango tree and was stooping to pick up the other when I received a heavy blow on the back of the head. A second or two later, the mother owl swooped down on Grandfather but he was quite agile and ducked out of the way.

Quickly, I placed the second owl under the mango tree. Then from a safe distance we watched the mother fly down and lead her offspring into the long grass at the edge of the garden. We thought she would take her family away from our rather strange household but next morning I found the two owlets perched on the hatstand in the veranda.

I ran to tell Grandfather and when we came back we found the mother sitting on the birdbath a few metres away. She was evidently feeling sorry for her behaviour the previous day because she greeted us with a soft 'whoo-whoo'.

'Now there's an unselfish mother for you,' said Grandfather. 'It's obvious she wants us to keep an eye on them. They're probably getting too big for her to manage.'

So the owlets became regular members of our household and were among the few pets that Grandmother took a liking to. She objected to all snakes, most monkeys and some crows—we'd had all these pets from time to time—but she took quite a fancy to the owlets and frequently fed them spaghetti!

They loved to sit and splash in a shallow dish provided by Grandmother. They enjoyed it even more if cold water was poured over them from a jug while they were in the bath. They would get thoroughly wet, jump out and perch on a towel rack, shake themselves and return for a second splash and sometimes a third. During the day they dozed on a hatstand. After dark, they had the freedom of the house and their nightly occupation was catching beetles, the kitchen quarters being a happy hunting ground. With their razor sharp eyes and powerful beaks, they were excellent pest-destroyers.

Looking back on those childhood days, I carry in my mind a picture of Grandmother in her rocking chair with a contented owlet sprawled across her aproned lap. Once, on entering a room while she was taking an afternoon nap, I saw one of the owlets had crawled up her pillow till its head was snuggled under her ear.

Both Grandmother and the owlet were snoring.

ADVENTURES IN A BANYAN TREE

Though the house and grounds of our home in India were Grandfather's domain, the magnificent old banyan tree was mine—chiefly because Grandfather, at the age of sixty-five, could no longer climb it. Grandmother used to tease him about this, and would speak of a certain Countess of Desmond, an Englishwoman who lived to the age of 117, and would have lived longer if she hadn't fallen while climbing an apple tree. The spreading branches of the banyan tree, which curved to the ground and took root again, forming a maze of arches, gave me endless pleasure. The tree was older than the house, older than Grandfather, as old as the town of Dehra, nestling in a valley at the foot of the Himalayas.

My first friend and familiar was a small grey squirrel. Arching his back and sniffing into the air, he seemed at first to resent my invasion of his privacy. But, when he found that I did not arm myself with a catapult or air-gun, he became friendlier. And, when I started leaving him pieces of cake and biscuit, he grew bolder, and finally became familiar enough to take food from my hands.

Before long he was delving into my pockets and helping himself to whatever he could find. He was a very young squirrel, and his friends and relatives probably thought him headstrong and foolish for trusting a human.

In the spring, when the banyan tree was full of small red figs, birds of all kinds would flock into its branches, the red-bottomed bulbul, cheerful and greedy; gossiping rosy-pastors; and parrots and crows, squabbling with each other all the time. During the fig season, the banyan tree was the noisiest place on the road.

Halfway up the tree I had built a small platform on which I would often spend the afternoons when it wasn't too hot. I could read there, propping myself up against the bole of the tree with cushions taken from the drawing room. *Treasure Island*, *Huck Finn*, the *Mowgli Stories*, and the novels of Edgar Wallace, Edgar Rice Burroughs and Louisa May Alcott made up my bag of very mixed reading.

When I didn't want to read, I could look down through the banyan leaves at the world below, at Grandmother hanging up or taking down the washing, at the cook quarrelling with a fruit vendor or at Grandfather grumbling at the hardy Indian marigolds which insisted on springing up all over his very English garden. Usually nothing very exciting happened while I was in the banyan tree, but on one particular afternoon I had enough excitement to last me through the summer.

That was the time I saw a mongoose and a cobra fight to death in the garden, while I sat directly above them in the banyan tree.

It was an April afternoon. And the warm breezes of approaching summer had sent everyone, including Grandfather, indoors. I was feeling drowsy myself and was wondering if I should go to the pond behind the house for a swim, when I saw a huge black cobra gliding out of a clump of cactus and making for some cooler part of the garden. At the same time a mongoose (whom I had often seen) emerged from the bushes and went straight for the cobra.

In a clearing beneath the tree, in bright sunshine, they came face to face.

The cobra knew only too well that the grey mongoose, three feet long, was a superb fighter, clever and aggressive. But the cobra was a skilful and experienced fighter too. He could move swiftly and strike with the speed of light, and the sacs behind his long, sharp fangs were full of deadly venom.

It was to be a battle of champions.

Hissing defiance, his forked tongue darting in and out, the cobra raised three of his six feet off the ground, and spread his broad, spectacled hood. The mongoose bushed his tail. The long hair on his spine stood up (in the past, the very thickness of his hair had saved him from bites that would have been fatal to others).

Though the combatants were unaware of my presence in the banyan tree, they soon became aware of the arrival of two other spectators. One was a myna, and the other a jungle crow (not the wily urban crow). They had seen these preparations for battle, and had settled on the cactus to watch the outcome. Had they been content only to watch, all would have been well with both of them.

The cobra stood on the defensive, swaying slowly from side to side, trying to mesmerize the mongoose into marking a false move. But the mongoose knew the power of his opponent's glassy, unwinking eyes, and refused to meet them. Instead he fixed his gaze at a point just below the cobra's hood, and opened the attack.

Moving forward quickly until he was just within the cobra's reach, he made a feint to one side. Immediately the cobra struck. His great hood came down so swiftly that I thought nothing could save the mongoose. But the little fellow jumped neatly to one side, and darted in as swiftly as the cobra, biting the snake on the back and darting away again out of reach.

The moment the cobra struck, the crow and the myna hurled themselves at him, only to collide heavily in mid-air. Shrieking at each other, they returned to the cactus plant.

A few drops of blood glistened on the cobra's back.

The cobra struck again and missed. Again the mongoose sprang aside, jumped in and bit. Again the birds dived at the snake, bumped into each other instead, and returned shrieking to the safety of the cactus.

The third round followed the same course as the first but with one dramatic difference. The crow and the myna, still determined to take part in the proceedings, dived at the cobra, but this time they missed each other as well as their mark. The myna flew on and reached its perch, but the crow tried to pull up in mid-air and turn back. In the second that it took him to do this, the cobra whipped his head back and struck with great force, his snout thudding against the crow's body.

I saw the bird flung nearly twenty feet across the garden, where, after fluttering about for a while, it lay still. The myna remained on the cactus plant, and when the snake and the mongoose returned to the fray, it very wisely refrained from interfering again!

The cobra was weakening, and the mongoose, walking

fearlessly up to it, raised himself on his short legs, and with a lightning snap had the big snake by the snout. The cobra writhed and lashed about in a frightening manner, and even coiled itself about the mongoose, but all to no avail. The little fellow hung grimly on, until the snake had ceased to struggle. He then smelt along its quivering length, and gripping it round the hood, dragged it into the bushes.

The myna dropped cautiously to the ground, hopped about, peered into the bushes from a safe distance, and then, with a shrill cry of congratulation, flew away.

When I had also made a cautious descent from the tree and returned to the house, I told Grandfather of the fight I had seen. He was pleased that the mongoose had won. He had encouraged it to live in the garden, to keep away the snakes, and fed it regularly with scraps from the kitchen. He had never tried taming it, because a wild mongoose was more useful than a domesticated one.

From the banyan tree I often saw the mongoose patrolling the four corners of the garden, and once I saw him with an egg in his mouth and knew he had been in the poultry house; but he hadn't harmed the birds, and I knew Grandmother would forgive him for stealing as long as he kept the snakes away from the house.

The banyan tree was also the setting for what we were to call the Strange Case of the Grey Squirrel and the White Rat.

The white rat was Grandfather's—he had bought it from the bazaar for four annas—but I would often take it with me into the banyan tree, where it soon struck up a friendship with one of the squirrels. They would go off together on little excursions among the roots and branches of the old tree.

Then the squirrel started building a nest. At first she tried building it in my pockets, and when I went indoors and changed my clothes I would find straw and grass falling out. Then one day Grandmother's knitting was missing. We hunted for it everywhere but without success.

Next day I saw something glinting in the hole in the banyan tree and, going up to investigate, saw that it was the end of Grandmother's steel knitting-needle. On looking further, I discovered that the hole was crammed with knitting. And amongst the wool were three baby squirrels—all of them white!

Grandfather had never seen white squirrels before, and we gazed at them in wonder. We were puzzled for some time, but when I mentioned the white rat's frequent visits to the tree, Grandfather told me that the rat must be the father. Rats and squirrels were related to each other, he said, and so it was quite possible for them to have offspring—in this case, white squirrels!

FROM MY NOTEBOOK

To know one's limitations and to do good work within them: more is achieved that way than by overreaching oneself. It is no use trying to write a masterpiece every year if you are so made as to write only one in ten years! In between, there are other good things that can be written—smaller things, but satisfying in their own way.

*

Any day now, I shall have to shut up shop and join the ranks of salaried clerks or teachers. Any day now, I shall find that I no longer make a living as a freelance. Any day now. . . .

I've had this dread for the past five years, but somehow, just when the going gets really rough and my bank balance touches rock-bottom, something does in fact turn up (Micawber would have envied me), and I can go on writing, not always in the way I Want to—because, if cheques are to be received, deadlines and editorial preferences must be met—but pretty much as I want to.

Any day now. . . .

*

Cyril Connolly, in a BBC interview, said:

'A good writer rises above everything and it's an alibi to say: "I can't write, I haven't got a room of my own. . ." or "I can't write, I haven't got a private income. . ." or "I can't write, I'm a journalist", and so on. These are all alibis. But I have seen in my contemporaries a great many who could have been much better if it hadn't been for two or three things: social climbing, drink, and unhappy love affairs due to flaws in themselves which made their love affairs go on for too long or become too unhappy.'

*

Graham Greene has said that, for the novelist taking his first clean sheet of paper, there is a 'correct' moment of experience at which to begin. For the writer for children this moment is often a moment of arrival. . . . Authors are now aware of the need to catch the child's interest and not frighten him off. The dreary beginning is a thing of the past, and for an example of it we have to turn back to something like *Children of the New Forest*. But modern writers can put the reader off in other ways. It is easy for them to lose half their potential readers on the first page. Rosemary Sutcliffe, a beautiful writer for children, unfortunately begins *The Hound of Ulster* with a catalogue of unfamiliar proper names. Now there can be no doubt that the Bible is one of the world's most beautiful books, and we usually skip the parts which go: 'And Jokshan begat Sheba, and Sheba begat Dedan', etc. But children don't like skipping. If they come up against something like this, they will leave the book altogether.

*

Down near the stream* I found wood-sorrel—tiny yellow flowers set among bunches of heart-shaped leaflets which are a beautiful pale green. The leaves are sweet and sour, and Anil likes to eat them. They seem to do him no harm. Then why should they cause diarrhoea in cows?

'All flesh is grass, is not only metaphorically, but literally, true; for all those creatures we behold, are but the herbs of the field, digested into flesh in them, or more remotely carnified in ourselves.' (Sir Thomas Browne, *Religio Medici*)

In a letter, P. L. Travers, (the author of *Mary Poppins*) says: 'I

---

*Some nature notes (made while living in Mussoorie; a writer who ignores the flora and fauna around him, does so at his own peril).

don't write for children. . . . Perhaps I write because a book wants to write itself in me . . . Then afterwards, if there are children and grown-ups who like it, I feel I am very lucky.

'To explain about writing, let me tell you what I saw one day, in the country . . .

'I was out very early on a summer morning and there suddenly at the edge of a clearing was a fox dancing, all by himself, up and down on his hind legs, bending like a rainbow, swinging his brush in the sun. There was no vixen near, the birds were not interested, nobody in the world cared. He was doing it for his own pleasure. Perhaps writers such as I are really foxes, dancing their own particular dance without any thought of a watching eye.'

*

This reminds me of my friend Pitambar, who was found one night dancing in the middle of the road.

'Why are you dancing in the road?' I asked.

'Because I am happy,' he said.

'And why are you so happy?'

He looked at me as if I were a moron.

'Because I am dancing on the road,' he said.

THUS SPOKE CROW

One summer evening, as storm-clouds gathered over the purple mountains, a glossy black jungle-crow settled on the window-sill, looked at me with his head cocked to one side, and said, 'You look worried today, chum. Anything I can do for you?'

I had been lolling in an easy chair near the window, looking pretty gloomy I suppose, for all was not well with life in general, when this Runyonesque character arrived and startled me out of my solitude.

'I beg your pardon?' I said politely. One must always be polite with strangers; nowadays some of them carry guns or knives.

'Just asked if anything was wrong,' said the crow. 'You're not your usual cheerful self.'

'No, I'm not. But there's nothing I can do about it. And it's got nothing to do with you.'

'You never can tell,' said my visitor.

'All right. And if it wasn't that I'm feverish and probably in delirium, I'd swear that you were talking to me.'

'Don't swear. Just listen. I've been around. I've even been human. Chang-tzu had me for a disciple. Epictetus had me for a friend. Saul of Tersus and I made tents together. I've knocked about with Kashyapa, father of demons. . . .'

'And now you're a crow. I suppose it's progress of a kind.'

'It's all because I went into politics the last time around. The result was this feathered reincarnation. But seriously, there's nothing wrong with being a crow. We are a much-maligned tribe. Do you realize that no other bird has our intelligence, our resilience. . . . We can make a living almost anywhere—and that's more than what you've been able to do of late!'

He had me there. I'd been struggling for some time, trying to make ends meet; but I wasn't getting anywhere.

'I'm doing my best,' I said.

'That's your trouble,' said Crow, moving nearer along the window-sill and looking me between the eyes. 'You do your best. You try too hard! That's fatal, friend. The secret of success lies in maximum achievement with minimum effort.'

'But that's ridiculous,' I protested. 'How am I to be a successful author if I don't *write*?'

'You misunderstand me. I am not recommending the idle life. Have you ever seen an idle crow? I bet you haven't. A hard-working crow? Most unlikely. And yet we've always got one eye open, and that eye's on the likeliest opportunity . . . 'And sidling up to me, he filched the remains of my sandwich from my hand. 'See that? Got what I wanted, didn't I? And with a minimum of effort. It's simply a question of being in the right place at the right time.'

I was not amused.

'That's all very well if your ambition is to pinch someone else's lunch,' I said. 'But how does it apply to successful authorship? Do I pinch other people's ideas?'

'Most people do but that's not the point. What I'm really advocating is pragmatism. The trouble with most people, and that includes writers, is that they want too much in the first place. A feast instead of a bite from a sandwich. And feasts are harder to come by and cost much more. So that's your first mistake—to be wanting too much, too soon.

'And the second mistake is to be pursuing things. What I'm saying, old chap, applies not only to authorship but to almost everything under the sun. Success is what you are pursuing, isn't it? Success is what most of us are pursuing.

'Now, I'm a successful crow, you must admit that. But I don't pursue. I wait, I watch, I collect! My motto is the same as that of any Boy Scout—"Be prepared"!

'I'm not a bird of prey. *You* are not a beast of prey. So it is not by pursuit that we succeed. Because if we became hunters, then we would automatically bring into being victims. And a victim's chief object is to get away! And so it is with success. Pursue it too avidly and it will elude you.'

'So what am I supposed to do? Write books and forget about them?'

'Exactly. I don't mean you have to tuck them away. Send them where you will—send them to the four corners of the earth—but don't fret over them, don't expect too much. That's the third mistake—fretting. Because when you keep fretting about something you've done, you can't give your mind to anything else.'

'You're right,' I had to admit. 'I do worry a lot. I'm the worrying kind.'

'All wrong. What have you to worry about?'

'Lots of little things.'

'Anything big?'

'Not at the moment.'

'But you expect something terrible to happen? You expect the worst?'

'Isn't it prudent to expect the worst?'

'Not in crow philosophy. We expect the best!' And hopping onto the side-table, he dipped his beak in my beermug and took a long, thoughtful sip. 'Always expecting the best! And I usually get it. By the way, if you can afford beer every day, you can't be too badly off.'

'I don't have it every day.'

'Almost every day. I've been watching you.'

'Why this sudden interest in my welfare? Why not someone more deserving?'

'Because I've taken a fancy to you,' he said, cocking his head to one side. 'You don't trouble crows.'

'I've never noticed them much.'

'A pity. If you'd taken the trouble to study crows, you'd have learnt something from them. Survival. Independence. Freedom from stress.' He took another sip of beer. 'No writer worth his salt can afford to ignore us. We're nature's greatest survivors!'

With a disdainful flap of his wings he took off and headed for the Woodstock school kitchens. I looked at the label on my bottle of beer. It seemed quite genuine. But you never know, these days.

ON THE ROAD

TRAVEL WRITINGS

GANGA DESCENDS

There has always been a mild sort of controversy as to whether the true Ganga (in its upper reaches) is the Alaknanda or the Bhagirathi. Of course the two rivers meet at Deoprayag and then both are Ganga. But there are some who assert that geographically the Alaknanda is the true Ganga, while others say that tradition should be the criterion, and traditionally the Bhagirathi is the Ganga.

I put the question to my friend Dr Sudhakar Misra, from whom words of wisdom sometimes flow; and, true to form, he answered: 'The Alaknanda is the Ganga, but the Bhagirathi is Gangaji.'

One sees what he means. The Bhagirathi is beautiful, almost caressingly so, and people have responded to it with love and respect, ever since Shiva released the waters of the goddess from his tangled locks and she sped plains-wards in the tracks of Prince Bhagirath's chariot.

> He held the river on his head,
> And kept her wandering, where,
> Dense as Himalayas woods were spread,
> The tangles of his hair.

Revered by Hindus, and loved by all, the goddess Ganga weaves her spell over all who come to her. Moreover, she issues from the very heart of the Himalayas. Visiting Gangotri in 1820, the writer and traveller Baillie Fraser noted: 'We are now in the centre of the Himalayas, the loftiest and perhaps the most rugged range of mountains in the world.'

Perhaps it is this realization that one is at the Very centre and heart of things, that gives one an almost primeval sense of belonging to these mountains and to this river valley in particular. For me, and for many who have been in the mountains, the Bhagirathi is the most beautiful of the four main river valleys of Garhwal. It will remain so provided we do not pollute its waters and strip it of its virgin forests.

The Bhagirathi seems to have everything—people of a gentle disposition, deep glens and forests, the ultra vision of an open valley graced with tiers of cultivation leading up by degrees to the peaks and glaciers at its head.

From some twenty miles above Tehri, as far as Bhatwari, a distance of about fifty-five miles along the valley, there are extensive forests of pine. It covers the mountains on both sides of the river and its affluents, filling the ravines and plateaus up to a height of about 5,000 feet. Above Bhatwari, forests of box, yew and cypress commence, and if we leave the valley and take the roads to Nachiketa Tal or Dodi Tal—little lakes at around 9,000 feet above sea level—we pass through dense forests of oak and chestnut. From Gangnani to Gangotri the deodar is the principal tree. The excelsa pine also extends eight miles up the valley above Gangotri, and birch is found in patches to within half a mile of the glacier.

On the right bank of the river, above Sukhi, the forest is nearly pure deodar, but on the left bank, with a northern aspect, there is a mixture of silver-fir, spruce and birch. The valley of the Jad-ganga is also full of deodar, and towards its head the valuable pencil-cedar is found. The only other area of Garhwal where the deodar is equally extensive is the Jaunsar-Bawar tract to the west.

It was the valuable timber of the deodar that attracted the adventurer Frederick 'Pahari' Wilson to the valley in the 1850's. He leased the forests from the Raja of Tehri in 1859, and in a few years, he had made a fortune.

The old forest rest-houses at Dharasu, Bhatwari and Harsil were all built by Wilson as staging-posts, for the only roads were narrow tracks linking one village to another. Wilson married a local girl, Gulabi, from the village of Mukhba, and the portraits of Mr and Mrs Wilson (early examples of the photographer's art) still hang in these sturdy little bungalows. At any rate, I found their pictures at

Bhatwari. Harsil is now out of bounds to civilians, and I believe part of the old house was destroyed in a fire a few years ago.*

Amongst other things, Wilson introduced the apple into this area, and 'Wilson apples'—large, red and juicy—are sold to travellers and pilgrims on their way to Gangotri. This fascinating man also acquired an encyclopaedic knowledge of the wildlife of the region, and his articles, which appeared in *Indian Sporting Life* in the 1860's, were later plundered by so-called wildlife experts for their own writings.

Bridge-building was another of Wilson's ventures. These bridges were meant to facilitate travel to Harsil and the shrine at Gangotri. The most famous of them was a 350-foot suspension bridge over the Jad-ganga at Bhaironghat, over 1,200 feet above the young Bhagirathi where it thunders through a deep defile. This rippling contraption of a bridge was at first a source of terror to travellers, and only a few ventured across it. To reassure people, Wilson would often mount his horse and gallop to and fro across the bridge. It has long since collapsed but local people will tell you that the hoofbeats of Wilson's horse can still be heard on full moon nights! The supports of the old bridge were complete tree-trunks, and they can still be seen to one side of the new motor-bridge put up by engineers of the Northern Railway.

Wilson's life is fit subject for a romance; but even if one were never written, his legend would live on, as it has done for over a hundred years. There has never been any attempt to commemorate him, but people in the valley still speak of him in awe and admiration, as though he had lived only yesterday. Some men leave a trail of legend behind them, because they give their spirit to the place where they have lived, and remain forever a part of the rocks and mountain streams.

In the old days, only the staunchest of pilgrims visited the shrines of Gangotri and Jamnotri. The roads were rocky and dangerous, winding along in some places, ascending and descending

---

*Wilson inspires one of my brief forays into historical fiction in the opening chapters to *Rosebud*.

the faces of deep precipices and ravines, at times leading along banks of loose earth where landslides had swept the original path away. There are still no large towns above Uttarkashi, and this absence of large centres of population may be one reason why the forests are better preserved than, say, those in the Alaknanda valley, or further downstream.

Gangotri is situated at just a little over 10,300 feet and on the right bank of the river is the Gangotri temple. It is a small neat building without too much ornamentation, built by Amar Singh Thapa, a Nepali general, early in the Nineteenth Century. It was renovated by the Maharaja of Jaipur in the 1920's. The rock on which it stands is called Bhagirath Shila and is said to be the place where Prince Bhagirath did penance in order that Ganga be brought down from her abode of eternal snow.

Here the rocks are carved and polished by ice and water, so smooth that in places they look like rolls of silk. The fast-flowing waters of this mountain torrent look very different from the huge sluggish river that finally empties its waters into the Bay of Bengal 1,500 miles away.

The river emerges from beneath a great glacier, thickly studded with enormous loose rocks and earth. The glacier is about a mile in width and extends upwards for many miles. The chasm in the glacier, through which the stream rushes into the light of day, is named Gaumukh, the cow's mouth, and is held in deepest reverence by Hindus. The regions of eternal frost in the vicinity were the scenes of many of their most sacred mysteries.

The Ganga enters the world no puny stream, but bursts from its icy womb a river thirty or forty yards in breadth. At Gauri Kund (below the Gangotri temple) it falls over a rock of considerable height, and continues tumbling over a succession of small cascades until it enters the Bhaironghati gorge.

A night spent beside the river, within sound of the fall, is an eerie experience. After some time it begins to sound, not like one fall but a hundred, and this sound permeates both one's dreams and walking hours. Rising early to greet the dawn proved rather pointless at Gangotri, for the surrounding peaks did not let the sun in till after 9 a.m. Everyone rushes about to keep warm, exclaiming delightedly at what they call *gulabi thand*,—literally, *rosy cold*. Guaranteed to turn the cheeks a rosy pink! A charming expression, but I prefer a rosy sunburn—and remained beneath a heavy quilt until the sun came up to throw its golden shafts across the river.

This is mid-October, and after Diwali the shrine and the small township will close for the winter, the pandits retreating to the relative warmth of Mukhba. Soon snow will cover everything, and even the hardy purple-plumaged whistling thrushes, lovers of deep shade, will move further down the valley. And down below the forest-line, the Garhwali farmers go about harvesting their ripening paddy, as they have done for centuries; their terraced fields form patterns of yellow, green and gold above the deep green of the river.

Yes, the Bhagirathi is a green river. Although deep and swift, it does not lose its serenity. At no place does it look hurried or confused—unlike the turbulent Alaknanda, fretting and frothing as it goes crashing down its boulder-strewn bed. The Alaknanda gives one a feeling of being trapped, because the river itself is trapped . The Bhagirathi is free-flowing, easy. At all times and places it seems to find its true level.

Uttarkashi, though a large and growing town, is as yet uncrowded. The seediness of over-populated towns like Rishikesh and Dehradun is not yet evident here. One can take a leisurely walk through its long (and well-supplied) bazaar, without being jostled by crowds or knocked over by three-wheelers. Here, too, the river is always with you, and you must live in harmony with its sound, as it goes rushing and humming along its shingly bed.

Uttarkashi is not without its own religious and historical importance, although all traces of its ancient capital called Barahat appear to have vanished. There are four important temples here, and on the occasion of Makar Sankranti, early in January, a week long fair is held, when thousands from the surrounding areas throng the roads to the town. To the beating of drums and blowing of trumpets, the Gods and Goddesses are brought to the fair in gaily decorated palanquins. The surrounding villages wear a deserted look that day as everyone flocks to the temples and bathing-ghats and to the entertainment of the fair itself.

We have to move far downstream to reach another large centre of population, the town of Tehri, and this is a very different place from Uttarkashi. Tehri has all the characteristics of a small town in the plains—crowds, noise, traffic congestion, dust and refuse, scrufty dhabas—with this difference, that here it is all ephemeral, for Tehri is destined to be submerged by the waters of the Bhagirathi when the Tehri dam is finally completed.

The rulers of Garhwal were often changing their capitals, and when, after the Gurkha Wars (1811-15) the former capital of Shrinagar became part of British Garhwal, Raja Sundershan Shah established his new capital at Tehri. It is said that when he reached this spot, his horse refused to go any further. This was enough for the king, it seems; or so the story goes.

Perhaps Prince Bhagirath's chariot will come to a halt here too, when the dam is built. The 246-metre high earthen dam, with forty-two square miles of reservoir capacity, will submerge the town and about thirty villages.

As we leave the town and cross the narrow bridge over the river, a mighty blast from above sends rocks hurtling down the defile, just to remind us that work is in progress.

Unlike the Raja's horse, I have no wish to be stopped in my tracks at Tehri. There are livelier places upstream.

BEAUTIFUL MANDAKINI

To see a river for the first time at its confluence with another great river is, for me, a special moment in time. And so it was with the Mandakini at Rudraprayag, where its waters were joined with the waters of the Alaknanda, the one having come from the glacial snows above Kedarnath, the other from the Himalayan heights beyond Badrinath. Both sacred rivers, both destined to become the holy Ganga further downstream.

I fell in love with the Mandakini at first sight. Or was it the valley that I fell in love with? I am not sure, and it doesn't really matter. The valley is the river.

While the Alaknanda valley, especially in its higher reaches, is a deep and narrow gorge where precipitous outcrops of rock hang threateningly over the traveller, the Mandakini valley is broader, gentler, the terraced fields wider, the banks of the river a green sward in many places.

Rudraprayag is hot. It is probably a pleasant spot in winter, but at the end of June it is decidedly hot. Perhaps its chief claim to fame is that it gave its name to the dreaded man-eating leopard of Rudraprayag who, in the course of seven years (1918-25), accounted for more than 300 victims. It was finally shot by the fifty-one-year-old Jim Corbett, who recounted the saga of his long hunt for the killer in his fine book, *The Man-eating Leopard of Rudraprayag*.

The place at which the leopard was shot was the village of Gulabrai, two miles south of Rudraprayag. Under a large mango tree stands a memorial raised to Jim Corbett by officers and men of the Border Roads Organisation. It is a happy gesture to one who loved Garhwal and India. Unfortunately several buffaloes are gathered close by, and one has to wade through slush and buffalo-dung to get to the memorial-stone. A board tacked on to the mango tree attracts the attention of motorists who might pass without noticing the memorial, which is off to one side.

The killer-leopard was noted for its direct method of attack on humans; and, in spite of being poisoned, trapped in a cave, and shot at innumerable times, it did not lose its contempt for man. Two English sportsmen covering both ends of the old suspension bridge over the Alaknanda fired several times at the man-eater but to little effect.

It was not long before the leopard acquired a reputation among the hill folk for being an evil spirit. A sadhu was suspected of turning into the leopard by night, and was only saved from being lynched by the ingenuity of Philip Mason, then Deputy Commissioner of Garhwal. Mason kept the sadhu in custody until the leopard made his next attack, thus proving the man innocent. Years later, when Mason turned novelist and (using the pen-name Philip Woodruff) wrote *The Wild Sweet Witch*, he had as his main character a beautiful young woman who turns into a man-eating leopard by night.

Corbett's host at Gulabrai was one of the few who survived an encounter with the leopard. It left him with a hole in his throat.

Apart from being a superb story-teller, Corbett displayed great compassion for people from all walks of life and is still a legend in Garhwal and Kumaon amongst people who have never read his books.

*

In June, one does not linger long in the steamy heat of Rudraprayag. But as one travels up the river, making a gradual ascent of the Mandakini valley, there is a cool breeze coming down from the snows, and the smell of rain is in the air.

The thriving little township of Agastmuni spreads itself along the wide riverbanks, and further upstream, near a little place called Chanderpuri, we cannot resist breaking our journey to sprawl on the tender green grass that slopes gently down to the swiftly flowing river. A small rest-house is in the making. Around it, banana fronds sway and poplar leaves dance in the breeze.

This is no sluggish river of the plains, but a fast moving current, tumbling over rocks, turning and twisting in its efforts to discover the easiest way for its frothy snowfed waters to escape the mountains. Escape is the word! For the constant plaint of many a Garhwali is that, while his hills abound in rivers the water runs down and away, and little if any reaches the fields and villages above it. Cultivation must depend on the rain and not on the river.

The road climbs gradually, still keeping to the river. Just outside Guptkashi my attention is drawn to a clump of huge trees sheltering a small but ancient temple. We stop here and enter the shade of the trees.

The temple is deserted. It is a temple dedicated to Shiva, and in the courtyard are several river-rounded stone lingams on which leaves and blossoms have fallen. No one seems to come here, which is strange, since it is on the pilgrim route. Two boys from a neighbouring field leave their yoked bullocks to come and talk to me, but they cannot tell me much about the temple except to confirm that it is seldom visited. 'The buses do not stop here.' That seems explanation enough. For where the buses go, the pilgrims go, and where the pilgrims go, other pilgrims will follow. Thus far and no further.

The trees seem to be magnolias, judging by the scent and shape of the flowers, and the boys call them Champa, Hindi for magnolia blossom. But I have never seen magnolia trees grow to such huge proportions. Perhaps they are something else. Never mind; let them remain a sweet-scented mystery.

Guptkashi in the evening is all a bustle. A coach-load of pilgrims (headed for Kedarnath) has just arrived, and the tea-shops near the bus-stand are doing brisk business. Then the 'local' bus—from Okhimath, across the river—arrives, and many of the passengers head for a tea-shop famed for its samosas. The local bus is called the *bhook-hartal*—the 'hunger strike' bus.

'How did it get that name?' I ask one of the samosa-eaters.

'Well, it's an interesting story. For a long time we had been asking the authorities to provide a bus service for the local people and for the villagers who live off the roads. All the buses came from

Srinagar or Rishikesh, and were taken up by pilgrims. The locals couldn't find room in them. But our pleas went unheard until the whole town—or most of it, anyway—decided to go on hunger-strike. That worked. And so the bus is named after our successful hunger-strike.'

'They nearly put me out of business too,' said the tea-shop owner cheerfully. 'Nobody ate any samosas for two days!'

There is no cinema or public place of entertainment at Guptkashi, and the town goes to sleep early. And wakes early.

At six, the hillside, green from recent rain, sparkles in the morning sunshine. Snow-capped Chaukhamba (23,400 ft.) is dazzling. The air is clear, no smoke or dust up here. The climate, I am told, is mild all the year round, Okhimath, on the other side of the river, lies in the shadow. It gets the sun at nine. In winter it must wait till afternoon. And yet it seems a bigger place, and by tradition the temple priest from Kedarnath passes winter there when the snows cover that distant shrine.

Guptkashi has not yet been rendered ugly by the barrack-type architecture that has come up in some growing hill towns. The old double-storeyed houses are built of stone, with grey slate roofs. They blend well with the hillside. Cobbled paths meander through the old bazaar.

One of these takes us to the famed Guptkashi temple, tucked away above the old part of the town. Here, as in Benares, Shiva is worshipped as Vishwanath, and two underground streams representing the sacred Yamuna and Bhagirathi rivers feed the pool sacred to the god. This temple gives the town its name—Guptkashi, the 'Invisible Benares,' just as Uttarkashi on the Bhagirathi is 'Upper Benares.'

Guptkashi and its environs have so many lingams that the saying *jitne kankar itne Sankar*—'As many stones, so many Shivas'—has become a proverb to describe its holiness.

From Guptkashi, pilgrims proceed north to Kedarnath, and the last stage of their journey—about a day's march—must be covered on foot or horseback. The temple of Kedarnath, situated at a height of 11,753 feet, is encircled by snowcapped peaks, and

Atkinson has conjectured that 'the symbol of the linga may have arisen from the pointed peaks around his (God Shiva's) original home.'

The temple is dedicated to Sadashiva, the subterranean form of the god, who, 'fleeing from the Pandavas took refuge here in the form of a he-buffalo.'

We leave the Mandakini to visit Tungnath on the Chandrashila range. But I will return to this river. It has captured my mind and heart.

217

THE MAGIC OF TUNGNATH

The mountains and valleys of Garhwal never fail to spring surprises on the traveller in search of the picturesque. It is impossible to know every corner of the Himalayas, which means that there are always new corners to discover; forest or meadow, mountain stream or wayside shrine.

The temple of Tungnath, at a little over 12,000 feet, is the highest shrine on the inner Himalayan range. It lies just below the Chandrashila peak. Some way off the main pilgrim routes, it is less frequented than Kedarnath or Badrinath, although it forms a part of the Kedar temple establishment. The priest here is a local man, a Brahmin from the village of Maku; the other Kedar temples have South Indian priests, a tradition begun by Sankaracharya, the eighth-century Hindu reformer and revivalist.

Tungnath's lonely eminence gives it a magic of its own. To get there (or beyond it), one passes through some of the most delightful temperate forest in the Garhwal Himalayas. Pilgrim or trekker, or just plain rambler like myself, one comes away a better man, forest refreshed and more aware of what the world was really like before mankind began to strip it bare.

Duiri Tal, a small lake, lies cradled on the hill above Okhimath at a height of 8,000 feet. It was a favourite spot of one of Garhwal's earliest British Commissioners, J.H. Batten, whose administration continued for twenty years (1836-56). He wrote:

The day I reached there it was snowing and young trees were laid prostrate under the weight of snow, the lake was frozen over to a depth of about two inches. There was no human habitation and the place looked a veritable wilderness. The next morning when the sun appeared, the

Chaukhamba and many other peaks extending as far as Kedarnath seemed covered with a new quilt of snow as if close at hand. The whole scene was so exquisite that one could not tire of gazing at it for hours. I think a person who has a subdued settled despair in his mind would all of a sudden feel a kind of bounding and exalting cheerfulness which will be imparted to his frame by the atmosphere of Duiri Tal.

This feeling of uplift can be experienced almost anywhere along the Tungnath range. Duiri Tal is still some way off the beaten track and anyone wishing to spend the night there should carry a tent. But further along this range, the road ascends to Dugalbeta (at about 9,000 feet) where a PWD rest-house, gaily painted, has come up like some exotic orchid in the midst of a lush meadow topped by excelsia pines and pencil cedars. Many an official who has stayed here has rhapsodized on the charms of Dugalbeta; and if you are unofficial (and therefore not entitled to stay in the bungalow), you can move on to Chopta, lusher still, where there is accommodation of a sort for pilgrims and other hardy souls. Two or three little tea-shops provide mattresses and quilts. The Garhwal Mandal is putting up a rest-house. These tourist rest-houses scattered over the length and breadth of Garhwal, are a great boon to the traveller; but during the pilgrim season (May–June) they are filled to overflowing and if you turn up unexpectedly you might have to take your pick of tea-shop or dharamshala, of a lucky dip, since they vary a good deal in comfort and cleanliness.

The trek from Chopta to Tungnath is only three and a half miles, but in that distance one ascends about 3,000 feet, and the pilgrim may be forgiven for feeling that at places he is on a perpendicular path. Like a ladder to heaven, I couldn't help thinking.

In spite of its steepness, my companion, the redoubtable Ganesh Saili, insisted that we take a short cut. After clawing our way up tufts of alpine grass which formed the rungs of our ladder, we were stuck and had to inch our way down again so that the ascent of Tungnath began to resemble a game of Snakes and Ladders.

*

A tiny guardian-temple dedicated to the god Ganesh spurred us on. Nor was I really fatigued for the cold fresh air and the verdant greenery surrounding us was like an intoxicant. Myriads of wild flowers grew on the hill slopes—buttercups, anemones, wild strawberries, forget-me-nots, rock-cress—enough to rival the Valley of Flowers at this time of the year.

Before reaching these alpine meadows, we climb through rhododendron forest and here one finds at least three species of this flower: the red flowering tree rhododendron (found throughout the Himalayas between 6,000 feet and 10,000 feet); a second variety, the almatta, with flowers that are light red or rosy in colour and the third, chimul or white variety found at heights ranging from between 10,000 feet and 13,000 feet. The chimul is a brushwood, seldom more than twelve feet high and growing slantingly due to the heavy burden of snow it has to carry for almost six months in the year.

Those brushwood rhododendrons are the last trees we see on our ascent for as we approach Tungnath the treeline ends and there is nothing between earth and sky except grass and rock and tiny flowers. Above us, a couple of crows dive-bomb a hawk who does his best to escape their attentions. Crows are the world's great survivors. They are capable of living at any height and in any climate; as much at home in the back streets of Delhi as on the heights of Tungnath.

Another survivor, up here at any rate, is the pika, a sort of mouse-hare, who looks like neither mouse nor hare but rather a tiny guinea-pig; small ears, no tail, grey-brown fur and chubby feet. They emerge from their holes under the rocks to forage for grasses on which to feed. Their simple diet and thick fur enable them to live in extreme cold and they have been found at 16,000 feet, which is higher than any other mammal lives. The Garhwalis call this little creature the runda—at any rate, that's what the temple priest called it, adding that it was not averse to entering his house and helping itself to grain and other delicacies. So perhaps there's more in it of mouse than of hare.

Those little rundas were with us all the way from Chopta to Tungnath, peering out from their rocks and scampering about on the hillside, seemingly unconcerned by our presence.

At Tungnath they live beneath the temple flagstones. The priest's grandchildren were having a game discovering their burrows; the rundas would go in at one hole and pop out at another—they must have had a system of underground passages.

When we arrived, clouds had gathered over Tungnath, as they do almost every afternoon. The temple looked austere in the gathering gloom.

To some, the name 'Tung' indicates 'lofty', from the position of the temple on the highest peak outside the main chain of the Himalayas; others derive it from the word *tangna*—to be suspended—in allusion to the form under which the deity is worshipped here. The form is the Swayambhu Ling; and on Shivaratri or night of Shiva, the true believer may, 'with the eye of faith', see the lingam increase in size; but 'to the evil-minded no such favour is granted.'

The temple, though not very large, is certainly impressive, mainly because of its setting and the solid slabs of grey granite from which it is built. The whole place somehow puts me in mind of Emily Brontë's Wuthering Heights—bleak, windswept, open to the skies. And as you look down from the temple at the little half-deserted hamlet that serves it in summer, the eye is met by grey slate roofs and piles of stones, with just a few hardy souls in residence—for the majority of pilgrims now prefer to spend the night down at Chopta.

*

Even the temple priest, attended by his son and grandsons,

complains bitterly of the cold. To spend every day barefoot on those flagstones must indeed be hardship. I wince after five minutes of it, made worse by stepping into a puddle of icy water. I shall never make a good pilgrim; no rewards for me, in this world or the next. But the priest's feet are literally thick-skinned; and the children seem oblivious to the cold. Still, in October they must be happy to descend to Maku, their home village on the slopes below Dugalbeta.

It begins to rain as we leave the temple. We pass herds of sheep huddled in a ruined dharamshala. The crows are still rushing about the grey weeping skies, although the hawk has very sensibly gone away. A runda sticks his nose out from his hole, probably to take a look at the weather. There is a clap of thunder and he disappears, like the White Rabbit in 'Alice in Wonderland'. We are halfway down the Tungnath 'ladder' when it begins to rain quite heavily. And now we pass our first genuine pilgrims, a group of intrepid Bengalis who are heading straight into the storm. They are without umbrellas or raincoats, but they are not to be deterred.

Oaks and rhododendrons flash past as we dash down the steep, winding path. Another shortcut and Ganesh Saili takes a tumble, but is cushioned by moss and buttercups. My wristwatch strikes a rock and the glass is shattered. No matter. Time here is of little or no significance. Away with time! Is this, I wonder, the 'bounding and exalting cheerfulness' experienced by Batten and now manifesting in me?

The tea-shop beckons. How would one manage in the hills without these wayside tea-shops? Miniature inns, they provide food, shelter and even lodging to dozens at a time.

We sit on a bench between a Gujjar herdsman and a pilgrim who is too feverish to make the climb to the temple. He accepts my offer of an aspirin to go with his tea. We tackle some buns— rock-hard, to match our environment—and wash the pellets with hot sweet tea.

There is a small shrine here, too, right in front of the tea-shop. It is a slab of rock roughly shaped like a lingam and it is daubed with vermilion and strewn with offerings of wild flowers. The mica in the rock gives it a beautiful sheen.

I suppose Hinduism comes closest to being a nature religion. Rivers, rocks, trees, plants, animals, and birds all play their part, both in mythology and in everyday worship. This harmony is most evident in those remote places where gods and mountains coexist. Tungnath, as yet unspoilt by materialistic society, exerts its magic on all who come there with open mind and heart.

ON THE ROAD TO BADRINATH

If you have travelled up the Mandakini valley, and then cross over into the valley of the Alaknanda, you are immediately struck by the contrast. The Mandakini is gentler, richer in vegetation, almost pastoral in places; the Alaknanda is awesome, precipitous, threatening—and seemingly inhospitable to those who must live, and earn a livelihood, in its confines.

Even as we left Chamoli and began the steady, winding climb to Badrinath, the nature of the terrain underwent a dramatic change. No longer did green fields slope gently down to the riverbed. Here they clung precariously to rocky slopes and ledges that grew steeper and narrower, while the river below, impatient to reach its confluence with the Bhagirathi at Deoprayag, thundered along the narrow gorge.

Badrinath is one of the four dhams, or four most holy places in India. (The other three are Rameshwaram, Dwarka and Jagannath Puri.) For the pilgrim travelling to this holiest of holies, the journey is exciting, possibly even uplifting; but for those who live permanently on these crags and ridges, life is harsh, a struggle from one day to the next. No wonder so many young men from Garhwal find their way into the Army. Little grows on these rocky promontories; and what does, is at the mercy of the weather. For most of the year the fields lie fallow. Rivers, unfortunately, run downhill and not uphill.

The harshness of this life, typical of much of Garhwal, was brought home to me at Pipalkoti, where we stopped for the night. Pilgrims stop here by the coach load, for the Garhwal Mandal Vikas Nigam's rest-house is fairly capacious, and small hotels and dharamshalas abound. Just off the busy road is a tiny hospital, and here, late in the evening, we came across a woman keeping vigil over the dead body of her husband. The body had been laid out on a bench in the courtyard. A few feet away the road was crowded with pilgrims in festival mood; no one glanced over the low wall to notice this tragic scene.

The woman came from a village near Helong. Earlier that day, finding her consumptive husband in a critical condition she had decided to bring him to the nearest town for treatment. As he was frail and emaciated, she was able to carry him on her back for several miles, until she reached the motor road. Then, at some expense, she engaged a passing taxi and brought him to Pipalkoti. But he was already dead when she reached the small hospital. There was no morgue; so she sat beside the body in the courtyard, waiting for dawn and the arrival of others from the village. A few men arrived next morning and we saw them wending their way down to the cremation ground. We did not see the woman again. Her children were hungry and she had to hurry home to look after them.

Pipalkoti is hot (and pipal trees are conspicuous by their absence), but Joshimath, the winter resort of the Badrinath temple establishment, is about 6,000 feet above sea level and has an equable climate. It is now a fairly large town, and although the surrounding hills are rather bare, it does have one great tree that has survived the ravages of time. This is an ancient mulberry, known as the Kalpa Vriksha (Immortal Wishing Tree), beneath which the great Sankaracharya meditated, a few centuries ago. It is reputedly over two thousand years old, and is certainly larger than my modest four-roomed flat in Mussoorie. Sixty pilgrims holding hands might just about encircle its trunk.

I have seen some big trees, but this is certainly the oldest and broadest of them. I am glad the Sankaracharya meditated beneath it and thus ensured its preservation. Otherwise it might well have gone the way of other great trees and forests that once flourished in this area.

A small boy reminds me that it is a Wishing Tree, so I make my wish. I wish that other trees might prosper like this one.

225

'Have you made a wish?' I ask the boy.

'I wish that you will give me one rupee,' he says.

His wish comes true with immediate effect. Mine lies in the uncertain future. But he has given me a lesson in wishing.

Joshimath has to be a fairly large place, because most of Badrinath arrives here in November, when the shrine is snowbound for six months. Army and PWD structures also dot the landscape. This is no carefree hill resort, but it has all the amenities for making a short stay quite pleasant and interesting. Perched on the steep mountainside above the junction of the Alaknanda and Dhauli rivers, it is now vastly different from what it was when Frank Smythe visited it fifty years ago and described it as 'an ugly little place . . . straggling unbeautifully over the hillside. Primitive little shops line the main street, which is roughly paved in places and in others has been deeply channelled by the monsoon rains. The pilgrims spend the night in single-storeyed rest-houses, not unlike the hovels provided for the kentish hop-pickers of former days, some of which are situated in narrow passages running off the main street and are filthy and evil-smelling.'

Those were Joshimath's former days. It is a different place today, with small hotels, modern shops, a cinema; and its growth and comparative modernity date from the early Sixties, when the old pilgrim footpath gave way to the motor road which takes the traveller all the way to Badrinath. No longer does the weary, footsore pilgrim sink gratefully down in the shade of the Kalpa-Vriksha. He alights from his bus or luxury coach and drinks a Cola or a Thums-up at one of the many small restaurants on the roadside.

Contrast this comfortable journey with the pilgrimage fifty years ago. Frank Smythe again: 'So they venture on their pilgrimage . . . Some borne magnificently by coolies, some toiling along in rags, some almost crawling, preyed on by disease and distorted by dreadful deformities . . . Europeans who have read and travelled cannot conceive what goes on in the minds of these simple folk, many of them from the agricultural parts of India, wonderment and fear must be the prime ingredients. So the pilgrimage becomes an adventure. Unknown dangers threaten the broad well-made path, at any moment the gods, who hold the rocks in leash, may unloose their wrath upon the hapless passerby. To the European it is a walk to Badrinath, to the Hindu pilgrim it is far, far more.'

Above Vishnuprayag, Smythe left the Alaknanda and entered the Bhyundar valley, a botanist's paradise, which he called the Valley of Flowers. He fell in love with the lush meadows of this high valley, and made it known to the world. It continues to attract the botanist and trekker. Primulas of subtle shades, wild geraniums, saxifrages clinging to the rocks, yellow and red potentillas, snow-white anemones, delphiniums, violets, wild roses, all these and many more flourish there, capturing the mind and heart of the flower-lover.

'Impossible to take a step without crushing a flower.' This may not be true any more, for many footsteps have trodden the Bhyundar in recent years. There are other areas in Garhwal where the hills are rich in flora—the Harki-doon, Harsil, Tungnath, and the Khiraun valley where the balsam grows to a height of eight feet—but the Bhyunder has both a variety and a concentration of wild flowers, especially towards the end of the monsoon. It would be no exaggeration to call it one of the most beautiful valleys in the world.

The Bhyundar is a digression for lovers of mountain scenery; but the pilgrim keeps his eyes fixed on the ultimate goal—Badrinath, where the gods dwelt and where salvation is to be found.

There are still a few who do it the hard way—mostly those who have taken sanyas and renounced the world. Here is one hardy soul doing penance. He stretches himself out on the ground, draws himself up to a standing position, then flattens himself out again. In this manner he will proceed from Badrinath to Rishikesh, oblivious of the sun and rain, the dust from passing buses, the sharp gravel of the footpath.

Others are not so hardy. One saffron robed scholar, speaking fair English, asks us for a lift to Badrinath, and we find a space for him. He rewards us with a long and involved commentary on the Vedas, which lasts through the remainder of the journey. His special field of study, he informs us, is the part played by Aeronautics in Vedic literature.

'And what,' I ask him, 'is the connection between the two?'

He looks at me pityingly.

'It is what I am trying to find out,' he replies.

The road drops to Pandukeshwar and rises again, and all the time I am scanning the horizon for the forests of the Badrinath region I had read about many years ago in Fraser's Himalaya Mountains! Walnuts growing up to 9,000 feet, deodars and 'Bilka' up to 9,500 feet, and 'Amesh' and 'Kiusu' fir up a similar height—but, apart from strands of long leaved excelsia pine, I do not see much, certainly no deodars. What has happened to them, I wonder. An endless variety of trees delighted us all the way from Dugalbeta to Mandal, a well-protected area but here on the high ridges above the Alaknanda, little seems to grow; or, if ever they did, have long since been bespoiled or swept away.

Finally we reach the wind-swept, barren valley which harbours Badrinath—a growing township, thriving, lively, but somewhat dwarfed by the snow capped peaks that tower above it. As at Joshimath, there is no dearth of hostelries and dharamshalas. Even so, every hotel or rest-house is filled to overflowing. It is the height of the pilgrim season, and pilgrims, tourists and mendicants of every description throng the river-front.

Just as Kedar is the most sacred of the Shiva temples in the Himalayas, so Badrinath is the supreme place of worship for the Vaishnav sects.

According to legend, when Sankaracharya in his digvijaya travels visited the Mana valley he arrived at the Narada-Kund and found fifty different images lying in its waters. These he rescued, and when he had done so, a voice from Heaven said, 'These are the images for the Kaliyug, establish them here.' Sankaracharya accordingly placed them beneath a mighty tree which grew there and whose shade extended from Badrinath to Nandprayag, a distance of over eighty miles. Close to it was the hermitage of Nar-Narayana (or Arjuna and Krishna), and in course of time temples were built in honour of these and other manifestations of Vishnu. It was here that Vishnu appeared to his followers in person, as the four-armed, crested and adorned with pearls and garlands. The faithful, it is said, can still see him on the peak of Nilkantha, on the great Kumbha day. It is, in fact, the Nilkantha peak that dominates this crater-like valley where a few hardy thistles and nettles manage to survive. Like cacti in the desert, the pricklier forms of life seem best equipped to live in a hostile environment.

Nilkantha means blue-necked, an allusion to the god Shiva's swallowing of a poison meant to destroy the world. The poison remained in his throat, which was rendered blue thereafter. It is a majestic and awe-inspiring peak, soaring to a height of 21,640 feet. As its summit is only five miles from Badrinath, it is justly held in reverence. From its ice-clad pinnacle three great ridges sweep down, of which the southern one terminates in the Alaknanda valley.

On the evening of our arrival we could not see the peak, as it was hidden in clouds. Badrinath itself was shrouded in mist. But we made our way to the temple, a gaily decorated building about fifty feet high, with a gilded roof. The image of Vishnu, carved in black stone, stands in the centre of the sanctum, opposite the door, in a Dhyana posture. An endless stream of people passes through the temple to pay homage and emerge the better for their proximity to the divine.

From the temple, flights of steps lead down to the rushing river and to the hot springs which emerge just above it. Another road leads through a long but tidy bazaar where pilgrims may buy mementos of their visit—from sacred amulets to pictures of the gods in vibrant technicolour. Here at last I am free to indulge my passion for cheap rings, with none to laugh at my foible. There are all kinds, from rings designed like a coiled serpent (my favourite) to twisted bands of copper and iron and others containing the pictures of gods, gurus and godmen. They do not cost more than two or three rupees each, and so I am able to fill my pockets. I never wear these rings. I simply hoard them away. My friends are convinced that in a previous existence I was a jackdaw, seizing upon and hiding away any kind of bright and shiny object: So be it. . . .

Even those who have renounced the world appear to be cheerful—like the young woman from Gujarat who had taken sanyas and who met me on the steps below the temple. She gave me a dazzling smile and passed me an exercise book. She had taken a vow of silence; but being, I think, of an extrovert nature, she seemed eager to remain in close communication with the rest of humanity, and did so by means of written questions and answers. Hence the exercise book.

Although, at Badrinath, I missed the sound of birds and the presence of trees, it was good to be part of the happy throng at its colourful little temple, and to see the sacred river close to its source. And early next morning I was rewarded with the liveliest experience of all.

Opening the window of my room, and glancing out, I saw the rising sun touch the snow clad summit of Nilkantha. At first the snows were pink; then they turned to orange and gold. All sleep vanished as I gazed up in wonder at that magnificent pinnacle in the sky. And had Lord Vishnu appeared just then on the summit, I would not have been in the least surprised.

FLOWERS ON THE GANGA

Flowers floating down the river: yellow and scarlet cannas, roses, jasmine, hibiscus. They are placed in boats made of broad leaves, then consigned to the waters with a prayer. The strong current carries them swiftly downstream, and they bob about on the water for fifty, sometimes a hundred yards, before being submerged in the river. Do the prayers sink too, or do they reach the hearts of the many gods who have favoured Hardwar—'Door of Hari, or Vishnu'—these several hundred years?

The river issues through a gorge in the mountains with a low booming sound. It does not break its banks until it levels out over the flat plains of Uttar Pradesh and Bihar. It is fast and muddy; but this does not deter thousands from descending the steps of the bathing-ghats, and plunging into the cold, snowfed waters. For the Ganga washes away all sin.

Says the *Mahabharata:* 'To repeat her name brings purity, to see her secures prosperity, to bathe in or drink her waters saves seven generations of our race. . . There is no place of pilgrimage like the Ganga, no god like Vishnu. . .'

Almost every child knows the story of how the Ganga descended from heaven. For 1,000 years King Sagara's great grandson stood with his hands upraised, praying for water to enable him to make the funeral oblations for the ashes of his 60,000 grand-uncles. Almost all the gods were involved in the affair. Finally, when the waters of the Ganga were released from heaven and the river reached the earth, the prince mounted his chariot and drove towards the spot where the ashes of his kinsmen lay. Wherever he went, the Ganga meekly followed. Gods, nymphs, demons, giants, sages, and great snakes, all joined in the procession, and as the river followed in the footsteps of the prince, the whole multitude

231

of created beings bathed in her sacred waters and washed away their sins.

*

The multitude that followed the prince could be the same multitude that throngs the riverfront today. I see no one who is not delighted at the prospect of entering the water. *'Ganga-Mai-Ki-Jai!'* The cry goes up mostly from the older people who have come here, many for the last time, to make their peace with the gods. Only their ashes will make the trip again.

It is a big crowd, although this is just an ordinary day of the week and not an occasion of special religious significance. Every day is a good day for bathing in the Ganga. But at the time of major festivals, such as Baisakhi, elaborate arrangements have to be made, including special trains and police reinforcements, to take care of the great influx of pilgrims. The number of pilgrims at the Baisakhi festival usually exceeds 100,000. During the Kumbh Mela, held every twelve years, there may be as many as 500,000 present on the great bathing-day. This is ten times the normal population of Hardwar. And when one realizes that the town is bounded by the steep Siwalik hills on one side and the river on the other, and has one main street leading to the riverfront, it is not surprising that in the past large numbers of people were crushed to death in stampedes at the narrow entrance to the ghats.

Fortunately the main street is a broad and pleasant thoroughfare. Although Hardwar is ancient (the Chinese traveller, Hiuen Tsang, records a visit made in the Seventh Century), little remains of earlier settlements. There are only two or three old temples. But the present buildings—tall, balconised structures put up in the Twenties and Thirties of this century—have a certain old-world charm. Even new houses follow the same pattern. This isn't conscious planning; it is simply that Hardwar is a conservative town and clings to its traditions.

Most of the buildings along the road are dharamsalas. The road is shaded by tall old peepul and banyan trees. In some places the trees reach right across the street to touch the roofs of the three-storey buildings on the other side. At several places I find small peepul saplings growing out of the walls of buildings. One young peepul has sprung up in the fork of an adult kadam tree and will probably throttle it in time. No one fells the sacred peepul. It is better that walls should crumble or kadam trees wither. At least this guarantees the survival of one species of tree in a world where forests are rapidly disappearing.

To fell a peepul is to invite trouble; for the tree is the abode of spirits, and the man who cuts so much as a branch is likely to be pursued by all the spirits he had disturbed.

*

Peepuls live for hundreds of years, and Hardwar's oldest trees must have been here before the present town reached maturity. Some will be as old as the eleventh-century Maya-devi temple, which is probably the oldest temple in Hardwar. On a sultry day there can be no pleasanter spot than the shade of a peepul tree; the leaves are perpetually in motion, even when there is no breeze, and spin around in currents of their own making. It is no wonder that the man who plants a peepul is blessed by generations of Hindus to come.

While I stand beneath one of these giant trees, a devout and elderly man approaches with a watering-can, and, circling the tree, waters the soil around the base of the trunk. I move out of the way of his sprinkler watching the ritual in some surprise. It has been raining steadily for some days, and the tree should have no need of water.

'Why are you watering it?' I ask.

'Why does one water anything?' asks the old man. 'So that it may grow and flourish, of course.'

'But it's been raining almost every day.'

'Rain is something else,' he says. 'I am not responsible for the rain, THIS is water from the Ganga, and I have fetched it myself. That makes a lot of difference.'

I cannot argue. He waters the tree with love; and his love for the tree, as much as rain-water or river-water, is what makes it flourish.

Leaving the main street, I enter the bazaar.

The Hardwar bazaar is a long, narrow, winding street, probably the oldest part of the town, and free of all vehicular traffic. The road is no more than four yards wide. The small shops are spilling over with sweets, pickles, bead-necklaces, sacred texts, ritual designs, festival images, and pictures of the gods in vibrant technicolour. There is something in these naïve, gaudy prints that acts as a transformer, making the more abstract Hindu philosophies comprehensible to anxious farmer or acquisitive taxi-driver.

The bazaar winds and turns back upon itself, and eventually I find myself back at the riverfront, gazing out across the river at the forested foothills. Few of the pilgrims on the bathing-steps can realize that sometimes at night a tiger stands on the opposite bank watching the bright illuminations of the temples, or that elephants listen to the rumbling of the trains bringing pilgrims to Hardwar from all parts of India.

It is evening now, and there are fewer people at the ghats. Most of the bathers are family people—farmers and small shopkeepers with their women and children and aged parents. One does not see many students, or young people in Western clothes. Hardwar is old-fashioned, and so are most of the people who come here.

*

Charity, too, is old-fashioned, and Hardwar thrives on charity: donations to the temples and alms to the beggars, mendicants and itinerant ash-smeared sadhus. The beggars do not follow one about, as in the larger cities. They are confident of receiving coins from the pilgrims who pass by on the steps to the river. They simply sit there, occasionally calling out, but preferring to listen to the music of small coins dropping into brass begging-bowls.

Close by are the money changers, squatting before baskets

which are brimming over with small change. In the rest of the country there is a shortage of small coins, and shopkeepers often decline to provide change; but in Hardwar you can change any number of notes for small coins. You are going to leave all the coins here anyway, when you distribute it along the river-front.

As the pilgrims leave the ghats, the joy of having accomplished their mission bursts forth in songs of praise: 'Henceforth no more pain, no more sickness; all will be well in future; *Ganga-mai-ki-jai.*'

More flowers are being sold; and now the leaf-boats are lit by 'diyas.' The little boats are swept away, sometimes travelling a considerable distance before being upset by submerged rocks or inquisitive fish.

I, too, send an offering down-stream, but my boat sails beneath the legs of a late bather, and disappears beneath the pilgrim. My boat is lost; but my rose-petals still float on the Ganga.

It has been said that if the Ganga ran dry, all life in India would cease. There is no likelihood of that happening. The Ganga is overgenerous as the annual floods will testify. So long as the Himalayas stand, this river will flow to the sea, and millions will come to immerse their bodies, their sins and their prayers in its sacred waters.

MATHURA'S HALLOWED HAUNTS

Mathura, most sacred of cities, stands on the right bank of the Yamuna northwest of Agra. All men speak of Mathura with reverence, and it has been said that 'if a man spend in Banaras all his lifetime, he has earned less merit than if he passes but a single day in the sacred city of Mathura.'

It is difficult to pierce the fog which hides the date of the city's birth; but sacred it has always been, as the capital of the kingdom of Braj and the birthplace of Lord Krishna: 'Teacher and Soul of the Universe. Destroyer of the earth's tyrant kings, and the First of the Spirits . . .'

I went to Mathura at the end of the rains. The fields and the trees were alive with strange, beautiful birds: the long-tailed king-crow; innumerable doves in shades of blue and green; kingfishers and bluejays and weaver-birds; and, resting on a telegraph pole, the great whiteheaded kite, which, some say, was Garuda, Vishnu's famous steed. Resplendent, too, were the green and gold parrots, from among whom Kamadeva, the god of love, chose his steed. Armed with his sugar cane bow with its string made of bees, Kamadeva still rides at night over the plains of Mathura. Many are the journeys he makes on nights approaching the full moon. He knows the ways of men and women, and his bow, like Cupid's, is always ready to assist the ardent lover.

In the tanks and 'jheels' around Mathura I saw a variety of game birds—wild duck, herbits, cranes and snipe—but all life is sacred for many miles around Mathura, and not even the bird trapper is permitted to lay his snares.

Strutting under an old tamarind tree are Krishna's birds, the brilliant peacocks. Centuries ago, they gave the city their name, and today Mathura is still known as the Peacock City. The peacocks seem to know that they are the chosen of Krishna. Spreading out their many-hued fantails, they glance at us drab mortals with an air of disdain.

Near Mathura is Brindavan in whose forests—they have gone now—the boy Krishna and his brother Balram ran wild, playing on their shepherds' pipes. The neighbours found Krishna very mischievous. He was extremely fond of butter and, going by stealth one day to the house of a neighbour, climbed onto a shelf to get at a large jar of butter. He ate the butter as far as he could reach, and then got into the jar. The owner, on returning, found him there and putting a cover on the jar to prevent the boy from escaping went to Krishna's father to make a complaint. But when he arrived at the house it was not the father who met him but the little butter-thief.

There is another story which tells us of the day Krishna stole his mother's curds, and finished them while no one was looking. 'O, you wicked one!' exclaimed his mother when she discovered what had happened. 'Come, let me see your mouth.' And when she looked into his mouth, she saw the Universe—the earth, sea and heavens; the sun and the moon, the planets and all the stars ...

Brindavan stands on a tongue of land surrounded by the river, which has curved here in a strange fashion. Legend tells us that Balram who was very strong, once led a dance on the Yamuna's bank, but moved his giant limbs so clumsily that the river laughed aloud and taunted him, saying: 'Enough, my clumsy child! How can you hope to dance as Krishna, who is divine?' Balram was very angry with the river, and taking his great plough he traced a furrow from the brink of the river; but so deep was the furrow that the river fell into it and was led far astray.

When the tyrant king Kamsa heard of the unusual exploits of Krishna and Balram, he planned to have them killed in case they became a danger to his power. He sent a message to the brothers, inviting them to a contest of arms in the royal city of Mathura. Krishna and Balram accepted the challenge.

On the day of the contest, King Kamsa sat on a lofty throne near the arena. As Krishna and Balram entered, a mighty elephant was sent against them. But Krishna, seizing the animal by the tail, swung it around his head and threw it to the ground. Then each of the brothers taking a tusk, they slew Kamsa's mightiest champions. Kamsa ordered his army to kill the boys, but Krishna sprang up the steps of the throne, seized the king by his hair and hurled him into a deep ravine.

Visitors to Mathura are still shown the mound where Kamsa's throne once stood. And still venerated is that part of the river front where the two boys rested after dragging the body of Kamsa down to the funeral pyre.

I wandered in the streets of the city past shops gleaming with brasswork or piled high with pedas, Mathura's famous sweets. From the bridge, I could see the riverfront with its innumerable temples. And below, hundreds of majestic tortoises watched the bathers and the boatmen with speculative eyes. Sometimes a boatman seized one of these longnecked creatures and held it up to view. The tortoise would immediately draw its legs into its shell—a vivid illustration of the theory that nothing is annihilated but only disappears, the effect being absorbed in the cause!

FOOTLOOSE IN AGRA

The cycle-rickshaw is the best way of getting about Agra. Its smooth gliding motion and leisurely rate of progress are in keeping with the pace of life in this old-world city. The rickshaw-boy juggles his way through the crowded bazaars, exchanging insults with tonga-drivers, pedestrians and other cyclists; but once on the broad Mall or Taj Road, his curses change to carefree song and he freewheels along the tree-lined avenues. Old colonial-style bungalows still stand in large compounds shaded by peepul, banyan, neem and jamun trees.

Looking up, I notice a number of bright paper kites that flutter, dip and swerve in the cloudless sky. I cannot recall seeing so many kites before.

'Is it a festival today?' I ask.

'No, sahib,' says the rickshaw-boy, 'not even a holiday.'

'Then why so many kites?'

He does not even bother to look up. 'You can see kites every day, sahib.'

'I don't see them in Delhi.'

'Ah, but Delhi is a busy place. In Agra, people still fly kites. There are kite-flying competitions every Sunday, and heavy bets are sometimes placed on the outcome.'

As we near the city, I notice kites stuck in trees or dangling from electric wires; but there are always others soaring up to take their place. I ask the rickshaw-boy to tell me something about the kite-fliers and the kitemakers, but the subject bores him.

'You had better see the Taj today, sahib.'

'All right take me to it. I can lunch afterwards.'

It is difficult to view the Taj at noon. The sun strikes the white marble, and there is a great dazzle of reflected light. I stand there with averted eyes, looking at everything—the formal gardens, the

239

surrounding walls of red sandstone, the winding river—
everything except the monument I have come to see.

It is there, of course, very solid and real, perfectly preserved,
with every jade, jasper or lapis lazuli playing its part in the overall
design; and after a while, I can shade my eyes and take in a vision
of shimmering white marble. The light rises in waves from the
paving-stones, and the squares of black and white marble create
an effect of running water. Inside the chamber it is cool and dark
but rather musty, and I waste no time in hurrying out again into
the sunlight.

I walk the length of a gallery and turn with some relief to
the river scene. The sluggish Yamuna winds past Agra on its way
to its union with the Ganga. I know the Yamuna well. I know
it where it emerges from the foothills near Kalsi, cold and blue
from the melting snows; I know it as it winds through fields
of wheat and sugar cane and mustard, across the flat plains of
Uttar Pradesh, sometimes placid, sometimes in flood. I know the
river at Delhi, where its muddy banks are a patchwork of clothes
spread out by the hundreds of washermen who serve the city
and I know it at Mathura, where it is alive with huge turtles;
Mathura, sacred city, whose beginnings are lost in antiquity.

And then the river winds its way to Agra, to this spot by
the Taj, where parrots flash in the sunshine, kingfishers swoop
low over the water and a proud peacock struts across the lawns
surrounding the monument.

I follow the peacock into a shady grove. It is quite tame and
does not fly away. It leads me to a small boy who is sitting in the
shade of a tree, feasting on a handful of small green fruit.

I have not seen the fruit before, and I ask the boy to tell me
what it is. He offers me what looks like a hard green plum.

'It is the fruity from the Ashoke tree,' says the boy. 'There
are many such trees in the garden.'

'Are you allowed to take the fruit?'

'I am allowed,' he says, grinning. 'My father is the head
gardener.'

I bite into the fruit. It is hard and sour but not unpleasant.

'Do you live here?' I ask.

'Over the wall,' he says. 'But I come here everyday, to help my father and to eat the fruit.'

'So you see the Taj Mahal every day?'

'I have seen it every day for as long as I can remember.'

'And I am seeing it for the first time. . . . you're very lucky.'

He shrugs. 'If you see it once, or a hundred times, it is the same. It doesn't change.'

'Don't you like looking at it, then?'

'I like looking at the people who come here. They are always different. In the evening there will be many people.'

'You must have seen people from almost every country in the world.'

'That is so. They all come here to look at the Taj. Kings and Queens and Presidents and Prime Ministers and film stars and poor people too. And I look at them. In that way it isn't boring.'

'Well, you have the Taj to thank for that.'

He gazes thoughtfully at the shimmering monument. His eyes are accustomed to the sharp sunlight. He sees the Taj every day, but at this moment he is really looking at it, thinking about it, wondering what magic it must possess to attract people from all comers of the earth, to bring them here walking through his father's well-kept garden so that he can have something new and fresh to look at each day.

A cloud—a very small cloud—passes across the face of the sun; and in the softened light I too am able to look at the Taj without screwing up my eyes.

As the boy said, it does not change. Therein lies beauty. For the effect on the traveller is the same today as it was three hundred years ago when Bernier wrote: 'Nothing offends the eye. . . . No part can be found that is not skilfully wrought, or that has not its peculiar beauty.'

And so, for a few moments, this poem in marble is on view to two unimportant people—the itinerant writer and the gardener's boy.

We say nothing; there is really nothing to be said. (But now, a

241

few months later, when I try to recapture the essence of that day, it is not the monument that I remember most vividly. The Taj is there of course; I still see it as a mirror for the sun. But what remains with me, more than anything else, is the passage of the river and the sharp flavour of the Ashoke fruit.)

In the afternoon I walk through the old bazaars which lie to the west of Akbar's great red sandstone fort, and I am not surprised to find a small street which is almost entirely taken up by kite-shops. Most of them sell the smaller, cheaper kites, but one small dark shop has in it a variety of odd and fantastic creations. Stepping inside, I find myself face to face with the doyen of Agra's kite-makers, Hosain Ali, a feeble old man whose long beard is dyed red with the juice of mehendi leaves. He has just finished making a new kite from bamboo, paper and thin silk, and it lies outside in the sun, firming up. It is a pale pink kite, with a small green tail.

The old man is soon talking to me, for he likes to talk and is not very busy. He complains that few people buy kites these days (I find this hard to believe), and tells me that I should have visited Agra twenty-five years ago, when kite-flying was the sport of kings and even grown men found time to spend an hour or two every day with these gay, dancing strips of paper. Now, he says, everyone hurries, hurries in a heat of hope, and delicate things like kites and day-dreams are trampled underfoot. 'Once I made a wonderful kite,' says Hosain Ali nostalgically. 'It was unlike any kite seen in Agra. It had a number of small, very light paper discs trailing on a thin bamboo frame. At the end of each disc I fixed a sprig of grass, forming a balance on both sides. On the first and largest disc I painted a face and gave it eyes made of two small mirrors. The discs, which grew smaller from head to tail, gave the kite the appearance of a crawling serpent. It was very difficult to get this great kite off the ground. Only I could manage it.

'Of course, everyone heard of the Dragon Kite I had made, and word went about that there was some magic in its making. A large crowd arrived on the maidan to watch me fly the kite.

'At first the kite would not leave the ground. The discs made a sharp wailing sound, the sun was trapped in the little mirrors. My kite had eyes and tongue and a trailing silver tail. I felt it come alive in my hands. It rose from the ground, rose steeply into the sky, moving farther and farther away, with the sun still glinting in its dragon eyes. And when it went very high, it pulled fiercely on the twine, and my son had to help me with the reel.

'But still the kite pulled, determined to be free—yes, it had become a living thing—and at last the twine snapped, and the wind took the kite, took it over the rooftops and the waving trees and the river and the far hills for ever. No one ever saw where it fell. Sahib, are you listening? The Dragon Kite is lost, but for you I'll make a bright new poem to fly.'

'Make me one,' I say, moved by his tale, or rather by the manner of its telling. 'I will collect it tomorrow, before I leave Agra. Let it be a beautiful kite. I won't fly it. I'll hang it on my wall, and will not give it a chance to get away.'

It is evening, and the winter sun comes slanting through the intricate branches of a banyan tree, as a cycle-rickshaw—a different one this time—brings me to a forgotten corner of Agra that I have always wanted to visit. This is the old Roman Catholic cemetery where so many early European travellers and adventurers lie buried.

Although it is quite probably the oldest Christian cemetery in northern India, it has none of that overgrown, crumbling look that is common to old cemeteries in monsoon lands. It is a bright, even cheerful place, and the jingle of tonga-bells and other street noises can be heard from any part of the grounds. The grass is cut, the gravestones are kept clean, and most of the inscriptions are still readable.

The caretaker takes me straight to the oldest grave—this is the oldest known European grave in northern India—and it happens to be that of an Englishman, John Mildenhall. The lettering stands out clearly:

Here lies John Mildenhall, Englishman, who left London in 1599 and travelling to India through Persia, reached Agra in 1605 and spoke with the Emperor Akbar. On a second visit in 1614 he fell ill at Lahore, died at Ajmere, and was buried here through the good offices of Thomas Kerridge Merchant.

During the seventeenth and eighteenth centuries, the Agra cemetery was considered blessed ground by Christians, and the dead were brought here from distant places. Thomas Kerridge must have put himself to considerable expense to bury his friend in Agra. Mildenhall was a romantic, who styled himself an envoy of Queen Elizabeth. Unfortunately he left no account of his travels, although a couple of his letters are quoted in the writings of Purchas, another English merchant, who lies buried in the Protestant cemetery a couple of furlongs away.

Nearby is the grave of the Venetian, Jerome Veronio, who died at Lahore. According to some old records, he had a hand in designing the Taj, modelling it on Humayun's tomb in Delhi. There had for long been a belief that this 'architect' of the Taj lay buried in the cemetery but no one knew where. Then in 1945, Father Hyacinth, Superior Regular of Agra, scraped the moss off a tombstone, revealing the simple epitaph: 'Here lies Jerome Veronio, who died at Lahore.'

Actually, there is no evidence that Veronio designed the Taj, and even if he had something to do with it, he was only one of a number of artists and architects who worked on its construction. The chief architect was Muhammed Sharif of Samarkand. Each drew a salary of one thousand rupees per month. Ismail Khan of Turkey was the dome-maker. A number of inlay workers, sculptors and masons were Hindus, including Manohar Singh of Lahore and Mohan Lal of Kanauj, both famous inlay-workers.

A man of more authentic accomplishments was the Italian lapidary, Horten Bronzoni, whose grave lies at a short distance from Veronio's. He died on 11 August 1677. According to Tavernier, it was Bronzoni who cut the Koh-i-noor diamond; and, says Tavernier, he cut the stone very badly.

Bronzoni is again mentioned as having manufactured a model ship of war for Aurangzeb, who had been annoyed by the depredations of Portuguese pirates and was anxious to create a navy. The ship was floated in a huge tank and manoeuvred by a number of European artillery-men. It made a ridiculous sight and convinced the Emperor that a navy was out of the question.

There are over eighty old Armenian graves in the cemetery, but the only one that interests me is the tomb of Shah Azar Khan, an expert in the art of moulding a heavy cannon. One of these, 'Zamzamah', earned a measure of immortality in Kipling's *Kim*, who hold *Zam-Zammah*, that 'fire-breathing dragon', hold the Punjab; for the great green-bronze piece is always first of the conqueror's loot. The gun was 14.6 feet long, and is still at Lahore.

Other historic tombs lie scattered about the cemetery, but the most striking and curious of them is the grave of Colonel Jon Hessing, who died in 1803. It is a miniature Taj Mahal, built of red sandstone. Although small compared to a Mughal tomb, it is large for a Christian grave, and could easily accommodate a living family of moderate proportions. Hessing came to India from Holland, and was one of a colourful band of freelance soldiers (most of them deserters) who served in Sindhia's Maratha army. Hessing, we are told, was a good, benevolent man and a great soldier. The tomb was built by his wife Alice, who it must be supposed, felt as tenderly towards the Colonel as Shah Jahan felt towards his queen. She could not afford marble. Even so, her 'Taj' cost a lakh of rupees.

Outside, in the street, people move about with casual unconcern.

Street-vendors occupy the pavement, unwilling that their rivals should take advantage of a brief absence. In the banyan tree, the sparrows and bulbuls are settling down for the night. A kite lies entangled in the upper branches.

STREET OF THE RED WELL

T he sun beats down on the sweltering city of Old Delhi. Not a breath of air stirs in the narrow, winding streets. This old walled city, now over three hundred years old, has no open spaces, no fountains, no sidewalks, no shady avenues. During the reign of Emperor Shah Jahan, a canal ran down the centre of the main thoroughfare, Chandni Chowk (Street of the Silversmiths); but the canal has long since been covered over, and the Jamuna river, from which the water was channelled, lies beyond the Emperor's fort, the Red Fort of Delhi, where the Prime Minister speaks to the multitude every year on Independence Day.

It is not water that I seek most, but shelter from the heat and glare of the overhead sun. I have chosen what is quite possibly the hottest day in May, the temperature over 105° Fahrenheit, to go walking in search of—what? A story, perhaps an adventure. Or that is what I set out to do. The heat of the day has willed otherwise. I may be ready for an adventure, but no one else is interested. I am the only one walking the streets from choice.

Shopkeepers nod drowsily beneath whirring ceiling-fans. The pavement barber has taken his customer into the shelter of an awning. A fortune-teller has decided that there is nothing to predict and has fallen asleep under the same awning. A vegetable-seller sprinkles water on his vegetables in a dispirited fashion. Those cauliflowers were fresh an hour ago, they look old already. Even the flies are drowsy. Instead of buzzing feverishly from place to place, they stagger about on tired legs.

It is the pigeons who have found all the coolest places. These birds have made the old city their own. New Delhi is for the crows who like to have a tree to sleep in, even if they take their meals from out of kitchens and verandas. But the pigeons prefer buildings, and the older the buildings the better. They are familiar with every cool alcove or shady recess in the crumbling walls of neglected mosques and mansions.

A fat, supercilious pigeon watches me from the window ledge above a jeweller's shop. The pigeon's forebears settled here long before the British thought of taking Delhi. Conquerors have come and gone. Nadir Shah the Persian, Madhav Rao the Maratha, Ghulam Kadir the Rohilla, and generations of goldsmiths and silversmiths. Hindus and Muslims have made and lost fortunes in the city, but nothing has disturbed the tranquil life of these pigeons. Their gentle cooing can always be heard when there is a lull in the jagged symphony of traffic noise. How do they manage to sound so cool?

But here's welcome relief for humans; a shady corner in Lal Kuan Bazaar (Street of the Red Well), where an old man provides drinking water to thirsty wayfarers such as myself. His water is stored in a surahi, an earthenware jug which keeps the water sweet and cool. I bend down, cup my hands, and receive the sparkling liquid as my benefactor tilts the surahi towards me.

Lal Kuan. The Red Well. Of course it is no longer here. But the street still bears its name. And I like to think that here, in the middle of the street, where a bullock has gone to sleep forcing the cyclists to make a detour, there was once a well made of dark red brick, where the water bubbled forth all day.

Imprisoned beneath the soil, held down by the crowded commercial houses of this old quarter, the water must still be there; it gives nourishment to an old peepul tree that grows beside a temple.

It is the only tree in the street. It juts out from the temple wall growing straight and tall, dwarfing the two-storey houses. One of its roots, breaking through the ground, has curled up to provide a smooth, well-worn seat.

And it is cool here, beneath the peepul. Even when there is no breeze, the slender heart-shaped leaves revolve prettily, creating their own currents of air. No wonder the sages of old found it a good tree to sit beneath. No wonder they called it sacred.

On the other side of the road, a tall iron doorway is set in a high wall. Doors like this were only built in the previous century, when a wealthy merchant's house had to be a miniature fortress as well as a residence. I cannot see over the wall and I would like to know what lies behind the door. Perhaps a side-street, perhaps a market, perhaps a garden, perhaps.

The door opens, not easily, because it has been left closed for a long time, but slowly and with much complaint. And beyond the door there is only an empty courtyard, covered with nibble, the ruins of an old house. I am about to turn away when I hear a deep tremendous murmur.

It is the cooing of many pigeons.

But where are they?

I advance further into the ruin, and there, opening out in front of me, ready to receive me as the rabbit hole was ready to receive Alice, is an old, disused well.

I peer down into its murky depths. It is dark, very dark, down there; but that is where the pigeons live, in the walls of this lost, long-forgotten well shut away from the rest of the city.

I cannot see any water. So I drop a pebble over the side. It strikes the wall, and then, with a soft plop, touches water. At that instant there is a rush of air and a tremendous beating of wings, and a flock of pigeons, thirty or forty of them, fly out of the well, streak upwards, circle the building, and then falling into formation, wheel overhead, the sun gleaming white on their underwings.

I have discovered their secret. Now I know why they always look so cool, so refreshed, while we who walk the streets of Old Delhi do so with parched mouths and drooping limbs.

The pigeons are the only ones who still know about the Red Well.

SONGS AND LOVE POEMS

LOST*

I boarded the big ship bound for the West,
The clean white liner.
In the noon-day heat
Coolies thronged the sun-drenched pier.
Yet I saw only
The village I had left,
And a boat at rest
On the river's shallow water
In the shade of the flowering
Long red-fingered poinsettia.
I saw not the big waves
But the ripple of running
Water in the reeds.

We came to London, lost in November mist:
In an ash-grey dawn at Tilbury dock
I longed for the warmth of a kiss
Of sunlight.

In the busy streets
Were cavalcades of people
Hurrying in a heat of hope.
But I saw only

The wheat-field, the tea-slope. . .
A cow at rest.
And longed for the soft, shoeless tread
Of a village boy. . .

---

*My first poem, published in the *Illustrated Weekly of India*, in 1952

251

LOVE LYRICS FOR BINYA DEVI

1

Your face streamed April rain,
As you climbed the steep hill,
Calling the white cow home.
You seemed very tiny
On the windswept mountainside;
A twist of hair lay
Strung across your forehead
And your torn blue skirt
Clung to your tender thighs.
You smiled through the blind white rain
And gave me the salt kiss of your lips,
Salt mingled with raindrop and mint,
And left me there, where I had come to fetch you—
So gallant in the blistering rain!
And you ran home laughing;
But it was worth the drenching.

2

Your feet, laved with dew,
Stood firm on the quickening grass.
There was a butterfly between us:
Red and gold its wings
And heavy with dew.
It could not move because of the weight of moisture.
And as your foot came nearer
And I saw that you would crush it,
I said: 'Stay. It has only a few days

In the sun, and we have many.'
'And if I spare it,' you said, laughing,
'What will you do for me, what will you pay?'

'Why, anything you say.'

'And will you kiss my foot?'

'Both feet,' I said; and did so happily.
For they were no less than the wings of butterflies.

3

All night our love
Stole sleep from dusty eyes.
What dreams were lost, I'll never know.
It seemed the world's last night had come
And there would never be a dawn.

Your touch soon swept the panting dark away—
Some suns are brighter by night than day!

4

Your eyes, glad and wondering,
Dwelt in mine,
And all that stood between us
Was a blade of grass
Shivering slightly
In the breath from our lips.

But grass will bend.

We turn and kiss,
And the world swings round,
The sky spins, the trees go hush
Hush, the mountain sings—

Though we must leave this place,
We've trapped forever
In the trembling air
The last sweet phantom kiss.

5

I know you'll come when the cherries
Are ripe;
But it is still November
And I must wait
For the green fruit to blush
At your approach.
And meanwhile the tree is visited
By robber bands, masked mynas
And yellow birds with beaks like daggers,
Determined not to leave one cherry
Whole for lovers.
But still I wait, hoping one day
You'll come to stain your lips
With cherry-juice, and climb my tree;
Bright goddess in dark green temple,
Thrusting your tongue at me.

6

Slender waisted, bright as a song,
Dark as the whistling-thrush at dawn,
Swift as the running days of November,
Lost like a dream too sweet to remember.

IT ISN'T TIME THAT'S PASSING

Remember the long ago when we lay together
In a pain of tenderness and counted
Our dreams: long summer afternoons
When the whistling-thrush released
A deep sweet secret on the trembling air;
Blackbird on the wing, bird of the forest shadows,
Black rose in the long ago summer,
This was your song:
It isn't time that's passing by,
It is you and I.

KITES

Are you listening to me, boy?
I am only your kitemaker,
My poems are flimsy things
Torn by the wind, caught in mango trees,
Gay sport for boys and dreamers.
My silent songs. But once I fashioned
A kite like a violin,
She sang most mournfully, like the wind
In tall deodars.

Are you listening? Remember
The Dragon Kite I made one summer?
No, you are too young. A great
Kite, with small mirrors to catch the sun
And eyes and a tongue, and gold
Trappings and a trailing silver tail.
A kite for the gods to ride!
And it rose most sweetly, but the wind
Came up from nowhere,

A wind in waiting for us,
My twine snapped and the wind took the kite,
Took it over the flat roofs
And the waving trees and the river
And the blue hills for ever.
No one knew where it fell. Boy, are you
Listening? All my kites
Are torn, but for you I'll make a bright
New poem to fly.

CHERRY TREE

Eight years have passed
Since I placed my cherry seed in the grass.
'Must have a tree of my own,' I said—
And watered it once and went to bed
And forgot; but cherries have a way of growing
Though no one's caring very much or knowing,
And suddenly that summer, near the end of May,
I found a tree had come to stay.
It was very small, a five months' child,
Lost in the tall grass running wild.
Goats ate the leaves, grasscutter's scythe
Split it apart, and a monsoon blight
Shrivelled the slender stem. . . Even so,
Next spring I watched three new shoots grow,
The young tree struggle, upwards thrust
Its arms in a fresh fierce lust
For light and air and sun.

I could only wait, as one
Who watches, wondering, while Time and the rain
Made a miracle from green growing pain. . .
I went away next year—
Spent a season in Kashmir—
Came back thinner, rather poor,
But richer by a cherry tree at my door.
Six feet high, my own dark cherry,
And—I could scarcely believe it—a berry,
Ripened and jewelled in the sun,
Hung from a branch—just one!

And next year there were blossoms, small
Pink, fragile, quick to fall
At the merest breath, the sleepiest breeze. . .

I lay on the grass, at ease,
Looked up through leaves, at the blue
Blind sky, at the finches as they flew
And flitted through the dappled green,
While bees in an ecstasy drank
Of nectar from each bloom, and the sun sank
Swiftly, and the stars turned in the sky,
And moon-moths and singing crickets and I—
Yes, I!—praised night and stars and trees:
A small, tall cherry grown by me.

LOVERS OBSERVED

Lovers lie drowsy in the grass,
Sunk in bracken, swimming in pools
Of late afternoon sunshine;
All agitation past, they stay totally
Absorbed in grass.

Green grass, and growing from that place
A sweep of languid arm still bare
But for a lost ladybird.
Anonymous lover brushes a dragon
Fly from his face.

Brief thunder blossoms in the air,
A leaf between the thighs is caught
And crushed. Love comes like a thief,
Crouching among the bruised and broken clover.
All flesh in grass.

LONE FOX DANCING

As I walked home last night
I saw a lone fox dancing
In the cold moonlight.

I stood and watched. Then
Took the low road, knowing
The night was his by right.

Sometimes, when words ring true,
I'm like a lone fox dancing
In the morning dew.

SECONDHAND SHOP IN HILL STATION

The smell of secondhand goods
Is everywhere. Lost causes,
Lonely lives, and deaths in small cottages
Among the pines, meet here in the mildewed dark
Of his shop—Abdul Salaam, Proprietor.
Tales of a hundred failures
And ten hundred broken dreams.

A hat-pin and an Iron Cross
Lie down with a blackened pistol,
While a bronze Buddha smiles across
At a plastic doll from Bristol.

Old clothes, old books (perhaps a first edition?),
A dressing-gown, a dagger marked with rust.
A card for some lost Christmas,
And inside, a letter:
'Dear Jane, I am getting better.'
A Chinese vase and a china-dog.

The shop is cold and thick with dust,
The Mall is far from Grand;
But Abdul Salaam grows prosperous,
In a suit that's secondhand.

A FROG SCREAMS

Standing near a mountain stream
I heard a sound like the creaking
Of a branch in the wind.
It was a frog screaming
In the jaws of a long green snake.

I couldn't bear that hideous cry.
And taking two sharp sticks,
I made the twisting snake disgorge the frog,
Who hopped quite spry out of the snake's mouth
And sailed away on a floating log.

Pleased with the outcome,
I released the green grass-snake,
Stood back and spoke aloud:
'Is this what it feels like to be God?'

'Only what it's like to be English,'
Said God (speaking for a change in French);
'*I* would have let the snake finish his lunch!'

A SONG FOR LOST FRIENDS

The past is always with us, for it feeds the present . . .

1

As a boy I stood on the edge of the railway-cutting,
Outside the dark tunnel, my hands touching
The hot rails, waiting for them to tremble
At the coming of the noonday train.
The whistle of the engine hung on the forest's silence.
Then out of the tunnel, a green-gold dragon
Came plunging, thundering past—
Out of the tunnel, out of the grinning dark.

And the train rolled on, every day
Hundreds of people coming or going or running away—
Goodbye, goodbye!
I haven't seen you again, bright boy at the carriage window,
Waving to me, calling,
But I've loved you all these years and looked for you everywhere,
In cities and villages, beside the sea,
In the mountains, in crowds at distant places;
Returning always to the forest's silence,
To watch the windows of some passing train. . . .

2

My father took me by the hand and led me
Among the ruins of old forts and palaces.

We lived in a tent near the tomb of Humayun
Among old trees. Now multi-storeyed blocks
Rise from the plain—tomorrow's ruins. . . .
You can explore them, my son, when the trees
Take over again and the thorn-apple grows
In empty windows. There were seven cities before. . . .

Nothing my father said could bring my mother home;
She had gone with another. He took me to the hills
In a small train, the engine having palpitations
As it toiled up the steep slopes peopled
With pines and rhododendrons. Through tunnels
To Simla. Boarding-school. He came to see me
In the holidays. We caught butterflies together.
'Next year,' he said, 'when the War is over,
We'll go to England.' But wars are never over
And I have yet to go to England with my father.
He died that year
And I was dispatched to my mother and stepfather—
A long journey through a dark tunnel.

No one met me at the station. So I wandered
Round Dehra in a tonga, looking for a house
With lichi trees. She'd written to say there were lichis
In the garden.
But in Dehra all the houses had lichi trees,
The tonga-driver charged five rupees
for taking me back to the station.
They were looking for me on the platform:
'We thought the train would be late as usual.'
It had arrived on time, upsetting everyone's schedule.

In my new home I found a new baby in a new pram.
Your little brother, they said; which made me a hundred.
But he too was left behind with the servants
When my mother and Mr H went hunting

Or danced late at the casino, our only wartime night-club.
Tommies and Yanks scuffled drunk and disorderly
In a private war for the favours of stale women.

Lonely in the house with the servants and the child
And books I'd read twice and my father's letters
Treasured secretly in the small trunk beneath my bed:
I wrote to him once but did not post the letter
For fear it might come back 'Return to sender...'

One day I slipped into the guava orchard next door—
It really belonged to Seth Hari Kishore
Who'd gone to the Ganga on a pilgrimage—
The guavas were ripe and ready for boys to steal
(Always sweeter when stolen)
And a bare leg thrust at me as I climbed:

There's only room for one,' came a voice.
I looked up at a boy who had blackberry eyes
And guava juice on his chin, grabbed at him
And we both tumbled out of the tree
On to the ragged December grass. We rolled and fought
But not for long. A gardener came shouting,
And we broke and ran—over the gate and down the road
And across the fields and a dry river bed,
Into the shades of afternoon...
'Why didn't you run home?' he said.
'Why didn't you?'
'There's no one there, my mother's out.'
'And mine's at home.'

3

His mother was Burmese; his father
An English soldier killed in the War.
They were waiting for it to be over.

Every day, beyond the gardens, we loafed:
Time was suspended for a time.
On heavy wings, ringed pheasants rose
At our approach.
The fields were yellow with mustard,
Parrots wheeled in the sunshine, dipped and disappeared
Into the morning mist on the foothills.
We found a pool, fed by a freshet
Of cold spring water. 'One day when we are men,'
He said, 'We'll meet here at the pool again.
Promise?' 'Promise,' I said. And we took a pledge
In blood, nicking our fingers on a penknife
And pressing them to each other's lips. Sweet salty kiss.
Late evening, past cowdust time, we trudged home:
He to his mother, I to my dinner.

One wining—dancing night I thought I'd stay out too.
We went to the pictures—*Gone with the Wind*—
A crashing bore for boys, and it finished late.
So I had dinner with them, and his mother said:
'It's past ten. You'd better stay the night.
 But will they miss you?'
I did not answer but climbed into my friend's bed—
I'd never slept with anyone before, except my father—
And when it grew cold, after midnight,
He put his arms around me and looped a leg
Over mine and it was nice that way
But I stayed awake with the niceness of it
My sleep stolen by his own deep slumber. . .
What dreams were lost, I'll never know!
But next morning, just as we'd started breakfast,
A car drew up, and my parents, outraged,
Chastised me for staying out and hustled me home.
Breakfast unfinished. My friend unhappy. My pride wounded.

We met sometimes, but a constraint had grown upon us,
And the following month I heard he'd gone
To an orphanage in Kalimpong.

4

I remember you well, old banyan tree,
As you stood there spreading quietly
Over the broken wall.
While adults slept, I crept away
Down the broad veranda steps, around
The outhouse and the melon-ground. . . .
In that winter of long ago, I roamed
The faded garden of my mother's home.
I must have known that giants have few friends
(The great lurk shyly in their private dens),
And found you hidden by a thick green wall
Of aerial roots.
Intruder in your pillared den, I stood
And shyly touched your old and wizened wood,
And as my heart explored you, giant tree,
I heard you singing!

The spirit of the tree became my friend,
Took me to his silent throbbing heart
And taught me the value of stillness.
My first tutor; friend of the lonely.

And the second was the tonga-man
Whose pony-cart came rattling along the road
Under the furthest arch of the banyan tree.
Looking up, he waved his whip at me
And laughing, called, 'Who lives up there?'
'I do,' I said.

And the next time he came along, he stopped the tonga
And asked me if I felt lonely in the tree.
'Only sometimes,' I said. 'When the tree is thinking.'
'I never think,' he said. 'You won't feel lonely with me.'
And with a flick of the reins he rattled away,
With a promise he'd give me a ride someday.
And from him I learnt the value of promises kept.

5

From the tree to the tonga was an easy drop.
I fell into life. Bansi, tonga-driver,
Wore a yellow waistcoat and spat red
Betel-juice the entire width of the road.
'I can spit further than any man,' he claimed.
It is natural for a man to strive to excel
At something; he spat with authority.

When he took me for rides, he lost a fare.
That was his way. He once said, 'If a girl
Wants five rupees for a fix, bargain like hell
And then give six.'
It was the secret of his failure, he claimed,
To give away more than he owned.
And to prove it, he borrowed my pocket-money
In order to buy a present for his mistress.

A man who fails well is better than one who succeeds badly.

The rattletrap tonga and the winding road
Through the valley, to the river-bed,
With the wind in my hair and the dust
Rising, and the dogs running and barking
And Bansi singing and shouting in my ear,
And the pony farting as it cantered along,
Wheels creaking, seat shifting,

Hood slipping off, the entire contraption
Always about to disintegrate, collapse,
But never quite doing so—like the man himself. . . .
All this was music,
And the ragtime-raga lingers in my mind.

Nostalgia comes swiftly when one is forty,
Looking back at boyhood years.
Even unhappiness acquires a certain glow.

It was shady in the cemetery, and the mango trees
Did well there, nourished by the bones
Of long-dead Colonels, Collectors, Magistrates and Memsahibs.
For here, in dusty splendour, lay the graves
Of those who'd brought their English dust
To lie with Ganges soil: some tombs were temples,
Some were cenotaphs; and one, a tiny Taj.
Here lay sundry relatives, including Uncle Henry,
Who'd been for many years a missionary.
'Sacred to the Memory
Of Henry C. Wagstaff,
Who translated the Gospels into Pashtu,
And was murdered by his own *Chowkidar*.
'Well done, thou good and faithful servant'—
So ran his epitaph.

The gardener, who looked after the trees,
Also dug graves. One day
I found him working at the bottom of a new cavity,
'They never let me know in time,' he grumbled.
'Last week I dug two graves, and now, without warning,
Here's another. It isn't even the season for dying.
There's enough work all summer, when cholera's about—
Why can't they keep alive through the winter?'

269

Near the railway-lines, watching the trains
(There were six every day, coming or going),
And across the line, the leper colony. . .
I did not know they were lepers till later
But I knew they were different: some
Were without fingers or toes
And one had no nose
And a few had holes in their faces
And yet some were beautiful
They had their children with them
And the children were no different
From other children.
I made friends with some
And won most of their marbles
And carried them home in my pockets.

One day my parents found me
Playing near the leper colony.
There was a big scene.
My mother shouted at the lepers
And they hung their heads as though it was all their fault,
And the children had nothing to say.
I was taken home in disgrace
And told all about leprosy and given a bath.
My clothes were thrown away
And the servants wouldn't touch me for days.
So I took the marbles I'd won
And put them in my stepfather's cupboard,
Hoping he'd catch leprosy from them.

6

A slim dark youth with quiet
Eyes and a gentle quizzical smile,
Manohar. Fifteen, working in a small hotel.

He'd come from the hills and wanted to return,
I forget how we met
But I remember walking the dusty roads
With this gentle boy, who held my hand
And told me about his home, his mother,
His village, and the little river
At the bottom of the hill where the water
Ran blue and white and wonderful,
'When I go home, I'll take you with me.'
But we hadn't enough money.
So I sold my bicycle for thirty rupees
And left a note in the dining room:
'Going away. Don't worry—(hoping they would)—
I'll come home
When I've grown up.'

We crossed the rushing waters of the Ganga
Where they issued from the doors of Vishnu
Then took the pilgrim road, in those days
Just a stony footpath into the mountains:
Not all who ventured forth returned;
Some came to die, of course,
Near the sacred waters or at their source.
We took this route and spent a night
At a wayside inn, wrapped tight
In the single blanket I'd brought along;
Even then we were cold
It was not the season for pilgrim
And the inn was empty, except for the locals
Drinking a local brew.
We drank a little and listened
To an old soldier from the hills
Talking of the women he'd known
In the first Great War, when stationed in Rome;

271

His memories were good for many drinks
In many inns; his face pickled in the suns
Of many mountain summers.
The mule-drivers slept in one room
And talked all night over hookahs.
Manohar slept bravely, but I lay watching
A bright star through the tiny window
And wished upon it, already knowing that wishes
Had no power, but wishing all the same. . . .
And next morning we set off again
Leaving the pilgrim-route to march
Down a valley, above a smaller river,
Walking until I felt
We'd walk and walk for ever.
Late at night, on a cold mountain,
Two lonely figures, we saw the lights
Of scattered houses and knew we had arrived.

7

'Not death, but a summing-up of life,'
Said the village patriarch, as we watched him
Treasure a patch of winter sunshine
On his string cot in the courtyard.
I remember his wisdom.
And I remember faces.
For it's faces I remember best.
The people were poor, and the patriarch said:
'I have heard it told that the sun
Sets in splendour in Himalaya—
But who can eat sunsets?'
The patriarch was old in years,
But some grew old at their mother's breasts.

Perhaps, if I'd stayed longer,
I would have yearned for creature comforts.

We were hungry sometimes, eating wild berries
Or slyly milking another's goat,
Or catching small fish in the river. . . .
But I did not long for home.
Could I have grown up a village boy,
Grazing sheep and cattle, while the Collected Works
Of W. Shakespeare lay gathering dust
In Dehra? Who knows? But it was nice
Of my stepfather to send his office manager
Into the mountains to bring me home!

Manohar.
He called goodbye and waved
As I looked back from the bend in the road.
Bright boy on the mountainside,
Waving to me, calling, and I've loved you
All these years and looked for you everywhere,
In the mountains, in crowds at distant places,
In cities and villages, beside the sea.
And the trains roll on, every day
Hundreds of people coming or going or running away—
Goodbye, goodbye!
Into the forest's silence,
Outside the dark tunnel,
Out of the tunnel, out of the dark. . . .

SCENES FROM THE NOVELS

SCENES FROM THE NOVELS

EXTRACT FROM *A FLIGHT OF PIGEONS*

T he sun rose in a cloudless, shimmering sky, and only those who had risen at dawn had been lucky enough to enjoy the cool breeze that had blown across the river for a brief spell. At seven o'clock the church bell began to toll, and people could be seen making their way towards the small, sturdily built cantonment church. Some, like Mr Labadoor and his daughter, were on foot, wearing their Sunday clothes. Others came in carriages, or were borne aloft in doolies manned by sweating doolie-bearers.

St Mary's, the little church in Shahjahanpur, is situated on the southern boundary of the cantonment, near an ancient mangogrove. There are three entrances: one to the south, facing a large compound known as Buller's; another to the west, below the steeple; and the vestry door opening to the north. A narrow staircase leads up to the steeple. To the east there were open fields sloping down to the river, cultivated with melon; to the west, lay an open plain bounded by the city; while the parade ground stretched away to the north until it reached the barracks of the sepoys. The bungalows scattered about the side of the parade ground belonged to the regimental officers, Englishmen who had slept soundly, quite unaware of an atmosphere charged with violence.

I will let Ruth take up the story. . . ..

At The Church

Father and I had just left the house when we saw several sepoys crossing the road, on their way to the river for their morning bath. They stared so fiercely at us that I pressed close to my father and whispered, 'Papa, how strange they look!' But their appearance did not strike him as unusual; the sepoys usually passed that way when going to the River Khannaut, and I suppose Father was used to meeting them on his way to office.

277

We entered the church from the south porch, and took our seats in the last pew to the right. A number of people had already arrived, but I did not particularly notice who they were. We had knelt down, and were in the middle of the Confession, when we heard a tumult outside and a lot of shouting, that seemed nearer every moment. Everyone in the church got up, and Father left our pew and went and stood at the door, where I joined him.

There were six or seven men on the porch. Their faces were covered up to their noses, and they wore tight loincloths as though they had prepared for a wrestling bout; but they held naked swords in their hands. As soon as they saw us, they sprang forward, and one of them made a cut at us. The sword missed us both and caught the side of the door where it buried itself in the wood. My father had his left hand against the door, and I rushed out from under it, and escaped into the church compound.

A second and third cut were made at my father by the others, both of which caught him on his right cheek. Father tried to seize the sword of one of his assailants, but he caught it high up on the blade, and so firmly, that he lost two fingers from his right hand. These were the only cuts he received; but though he did not fall, he was bleeding profusely. All this time I had stood looking on from the porch, completely bewildered and dazed by what had happened. I remember asking my father what had happened to make him bleed so much.

'Take the handkerchief from my pocket and bandage my face,' he said.

When I had made a bandage from both our handkerchiefs and tied it about his head, he said he wished to go home. I took him by the hand and tried to lead him out of the porch; but we had gone only a few steps when he began to feel faint, and said, 'I can't walk, Ruth. Let us go back to the church.'

The armed men had made only one rush through the church, and had then gone off through the vestry door. After wounding my father, they had run up the centre of the aisle, slashing right and left.

They had taken a cut at Lieutenant Scott, but his mother threw herself over him and received the blow on her ribs; her tight clothes saved her from a serious injury. Mr Ricketts, Mr Jenkins, the Collector, and Mr MacCullam, the Minister, ran out through the vestry.

The rest of the congregation had climbed up to the belfry, and on my father's urging me to do so, I joined them there. We saw Captain James riding up to the church, quite unaware of what was happening. We shouted him a warning, but as he looked up at us, one of the sepoys, who were scattered about on the parade ground, fired at him, and he fell from his horse. Now two other officers came running from the Mess, calling out to the sepoys: 'Oh! children, what are you doing?' They tried to pacify their men, but no one listened to them. They had, however, been popular officers with the sepoys, who did not prevent them from joining us in the turret with their pistols in their hands.

Just then we saw a carriage coming at full speed towards the church. It was Dr Bowling's, and it carried him, his wife and child, and the nanny. The carriage had to cross the parade ground, and they were halfway across, when a bullet hit the doctor who was sitting on the coach box. He doubled up in his seat, but did not let go of the reins, and the carriage had almost reached the church, when a sepoy ran up and made a slash at Mrs Bowling, missing her by inches. When the carriage reached the church, some of the officers ran down to help Dr Bowling off the coach box. He struggled in their arms for a while, and was dead when they got him to the ground.

I had come down from the turret with the officers, and now ran to where my father lay. He was sitting against the wall, in a large pool of blood. He did not complain of any pain, but his lips were parched, and he kept his eyes open with an effort. He told me to go home, and to ask Mother to send someone with a cot, or a doolie, to carry him back. So much had happened so quickly that I was completely dazed, and though Mrs Bowling and the other women were weeping, there wasn't a tear in my eye. There were two great wounds on my father's face, and I was reluctant to leave him, but to run home and fetch a doolie seemed to be the only way in which I could help him.

Leaving him against the stone wall of the church, I ran round to the vestry side and almost fell over Mr Ricketts, who was lying about twelve feet from the vestry door. He had been attacked by an expert and powerful swordsman, whose blow had cut through the trunk from the left shoulder separating the head and right hand from the rest of the body. Sick with horror, I turned from the spot and began running home through Buller's compound.

Nobody met me on the way. No one challenged me, or tried to intercept or molest me. The cantonment seemed empty and deserted; but just as I reached the end of Buller's compound, I saw our house in flames. I stopped at the gate, looking about for my mother, but could not see her anywhere. Granny, too, was missing, and the servants. Then I saw Lala Ramjimal walking down the road towards me.

'Don't worry, my child,' he said. 'Mother, Granny and the others are all safe. Come, I will take you to them.'

There was no question of doubting Lala Ramjimal's intentions. He had held me on his knee when I was a baby, and I had grown up under his eyes. He led me to a hut some thirty yards from our old home. It was a mud house, facing the road, and its door was closed. Lala knocked on the door, but received no answer; then he put his mouth to a chink and whispered, 'Missy-baba is with me, open the door.'

The door opened, and I rushed into my mother's arms.

'Thank God!' she cried. 'At least one is spared to me.'

'Papa is wounded at the church,' I said. 'Send someone to fetch him.'

Mother looked up at Lala and he could not resist the appeal in her eyes.

'I will go,' he said. 'Do not move from here until I return.'

'You don't know where he is,' I said. 'Let me come with you and help you.'

'No, you must not leave your mother now,' said Lala. 'If you are seen with me, we shall both be killed.'

He returned in the afternoon, after several hours. 'Sahib is dead,' he said, very simply. 'I arrived in time to see him die. He had lost so much blood that it was impossible for him to live. He could not speak, and his eyes were becoming glazed, but he looked at me in such a way that I am sure he recognized me . . .'

Lata Ramjimal

Lala left us in the afternoon, promising to return when it grew dark, then he would take us to his own house. He ran a grave risk in doing so, but he had promised us his protection, and he was a man who, once he had decided on taking a certain course of action, could not be shaken from his purpose. He was not a Government servant and owed no loyalties to the British; not had he conspired with the rebels, for his path never crossed theirs. He had been content always to go about his business (he owned several doolies and carriages, which he hired out to Europeans who could not buy their own) in a quiet and efficient manner, and was held in some respect by those he came into contact with; his motives were always personal, and if he helped us, it was not because we belonged to the ruling class—my father was probably the most junior officer in Shahjahanpur—but because he had known us for many years, and had grown fond of my mother, who had always treated him as a friend and equal.

I realized that I was now fatherless, and my mother, a widow; but we had no time to indulge in our private sorrow. Our own lives were in constant danger. From our hiding place we could hear the crackling of timber coming from our burning house. The road from the city to the cantonment was in an uproar, with people shouting on all sides. We heard the tramp of men passing up and down the road, just in front of our door; a moan or a sneeze would have betrayed us, and then we would have been at the mercy of the most ruffianly elements from the bazaar, whose swords flashed in the dazzling sunlight.

There were eight of us in the little room: Mother, Granny, myself; my cousin, Anet; my mother's half-brother, Pilloo, who was about my age, and his mother; our servants, Champa and Lado; as well as two of our black and white spaniels, who had followed close on Mother's heels when she fled from the house.

The mud hut in which we were sheltering was owned by Tirloki, a mason who had helped build our own house. He was well-known to us. Weeks before the outbreak, when Mother used to gossip with her servants and others about the possibility of trouble in Shahjahanpur, Tirloki had been one of those who had offered his house for shelter should she ever be in need of it. And Mother, as a precaution, had accepted his offer, and taken the key from him.

Mother afterwards told me that, as she sat on the veranda that morning, one of the gardener's sons had come running to her in great haste, and had cried out: 'Mutiny broken out, Sahib and Missy-baba killed!' Hearing that we had both been killed, Mother's first impulse was to throw herself into the nearest well; but Granny caught hold of her, and begged her not to be rash, saying,' And what will become of the rest of us if you do such a thing?' And so she had gone across the road, followed by the others, and had entered Tirloki's house and chained the door from within.

We were shut up in the hut all day, expecting, at any moment, to be discovered and killed. We had no food at all, but we could not have eaten any had it been there. My father gone, our future appeared a perfect void, and we found it difficult to talk. A hot wind blew through the cracks in the door, and our throats were parched. Late in the afternoon, a chatti of cold water was let down to us from a tree outside a window at the rear of the hut. This was an act of compassion on the part of a man called Chinta, who had worked for us as a labourer when our bungalow was being built.

At about ten o'clock, Lala returned, accompanied by Dhani, our old bearer. He proposed to take us to his own house. Mother hesitated to come out into the open, but Lala assured her that the roads were quite clear now, and there was little fear of our being molested. At last, she agreed to go.

We formed two batches. Lala led the way with a drawn sword in one hand, his umbrella in the other. Mother and Anet and I followed, holding each other's hands. Mother had thrown over us a counterpane which she had been carrying with her when she left the house. We avoided the main road, making our way round the sweeper settlement, and reached Lala's house after a fifteen-minute walk. On our arrival there, Lala offered us a bed to sit upon, while he squatted down on the ground with his legs crossed.

Mother had thrown away her big bunch of keys as we left Tirloki's house. When I asked her why she had done so, she pointed to the smouldering ruins of our bungalow and said: 'Of what possible use could they be to us now?'

The bearer, Dhani, arrived with the second batch, consisting of dear Granny, Pilloo and his mother, and Champa and Lado, and the dogs. There we were, eight of us in Lala's small house; and, as far as I could tell, his own family was as large as ours.

We were offered food, but we could not eat. We lay down for the night—Mother, Granny and I on the bed, the rest on the ground. And in the darkness, with my face against my mother's bosom, I gave vent to my grief and wept bitterly. My mother wept, too, but silently, and I think she was still weeping when at last I fell asleep.

In Lala's House

Lala Ramjimal's family consisted of himself, his wife, mother, aunt and sister. It was a house of women, and our unexpected arrival hadn't changed that. It must indeed have been a test of Lala's strength and patience, with twelve near-hysterical females on his hands!

His family, of course, knew who we were, because Lala's mother and aunt used to come and draw water from our well, and offer bel leaves at the little shrine near our house. They were at first shy of us; and we, so immersed in our own predicament, herded together in a corner of the house, and looked at each other's faces, and wept. Lala's wife would come and serve us food in platters made of stitched leaves. We ate once in twenty-four hours, a little after noon, but we were satisfied with this one big meal.

The house was an ordinary mud building, consisting of four flat-roofed rooms, with a low veranda in the front, and a courtyard at the back. It was small and unpretentious, occupied by a family of small means.

Lala's wife was a young woman, short in stature, with a fair complexion. We didn't know her name, because it is not customary for a husband or wife to call the other by name; but her mother-in-law would address her as Dulhan, or bride.

Ramjimal himself was a tall, lean man, with long moustaches. His speech was always very polite, like that of most Kayasthas but he had an air of determination about him that was rare in others.

On the second day of our arrival, I overheard his mother speaking to him: 'Lalaji, you have made a great mistake in bringing these Angrezans into our house. What will people say? As soon as the rebels hear of it, they will come and kill us.'

'I have done what is right,' replied Lala very quietly. 'I have not given shelter to Angrezans. I have given shelter to friends. Let people say or think as they please.'

He seldom went out of the house, and was usually to be seen seated before the front door, either smoking his small hookah, or playing chess with some friend who happened to drop by. After a few days, people began to suspect that there was somebody in the house about whom Lala was being very discreet, but they had no idea who these guests could be. He kept a close watch on his family, to prevent them from talking too much; and he saw that no one entered the house, keeping the front door chained at all times.

It is a wonder that we were able to live undiscovered for as long as we did, for there were always the dogs to draw attention to the house. They would not leave us, though we had nothing to offer them except the leftovers from our own meals. Lala's aunt told Mother that the third of our dogs, who had not followed us, had been seen going round and round the smoking ruins of our bungalow, and that on the day after the outbreak, he was found dead, sitting up—waiting for his master's return!

One day, Lala came in while we were seated on the floor talking about the recent events. Anxiety for the morrow had taken the edge off our grief, and we were able to speak of what had happened without becoming hysterical.

Lala sat down on the ground with a foil in his hand—the weapon had become his inseparable companion, but I do not think he had yet had occasion to use it. It was not his own, but one that he had found on the floor of the looted and ransacked courthouse.

'Do you think we are safe in your house, Lala?' asked Mother. 'What is going on outside these days?'

'You are quite safe here,' said Lala, gesturing with the foil. 'No one comes into this house except over my dead body. It is true, though, that I am suspected of harbouring kafirs. More than one person has asked me why I keep such a close watch over my house. My reply is that as the outbreak has put me out of employment, what would they have me do except sit in front of my house and look after my women? Then they ask me why I have not been to the Nawab, like everyone else.'

'What Nawab, Lala?' asked Mother.

'After the sepoys entered the city, their leader, the Subedar Major, set up Qadar Ali Khan as the Nawab, and proclaimed it throughout the city. Nizam Ali, a pensioner, was made Kotwal, and responsible posts were offered to Javed Khan, and to Nizam Ali Khan, but the latter refused to accept office.'

'And the former?'

'He has taken no office yet, because he and Azzu Khan have been too busy plundering the sahibs' houses. Javed Khan also instigated an attack on the treasurer. It was like this. . . .'

'Javed Khan, as you now, is one of the biggest ruffians in the city. When the sepoys had returned to their lines after proclaiming the Nawab, Javed Khan paid a visit to their commander. On learning that the regiment was preparing to leave Shahjahanpur and join the Bareilly brigade, he persuaded the Subedar-major, Ghansham Singh, to make a raid on the Rosa Rum Factory before leaving. A detachment, under Subedar Zorawar Singh, accompanied Javed Khan, and they took the road which passes by Jhunna Lal, the treasurer's house. There they halted, and demanded a contribution from Jhunna Lal. It so happened that he had only that morning received a sum of six thousand rupees from the Tehsildar of Jalalabad, and this the Subedar seized at once. As Jhunna Lal refused to part with any more, he was tied hand and foot and suspended from a tree by his legs. At the same time Javed Khan seized all his account books and threw them into a well saying, "Since you won't give us what we need, there go your accounts! We won't leave you with the means of collecting money from others!"

'After the party had moved on, Jhunna Lal's servants took him down from the tree. He was half-dead with fright, and from the rush of blood to his head. But when he came to himself, he got his servants to go down the well and fish up every account book!'

'And what about the Rosa Factory?' I asked.

'Javed Khan's party set fire to it, and no less than 70,000 gallons of rum, together with a large quantity of loaf sugar, were destroyed. The rest was carried away. Javed Khan's share of loaf sugar was an entire cart-load!'*

The next day when Lala came in and sat beside us—he used to spend at least an hour in our company every day—I asked him a question that had been on my mind much of the time, but the answer to which I was afraid of hearing: the whereabouts of my father's body.

'I would have told you before, Missy-baba,' he said, 'but I was afraid of upsetting you. The day after I brought you to my house I went again to the church, and there I found the body of your father, of the Collector-Sahib, and the doctor, exactly where I had seen them the day before. In spite of their exposure and the great heat they had not decomposed at all, and neither the vultures nor the jackals had touched them. Only their shoes had gone.

'As I turned to leave I saw two persons, Muslims, bringing in the body of Captain James, who had been shot a little distance from the church. They laid it beside that of your father and Dr Bowling. They told me that they had decided to bury the mortal

---

*The Rosa Rum Factory recovered, and survives to this day.

remains of those Christians who had been killed. I told them that they were taking a risk in doing so, as they might be accused by the Nawab's men of being in sympathy with the Firangis. They replied that they were aware of the risk, but that something had impelled them to undertake this task, and that they were willing to face the consequences.

'I was put to shame by their intentions, and, removing my long coat, began to help them carry the bodies to a pit they had dug outside the church. Here I saw, and was able to identify, the bodies of Mr MacCullam, the Padri-Sahib, and Mr Smith, the Assistant Collector. All six were buried side-by-side, and we covered the grave with a masonry slab upon which we drew parallel lines to mark each separate grave. We finished the work within an hour, and when I left the place I felt a satisfaction which I cannot describe . . .

Later, when we had recovered from the emotions which Ramjimal's words had aroused in us, I asked him how Mr MacCullam, the chaplain, had me this death; for I remembered seeing him descending from his pulpit when the ruffians entered the church, and running through the vestry with Mr Ricketts' mother.

'I cannot tell you much,' said Lala. 'I only know that while the sepoys attacked Mr Ricketts, Mr MacCullam was able to reach the melon field and conceal himself under some creepers. But another gang found him there, and finished him off with their swords.'

'Poor Mr MacCullam!' sighed Mother. 'He was such a harmless little man. And what about Arthur Smith, Lala?' Mother was determined to find out what had happened to most of the people we had known.

'Assistant Sahib was murdered in the city,' said Lala. 'He was in his bungalow, ill with fever, when the trouble broke out. His idea was to avoid the cantonment and make for the city, thinking it was only the sepoys who had mutinied. He went to the courts, but found them a shambles, and while he was standing in the street, a mob collected round him and began to push him about. Somebody prodded him with the hilt of his sword. Mr Smith lost his temper and, in spite of his fever, drew his revolver and shot at the man. But alas for Smith-Sahib, the cap snapped and the charge refused to explode. He levelled again at the man, but this time the bullet had no effect, merely striking the metal clasp of the man's belt and falling harmlessly to the ground. Mr Smith flung away his revolver in disgust, and now the man cut at him with his sword and brought him to his knees. Then the mob set upon him. Fate was against Smith-Sahib. The Company Bahadur's prestige has gone, for who ever heard of a revolver snapping, or a bullet being resisted by a belt?'

EXTRACT FROM *THE ROOM ON THE ROOF*

In his room, Rusty was a king. His domain was the sky and everything he could see. His subjects were the people who passed below, but they were his subjects only while they were below and he was on the roof; and he spied on them through the branches of the banyan tree. His close confidants were the inhabitants of the banyan tree; which, of course, included Kishen.

It was the day of the picnic, and Rusty had just finished bathing at the water-tank. He had become used to the people at the tank and had made friends with the ayahs and their charges. He had come to like their bangles and bracelets and ankle-bells. He liked to watch one of them at the tap, squatting on her haunches, scrubbing her feet, and making much music with the bells and bangles, she would roll her sari up to the knees to give her legs greater freedom, and crouch forward so that her jacket revealed a modest expanse of waist.

It was the day of the picnic, and Rusty had bathed, and now he sat on a disused chimney, drying himself in the sun.

Summer was coming. The lichis were almost ready to eat, the mangoes ripened under Kishen's greedy eye. In the afternoons the sleepy sunlight stole through the branches of the banyan tree, and made a patchwork of arched shadows on the walls of the house. The inhabitants of the trees knew it, and slapped lazily against his heels; and Kishen grumbled and became more untidy, and even Suri seemed to be taking a rest from his private investigations. Yes, summer was coming.

And it was the day of the picnic.

The car had been inspected, and the two bottles that Kapoor had hidden in the dickey had been found and removed; Kapoor was put in top khaki drill trousers and a bush-shirt and pronounced fit to drive; a basket of food and a gramophone were in the dickey.

Suri had a camera slung over his shoulders; Kishen was sporting a Gurkha hat; and Rusty had on a thick leather belt reinforced with steel knobs. Meena had dressed in a hurry, and looked the better for it. And for once, Somi had tied his turban to perfection.

'Everyone present?' said Meena. 'If so, get into the car.'

'I'm waiting for my dog,' said Suri, and he had hardly made the announcement when from around the corner came a yapping mongrel.

'He's called Prickly-Heat,' said Suri. 'We'll put him in the back seat.'

'He'll go in the dickey,' said Kishen. 'I can see the lice from here.'

Prickly Heat wasn't any particular kind of dog, just a kind of dog; he hadn't even the stump of a tail. But he had sharp, pointed ears that wagged as well as any tail, and they were working furiously this morning.

Suri and the dog were both deposited in the dickey; Somi, Kishen and Rusty made themselves comfortable in the back seat, and Meena sat next to her husband in the front. The car belched and lurched forward, and stirred up great clouds of dust; then, accelerating, sped out of the compound and across the narrow wooden bridge that spanned the canal.

The sun rose over the forest, and a spiral of smoke from a panting train was caught by a slanting ray spangled with gold. The air was fresh and exciting. It was ten miles to the river and the sulphur springs, ten miles of intermittent grumbling and gaiety with Prickly Heat yapping in the dickey and Kapoor whistling the wheel and Kishen letting fly from the window with a catapult.

Somi said: 'Rusty, your pimples will leave you if you bathe in the sulphur springs.'

'I would rather have pimples than pneumonia,' replied Rusty.

'But it's not cold,' said Kishen. 'I would bathe myself, but I don't feel very well.'

'Then you shouldn't have come,' said Meena from the front.

'I didn't want to disappoint you all,' said Kishen.

Before reaching the springs, the car had to cross one or two river-beds, usually dry at this time of the year. But the mountains had tricked the party, for there was a good deal of water to be seen, and the current was strong.

'It's not very deep,' said Kapoor, at the first river-bed, 'I think we can drive through easily.'

The car dipped forward, rolled down the bank, and entered the current with a great splash. In the dickey, Suri got a soaking.

'Got to go fast,' said Mr Kapoor, 'or we'll stick.'

He accelerated, and a great spray of water rose on both sides of the car. Kishen cried out for sheer joy, but at the back Suri was having a fit of hysterics.

'I think the dog's fallen out,' said Meena.

'Good,' said Somi.

'I think Suri's fallen out', said Rusty.

'Good,' said Somi.

Suddenly the engines spluttered and choked, and the car came to a standstill.

'We have stuck,' said Kapoor.

'That,' said Meena bitingly, 'is obvious. Now I suppose you want us at all to get out and push?'

'Yes, that's a good idea.'

'You're a genius.'

Kishen had his shoes off in a flash, and was leaping about in the water with great abandon. The water reached up to his knees and, as he hadn't been swept off his feet, the others followed his example.

Meena rolled her sari up to the thighs, and stepped gingerly into the current. Her legs, so seldom exposed, were very fair in contrast to her feet and arms, but they were strong and nimble, and she held herself erect. Rusty stumbled to her side, intending to aid her; but ended by clinging to her dress for support. Suri was not to be seen anywhere.

'Where is Suri?' said Meena.

'Here,' said a muffled voice from the floor of the dickey. 'I've got sick. I can't push.'

'All right,' said Meena. 'But you'll clean up the mess yourself.'

291

Somi and Kishen were looking for fish. Kapoor tooted the horn.

'Are you all going to push?' he said. 'Or are we going to have the picnic in the middle of the river?'

Rusty was surprised at Kapoor's unusual display of common sense; when sober, Mr Kapoor did sometimes have moments of sanity.

Everyone put their weight against the car, and pushed with all their strength; and, as the car moved slowly forward, Rusty felt a thrill of health and pleasure run through his body. In front of him, Meena pushed silently, the muscles of her thighs trembling with the strain. They all pushed silently, with determination; the sweat ran down Somi's face and neck, and Kishen's jaws worked desperately on his chewing-gum. But Kapoor sat in comfort behind the wheel, pressing and pulling knobs, and saying 'harder, push harder', and Suri began to be sick again. Prickly Heat was strangely quiet, and it was assumed that the dog was sick too.

With one last final heave, the car was moved up the opposite bank and on to the straight. Everyone groaned and flopped to the ground. Meena's hands were trembling.

'You shouldn't have pushed,' said Rusty.

'I enjoyed it,' she said, smiling at him. 'Help me to get up.'

He rose and, taking her hand, pulled her to her feet. They stood together, holding hands. Kapoor fiddled around with starters and chokes and things.

'It won't go,' he said. 'I'll have to look at the engine. We might as well have the picnic here.'

So out came the food and lemonade bottles and, miraculously enough, out came Suri and Prickly Heat, looking as fit as ever.

'Hey,' said Kishen, 'we thought you were sick. I suppose you were just making room for lunch.'

'Before he eats anything,' said Somi, 'he's going to get wet. Let's take him for a swim.'

Somi, Kishen and Rusty caught hold of Suri and dragged him along the river-bank to a spot downstream where the current was mild and the water warm and waist-high. They unrobed Suri, took off their own clothes, and ran down the sandy slope to the water's edge; feet splashed ankle-deep, calves thrust into the current, and then the ground suddenly disappeared beneath their feet.

Somi was a fine swimmer; his supple limbs cut through the water and, when he went under, he was almost as powerful; the chequered colours of his body could be seen first here and then there, twisting and turning, diving and disappearing for what seemed like several minutes, and then coming up under someone's feet.

Rusty and Kishen were amateurs. When they tried swimming underwater, their bottoms remained on the surface, having all the appearance of floating buoys. Suri couldn't swim at all but, though he was often out of his depth and frequently ducked, managed to avoid his death by drowning.

They heard Meena calling them for food, and scrambled up the bank, the dog yapping at their heels. They ate in the shade of a poinsettia tree, whose red long-fingered flowers dropped sensually to the running water; and when they had eaten, lay down to sleep or drowse the afternoon away.

When Rusty awoke, it was evening, and Kapoor was tinkering about with the car, muttering to himself, a little cross because he hadn't had a drink since the previous night. Somi and Kishen were back in the river, splashing away, and this time they had Prickly Heat for company. Suri wasn't in sight. Meena stood in a clearing at the edge of the forest.

Rusty went to Meena, but she wandered into the thicket. The boy followed. She must have expected him, for she showed no surprise at his appearance.

'Listen to the jungle,' she said.

'I can't hear anything.'

They were surrounded by silence; a dark, pensive silence, heavy, scented with magnolia and jasmine.

It was shattered by a piercing shriek, a cry that rose on all sides, echoing against the vibrating air; and, instinctively, Rusty put his arm round Meena—whether to protect her or to protect himself,' he did not really know—and held her tight.

'It is only a bird,' she said, 'of what are you afraid?'

But he was unable to release his hold, and she made no effort to free herself. She laughed into his face, and her eyes danced in the shadows. But he stifled her laugh with his lips.

It was a clumsy, awkward kiss, but fiercely passionate, and Meena responded, tightening her embrace, returning the fervour of the kiss. They stood together in the shadows, Rusty intoxicated with beauty and sweetness, Meena with freedom and the comfort of being loved.

A monkey chattered shrilly in a branch above them, and the spell was broken.

'Oh, Meena. . . .'

'Shh. . . . you spoil these things by saying them'.

'Oh, Meena. . . .'

They kissed again, but the monkey set up such a racket that they feared it would bring Kapoor and the others to the spot. So they walked through the trees, holding hands.

They were barefooted, but they did not notice the thorns and brambles that pricked their feet; they walked through heavy foliage, nettles and long grass, until they came to a clearing and a stream.

Rusty was conscious of a wild urge, a desire to escape from the town and its people, and live in the forest with Meena, with no one but Meena. . . .

As though conscious of his thoughts, she said: 'This is where we drink. In the trees we eat and sleep, and here we drink.'

She laughed, but Rusty had a dream in his heart. The pebbles on the bed of the stream were round and smooth, taking the flow of water without resistance. Only weed and rock could resist water: only weed or rock could resist life.

'It would be nice to stay in the jungle,' said Meena.

'Let us stay. . . .'

'We will be found. We cannot escape—from—others. . . .

'Even the world is too small. Maybe there is more freedom in your little room than in all the jungle and all the world.'

Rusty pointed to the stream and whispered, 'Look!'

Meena looked, and at the same time a deer looked up. They

looked at each other with startled, fascinated eyes, the deer and Meena. It was a spotted cheetal, a small animal with delicate, quivering limbs and muscles, and young green antlers.

Rusty and Meena did not move; nor did the deer; they might have gone on staring at each other all night if somewhere a twig hadn't snapped sharply. At the snap of the twig, the deer jerked its head up with a start, lifted one foot pensively, sniffed the air; then leapt the stream and, in a single bound, disappeared into the forest.

The spell was broken, the magic lost. Only, the water ran on and life ran on.

'Let's go back,' said Meena.

They walked back through the dappled sunlight, swinging their clasped hands like two children who had only just discovered love.

Their hands parted as they reached the river-bed.

Miraculously enough, Kapoor had started the car, and was waving his arms and shouting to everyone to come home. Everyone was ready to start back except for Suri and Prickly Heat, who were nowhere to be seen. Nothing, thought Meena, would have been better than for Suri to disappear for ever, but unfortunately she had taken full responsibility for his well-being, and did not relish the thought of facing his strangely affectionate mother. So she asked Rusty to shout for him.

Rusty shouted, and Meena shouted, and Somi shouted, and then they all shouted together, only Suri didn't shout.

'He's up to his tricks,' said Kishen. 'We shouldn't have brought him. Let's pretend we're leaving, then he'll be scared.

So Kapoor started the engine, and everyone got in, and it was only then that Suri came running from the forest, the dog at his heels, his shirt-tails flapping in the breeze, his hair wedged between his eyes and his spectacles.

'Hey,' wait for us!' he cried. 'Do you want me to die?'

Kishen mumbled in the affirmative, and swore quietly.

'We thought you were in the dickey,' said Rusty.

Suri and Prickly Heat climbed into the dickey, and at the same time the car entered the river with a determined splashing and churning of wheels, to emerge the victor.

Everyone cheered, and Somi gave Kapoor such an enthusiastic slap on the back that the pleased recipient nearly caught his head in the steering-wheel.

It was dark now, and all that could be seen of the countryside was what the headlights showed. Rusty had hopes of seeing a panther or tiger, for this was their territory, but only a few goats blocked the road. However, for the benefit of Suri, Somi told a story of a party that had gone for an outing in a car and, on returning home, had found a panther in the dickey.

Kishen fell asleep just before they reached the outskirts of Dehra, his fuzzy head resting on Rusty's shoulder. Rusty felt protectively towards the boy, for a bond of genuine affection had grown between the two. Somi was Rusty's best friend, in the same way that Ranbir was a friend, and their friendship was on a high emotional plane. But Kishen was a brother more than a friend. He loved Rusty, but without knowing or thinking or saying it, and that is the love of a brother.

Somi began singing. The town came in sight, the bazaar lights twinkling defiance at the starry night.

THE LAFUNGA*

'If you have nothing to do,' said Devinder, 'will you come with me on my rounds?'

'First we will see Hathi. If he has not left yet, I can accompany him to Lansdowne.'

Rusty set out with Devinder in the direction of the bazaar. As it was early morning, the shops were just beginning to open. Vegetable vendors were busy freshening their stock with liberal sprinklings of water, calling their prices and their wares; children dawdled in the road on their way to school, playing hopscotch or marbles. Girls going to college chattered in groups like gay, noisy parrots. Men cycled to work, and bullock-carts came in from the villages, laden with produce. The dust, which had taken all night to settle, rose again like a mist.

Rusty and Devinder stopped at the tea-shop to eat thickly buttered buns and drink strong, sweet tea. Then they looked for Hathi's room, and found it above a cloth shop, lying empty, with its doors open. The string bed leant against the wall. On shelves and window-ledges, in corners and on the floor, lay little coloured toys made of clay—elephants and bulls, horses and peacocks, and images of Krishna and Ganesha; a blue Krishna, with a flute to his lips, a jolly Ganesha with a delightful little trunk. Most of the toys were rough and unfinished, more charming than the completed pieces. Most of the finished products would now be on sale in the bazaar.

It came as a surprise to Rusty to discover that Hathi, the big wrestler, made toys for a living. He had not imagined there would be delicacy and skill in his friend's huge hands. The pleasantness of the discovery offset his disappointment at finding Hathi had gone.

*From *Vagrants in the Valley*.

'He has left already,' said Rusty. 'Never mind. I know he will welcome me, even if I arrive unexpectedly.'

He left the bazaar with Devinder, making for the residential part of the town. As he would be leaving Dehra soon, there was no point in his visiting the school again; later, though, he would see Mr Pettigrew.

When they reached the Clock Tower, someone whistled to them from across the street, and a tall young man came striding towards them.

He looked taller than Devinder, mainly because of his long legs. He wore a loose-fitting bush-shirt that hung open in front. His face was long and pale, but he had quick, devilish eyes, and he smiled disarmingly.

'Here comes Sudheer the Lafunga,' whispered Devinder. 'Lafunga means loafer. He probably wants some money. He is the most charming and the most dangerous person in town.' Aloud, he said, 'Sudheer, when are you going to return the twenty rupees you owe me?'

'Don't talk that way, Devinder,' said the Lafunga, looking offended. 'Don't hurt my feelings. You know your money is safer with me than it is in the bank. It will even bring you dividends, mark my words. I have a plan that will come off in a few days, and then you will get back double your money. Please tell me, who is your friend?'

'We stay together,' said Devinder, introducing Rusty. 'And he is bankrupt too, so don't get any ideas.'

'Please don't believe what he says of me,' said the Lafunga with a captivating smile that showed his strong teeth. 'Really I am not very harmful.'

'Well, completely harmless people are usually dull,' said Rusty.

'How I agree with you! I think we have a lot in common.'

'No, he hasn't got anything,' put in Devinder.

'Well then, he must start from the beginning. It is the best way to make a fortune. You will come and see me, won't you, mister Rusty? We could make a terrific combination, I am sure. You are the kind of person people trust! They take only one look at me and then feel their pockets to see if anything is missing!.'

Rusty instinctively put his hand to his own pocket, and all three of them laughed.

'Well, I must go,' said Sudheer the Lafunga, now certain that Devinder was not likely to produce any funds. 'I have a small matter to attend to. It may bring me a fee of twenty or thirty rupees.'

'Go,' said Devinder. 'Strike while the iron is hot.'

'Not I,' said the Lafunga, grinning and moving off. 'I make the iron hot by striking.'

*

'Sudheer is not too bad,' said Devinder, as they walked away from the Clock tower. 'He is a crook, of course—*Shree 420*—but he would not harm people like us. As he is quite well educated, he manages to gain the confidence of some well-to-do people, and acts on their behalf in matters that are not always respectable. But he spends what he makes, and is too generous to be successful.'

They had reached a quiet, tree-lined road, and walked in the shade of neem, mango, jamun and eucalyptus trees. Clumps of tall bamboo grew between the trees. Nowhere, but in Dehra, had Rusty seen so many kinds of trees. Trees that had no names. Tall, straight trees, and broad, shady trees. Trees that slept or brooded in the afternoon stillness. And trees that shimmered and moved and whispered even when the winds were asleep.

Some marigolds grew wild on the footpath, and Devinder picked two of them, giving one to Rusty.

'There is a girl who lives at the bottom of the road,' he said. 'She is a pretty girl. Come with me and see her.'

They walked to the house at the end of the road and, while Rusty stood at the gate, Devinder went up the path. Devinder stood at the bottom of the veranda steps, a little to one side, where he could be seen from a window, and whistled softly.

Presently a girl came out on the veranda. When she saw Devinder she smiled. She had a round, fresh face, and long black hair, and she was not wearing any shoes.

Devinder gave her the marigold. She took it in her hand and, not knowing what to say, ran indoors.

That morning Devinder and Rusty walked about four miles. Devinder's customers ranged from decadent maharanis and the wives of government officials to gardeners and sweeper women. Though his merchandise was cheap, the well-to-do were more finicky about a price than the poor. And there were a few who bought things from Devinder because they knew his circumstances and liked what he was doing.

A small girl with flapping pigtails came skipping down the road. She stopped to stare at Rusty, as though he were something quite out of the ordinary, but not unpleasant.

Rusty took the other marigold from his pocket, and gave it to the girl. It was a long time since he had been able to make anyone a gift.

*

After some time they parted, Devinder going back to the town, while Rusty crossed the river-bed. He walked through the tea-gardens until he found Mr Pettigrew's bungalow.

The old man was not in the veranda, but a young servant salaamed Rusty and asked him to sit down. Apparently Mr Pettigrew was having his bath.

'Does he always bathe in the afternoon?' asked Rusty.

'Yes, the sahib likes his water to be put in the sun to get warm. He does not like cold baths or hot baths. The afternoon sun gives his water the right temperature.'

Rusty walked into the drawing-room and nearly fell over a small table. The room was full of furniture and pictures and bric-à-brac. Tiger-heads, stuffed and mounted, snarled down at him from the walls. On the carpet lay several cheetal skins, a bit worn at the sides. There were several shelves filled with books bound in morocco or calf. Photographs adorned the walls—one of a much younger Mr Pettigrew standing over a supine leopard, another of

Mr Pettigrew perched on top of an elephant, with his rifle resting on his knees . . . Remembering his own experiences, Rusty wondered how such an active shikari ever found time for reading. While he was gazing at the photographs, Pettigrew himself came in, a large bathrobe wrapped round his thin frame, his grizzly chest looking very raw and red from the scrubbing he had just given it.

'Ah, there you are!' he said. 'The bearer told me you were here. Glad to see you again. Sit down and have a drink.'

Mr Pettigrew found the whisky and poured out two stiff drinks. Then, still in his bathrobe and slippers, he made himself comfortable in an armchair. Rusty said something complimentary about one of the mounted tiger-heads.

'Bagged it in Assam,' he said. 'Back in 1928, that was. I spent three nights on a machan before I got a shot at it.'

'You have a lot of books,' observed Rusty.

'A good collection, mostly flora and fauna. Some of them are extremely rare. By the way,' he said, looking around at the wall, 'did you ever see a picture of your father?'

'Have you got one?' asked Rusty. 'I've only a faint memory of what he looked like.'

'He's in that group photograph over there,' said Mr Pettigrew, pointing to a picture on the wall.

Rusty went over to the picture and saw three men dressed in white shirts and flannels, holding tennis rackets, and looking very self-conscious.

'He's in the middle,' said Pettigrew. 'I'm on his right.'

Rusty saw a young man with fair hair and a fresh face. He was the only player who was smiling. Mr Pettigrew, sporting a fierce moustache, looked as though he was about to tackle a tiger with his racket. The third person was bald and uninteresting.

'Of course, he's very young in that photo,' said Pettigrew. 'It was taken long before you were ever thought of—before your father married.'

Rusty did not reply. He was trying to imagine his father in action on a tennis court, and wondered if he was a better player than Pettigrew.

'Who was the best player among you?' he asked.

'Ah, well, we were both pretty good, you know. Except for poor old Wilkie on the left. He got in the picture by mistake.'

'Did my father talk much?' asked Rusty.

'Well, we all talked a lot, you know, especially after a few drinks. He talked as much as any of us. He could sing, when he wanted to. His rendering of the "Kashmiri Love Song" was always popular at parties, but it wasn't often he sang, because he didn't like parties . . . Do you remember it? "Pale hands I love, beside the Shalimar . . ." '

Pettigrew began singing in a cracked, wavering voice, and Rusty was forced to take his eyes off the photograph. Half-way through the melody, Pettigrew forgot the words, so he took another gulp of whisky and began singing 'The Rose of Tralee'. The sight of the old man singing love songs in his bathrobe, with a glass of whisky in his hand, made Rusty smile.

'Well,' said Pettigrew, breaking off in the middle of the song, 'I don't sing as well as I used to. Never mind. Now tell me, boy, when are you going to Garhwal?'

'Tomorrow, perhaps.'

'Have you any money?'

'Enough to travel with. I have a friend in the hills, with whom I can stay for some time.'

'And what about money?'

'I have enough.'

'Well, I'm lending you twenty rupees,' he said, thrusting an envelope into the boy's hands. 'Come and see me when you return, even if you don't find what you're looking for.'

'I'll do that, Mr Pettigrew.'

The old man looked at the boy for some time, as though summing him up.

'You don't really have to find out much about your father,' he said. 'You're just like him, you know.'

*

Returning to the bazaar, Devinder found Sudheer at a paan shop, his lips red with betel juice. Devinder went straight to the point.

'Sudheer,' he said, 'you owe ne twenty rupees. I need it, not for myself, but for Rusty, who has to leave Dehra very urgently. You must get me the money by tonight.'

The Lafunga scratched his head.

'It will be difficult,' he said, 'but perhaps it can be managed. He really needs the money? It is not just a trick to get your own money back?'

'He is going to the hills. There may be money for him there, if he finds the person he is looking for.'

'Well, that's different,' said the Lafunga, brightening up, 'That makes Rusty an investment. Meet me at the Clock Tower at six o' clock, and I will have the money for you. I am glad to find you making useful friends for a change.'

He stuffed another roll of paan into his mouth, and taking leave of Devinder with a bright red smile, strolled leisurely down the bazaar road.

As far as appearances went, he had little to do but loll around in the afternoon sunshine, frequenting tea-shops, and gambling with cards in small back rooms. All this he did very well—but it did not make him a living.

To say that he lived on his wits would be an exaggeration. He lived a great deal on other people's wits. There was the Seth for instance, Rusty's former landlord, who owned much property and dabbled in many shady transactions, and who was often represented by the Lafunga in affairs of an unsavoury nature.

Sudheer came originally from the Frontier, where little value was placed on human life; and while still a boy, he had wandered, a homeless refugee, over the border into India. A smuggler adopted him, taught him something of the trade, and introduced him to some of the best hands in the profession; but in a border-foray with the police, Sudheer's foster-father was shot dead, and the youth was once again on his own. By this time he was old enough to look after himself. With the help of his foster-father's connections, he soon attained the service and confidence of the Seth.

Sudheer was no petty criminal. He practised crime as a fine art, and believed that thieves, and even murderers, had to have certain principles. If he stole, then he stole from a rich man, who could afford to be robbed, or from a greedy man, who deserved to be robbed. And if he did not rob poor men, it was not because of any altruistic motive—it was because poor men were not worth robbing.

He was good to those friends, like Devinder, who were good to him. Perhaps his most valuable friends, as sources of both money and information, were the dancing-girls who followed their profession in an almost inaccessible little road in the heart of the bazaar. His best friends were Hastini and Mrinalini. He borrowed money from them very freely, and seldom paid back more than half of it.

Hastini could twang the sitar, and dance—with a rather heavy tread—among various other accomplishments.

Mrinalini, a much smaller woman, had grown up in the profession. She was looked after by her mother, a former entertainer; who kept most of the money that Mrinalini made.

Sudheer awoke Hastini in the middle of her afternoon siesta by tickling her under the chin with a feather.

'And who were you with last night, little brother?' she asked running her fingers through his thick brown hair. 'You are smelling of some horrible perfume.'

'You know I do not spend my nights with anyone,' said Sudheer. 'The perfume is from yesterday.'

'Someone new?'

'No, my butterfly. I have known her for a week.'

'Too long a time,' said Hastini petulantly. 'A dangerously long time. How much have you spent on her?'

'Nothing so far. But that is not why I came to see you. Have you got twenty rupees?'

'Villain!' cried Hastini. 'Why do you always borrow from me when you want to entertain some stupid young thing? Are you so heartless?

'My little lotus flower!' protested Sudheer, pinching her rosy cheeks. 'I am not borrowing for any such reason. A friend of mine has to leave Dehra urgently, and I must get the money for his train fare. I owe it to him.'

'Since when did you have a friend?'

'Never mind that. I have one. And I come to you for help because I love you more than any one. Would you prefer that I borrow the money from Mrinalini?'

'You dare not,' said Hastini. 'I will kill you if you do.'

Between Hastini, of the broad hips, and Mrinalini, who was small and slender, there existed a healthy rivalry for the affections of Sudheer. Perhaps it was the great difference in their proportions that animated the rivalry. Mrinalini envied the luxuriousness of Hastini's soft body, while Hastini envied Mrinalini's delicacy, poise, slenderness of foot, and graceful walk. Mrinalini was the colour of milk and honey; she had the daintiness of a deer, while Hastini possessed the elegance of an elephant.

Sudheer could appreciate both these qualities.

He stood up, looking young even for his twenty-two years, and smiled a crooked smile. He might have looked effeminate had it not been for his hands—they were big, long-fingered, strong hands.

'Where is the money?' he asked.

'You are so impatient! Sit down, sit down. I have it here beneath the mattress.'

Sudheer's hand made its way beneath the mattress and probed about in search of the money.

'Ah, here it is! You have a fortune stacked away here. Yes, ten rupees, fifteen, twenty—and one for luck. . . . Now give me a kiss!

*

About an hour later Sudheer was in the street again, whistling cheerfully to himself. He walked with a long, loping stride, his shirt hanging open. Warm sunshine filled one side of the narrow street, and crept up the walls of shops and houses.

Sudheer passed a fruit stand, where the owner was busy talking to a customer, and helped himself to a choice red Kashmiri apple. He continued on his way down the bazaar road, munching the apple.

The bazaar continued for a mile, from the Clock Tower to the railway station, and Sudheer could hear the whistle of a train. He turned off at a little alley, throwing his half-eaten apple to a stray dog. Then he climbed a flight of stairs—wooden stairs that were loose and rickety, liable to collapse at any moment . . .

Mrinalini's half-deaf mother was squatting on the kitchen floor, making a fire in an earthen brazier. Sudheer poked his head round the door and shouted: 'Good morning, Mother, I hope you are making me some tea. You look fine today!' And then, in a lower tone, so that she could not hear: 'You look like a dried-up mango.'

'So it's you again,' grumbled the old woman. 'What do you want now?'

'Your most respectable daughter is what I want,' said Sudheer.

'What's that?' She cupped her hand to her ear and leaned forward.

'Where's Mrinalini?' shouted Sudheer.

'Don't shout like that! She is not here.'

'That's all I wanted to know,' said Sudheer, and he walked through the kitchen, through the living-room, and on to the veranda balcony, where he found Mrinalini sitting in the sun, combing out her long silken hair.

'Let me do it for you,' said Sudheer, and he took the comb from her hand and ran it through the silky black hair. 'For one so little, so much hair. You could conceal yourself in it, and not be seen, except for your dainty little feet.'

'What are you after, Sudheer? You are so full of compliments this morning. And watch out for Mother—if she sees you combing my hair, she will have a fit!'

'And I hope it kills her.'

'Sudheer!'

'Don't be so sentimental about your mother. You are her little gold mine, and she treats you as such—soon I will be having to fill in application forms before I can see you! It is time you kept your earnings for yourself.'

'So that it will be easier for you to help yourself?'

'Well, it would be more convenient. By the way, I have come to you for twenty rupees.'

Mrinalini laughed delightedly, and took the comb from Sudheer. 'What were you saying about my little feet?' she asked slyly.

'I said they were the feet of a princess, and I would be very happy to kiss them.'

'Kiss them, then.'

She held one delicate golden foot in the air, and Sudheer took it in his hands (which were as large as her feet) and kissed her ankle.

'That will be twenty rupees,' he said.

She pushed him away with her foot. 'But, Sudheer, I gave you fifteen rupees only three days ago. What have you done with it?'

'I haven't the slightest idea. I only know that I must have more. It is most urgent, you can be sure of that. But if you cannot help me, I must try elsewhere.'

'Do that, Sudheer. And may I ask, whom do you propose to try?'

'Well, I was thinking of Hastini.'

'Who?'

'You know, Hastini, the girl with the wonderful figure. . . .'

'I should think I do! Sudheer, if you so much as dare to take a rupee from her, I'll never speak to you again!'

'Well then, what shall I do?'

Mrinalini beat the arms of the chair with her little fists, and cursed Sudheer under her breath. Then she got up and went into the kitchen. A great deal of shouting went on in the kitchen before Mrinalini came back with flushed cheeks and fifteen rupees.

'You don't know the trouble I had getting it,' she said. 'Now don't come asking for more until at least a week has passed.'

'After a week, I will be able to supply you with funds. I am engaged tonight on a mission of some importance. In a few days I will place golden bangles on your golden feet.'

'What mission?' asked Mrinalini, looking at him with an anxious frown. 'If it is anything to do with the Seth, please leave it alone. You know what happened to Satish Dayal. He was smuggling opium for the Seth, and now he is sitting in jail, while the Seth continues as always.'

'Don't worry about me. I can deal with the Seth.'

'Then be off! I have to entertain a foreign delegation this evening. You can come tomorrow morning, if you are free.'

'I may come. Meanwhile, goodbye!'

He walked backwards into the living-room, pivoted into the kitchen and, bending over the old woman, kissed her on the forehead.

'You dried-up old mango,' he said. And went away, whistling.

EXTRACT FROM *ROSEBUD*

One

The Duel

'Eight annas in the rupee,' sneered Major Crump for the hundredth time, as I walked into the officers' mess of Her Majesty's 32nd Foot in Meerut.

He thought the remark was hilarious, and although hardly anyone smiled, he roared with laughter at his own crude joke.

I had always ignored this sort of jibe, but that evening I was in a black mood, having just been refused leave to visit my sick sister in Bareilly. The younger British officers of my own age never made remarks about my forebears or the fact that my parentage was mixed; but the Major, for reasons that I found difficult to fathom, went out of his way to be offensive. Eight annas in the rupee—half a rupee—implied a half-breed, and of course I had an Indian mother and an English father and made no secret of the fact. But it seemed to afford endless amusement to Major Crump.

As I was only a lieutenant, I could hardly engage in a war of words with my superior officer. But the more I controlled myself and tried to suppress my anger, the more certain I became that I would erupt one day, and then heaven only knew what the consequences would be.

My mother came from a respected Muslim-Christian family near Bareilly. My father, an English officer in the East India Company's service, had been killed during the 1857 uprising. I had only vague, disjointed memories of him. My mother and I had survived the holocaust; I went to school in Lucknow, and when I was eighteen I joined the 32nd Foot, my father's regiment. I had my father's fair complexion; but I also had my mother's passionate nature and fiery temper. I was not very tall, but I was strong, quick on my feet, and a good fighter. But you did not strike a senior officer no matter how great the provocation.

Except that I did. I was sick of Major Crump, who was in the habit of using his boots on servants, street-vendors and dogs, and my fist caught him between the eyes and sent him reeling against the billiard-table.

He came at me in a clumsy fashion, but like most bullies he was confused by a direct attack; I moved aside and helped him on his way, so that the velocity of his rush took him spinning across the room. He fell over a chair, which broke, and ended up on the floor with blood from his nose dripping onto his sandy moustache.

'I'll have you court-martialled for this, Wilson!' he choked the words out.

'Challenge him to a duel,' called out a slightly tipsy onlooker. 'Cut him down to size!'

'Yes,' I said. 'That's the only way to salvage your honour. Dignity you have already lost. Being knocked down by a half-breed junior officer—why, you'd be the laughing-stock of a court-martial. They couldn't shoot me for it, you know that. Just kick me out of the regiment. Who cares?'

'You're right,' said Major Crump, getting up and dusting himself down. 'I'd rather do the shooting myself.'

'So it's pistols, then? I heard you were something of a terror with a sword.'

'You wouldn't have much chance with a sword,' he said with a sneer. The effect of this was lost, because as he picked up his wineglass with a flourish, more blood from his nose dripped into it. 'We meet in the Company gardens at five tomorrow morning. I doubt if any officer will want to be your second—'

'One of the men will do,' I said with a laugh. 'I'm no stickler for convention.'

I walked out of the mess-room in a casual, off-hand manner. But I did not feel all that confident. The Major had many years of tiger-shooting behind him, and was reputed to be a good shot. He had reduced the tiger population by at least twenty, I'd been told. And he wasn't the type who would shoot to wing or disable an opponent. He would aim at the heart.

But I was certain of one thing : death would not overtake me hiding in a corner.

*

I woke early in the September dawn. A brain-fever bird had kept me awake for most of the night, and so had thoughts of the impending duel. My orderly came at five and began to set out my uniform.

'Don't bother with that,' I said. 'Whatever happens, I won't be wearing the Queen's uniform again.'

I knew that if I killed, or even wounded, Major Crump, I would be up for a court-martial. And that if I got the worst of it, I would not need a uniform, except possibly to be buried in.

When I reached the gardens, the Major was pacing about alongside a bed of canna-lilies, while a friend of his loaded and primed the pistols. They were of the old-fashioned type, but still used in duels. A young subaltern, who had offered to be my second, handed me a pistol. It appeared to be in good order. He then measured out twenty paces from where Major Crump stood, and positioned me there.

'Are you ready, gentlemen?' asked the Major's second. 'Death before dishonour and all that. And don't fire until I give the word!'

We raised our pistols and aimed at each other. My hand was trembling a little, so I did not aim too high. Major Crump's midriff presented the best target.

'Cock your locks!' shouted the Major's aide. 'Take good aim! Fire!'

I have no idea where the Major's ball went. If his aim was poor that day it was probably because of some heavy drinking the night before.

My shot proved quite effective, passing through both his cheeks—he must have turned side-on at the last moment—and knocking out all his teeth. When I walked up to him, he was lying on the dew-fresh grass, screaming blue murder.

'Well, that was on behalf of the tigers,' I said, adding a little insult to injury.

He spat out two or three mouthfuls of blood and flung his pistol away in disgust. It landed amongst the canna-lilies.

'You'd better be off,' said the young subaltern quietly. 'There'll be no hushing this up. He said that if he did not humiliate you today, he'd have you hanged for mutiny!'

Two

The Outlaw

I collected my horse from the stables, and without bothering to return to my quarters for my few belongings, rode out of the sleeping cantonment and took the Saharanpur road.

I made good progress before sunrise, knowing that it would be some time before anyone was sent after me. By the time the sun was up, I was in the sugar cane country near Sardhana. I thought of stopping there for a while—a cousin of mine was in the Begum's service—but decided that this would be too risky! Sardhana was only forty miles from Meerut.

I rode on, and it became hot and dusty. At a small irrigation canal I stopped to allow my horse to drink. Then we were off again, at a steady canter. I avoided the main towns, in case a telegraph message had been sent to one of them. Taking the village roads, I went unnoticed except by half-naked children who ran behind me for short distances, either cheering my progress or shouting imprecations.

My friend McNulty lived on the outskirts of Saharanpur, where he had some land and a large mango grove. It was good country for mangoes. Saharanpur was then a sleepy little town a few miles from the foothills, and my friend's home was an old Rohilla fortress which he had converted into a residence.

It was evening when I rode up to his house. He was glad to see me, for he was lonely on his estate. His wife, tired of their isolated existence had packed up and gone back to England the year before. McNulty was helping the Botanical Survey with its collection of plants from Nepal and the Indian foothills.

As dusk descended over the mango trees, and the flying-foxes began their nocturnal journeys to and fro, we sat out on his lawn and drank the local punch. I told him what had happened, and he said, 'The Army was never for you, my boy. You should be in the mountains, collecting plants for English gardens. Of course you'll have to lie low for a while. And you can't be seen in Saharanpur. This is the last outpost of the Empire, my boy. Go into the hills for some time, that's my advice to you. There's a hill raja who owes the British a favour or two, but he won't bother you. He can't really. There are no roads. It's a wonder he manages to collect any taxes. I shall lend you a few rupees. They'll go a long way. People are poor in these hills. But they are usually peacable, and they don't ask too many questions.'

I slept under the stars, on the ramparts of that strange old fort, and got up at the crack of dawn, when my good friend McNulty brought me a cup of sweet-scented Kashmiri tea.

We rode out together, reaching the foothills even as the sun drew an open wound across the sky. We forded a river on our horses. Then McNulty said, 'Well, this is where you take the high road and I take the low road. You'll be better off on foot now. This thoroughbred will only come to grief on these steep hillsides. I'll look after it for you.'

We shook hands, and he rode back across the river. The volume of water had abated since the end of the rains, and the two horses were never more than knee-deep in the water. And here the river opened out and lost some of its velocity. Higher up in the mountains the river would be an altogether different sort of creature.

Even though I had now been left entirely on my own, I began to grow in confidence. The greater freedom of the mountains lay ahead of me. Thinly populated, with scattered villages seldom visited by anyone from the plains, these sweeping ranges would, I felt sure, offer me refuge and shelter. Once across the valley I would be outside British territory. I wasn't quite sure whose territory I would be in, but where there are no roads it doesn't matter so much.

A path rose from the banks of the river and I followed it

upstream until the river was far below and the sky suddenly much nearer and clearer. There were hardly any trees on this particular range, just clumps of cacti, and as the sun rose higher, I began to look for shade. I found it near a spring, a mere trickle that came from the hillside near a stunted medlar tree.

I drank from the spring. The water was sweet and cool. This was better than the turgid waters of Meerut: I emptied my water-bottle (given to me by McNulty) and refilled it from the spring. Then I sat down to make an inventory of my belongings—all given or lent to me by my friend.

I had a .12-bore gun and a belt full of cartridges; some with ball and some with small shot. I could hunt for my food if need be. McNulty had also provided me with a variety of useful odds and ends—a blanket, a clasp-knife, a tin plate, a tin cup, a fork, a spoon, a towel; and, not least, a list of plants he wanted me to collect, described in some detail. The fork and spoon seemed a little superfluous at the time. I did not expect to find a dining-table laid out for me in the mountains. Nor would I need them for the sugar-coated Huntley and Palmer biscuits that I found in a tin, or for the bag of dried figs that I found at the bottom of the haversack.

The mountains had always beckoned to me, drawn me towards them. Well, they lay before me now, the whole vast expanse of the Himalayas, and to save my skin I had no alternative but to go as far as possible into their remotest regions. A plant-hunter I would be!

As I chewed a fig and contemplated a small white butterfly resting on the shining barrel of my gun, I heard the distant clatter of falling rocks. Looking down, I saw three horsemen on the other side of the river, trying to ride up a steep incline. They wore the uniforms of my regiment. And they had, apparently, decided to pursue me as far as they could, probably to take me back for a court-martial if they could take me alive.

I loaded my gun with two cartridges of small shot, and fired a warning shot across the river.

Some of the shot must have struck someone, or something, because a horse neighed and reared, and there was a shout, either of pain or of anger. Then someone called up the ravine, and his words carried quite distinctly in the clear air, on a breeze that was no more than a zephyr.

'You're a traitor, Wilson! Come back and take your medicine like a man!'

A rifle shot rang out, and a bullet snapped a branch off the medlar free. Perhaps I had been too considerate in using small shot on them!

Fortunately an outcrop of rock prevented them from getting a clear view of me. Creeping closer to the rocks, and taking more careful aim, I fired my second cartridge. The shot must have sprayed someone's arm, for I heard the sound of a rifle clattering to the ground. A volley of curses, followed by a volley of wild shooting, disturbed the peace of the hillside. Ravens and hawks flew up in alarm and disgust. Down in the gully the men were at a disadvantage, and they knew it. As the ground grew steeper, a man on foot would always have an advantage over a man on horseback.

The expedition retreated. They were unfamiliar with the terrain and once across the river they would be on someone else's territory. One horseman even shook his fist in my direction! Shades of the playing fields of Eton. They disappeared round a bend of the river and I was left alone on the hillside. The hawks and ravens returned to their resting-places. A horny-backed lizard stared balefully at me from a rock. I ate a fig and a biscuit, and decided it would be better to move further into the hills before taking a long rest.*

---

*Author's note: If I continue with this narrative, Wilson will move further into the interior, collecting plants and making friends. In a remote village he will meet the beautiful Gulabi (Rosebud) and fall in love with her. What enchanted him was her smile. It dropped over her face slowly, like sunshine moving over brown hills.

TIME STOPS AT SHAMLI

TIME STOPS AT SHAMLI

T he Dehra Express usually drew into Shamli at about five o'clock in the morning, at which time the station would be dimly lit and the jungle across the tracks would just be visible in the faint light of dawn. Shamli is a small station at the foot of the Siwalik hills, and the Siwaliks lie at the foot of the Himalayas, which in turn lie at the feet of God.

The station, I remember, had only one platform, an office for the station-master, and a waiting-room. The platform boasted a tea-stall, a fruit vendor, and a few stray dogs; not much else was required, because the train stopped at Shamli for only five minutes before rushing on into the forests.

Why it stopped at Shamli, I never could tell. Nobody got off the train and nobody got in. There were never any coolies on the platform. But the train would stand there a full five minutes, and the guard would blow his whistle, and presently Shamli would be left behind and forgotten. . . . until I passed that way again.

I was paying my relations in Saharanpur an annual visit, when the night train stopped at Shamli. I was thirty-six at the time, and still single.

On this particular journey, the train came into Shamli just as I awoke from a restless sleep. The third class compartment was crowded beyond capacity, and I had been sleeping in an upright position, with my back to the lavatory door. Now someone was trying to get into the lavatory. He was obviously hard pressed for time.

'I'm sorry, brother,' I said, moving as much as I could do to one side.

He stumbled into the closet without bothering to close the door.

'Where are we now?' I asked the man sitting beside me. He

319

was smoking a strong aromatic bidi.

'Shamli station,' he said, rubbing the palm of a large calloused hand over the frosted glass of the window.

I let the window down and stuck my head out. There was a cool breeze blowing down the platform, a breeze that whispered of autumn in the hills. As usual there was no activity, except for the fruit-vendor walking up and down the length of the train with his basket of mangoes balanced on his head. At the tea-stall, a kettle was streaming, but there was no one to mind it. I rested my forehead on the window-ledge, and let the breeze play on my temples. I had been feeling sick and giddy but there was a wild sweetness in the wind that I found soothing.

'Yes,' I said to myself, 'I wonder what happens in Shamli, behind the station walls.'

My fellow passenger offered me a beedi. He was a farmer, I think, on his way to Dehra. He had a long, untidy, sad moustache.

We had been more than five minutes at the station, I looked up and down the platform, but nobody was getting on or off the train. Presently the guard came walking past our compartment.

'What's the delay?' I asked him.

'Some obstruction further down the line,' he said.

'Will we be here long?'

'I don't know what the trouble is. About half-an-hour, at the least.'

My neighbour shrugged, and, throwing the remains of his beedi out of the window, closed his eyes and immediately fell asleep. I moved restlessly in my seat, and then the man came out of the lavatory, not so urgently now, and with obvious peace of mind. I closed the door for him.

I stood up and stretched; and this stretching of my limbs seemed to set in motion a stretching of the mind, and I found myself thinking: 'I am in no hurry to get to Saharanpur, and I have always wanted to see Shamli, behind the station walls. If I get down now, I can spend the day here, it will be better than sitting in this train for another hour. Then in the evening I can catch the next train home.'

In those days I never had the patience to wait for second

thoughts, and so I began pulling my small suitcase out from under the seat.

The farmer woke up and asked, 'What are you doing, brother?'

'I'm getting out,' I said.

He went to sleep again.

It would have taken at least fifteen minutes to reach the door, as people and their belongings cluttered up the passage; so I let my suitcase down from the window and followed it onto the platform.

There was no one to collect my ticket at the barrier, because there was obviously no point in keeping a man there to collect tickets from passengers who never came; and anyway, I had a through-ticket to my destination, which I would need in the evening.

I went out of the station and came to Shamli.

*

Outside the station there was a neem tree, and under it stood a tonga. The tonga-pony was nibbling at the grass at the foot of the tree. The youth in the front seat was the only human in sight; there were no signs of inhabitants or habitation. I approached the tonga, and the youth stared at me as though he couldn't believe his eyes.

'Where is Shamli?' I asked.

'Why, friend, this is Shamli,' he said.

I looked around again, but couldn't see any signs of life. A dusty road led past the station and disappeared in the forest.

'Does anyone live here?' I asked.

'I live here,' he said, with an engaging smile. He looked an amiable, happy-go-lucky fellow. He wore a cotton tunic and dirty white pyjamas.

'Where?' I asked.

'In my tonga, of course,' he said. 'I have had this pony five years now. I carry supplies to the hotel. But today the manager has not come to collect them. You are going to the hotel? I will take you.'

'Oh, so there's a hotel?'

'Well, friend, it is called that. And there are a few houses too, and some shops, but they are all about a mile from the station. If

321

they were not a mile from here, I would be out of business.'

I felt relieved, but I still had the feeling of having walked into a town consisting of one station, one pony and one man.

'You can take me,' I said. 'I'm staying till this evening.'

He heaved my suitcase into the seat beside him and I climbed in at the back. He flicked the reins and slapped his pony on the buttocks, and, with a roll and a lurch, the buggy moved off down the dusty forest road.

'What brings you here?' asked the youth.

'Nothing,' I said. 'The train was delayed, I was feeling bored, and so I got off.'

He did not believe that; but he didn't question me further. The sun was reaching up over the forest, but the road lay in the shadow of tall trees, eucalyptus, mango and neem.

'Not many people stay in the hotel,' he said. 'So it is cheap, you will get a room for five rupees.'

'Who is the manager?'

'Mr Satish Dayal. It is his father's property. Satish Dayal could not pass his exams or get a job, so his father sent him here to look after the hotel.'

The jungle thinned out, and we passed a temple, a mosque, a few small shops. There was a strong smell of burnt sugar in the air, and in the distance I saw a factory chimney: that, then, was the reason for Shamli's existence. We passed a bullock-cart laden with sugar cane. The road went through fields of cane and maize, and then, just as we were about to re-enter the jungle, the youth pulled his horse to a side road and the hotel came in sight.

It was a small white bungalow, with a garden in the front, banana trees at the sides, and an orchard of guava trees at the back. We came jingling up to the front veranda. Nobody appeared, nor was there any sign of life on the premises.

'They are all asleep,' said the youth.

I said, 'I'll sit in the veranda and wait.' I got down from the tonga, and the youth dropped my case on the veranda steps. Then he stooped in front of me, smiling amiably, waiting to be paid.

'Well, how much?' I asked.

'As a friend, only one rupee.'

'That's too much,' I complained. 'This is not Delhi.'

'This is Shamli,' he said. 'I am the only tonga in Shamli. You may not pay me anything, if that is your wish. But then, I will not take you back to the station this evening, you will have to walk.'

I gave him the rupee. He had both charm and cunning, an effective combination.

'Come in the evening at about six,' I said.

'I will come,' he said, with an infectious smile, 'Don't worry.' I waited till the tonga had gone round the bend in the road before walking up the veranda steps.

The doors of the house were closed, and there were no bells to ring. I didn't have a watch, but I judged the time to be a little past six o'clock. The hotel didn't look very impressive; the whitewash was coming off the walls, and the cane-chairs on the veranda were old and crooked. A stag's head was mounted over the front door, but one of its glass eyes had fallen out; I had often heard hunters speak of how beautiful an animal looked before it died, but how could anyone with true love of the beautiful care for the stuffed head of an animal, grotesquely mounted, with no resemblance to its living aspect?

I felt too restless to take any of the chairs. I began pacing up and down the veranda, wondering if I should start banging on the doors. Perhaps the hotel was deserted; perhaps the tonga-driver had played a trick on me. I began to regret my impulsiveness in leaving the train. When 'I saw the manager I would have to invent a reason for coming to his hotel. I was good at inventing reasons. I would tell him that a friend of mine had stayed here some years ago, and that I was trying to trace him. I decided that my friend would have to be a little eccentric (having chosen Shamli to live in), that he had become a recluse, shutting himself off from the world; his parents—no, his sister—for his parents would be dead—had asked me to find him if I could; and, as he had last been heard of in Shamli, I had taken the opportunity to enquire after him. His name would be Major Roberts, retired.

I heard a tap running at the side of the building, and walking around, found a young man bathing at the tap. He was strong and well-built, and slapped himself on the body with great enthusiasm. He had not seen me approaching, and I waited until he had finished bathing and had begun to dry himself.

'Hullo,' I said.

He turned at the sound of my voice, and looked at me for a few moments with a puzzled expression. He had a round, cheerful face and crisp black hair. He smiled slowly, but it was a more genuine smile than the tonga-driver's. So far I had met two people in Shamli, and they were both smilers; that should have cheered me, but it didn't. 'You have come to stay?' he asked, in a slow easygoing voice.

'Just for the day,' I said. 'You work here?'

'Yes, my name is Daya Ram. The manager is asleep just now, but I will find a room for you.'

He pulled on his vest and pyjamas, and accompanied me back to the veranda. Here he picked up my suitcase and, unlocking a side door, led me into the house. We went down a passage way; then Daya Ram stopped at the door on the right, pushed it open, and took me into a small, sunny room that had a window looking out on the orchard. There was a bed, a desk, a couple of cane-chairs, and a frayed and faded red carpet.

'Is it all right?' said Daya Ram.

'Perfectly all right.'

They have breakfast at eight o'clock. But if you are hungry, I will make something for you now.'

'No, it's all right. Are you the cook too?'

'I do everything here.'

'Do you like it?'

'No,' he said, and then added, in a sudden burst of confidence, 'there are no women for a man like me.'

'Why don't you leave, then?'

'I will,' he said, with a doubtful look on his face. 'I will leave....'

After he had gone I shut the door and went into the bathroom to bathe. The cold water refreshed me and made me feel one with the world. After I had dried myself, I sat on the bed, in front of the

324

open window. A cool breeze, smelling of rain, came through the window and played over my body. I thought I saw a movement among the trees.

And getting closer to the window, I saw a girl on a swing. She was a small girl, all by herself, and she was swinging to and fro, and singing, and her song carried faintly on the breeze.

I dressed quickly, and left my room. The girl's dress was billowing in the breeze, her pigtails flying about. When she saw me approaching, she stopped swinging, and stared at me. I stopped a little distance away.

'Who are you?' she asked.

'A ghost,' I replied.

'You look like one,' she said.

I decided to take this as a compliment, as I was determined to make friends. I did not smile at her, because some children dislike adults who smile at them all the time.

'What's your name?' I asked.

'Kiran,' she said, 'I'm ten.'

'You are getting old.'

'Well, we all have to grow old one day. Aren't you coming any closer?'

'May I?' I asked.

'You may. You can push the swing.'

One pigtail lay across the girl's chest, the other behind her shoulder. She had a serious face, and obviously felt she had responsibilities; she seemed to be in a hurry to grow up, and I suppose she had no time for anyone who treated her as a child. I pushed the swing, until it went higher and higher, and then I stopped pushing, so that she came lower each time and we could talk.

'Tell me about the people who live here,' I said.

'There is Heera,' she said. 'He's the gardener. He's nearly a hundred. You can see him behind the hedges in the garden. You can't see him unless you look hard. He tells me stories, a new story every day. He's much better than the people in the hotel, and so is Daya Ram.'

'Yes, I met Daya Ram.'

'He's my bodyguard. He brings me nice things from the kitchen when no one is looking.'

'You don't stay here?'

'No, I live in another house, you can't see it from here. My father is the manager of the factory.'

'Aren't there any other children to play with?' I asked.

'I don't know any,' she said.

'And the people staying here?'

'Oh, *they*.' Apparently Kiran didn't think much of the hotel guests. 'Miss Deeds is funny when she's drunk. And Mr Lin is the *strangest*.'

'And what about the manager, Mr Dayal?'

'He's mean. And he gets frightened of slightest things. But Mrs Dayal is nice, she lets me take flowers home. But she doesn't talk much.'

I was fascinated by Kiran's ruthless summing up of the guests. I brought the swing to a stand-still and asked, 'And what do you think of me?'

'I don't know as yet,' said Kiran quite seriously. 'I'll think about you.'

*

As I came back to the hotel, I heard the sound of a piano in one of the front rooms. I didn't know enough about music to be able to recognize the piece, but it had sweetness and melody, though it was played with some hesitancy. As I came nearer, the sweetness deserted the music, probably because the piano was out of tune.

The person at the piano had distinctive Mongolian features, and so I presumed he was Mr Lin. He hadn't seen me enter the room, and I stood beside the curtains of the door, watching him play. He had full round lips, and high slanting cheekbones. His eyes were large and round and full of melancholy. His long, slender fingers hardly touched the keys.

I came nearer; and then he looked up at me, without any show of surprise or displeasure, and kept on playing.

'What are you playing?' I asked.

'Chopin,' he said.

'Oh, yes. It's nice, but the piano is fighting it.'

'I know. This piano belonged to one of Kipling's aunts. It hasn't been tuned since the last century.'

'Do you live here?'

'No, I come from Calcutta,' he answered readily. 'I have some business here with the sugar cane people, actually, though I am not a businessman.' He was playing softly all the time, so that our conversation was not lost in the music. 'I don't know anything about business. But I have to do something.'

'Where did you learn to play the piano?'

'In Singapore. A French lady taught me. She had great hopes of my becoming a concert pianist when I grow up. I would have toured Europe and America.'

'Why didn't you?'

'We left during the War, and I had to give up my lessons.'

'And why did you go to Calcutta?'

'My father is a Calcutta businessman. What do you do, and why do you come here?' he asked. 'If I am not being too inquisitive.'

Before I could answer, a bell rang, loud and continuously, drowning the music and conversation.

'Breakfast,' said Mr Lin.

A thin dark man, wearing glasses, stepped nervously into the room and peered at me in an anxious manner.

'You arrived last night?'

'That's right,' I said, 'I just want to stay the day. I think you're the manager?'

'Yes. Would you like to sign the register?'

I went with him past the bar and into the office. I wrote my name and Mussoorie address in the register, and the duration of my stay. I paused at the column marked 'Profession', thought it would be best to fill it with something and wrote 'Author'.

'You are here on business?' asked Mr Dayal.

'No, not exactly. You see, I'm looking for a friend of mine who was heard of in Shamli, about three years ago. I thought I'd make a few enquiries in case he's still here.'

'What was his name? Perhaps he stayed here.'

'Major Roberts,' I said. 'An Anglo-Indian.'

'Well, you can look through the old registers after breakfast.'

He accompanied me into the dining-room. The establishment was really more of a boarding-house than a hotel, because Mr Dayal ate with his guests. There was a round mahogany dining-table in the centre of the room, and Mr Lin was the only one seated at it. Daya Ram hovered about with plates and trays. I took my seat next to Lin, and, as I did so, a door opened from the passage, and a woman of about thirty-five came in.

She had on a skirt and blouse, which accentuated a firm, well-rounded figure, and she walked on high-heels, with a rhythmical swaying of the hips. She had an uninteresting face, camouflaged with lipstick, rouge and powder—the powder so thick that it had become embedded in the natural lines of her face—but her figure compelled admiration.

'Miss Deeds,' whispered Lin.

There was a false note to her greeting.

'Hallo, everyone,' she said heartily, straining for effect. 'Why are you all so quiet? Has Mr Lin been playing the Funeral March again?' She sat down and continued talking. 'Really, we must have a dance or something to liven things up. You must know some good numbers, Lin, after your experience of Singapore night-clubs. What's for breakfast? Boiled eggs. Daya Ram, can't you make an omelette for a change? I know you're not a professional cook, but you don't have to give us the same thing every day, and there's absolutely no reason why you should burn the toast. You'll have to do something about a cook, Mr Dayal.' Then she noticed me sitting opposite her. 'Oh, hallo,' she said, genuinely surprised. She gave me a long appraising look.

'This gentleman,' said Mr Dayal introducing me, 'is an author.'

'That's nice,' said Miss Deeds. 'Are you married?'

'No,' I said. 'Are you?'

'Funny, isn't it,' she said, without taking offence, 'no one in this house seems to be married.'

'I'm married,' said Mr Dayal.

'Oh yes, of course,' said Miss Deeds. 'And what brings you to Shamli?' she asked, turning to me.

'I'm looking for a friend called Major Roberts.'

Lin gave an exclamation of surprise. I thought he had seen through my deception.

But another game had begun.

'I knew him,' said Lin. 'A great friend of mine.'

*

'Yes,' continued Lin. 'I knew him. A good chap, Major Roberts.'

Well, there I was, inventing people to suit my convenience, and people like Mr Lin started inventing relationships with them. I was too intrigued to try and discourage him. I wanted to see how far he would go.

'When did you meet him?' asked Lin, taking the initiative.

'Oh, only about three years back. Just before he disappeared. He was last heard of in Shamli.'

'Yes, I heard he was here,' said Lin. 'But he went away, when he thought his relatives had traced him. He went into the mountains near Tibet.'

'Did he?' I said, unwilling to be instructed further. 'What part of the country? I come from the hills myself. I know the Mana and Niti passes quite well. If you have any idea of exactly where he went, I think I could find him.' I had the advantage in this exchange, because I was the one who had originally invented Roberts. Yet I couldn't bring myself to end his deception, probably because I felt sorry for him. A happy man wouldn't take the trouble of inventing friendships with people who didn't exist, he'd be too busy with friends who did.

'You've had a lonely life, Mr Lin?' I asked.

'Lonely?' said Mr Lin, with forced incredulousness. 'I'd never been lonely till I came here a month ago. When I was in Singapore . . .'

'You never get any letters though, do you?' asked Miss Deeds suddenly.

Lin was silent for a moment. Then he said: 'Do you?'

Miss Deeds lifted her head a little, as a horse does when it is annoyed, and I thought her pride had been hurt; but then she laughed unobtrusively and tossed her head.

'I never write letters,' she said. 'My friends gave me up as hopeless years ago. They know it's no use writing to me, because they rarely get a reply. They call me the Jungle Princess.'

Mr Dayal tittered, and I found it hard to suppress a smile. To cover up my smile I asked, 'You teach here?'

'Yes, I teach at the girls' school,' she said with a frown. 'But don't talk to me about teaching. I have enough of it all day.'

'You don't like teaching?'

She gave an aggressive look. 'Should I?' she asked.

'Shouldn't you?' I said.

She paused, and then said, 'Who are you, anyway, the Inspector of Schools?'

'No,' said Mr Dayal who wasn't following very well, 'he's a journalist.'

'I've heard they are nosey,' said Miss Deeds.

Once again Lin interrupted to steer the conversation away from a delicate issue.

'Where's Mrs Dayal this morning?' asked Lin.

'She spent the night with our neighbours,' said Mr Dayal. 'She should be here after lunch.'

It was the first time Mrs Dayal had been mentioned. Nobody spoke either well or ill of her; I suspected that she kept her distance from the others, avoiding familiarity. I began to wonder about Mrs Dayal.

*

Dayaram came in from the veranda looking worried.

'Heera's dog has disappeared,' he said. 'He thinks a leopard took it.'

Heera, the gardener, was standing respectfully outside on the veranda steps. We all hurried out to him, firing questions which he didn't try to answer.

'Yes. It's a leopard,' said Kiran, appearing from behind Heera. 'It's going to come into the hotel,' she added cheerfully.

'Be quiet,' said Satish Dayal crossly.

'There are pug marks under the trees,' said Daya Ram.

Mr Dayal, who seemed to know little about leopards or pug marks, said, 'I will take a look,' and led the way to the orchard, the rest of us trailing behind in an ill-assorted procession.

There were marks on the soft earth in the orchard (they could have been a leopard's) which went in the direction of the river-bed. Mr Dayal paled a little and went hurrying back to the hotel. Heera returned to the front garden, the least excited, the most sorrowful. Everyone else was thinking of a leopard, but he was thinking of the dog.

I followed him, and watched him weeding the sunflower beds. His face was wrinkled like a walnut, but his eyes were clear and bright. His hands were thin, and bony, but there was a deftness and power in the wrist and fingers, and the weeds flew fast from his spade. He had a cracked, parchment-like skin. I could not help thinking of the gloss and glow of Daya Ram's limbs, as I had seen them when he was bathing, and wondered if Heera's had once been like that and if Daya Ram's would ever be like this, and both possibilities—or were they probabilities—saddened me. Our skin, I thought, is like the leaf of a tree, young and green and shiny; then it gets darker and heavier, sometimes spotted with disease, sometimes eaten away; then fading, yellow and red, then falling, crumbling into dust or feeding the flames of fire. I looked at my own skin, still smooth, not coarsened by labour; I thought of Kiran's fresh rose-tinted complexion; Miss Deed's skin, hard and dry; Lin's pale taut skin, stretched tightly across his prominent cheeks and forehead; and Mr Dayal's grey skin, growing thick hair. And I wondered about Mrs Dayal and the kind of skin she would have.

'Did you have the dog for long?' I asked Heera.

He looked up with surprise, for he had been unaware of my

presence.

'Six years, sahib,' he said. 'He was not a clever dog, but he was very friendly. He followed me home one day, when I was coming back from the bazaar. I kept telling him to go away, but he wouldn't. It was a long walk and so I began talking to him. I liked talking to him, and I have always talked with him, and we have understood each other. That first night, when I came home, I shut the gate between us. But he stood on the other side, looking at me with trusting eyes. Why did he have to look at me like that?'

'So you kept him?'

'Yes, I could never forget the way he looked at me. I shall feel lonely now, because he was my only companion. My wife and son died long ago. It seems I am to stay here forever, until everyone has gone, until there are only ghosts in Shamli. Already the ghosts are here. . . .'

I heard a light footfall behind me and turned to find Kiran. The bare-footed girl stood beside the gardener, and with her toes began to pull at the weeds.

'You are a lazy one,' said the old man. 'If you want to help me, sit down and use your hands.'

I looked at the girl's fair round face, and in her bright eyes I saw something old and wise; and I looked into the old man's wise eyes, and saw something forever bright and young. The skin cannot change the eyes; the eyes are the true reflection of a man's age and sensibilities; even a blind man has hidden eyes.

'I hope we shall find the dog,' said Kiran. 'But I would like a leopard. Nothing ever happens here.'

'Not now,' sighed Heera. 'Not now. . . . Why, once there was a band and people danced till morning, but now. . . .' He paused, lost in thought, and then said: 'I have always been here. I was here before Shamli.'

'Before the station?'

'Before there was a station, or a factory, or a bazaar. It was a village then, and the only way to get here was by bullock-cart. Then a bus service was started, then the railway lines were laid and a station built, then they started the sugar factory, and for a few years

Shamli was a town. But the jungle was bigger than the town. The rains were heavy and malaria was everywhere. People didn't stay long in Shamli. Gradually, they went back into the hills. Sometimes I too wanted to go back to the hills, but what is the use when you are old and have no one left in the world except a few flowers in a troublesome garden. I had to choose between the flowers and the hills, and I chose the flowers. I am tired now, and old, but I am not tired of flowers.'

I could see that his real world was the garden; there was more variety in his flower-beds than there was in the town of Shamli. Every month, every day, there were new flowers in the garden, but there were always the same people in Shamli.

I left Kiran with the old man, and returned to my room. It must have been about eleven o'clock.

*

I was facing the window when I heard my door being opened. Turning, I perceived the barrel of a gun moving slowly round the edge of the door. Behind the gun was Satish Dayal, looking hot and sweaty. I didn't know what his intentions were; so, deciding it would be better to act first and reason later, I grabbed a pillow from the bed and flung it in his face. I then threw myself at his legs and brought him crashing down to the ground.

When we got up, I was holding the gun. It was an old Enfield rifle, probably dating back to the Afghan wars, the kind that goes off at the least encouragement.

'But—but—why?' stammered the dishevelled and alarmed Mr Dayal.

'I don't know,' I said menacingly. 'Why did you come in here pointing this at me?'

'I wasn't pointing it at you. It's for the leopard.'

'Oh, so you came into my room looking for a leopard? You have, I presume been stalking one about the hotel?' (By now I was convinced that Mr Dayal had taken leave of his senses and was hunting imaginary leopards.)

'No, no,' cried the distraught man, becoming more confused, 'I was looking for you. I wanted to ask you if you could use a gun. I was thinking we should go looking for the leopard that took Heera's dog. Neither Mr Lin nor I can shoot.'

'Your gun is not up-to-date,' I said. 'It's not at all suitable for hunting leopards. A stout stick would be more effective. Why don't we arm ourselves with lathis and make a general assault?'

I said this banteringly, but Mr Dayal took the idea quite seriously. 'Yes, yes,' he said with alacrity, 'Daya Ram has got one or two lathis in the godown. The three of us could make an expedition. I have asked Mr Lin but he says he doesn't want to have anything to do with leopards.'

'What about our Jungle Princess?' I said. 'Miss Deeds should be pretty good with a lathi.'

'Yes, yes,' said Mr Dayal humourlessly 'but we'd better not ask her.'

Collecting Daya Ram and two lathis, we set off for the orchard and began following the pug marks through the trees. It took us ten minutes to reach the river-bed, a dry hot rocky place; then we went into the jungle, Mr Dayal keeping well to the rear. The atmosphere was heavy and humid, and there was not a breath of air amongst the trees. When a parrot squawked suddenly, shattering the silence, Mr Dayal let out a startled exclamation and started for home.

'What was that?' he asked nervously.

'A bird,' I explained.

'I think we should go back now,' he said. 'I don't think the leopard's here.'

'You never know with leopards,' I said, 'they could be anywhere.'

Mr Dayal stepped away from the bushes. 'I'll have to go,' he said. 'I have a lot of work. You keep a lathi with you, and I'll send Daya Ram back later.'

'That's very thoughtful of you,' I said.

Daya Ram scratched his head and reluctantly followed his employer back through the trees. I moved on slowly, down the little-used path, wondering if I should also return. I saw two monkeys playing on the branch of a tree, and decided that there could be no danger in the immediate vicinity.

Presently I came to a clearing where there was a pool of fresh clear water. It was fed by a small stream that came suddenly, like a snake, out of the long grass. The water looked cool and inviting; laying down the lathi and taking off my clothes, I ran down the bank until I was waist-deep in the middle of the pool. I splashed about for some time, before emerging; then I lay on the soft grass and allowed the sun to dry my body. I closed my eyes and gave myself up to beautiful thoughts. I had forgotten all about leopards.

I must have slept for about half-an-hour because when I awoke, I found that Daya Ram had come back and was vigorously threshing about in the narrow confines of the pool. I sat up and asked him the time.

Twelve o'clock,' he shouted, coming out of water, his dripping body all gold and silver in sunlight. 'They will be waiting for dinner.'

'Let them wait,' I said.

It was a relief to talk to Daya Ram, after the uneasy conversations in the lounge and dining-room.

'Dayal sahib will be angry with me.'

'I'll tell him we found the trail of the leopard, and that we went so far into the jungle that we lost our way. As Miss Deeds is so critical of the food, let her cook the meal.'

'Oh, she only talks like that,' said Daya Ram. 'Inside she is very soft. She is too soft in some ways.'

'She should be married.'

'Well, she would like to be. Only there is no one to marry her. When she came here she was engaged to be married to an English army captain; I think she loved him, but she is the sort of person who cannot help loving many men all at once, and the captain could not understand that—it is just the way she is made, I suppose. She is always ready to fall in love.'

'You seem to know,' I said.

'Oh, yes.'

We dressed and walked back to the hotel. In a few hours, I

335

thought, the tonga will come for me and I will be back at the station; the mysterious charm of Shamli will be no more, but whenever I pass this way I will wonder about these people, about Miss Deeds and Lin and Mrs. Dayal.

Mrs Dayal. . . . She was the one person I had yet to meet; it was with some excitement and curiosity that I looked forward to meeting her; she was about the only mystery left to Shamli, now, and perhaps she would be no mystery when I met her. And yet. . . I felt that perhaps she would justify the impulse that made me get down from the train.

I could have asked Daya Ram about Mrs Dayal, and so satisfied my curiosity; but I wanted to discover her for myself. Half the day was left to me, and I didn't want my game to finish too early.

I walked towards the veranda, and the sound of the piano came through the open door.

'I wish Mr Lin would play something cheerful,' said Miss Deeds. 'He's obsessed with the Funeral March. Do you dance?'

'Oh no,' I said.

She looked disappointed. But when Lin left the piano, she went into the lounge and sat down on the stool. I stood at the door watching her, wondering what she would do. Lin left the room, somewhat resentfully.

She began to play an old song, which I remembered having heard in a film or on a gramophone record. She sang while she played, in a slightly harsh but pleasant voice:

Rolling round the world
Looking for the sunshine
I know I'm going to find some day. . . .

Then she played 'Am I blue?' and 'Darling, Je Vous Aime Beaucoup.' She sat there singing in a deep husky voice, her eyes a little misty, her hard face suddenly kind and sloppy. When the dinner gong rang, she broke off playing, and shook off her sentimental mood, and laughed derisively at herself.

I don't remember that lunch. I hadn't slept much since the previous night and I was beginning to feel the strain of my journey.

The swim had refreshed me, but it had also made me drowsy. I ate quite well, though, of rice and kofta curry, and then, feeling sleepy, made for the garden to find a shady tree.

There were some books on the shelf in the lounge, and I ran my eye over them in search of one that might condition sleep. But they were too dull to do even that. So I went into the garden, and there was Kiran on the swing, and I went to her tree and sat down on the grass.

'Did you find the leopard?' she asked.

'No,' I said, with a yawn.

'Tell me a story.'

'You tell me one,' I said.

'All right. Once there was a lazy man with long legs, who was always yawning and wanting to fall asleep. . . .'

I watched the swaying motions of the swing and the movements of the girl's bare legs, and a tiny insect kept buzzing about in front of my nose. . . . 'and fall asleep, and the reason for this was that he liked to dream.' I blew the insect away, and the swing became hazy and distant, and Kiran was a blurred figure in the trees. . . . 'liked to dream, and what do you think he dreamt about. . . .' dreamt about, dreamt about. . . .

*

When I awoke there was that cool rain-scented breeze blowing across the garden. I remember lying on the grass with my eyes closed, listening to the swishing of the swing. Either I had not slept long, or Kiran had been a long time on the swing; it was moving slowly now, in a more leisurely fashion, without much sound. I opened my eyes and saw that my arm was stained with the juice of the grass beneath me. Looking up, I expected to see Kiran's legs waving above me. But instead I saw dark slim feet and above them the folds of a sari. I straightened up against the trunk of the tree to look closer at Kiran, but Kiran wasn't there, it was someone else in the swing, a young woman in a pink sari and with a red rose in her hair.

She had stopped the swing with her foot on the ground, and she was smiling at me.

It wasn't a smile you could see, it was a tender fleeting movement that came suddenly and was gone at the same time, and its going was sad. I thought of the others' smiles, just as I had thought of their skins: the tonga-driver's friendly, deceptive; Daya Ram's wide sincere smile; Miss Deed's cynical, derisive-smile. And looking at Sushila, I knew a smile could never change. She had always smiled that way.

'You haven't changed,' she said.

I was standing up now, though still leaning against the tree for support. Though I had never thought much about the *sound* of her voice, it seemed as familiar as the sounds of yesterday.

'You haven't changed either,' I said. 'But where did you come from?' I wasn't sure yet if I was awake or dreaming.

She laughed, as she had always laughed at me.

'I came from behind the tree. The little girl has gone.'

'Yes, I'm dreaming,' I said helplessly.

'But what brings you here?'

'I don't know. At least I didn't know when I came. But it must have been you. The train stopped at Shamli, and I don't know why, but I decided I would spend the day here, behind the station walls. You must be married now, Sushila.'

'Yes, I am married to Mr Dayal, the manager of the hotel. And what has been happening to you?'

'I am still a writer, still poor, and still living in Mussoorie.'

'When were you last in Delhi?' she asked. 'I don't mean Delhi, I mean at home.'

'I have not been to your home since you were there.'

'Oh, my friend,' she said, getting up suddenly and coming to me, 'I want to talk about our home and Sunil and our friends and all those things that are so far away now. I have been here two years, and I am already feeling old. I keep remembering our home, how young I was, how happy, and I am all alone with memories. But now you are here! It was a bit of magic, I came through the trees after Kiran had gone, and there you were, fast asleep under the tree. I didn't wake you then, because I wanted to see you wake up.'

'As I used to watch you wake up . . .'

She was near me and I could look at her more closely. Her cheeks did not have the same freshness; they were a little pale, and she was thinner now, but her eyes were the same, smiling the same way. Her voice was the same. Her fingers, when she took my hand, were the same warm delicate fingers.

'Talk to me,' she said. 'Tell me about yourself.'

'You tell me,' I said.

'I am here,' she said. 'That is all there is about myself.'

'Then let us sit down and I'll talk.'

'Not here,' she took my hand and led me through the trees. 'Come with me.'

I heard the jingle of a tonga-bell and a faint shout. I stopped and laughed.

'My tonga,' I said, 'It has come to take me back to the station.'

'But you are not going,' said Sushila, immediately downcast.

'I will tell him to come in the morning,' I said. 'I will spend the night in your Shamli.'

I walked to the front of the hotel where the tonga was waiting. I was glad no one else was in sight. The youth was smiling at me in his most appealing manner.

'I'm not going today,' I said. 'Will you come tomorrow morning?'

'I can come whenever you like, friend. But you will have to pay for every trip, because it is a long way from the station even if my tonga is empty.'

'All right, how much?'

'Usual fare, friend, one rupee.'

I didn't try to argue but resignedly gave him the rupee. He cracked his whip and pulled on the reins, and the carriage moved off.

'If you don't leave tomorrow,' the youth called out after me, 'you'll never leave Shamli!'

I walked back to trees, but I couldn't find Sushila.

'Sushila, where are you?' I called, but I might have been

speaking to the trees, for I had no reply. There was a small path going through the orchard, and on the path I saw a rose petal. I walked a little further and saw another petal. They were from Sushila's red rose. I walked on down the path until I had skirted the orchard, and then the path went along the frame of the jungle, past a clump of bamboos, and here the grass was a lush green as though it had been constantly watered. I was still finding rose petals. I heard the chatter of seven-sisters, and the call of a hoopoe. The path bent to meet a stream, there was a willow coming down to the water's edge, and Sushila was waiting there.

'Why didn't you wait?' I said.

'I wanted to see if you were as good at following me as you used to be.'

'Well, I am,' I said, sitting down beside her on the grassy bank of the stream. 'Even if I'm out of practice.'

'Yes, I remember the time you climbed onto an apple tree to pick some fruit for me. You got up all right but then you couldn't come down again. I had to climb up myself and help you.'

'I don't remember that,' I said.

'Of course you do.'

'It must have been your other friend, Pramod.

'I never climbed trees with Pramod.'

'Well, I don't remember.'

I looked at the little stream that ran past us. The water was no more than ankle-deep, cold and clear and a sparkling, like the mountain-stream near my home. I took off my shoes, rolled up my trousers, and put my feet in the water. Sushila's feet joined mine.

At first I had wanted to ask her about her marriage, whether she was happy or not, what she thought of her husband; but now I couldn't ask her these things, they seemed far away and of little importance. I could think of nothing she had in common with Mr Dayal; I felt that her charm and attractiveness and warmth could not have been appreciated, or even noticed, by that curiously distracted man. He was much older than her, of course; probably older than me; he was obviously not her choice but her parents'; and so far they were childless. Had there been children, I don't think

Sushila would have minded Mr Dayal as her husband. Children would have made up for the absence of passion—or was there passion in Satish Dayal?. . . . I remembered having heard that Sushila had been married to a man she didn't like; I remembered having shrugged off the news, because it meant she would never come my way again, and I have never yearned after something that has been irredeemably lost. But she *had* come my way again. And was she still lost? That was what I wanted to know. . . .

'What do you do with yourself all day?' I asked.

'Oh, I visit the school and help with the classes. It is the only interest I have in this place. The hotel is terrible. I try to keep away from it as much as I can.'

'And what about the guests?'

'Oh, don't let us talk about them. Let us talk about ourselves. Do you have to go tomorrow?'

'Yes, I suppose so. Will you always be in this place?'

'I suppose so.'

That made me silent. I took her hand, and my feet churned up the mud at the bottom of the stream. As the mud subsided, I saw Sushila's face reflected in the water; and looking up at her again, into her dark eyes, the old yearning returned and I wanted to care for her and protect her, I wanted to take her away from that place, from sorrowful Shamli; I wanted her to live again. Of course, I had forgotten all about my poor finances, Sushila's family, and the shoes I wore, which were my last pair. The uplift I was experiencing in this meeting with Sushila, who had always, throughout her childhood and youth, bewitched me as no other had ever bewitched me, made me reckless and impulsive.

I lifted her hand to my lips and kissed her in the soft of the palm.

'Can I kiss you?' I said.

'You have just done so.'

'Can I kiss you?' I repeated.

'It is not necessary.'

I leaned over and kissed her slender neck. I knew she would like this, because that was where I had kissed her often before. I kissed her in the soft of the throat, where it tickled.

'It is not necessary,' she said, but she ran her fingers through my hair and let them rest there. I kissed her behind the ear then, and kept my mouth to her ear and whispered, 'Can I kiss you?'

She turned her face to me so that we were deep in each other's eyes, and I kissed her again, and we put our arms around each other and lay together on the grass, with the water running over our feet; and we said nothing at all, simply lay there for what seemed like several years, or until the first drop of rain.

It was a big wet drop, and it splashed on Sushila's cheek, just next to mine, and ran down to her lips, so that I had to kiss her again. The next big drop splattered on the tip of my nose, and Sushila laughed and sat up. Little ringlets were forming on the stream where the rain-drops hit the water, and above us there was a pattering on the banana leaves.

'We must go,' said Sushila.

We started homewards, but had not gone far before it was raining steadily, and Sushila's hair came loose and streamed down her body. The rain fell harder, and we had to hop over pools and avoid the soft mud. Sushila's sari was plastered to her body, accentuating her ripe, thrusting breasts, and I was excited to passion, and pulled her beneath a big tree and crushed her in my arms and kissed her rain-kissed mouth. And then I thought she was crying, but I wasn't sure, because it might have been the rain-drops on her cheeks.

'Come away with me,' I said. 'Leave this place. Come away with me tomorrow morning. We will go somewhere where nobody will know us or come between us.'

She smiled at me and said, 'You are still a dreamer, aren't you?'

'Why can't you come?'

'I am married, it is as simple as that.'

'If it is that simple you can come.'

'I have to think of my parents, too. It would break my father's heart if I were to do what you are proposing. And you are proposing it without a thought for the consequences.'

342

'You are too practical,' I said.

'If women were not practical, most marriages would be failures.'

'So your marriage is a success?'

'Of course it is, as a marriage. I am not happy and I do not love him, but neither am I so unhappy that I should hate him. Sometimes, for our own sakes, we have to think of the happiness of others. What happiness would we have living in hiding from everyone we once knew and cared for. Don't be a fool. I am always here and you can come to see me, and nobody will be made unhappy by it. But take me away and we will only have regrets.'

'You don't love me,' I said foolishly.

'That sad word *love*,' she said, and became pensive and silent.

I could say no more. I was angry again, and rebellious, and there was no one and nothing to rebel against. I could not understand someone who was afraid to break away from an unhappy existence lest that existence should become unhappier; I had always considered it an admirable thing to break away from security and respectability. Of course it is easier for a man to do this, a man can look after himself, he can do without neighbours and the approval of the local society. A woman, I reasoned, would do anything for love provided it was not at the price of security; for a woman loves security as much as a man loves independence.

'I must go back now,' said Sushila. 'You follow a little later.'

'All you wanted to do was talk,' I complained.

She laughed at that, and pulled me playfully by the hair; then she ran out from under the tree, springing across the grass, and the wet mud flew up and flecked her legs. I watched her through the thin curtain of rain, until she reached the veranda. She turned to wave to me, and then skipped into the hotel. She was still young; but I was no younger.

*

The rain had lessened, but I didn't know what to do with myself. The hotel was uninviting, and it was too late to leave Shamli. If the grass hadn't been wet I would have preferred to sleep under a tree rather than return to the hotel to sit at that alarming dining-table.

I came out from under the trees and crossed the garden. But instead of making for the veranda I went round to the back of the hotel. Smoke issuing from the barred window of a back room told me I had probably found the kitchen. Daya Ram was inside, squatting in front of a stove, stirring a pot of stew. The stew smelt appetizing. Daya Ram looked up and smiled at me.

'I thought you must have gone,' he said.

'I'll go in the morning,' I said pulling myself up on an empty table. Then I had one of my sudden ideas and said, 'Why don't you come with me? I can find you a good job in Mussoorie. How much do you get paid here?'

'Fifty rupees a month. But I haven't been paid for three months.'

'Could you get your pay before tomorrow morning?'

'No, I won't get anything until one of the guests pays a bill. Miss Deeds owes about fifty rupees on whisky alone. She will pay up, she says, when the school pays her salary. And the school can't pay her until they collect the children's fees. That is how bankrupt everyone is in Shamli.'

'I see,' I said, though I didn't see. 'But Mr Dayal can't hold back your pay just because his guests haven't paid their bills.'

'He can, if he hasn't got any money.'

'I see,' I said. 'Anyway, I will give you my address. You can come when you are free.'

'I will take it from the register,' he said.

I edged over to the stove and, leaning over, sniffed at the stew. 'I'll eat mine now,' I said; and without giving Daya Ram a chance to object, I lifted a plate off the shelf, took hold of the stirring-spoon and helped myself from the pot.

'There's rice too,' said Daya Ram.

I filled another plate with rice and then got busy with my fingers. After ten minutes I had finished. I sat back comfortably in the hotel, in a ruminative mood. With my stomach full I could take a more tolerant view of life and people. I could understand Sushila's apprehensions, Lin's delicate lying, and Miss Deeds' aggressiveness. Daya Ram went out to sound the dinner-gong, and I trailed back to my room.

From the window of my room I saw Kiran running across the lawn, and I called to her, but she didn't hear me. She ran down the path and out of the gate, her pigtails beating against the wind.

The clouds were breaking and coming together again, twisting and spiralling their way across a violet sky. The sun was going down behind the Siwaliks. The sky there was blood-shot. The tall slim trunks of the eucalyptus tree were tinged with an orange glow; the rain had stopped, and the wind was a soft, sullen puff, drifting sadly through the trees. There was a steady drip of water from the eaves of the roof onto the window-sill. Then the sun went down behind the old, old hills, and I remembered my own hills, far beyond these.

The room was dark but I did not turn on the light. I stood near the window, listening to the garden. There was a frog warbling somewhere, and there was a sudden flap of wings overhead. Tomorrow morning I would go, and perhaps I would come back to Shamli one day, and perhaps not; I could always come here looking for Major Roberts, and, who knows, one day I might find him. What should he be like, this lost man? A romantic, a man with a dream, a man with brown skin and blue eyes, living in a hut on a snowy mountain-top, chopping wood and catching fish and swimming in cold mountain streams; a rough, free man with a kind heart and a shaggy beard, a man who owed allegiance to no one, who gave a. damn for money and politics and cities, and civilizations, who was his own master, who lived at one with nature knowing no fear. But that was not Major Roberts—that was the man I wanted to be. He was not a Frenchman or an Englishman, he was me, a dream of myself. If only I could find Major Roberts.

*

When Daya Ram knocked on the door and told me the others had finished dinner, I left my room and made for the lounge. It was quite lively in the lounge. Satish Dayal was at the bar, Lin at the piano, and Miss Deeds in the centre of the room, executing a tango on her own. It was obvious she had been drinking heavily.

'All on credit,' complained Mr Dayal to me. 'I don't know when I'll be paid, but I don't dare to refuse her anything for fear she'll start breaking up the hotel.'

'She could do that, too,' I said. 'It comes down without much encouragement.'

Lin began to play a waltz (I think it was a waltz), and then I found Miss Deeds in front of me, saying, 'Wouldn't you like to dance, old boy?'

'Thank you,' I said, somewhat alarmed. 'I hardly know how to.'

'Oh, come on, be a sport,' she said, pulling me away from the bar. I was glad Sushila wasn't present; she wouldn't have minded, but she'd have laughed as she always laughed when I made a fool of myself.

We went round the floor in what I suppose was waltz-time, though all I did was mark time to Miss Deeds' motions; we were not very steady—this because I as trying to keep her at arm's length, whilst she was determined to have me crushed to her bosom. At length Lin finished the waltz. Giving him a grateful look, I pulled myself free. Miss Deeds went over to the piano, leant right across it, and said, 'Play something lively, dear Mr Lin, play some hot stuff.'

To my surprise Mr Lin without so much as an expression of distaste or amusement, began to execute what I suppose was the frug or the jitterbug. I was glad she hadn't asked me to dance that one with her.

It all appeared very incongruous to me. Miss Deeds letting herself go in crazy abandonment, Lin playing the piano with great seriousness, and Mr Dayal watching from the bar with an anxious frown. I wondered what Sushila would have thought of them now.

Eventually Miss Deeds collapsed on the couch breathing heavily. 'Give me a drink,' she cried.

With the noblest of intentions I took her a glass of water. Miss Deeds took a sip and made a face. 'What's this stuff?' she asked. 'It

346

is different.'

'Water,' I said.

'No,' she said, 'now don't joke, tell me what it is.'

'It's water, I assure you,' I said.

When she saw that I was serious, her face coloured up, and I thought she would throw the water at me; but she was too tired to do this, and contented herself by throwing the glass over her shoulder. Mr Dayal made a dive for the flying glass, but he wasn't in time to rescue it, and it hit the wall and fell to pieces on the floor.

Mr Dayal wrung his hands. 'You'd better take her to her room,' he said, as though I were personally responsible for her behaviour just because I'd danced with her.

'I can't carry her alone,' I said, making an unsuccessful attempt at helping Miss Deeds up from the couch.

Mr Dayal called for Daya Ram, and the big amiable youth came lumbering into the lounge. We took an arm each and helped Miss Deeds, feet dragging, across the room. We got her to her room and onto her bed. When we were about to withdraw she said, 'Don't go, my dear, stay with me a little while.'

Daya Ram had discreetly slipped outside. With my hand on the door-knob I said, 'Which of us?'

'Oh, are there two of you,' said Miss Deeds, without a trace of disappointment.

'Yes, Daya Ram helped me carry you here.'

'Oh, and who are you?'

'I'm the writer. You danced with me, remember?'

'Of course. You dance divinely, Mr Writer. Do stay with me. Daya Ram can stay too if he likes.'

I hesitated, my hand on the door-knob. She hadn't opened her eyes all the time I'd been in the room, her arms hung loose, and one bare leg hung over the side of the bed. She was fascinating somehow, and desirable, but I was afraid of her. I went out of the room and quietly closed the door.

*

347

As I lay awake in bed I heard the jackal's 'pheau', the cry of fear, which it communicates to all the jungle when there is danger about, a leopard or a tiger. It was a weird howl, and between each note there was a kind of low gurgling. I switched off the light and peered through the closed window. I saw the jackal at the edge of the lawn. It sat almost vertically on its haunches, holding its head straight up to the sky, making the neighbourhood vibrate with the eerie violence of its cries. Then suddenly it started up and ran off into the trees.

Before getting back into bed I made sure the window was fast. The bull-frog was singing again, 'ing-ong, ing-ong', in some foreign language. I wondered if Sushila was awake too, thinking about me. It must have been almost eleven o'clock. I thought of Miss Deeds, with her leg hanging over the edge of the bed. I tossed restlessly, and then sat up. I hadn't slept for two nights but I was not sleepy. I got out of bed without turning on the light and, slowly opening my door, crept down the passage-way. I stopped at the door of Miss Deed's room. I stood there listening, but I heard only the ticking of the big clock that might have been in the room or somewhere in the passage, I put my hand on the door-knob, but the door was bolted. That settled the matter.

I would definitely leave Shamli the next morning. Another day in the company of these people and I would be behaving like them. Perhaps I was already doing so! I remembered the tonga-driver's words, 'Don't stay too long in Shamli or you will never leave!'

When the rain came, it was not with a preliminary patter or shower, but all at once, sweeping across the forest like a massive wall, and I could hear it in the trees long before it reached the house. Then it came crashing down on the corrugated roofing, and the hailstones hit the window panes with a hard metallic sound, so that I thought the glass would break. The sound of thunder was like the booming of big guns, and the lightning kept playing over the garden, at every flash of lightning I sighted the swing under the tree, rocking and leaping in the air as though some invisible, agitated being was sitting on it. I wondered about Kiran. Was she sleeping through all this, blissfully unconcerned, or was she lying awake in bed, starting at every clash of thunder, as I was; or was she up and about, exulting in the storm? I half expected to see her come running through the trees, through the rain, to stand on the swing with her hair blowing wild in the wind, laughing at the thunder and the angry skies. Perhaps I did see her, perhaps she was there. I wouldn't have been surprised if she were some forest nymph, living in the bole of a tree, coming out sometimes to play in the garden.

A crash, nearer and louder than any thunder so far, made me sit up in the bed with a start. Perhaps lightning had struck the house. I turned on the switch, but the light didn't come on. A tree must have fallen across the line.

I heard voices in the passage, the voices of several people. I stepped outside to find out what had happened, and started at the appearance of a ghostly apparition right in front of me; it was Mr Dayal standing on the threshold in an oversized pyjama suit, a candle in his hand.

'I came to wake you,' he said. 'This storm.'

He had the irritating habit of stating the obvious.

'Yes, the storm,' I said. 'Why is everybody up?'

'The back wall has collapsed and part of the roof has fallen in. We'd better spend the night in the lounge, it is the safest room. This is a very old building,' he added apologetically.

'All right,' I said. 'I am coming.'

The lounge was lit by two candles; one stood over the piano, the other on a small table near the couch. Miss Deeds was on the couch, Lin was at the piano-stool, looking as though he would start playing Stravinsky any moment, and Dayal was fussing about the room. Sushila was standing at a window, looking out at the stormy night. I went to the window and touched her, she didn't took round or say anything. The lightning flashed and her dark eyes were pools of smouldering fire.

'What time will you be leaving?' she said.

'The tonga will come for me at seven.'

'If I come,' she said. 'If I come with you, I will be at the station before the train leaves.'

'How will you get there?' I asked, and hope and excitement rushed over me again.

'I will get there,' she said. 'I will get there before you. But if I am not there, then do not wait, do not come back for me. Go on your way. It will mean I do not want to come. Or I will be there.'

'But are you sure?'

'Don't stand near me now. Don't speak to me unless you have to.' She squeezed my fingers, then drew her hand away. I sauntered over to the next window, then back into the centre of the room. A gust of wind blew through a cracked window-pane and put out the candle near the couch.

'Damn the wind,' said Miss Deeds.

The window in my room had burst open during the night, and there were leaves and branches strewn about the floor. I sat down on the damp bed, and smelt eucalyptus. The earth was red, as though the storm had bled it all night.

After a little while I went into the veranda with my suitcase, to wait for the tonga. It was then that I saw Kiran under the trees. Kiran's long black pigtails were tied up in a red ribbon, and she looked fresh and clean like the rain and the red earth. She stood looking seriously at me.

'Did you like the storm?' she asked.

'Some of the time,' I said. 'I'm going soon. Can I do anything for you?'

'Where are you going?'

'I'm going to the end of the world. I'm looking for Major Roberts, have you seen him anywhere?'

'There is no Major Roberts,' she said perceptively. 'Can I come with you to the end of the world?'

'What about your parents?'

'Oh, we won't take them.'

'They might be annoyed if you go off on your own.'

'I can stay on my own. I can go anywhere.'

'Well, one day I'll come back here and I'll take you everywhere and no one will stop us. Now is there anything else I can do for you?'

'I want some flowers, but I can't reach them,' she pointed to a hibiscus tree that grew against the wall. It meant climbing the wall to reach the flowers. Some of the red flowers had fallen during the night and were floating in a pool of water.

'All right,' I said and pulled myself up on to the wall. I smiled down into Kiran's serious upturned face. 'I'll throw them to you and you can catch them.'

I bent a branch, but the wood was young and green, and I had to twist it several times before it snapped.

'I hope nobody minds,' I said, as I dropped the flowering branch to Kiran.

'It's nobody's tree,' she said.

'Sure?'

She nodded vigorously. 'Sure, don't worry.'

I was working for her and she felt immensely capable of protecting me. Talking and being with Kiran, I felt a nostalgic longing for the childhood emotions that had been beautiful because they were never completely understood.

'Who is your best friend?' I said.

'Daya Ram,' she replied. 'I told you so before.'

She was certainly faithful to her friends.

'And who is the second best?'

She put her finger in her mouth to consider the question; her head dropped sideways in connection.

'I'll make you the second best,' she said.

I dropped the flowers over her head. 'That is so kind of you. I'm proud to be your second best.'

I heard the tonga bell, and from my perch on the wall saw the carriage coming down the driveway. 'That's for me,' I said. 'I must go now.'

I jumped down the wall. And the sole of my shoe came off at last.

'I knew that would happen,' I said.

'Who cares for shoes?' said Kiran.

'Who cares?' I said.

I walked back to the veranda, and Kiran walked beside me,

351

and stood in front of the hotel while I put my suitcase in the tonga.

'You nearly stayed one day too late,' said the tonga-driver. 'Half the hotel has come down, and tonight the other half will come down.'

I climbed into the back seat. Kiran stood on the path, gazing intently at me.

'I'll see you again,' I said.

'I'll see you in Iceland or Japan,' she said. 'I'm going everywhere.'

'Maybe,' I said, 'maybe you will.'

We smiled, knowing and understanding each other's importance. In her bright eyes I saw something old and wise. The tonga-driver cracked his whip, the wheels creaked, the carriage rattled down the path. We kept waving to each other. In Kiran's hand was a sprig of hibiscus. As she waved, the blossoms fell apart and danced a little in the breeze.

*

Shamli station looked the same as it had the day before. The same train stood at the same platform, and the same dogs prowled beside the fence. I waited on the platform until the bell clanged for the train to leave, but Sushila did not come.

Somehow, I was not disappointed. I had never really expected her to come. Unattainable, Sushila would always be more bewitching and beautiful than if she were mine.

Shamli would always be there. And I could always come back, looking for Major Roberts.

DELHI IS NOT FAR

'Oh yes, I have known love, and again love, and many other kinds of love; but of that tenderness I felt then, is there nothing I can say?'

Andre Gide, *Fruits of the Earth*

'If I am not for myself, who will be for me?
And if I am not for others, what am I?
And if not now, when?'

Hillel (Ancient Hebrew sage)

ONE

My balcony is my window on the world.
The room has one window, a square hole in the wall
crossed by three iron bars.

The view from it is a restricted one. If I crane my neck
sideways, and put my nose to the bars, I can see the extremities
of the building; below, a narrow courtyard where children—the
children of all classes of people—play together. It is only when
they are older that they become conscious of the barriers of class
and caste.

Across the courtyard, on a level with my room, are three
separate windows, belonging to three separate rooms, each
window barred in the same unimaginative way. During the day
it is difficult to look into these rooms. The harsh, cruel sunlight
fills the courtyard, mailing the windows patches of darkness.

My room is very small. I have paced about in it so often
that I know its exact measurements. My foot, from heel to toe,
is eleven inches. That makes the room just over fifteen feet in
length; when I measure the last foot, my toes turn up against the
wall. In breadth, the room is exactly eight feet.

The plaster has been peeling off the walls, and there are
many greasy stains and patches which are difficult to hide. I
cover the worst stains with pictures cut from magazines, but as
there is no symmetry about the stains there is none about the
pictures. My personal effects are few, and none of them precious.

On a shelf in the wall are a pile of paper-backs, in
English, Hindi and Urdu; among them my two Urdu
thrillers, *Khoon* (Blood) and *Jasoosi* (Detective). They did not
take long to write. Some passages were my own, some free
translations from English authors. Having been brought
up in a Hindu home in a Muslim city—and in an English

school—I was fairly proficient in three languages. The books have sold quite well—for my publisher . . .

My publisher, who operated from a Meerut by-lane, paid me two hundred rupees for each book; a flat and final payment, no royalties. I could not get better terms from any other publisher. It is a good country for publishers but not for writers. To quote Byron: 'Now Barabbas was a publisher . . .'

'If you want to make money,' he confided in me when he handed me my last cheque, 'publish your own books. Not detective stories. They have a limited market. Haven't you realized that India in fuller than ever of young people trying to pass exams? It is a desperate matter, this race for academic qualifications. Half the entrants fall by the wayside. The other half are even more unfortunate. They pass their exams and then they fall by the wayside. The point is, millions are sitting for exams, for MA, BSc, Ph.D., and other degrees. They all want to get these degrees the easy way, without reading too many books or attending more than half a dozen lectures—and that's where a smart person like you comes in! Why should they wade through five volumes of political history when they can get a dozen model-answer papers? They are seldom wrong, the guess-papers. All you have to do is make friends with someone on the University Board, write your papers, print them cheaply—never mind a few printing errors—and flood the market. They'll sell like hot cakes,' he concluded, using an English expression.

I told him I would think about his proposal, but I never really liked the idea. I preferred spilling the blood of fictitious prostitutes to spoon-feeding the brains of misguided students.

Besides, it would have been very boring.

A friend who shall be nameless offered to teach me the art of pickpocketing. But I had to give up after a few clumsy attempts on his pocket. The pick someone's pocket successfully is definitely an art. My friend practised his craft at various railway stations and made a good living from it. I would have to stick to writing cheap thrillers.

TWO

The string of my charpai needs tightening. The dip in the middle of the bed is so pronounced that invariably I wake up in the morning with a backache. But I am hopeless at tightening charpai strings and will have to wait until one of the boys from the tea-shop pays me a visit.

Under the charpai is my tin trunk. Its contents range from old, rejected manuscripts to photographs, clothes, newspaper cuttings and all that goes with the floating existence of an itinerant bachelor.

I do not live entirely alone. Sometimes a beggar, if he is not diseased, spends the night on the balcony; during cold or rainy weather the boys from the tea-shop, who normally sleep on the pavement, crowd into my room. But apart from them, there are the lizards on the wall—friends, these—and a large rat who gets in and out of the window and carries away manuscripts and clothing; definitely an enemy.

*

June nights are the most uncomfortable of all. Mosquitoes emerge from all the ditches and gullies and ponds, and take over control of Pipalnagar. Bugs, finding it uncomfortable inside the woodwork of the charpai, scramble out at night and find their way under my sheet. I wrap myself up in the sheet like a corpse, but the mosquitoes bite through the thin material, and the bugs get in at the tears and holes.

The lizards wander listlessly over the walls, impatient for the monsoon rains, when they will be able to feast off thousands of insects.

Everyone is waiting for the cool, quenching relief of the monsoon. But two months from now, when roofs have fallen in, the

357

road is flooded, and the drinking water contaminated, we will be cursing the monsoon and praying for its speedy retreat.

To wake in the morning is not difficult, as sleep is fitful, uneasy, crowded with dreams and fantasies. I know it is five o'clock when I hear the first bus coming out of the shed. If I am to defecate in private, I must be up and away into the fields beyond the railway tracks. The public lavatory near the station hasn't been cleaned for over a week.

Afterwards I return to the balcony and, slipping out of my vest and pyjamas, rub down my body with mustard oil. If the boy from the tea-shop is awake, I get him to massage me, while I lie flat on my back or on my belly, dreaming of things less mundane than life in Pipalnagar.

As the passengers alight from the first bus, I sit in the barber shop and talk to Deep Chand while he lathers my face with soap. The knife moves cleanly across my cheeks and throat, and Deep Chand's breath, smelling of cloves and cardamoms—he is a perpetual eater of paan—plays on my face. In the next chair the sweetmeat-seller is having the hair shaved from under his great flabby armpits; he is looked after by Deep Chand's younger brother, Ramu, who is deputed to attend to the less popular customers. Ramu flashes a smile at me when I enter the shop; we have had a couple of natural excursions together.

Deep Chand is a short, thick-set man, very compact, dark and smooth-skinned from his waist upwards. Below his waist, from his hips to his ankles, he is a mass of soft black hair. An extremely virile man, he is very attractive to women.

Deep Chand and Ramu know all there is to know about me—in fact, all there is to know about Pipalnagar.

'When are you going to get married, brother?' Deep Chand asked me recently.

'Oh, after five or ten years,' I replied. 'Unless I find a woman rich enough to support me.'

'You are twenty-five now,' he said. 'This is the time to marry. Once you are thirty, it will not be so easy to find a wife. In Pipalnagar, when you are thirty you are old.'

I feel too old already,' I said. 'Don't talk to me of marriage, but give my head a massage. My brain is not functioning well these days. In my latest book I have killed three people in one chapter, and still it is dull.'

'Well, finish it soon,'said Deep Chand, beginning the ritual of the head-massage. 'Then you can clear your debts. When you have paid your debts you will leave Pipalnagar, won't you?'

I could not answer because he had started thumping my skull with his hard, communicative fingers, tugging at the roots of my hair, and squeezing my temples with the palms of his hands. No one gave a better massage than Deep Chand. Had his income been greater, he could have shifted his trade to another locality and made a decent living. Here, in our Mohalla, his principal customers were shopkeepers, truck drivers, labourers from the railway station. He charged only two rupees for a hair-cut; in other places it was three rupees.

While Deep Chand ran his fingers through my hair, exerting a gentle pressure on my temples, I made a mental inventory of all the people who owed me money and to whom I was in debt.

The amounts I had loaned out—to various bazaar acquaintances—were small compared to the amounts I owed others.

There was my landlord, Seth Govind Ram, who was in fact the landlord of half Pipalnagar and the proprietor of the dancing-girls—they did everything but dance—living in a dormitory near the bus stop; I owed him six months' rent. Sixty rupees.

He does not bother me just now, but in six months' time he will be after my blood, and I will have to pay up somehow.

Seth Govind Ram possesses a bank, a paunch and, allegedly, a mistress. The bank and the paunch are both conspicuous landmarks in Pipalnagar. Few people have seen his mistress. She is kept hidden away in an enormous Rajput-style house outside the city, and continues to be a challenge to my imagination.

Seth Govind Ram is a prominent member of the municipality. Publicly, he is a staunch supporter of the ruling party; privately, he supports all parties with occasional contributions towards their funds. He owns most of the buildings in the Pipalnagar Mohalla; and though he is always promising to pull them down and build new ones, he finds it more profitable to leave them as they are.

THREE

My efforts at making a fortune were many and varied. I had, for three days, kept a vegetable stall; invested in an imaginary tea-shop; and even tried my hand as a palmist. This last venture was a failure, not because I was a poor palmist—I had intuition enough to be able to guess what a man or woman would be happy to know—but because prospective customers were few in Pipalnagar. My friends and neighbours had grown far too cynical of the future to expect any bonuses.

'When a child is born,' asserted Deep Chand, 'his fists are clenched. They have been clenched for so long that little creases form on his palms. That is the only meaning in our lines. What have they to do with our future?'

I agreed with Deep Chand, but I thought fortune-telling might be an easy way of making money. Others did it, from saffron-robed sadhus to BAs and BComs, and did it fairly successfully, so that I felt I should try it too. It did not take me long to read a book on the subject, and to hang a board from my balcony, announcing my profession. That I did not succeed was probably due to the fact that I was too well-known in Pipalnagar. Half the Mohalla thought it was a joke; the other half, quite understandably, didn't believe in my genuineness.

The vegetable stall was more exciting. Down the road, near the clock tower, a widow kept a grocery store. She sold rice, spices, pulses, almost everything except meat and vegetables. The widow did not think vegetables were worth the risk of an initial investment, but she was determined to try them out, and persuaded me to put up the money.

I found it difficult to refuse. She was a strong woman, am-plebosomed, known to fight in public with any man who tried to get the better of her. But she was a persuasive saleswoman, too, and soon had me conjuring up visions of a vegetable stall of my own full of succulent fruits and fresh green vegetables.

Full it was, from beginning to end. I didn't sell a single cabbage or cauliflower or salad leaf. Before the vegetables went bad, I gave them away to Deep Chand, Pitamber, and other friends. The widow had insisted that I charge ten paise per kilo more than others charged, a disastrous thing to do in Pipalnagar, where the question of preferring quality to quantity did not arise. She said that for the extra ten paise customers would get cleaner and greener vegetables. She was wrong. Customers wanted them cleaner and greener *and* cheaper.

Still, it had been exciting on the first morning, getting up at five (I hadn't done this for years) and walking down to the vegetable market near the railway station, haggling with the wholesalers, piling the vegetables into baskets, and leading the coolie back to the bazaar with a proprietorial air.

The railway station, half a mile from the bus stop, had always attracted me. As a child I had been fascinated by trains (as I suppose most children are), and waved to the passengers as the trains flew through the fields, and was always delighted when one of them waved back to me. I had wondered about the people in the carriages—where they were going, and why . . . Trains had meant romance, escape into another world.

'What you should do,' advised Deep Chand, while he lathered my face with soap—(there were several reasons why I did not shave myself; laziness, the desire to gossip, the fact that Deep Chand used his razor as an artist uses a brush)—'What you should do, is marry a wealthy woman. It would solve all your problems. She would be only too happy to possess a young man of sexual accomplishments. You could then do your writing at leisure, with slaves to fan you and press your legs.'

'Not a bad idea,' I said, 'but where does one find such a woman? I expect Seth Govind Ram has a wife in addition to a mistress, but I have never seen her; and the Seth doesn't look as though he is going to die.'

'She doesn't have to be a widow. Find a young woman who is married to a fat and important millionaire. She will support you.'

Deep Chand was a married man himself, with several children. I had never bothered to count them.

His children, and others, give one the impression that in Pipalnagar children outnumber adults five to one. This is really the case, I suppose. The census tells us that one in four of our population is in the age-group of five to fifteen years. They swarm over the narrow streets, appearing to belong to one vast family—a race of pot-bellied little men, half-naked, dusty, quarrelling and laughing and crying and having so little in common with the race of adults who have brought them into the world.

On either side of my room there are families each with about a dozen members—each family living in a room a little bigger than mine, which is used for cooking, eating, sleeping and loving. The men work in the sugar factory and bring home about fifty rupees a month. The older children attend the Pipalnagar High School, and come home only for their food. The younger ones are in and out all day, their pockets full of stones and marbles and small coins.

Tagore wrote: 'Every child comes with the message that God is not yet discouraged of man.'

'I wonder why God ever bothered to make men, when he had the whole wide beautiful world to himself,' I said. 'Why did he find it necessary to share it with others?'

'Perhaps he felt lonely,' said Suraj.

At noon, when the shadows shift and cross the road, a band of children rush down the empty, silent street, shouting and waving their satchels. They have been at their desks from early morning, and now, despite the hot sun, they will have their fling while their elders sleep on string charpais beneath leafy neem trees.

On the soft sand near the river-bed boys wrestle or play leapfrog. At alley-corners, where tall buildings shade narrow passages, the favourite game is gulli-danda.

The gulli—small piece of wood, about four inches long, sharpened to a point at each end—is struck with the danda, a short stout stick. A player is allowed three hits, and his score is the distance, in danda lengths, he hits the gulli.

Boys who are experts at this game send the gulli flying far down the road; sometimes into a shop or through a window-pane, resulting in commotion, loud invective, and a dash for cover.

A game for both children and young men is kabbadi. It is a game that calls for good control of the breath and much agility. It is also known by such names as hootoo-too, kho-kho, and atyapatya. As it is essentially a village game, Pitamber excels at it. He is the Pipalnagar kho-kho champion.

The game is played by two teams, consisting of eight or nine members each, facing each other across a dividing line. Each side in turn sends out one of its players into the opponents' area. This person has to keep on saying 'kabbadi, kabbadi' or 'kho, kho' while holding his breath. If he returns to his side after touching an opponent, that opponent is 'dead' and out of the game. If, however, he is caught by an opponent and cannot struggle back to his side while holding his breath, he is 'dead'.

Pitamber, who is a wrestler, and knows all the holds, is particularly adept at capturing an opponent. He took me to his village where all the boys were long-limbed and sun-browned, erect and at the same time relaxed. There is a sense of vitality and confidence in Pitamber's village, which I have not seen in Pipalnagar.

In Pipalnagar there is not exactly despair, but resignation, an indifference to both living and dying. The town is almost truly reflected in the Pipalnagar Home, where in an open courtyard surrounded by mud walls a score of mental patients wander about, listless and bored. A man jabbers excitedly, but most of the inmates are quiet, sad and resentful—resentful because we do not try to understand their beautiful insane world.

*

Aziz visits me occasionally for a loan of two or three rupees, which he returns in kind, whenever I visit his junk shop. He is a Muslim boy of eighteen. He lives in a small room behind the junk shop.

The shop has mud walls and a tin roof. The walls are always in danger of being washed away during the monsoon, and the roof

363

of sailing away during a dust-storm. The rain comes in, anyway, and the floor is awash most of the time; bound copies of old English magazines gather mildew, and the pots and pans and spare parts grow rusty. Aziz, at eighteen, is beginning to collect dust and age and disease.

But he is an optimistic soul, even though there is nothing for him to be optimistic about, and he is always asking me when I intend keeping my vow of going to Delhi to make my fortune. I am to keep an eye out for a favourable shop-site near Chandni Chowk where he can open a more up-to-date junk shop. He is saving towards this end; but what he saves trickles away in paying for his wife's upkeep at the Home.

FOUR

I was walking through the fields beyond the railway tracks, when I saw someone lying on the footpath, his head and body hidden by the ripening wheat. The wheat was shaking where he lay, and as I came nearer I saw that one of his legs kept twitching convulsively.

Thinking that perhaps it was a case of robbery with violence, I prepared to run; but then, cursing myself for being a shallow coward, I approached the agitated person.

He was a youth of about eighteen, and he appeared to be in the throes of a violent fit.

His face was white, except where a little blood had trickled from his mouth. His leg kept twitching, and his hands moved restlessly, helplessly amongst the wheat.

I spoke to him: 'What is wrong?' I asked, but he was obviously unconscious and could not answer. So I ran down the path to the well, and dipping the end of my shirt in a shallow trough of water, soaked it well, and ran back to the boy.

By that time he seemed to have recovered from the fit. The twitching had ceased, and though he still breathed heavily, his face was calm and his hands still. I wiped the blood from his mouth, and he opened his eyes and stared at me without any immediate comprehension.

'You have bitten your tongue.' I said. 'There's no hurry. I'll stay here with you.'

We rested where we were for some minutes without saying anything. He was no longer agitated. Resting his chin on his knees, he passed his hands around his drawn-up legs.

'I am all right now,' he said.

'What happened?'

'It was nothing, it often happens. I don't know why. I cannot stop it.'

'Have you seen a doctor?'

'I went to the hospital when it first began. They gave me some pills. I had to take them every day. But they made me so tired and sleepy that I couldn't do any work. So I stopped taking them. I get the attack about once a week, but I am useless if I take those pills.'

He got to his feet, smiling as he dusted his clothes.

He was a thin boy, long-limbed and bony. There was a little fluff on his cheeks and the promise of a moustache. His pyjamas were short for him, accentuating the awkwardness of his long, bony feet. He had beauty, though; his eyes held secrets, his mouth hesitant smiles.

He told me that he was a student at the Pipalnagar College, and that his terminal examination would be held in August. Apparently his whole life hinged on the result of the coming examination. If he passed, there was the prospect of a scholarship, and eventually a place for himself in the world. If he failed, there was only the prospect of Pipalnagar, and a living eked out by selling combs and buttons and little vials of perfume.

I noticed the tray of merchandise lying on the ground. It usually hung at his waist, the straps going round his neck. All day he walked about Pipalnagar, covering ten to fifteen miles a day, selling odds and ends to people at their houses. He made about two rupees a day, which gave him enough for his food; and he ate irregularly, at little tea-shops, at the stalls near the bus stops, or on the roadside under shady jamun and mango trees. When the jamuns were ripe, he would sit in a tree, sucking the sour fruit till his lips were stained purple with their juice. There was always the fear that he would get a fit while sitting in a tree, and fall off; but the temptation to eat jamuns was too great for him, and he took the risk.

'Where do you stay?' I asked. 'I will walk back with you to your home.'

'I don't stay anywhere in particular. Sometimes in a dharamsala, sometimes in the Gurudwara, sometimes on the

Maidan. In the summer months I like to sleep on the Maidan, on the grass.'

'Then I'll walk with you to the Maidan,' I said.

There was nothing extraordinary about his being a refugee and an orphan. During the communal holocaust of 1947 thousands of homes had been destroyed, women and children killed. What was extraordinary was his sensitivity—or should I say sensibility—a rare quality in a Punjabi youth who had been brought up in the Frontier Provinces during one of the most cruel periods in the country's history. It was not his conversation that impressed me—though his attitude to life was one of hope, while in Pipalnagar people were too resigned even to be desperate— but the gentle persuasiveness of his voice, eyes, and also of his hands, long-fingered, gliding hands, and his smile which flickered with amusement and sometimes irony.

FIVE

One morning, when I opened the door of my room, I found Suraj asleep at the top of the steps. His tray lay a short distance away. I shook him gently, and he woke up immediately, blinking in the bright sunlight.

'Why didn't you come in,' I said. 'Why didn't you tell me?'

'It was late,' he said. 'I didn't want to disturb you.'

'Someone could have stolen your things while you slept.'

'So far no one has stolen from me.'

I made him promise to sleep in my room that night, and he came in at ten, curled up on the floor and slept fitfully, while I lay awake worrying if he was comfortable enough.

He came several nights, and left early in the morning, before I could offer him anything to eat. We would talk into the early hours of the morning. Neither of us slept much.

I liked Suraj's company. He dispelled some of my own loneliness, and I found myself looking forward to the sound of his footsteps on the stairs. He liked my company because I was full of stories, even though some of them were salacious; and because I encouraged his ambitions and gave him confidence.

I forget what it was I said that offended him and hurt his feelings—something unintentional, and, of course, silly: one of those things that you cannot remember afterwards but which seem terribly important at the time. I had probably been giving him too much advice, showing off my knowledge of the world and women, and joking about his becoming a prime minister one day: because the next night he didn't come to my room.

I waited till eleven o'clock for the sound of his footsteps, and then when he didn't come, I left the room and went in search of him. I couldn't bear the thought of an angry and unhappy Suraj sleeping alone on the Maidan. What if he should have another fit? I told myself that he had been through scores of fits without my being around to help him, but already I was beginning to feel protective towards him.

The shops had closed and lights showed only in upper windows. There were many sleeping on the sidewalk, and I peered into the faces of each, but I did not find Suraj. Eventually I found him on the Maidan, asleep on a bench.

'Suraj,' I said, and he awoke and sat up.

'What is it?'

'I've been looking for you for the last two hours. Come on home.'

'Why don't you spend the night here?' he said. 'This is my home.'

I felt angry at first, but then I felt ashamed of my anger.

I said, 'Thank you for your kind offer, dear friend, it will be a privilege to be your guest,' and sat down on the bench beside him.

We were silent for some time, while a big yellow moon played hide and seek with the clouds. Then it began to drizzle.

'It's raining,' I said. 'Why didn't you make a roof over your house? Now let us go back to mine.'

I thought he might still refuse to return with me, but he got up, smiling; perhaps it was my own sudden humility, or perhaps it was the rain. . . . I think it was my own humility, because it made him feel he had wronged me. He did not feel for himself that way, and so it was not the rain.

*

In the afternoon Pipalnagar is empty. The temperature has touched 106°F! To walk barefoot on the scorching pavement is possible only for the beggars and labourers whose feet have developed several layers of hard protective skin. And even they lie stretched out in the shade given by shops and walls, their open sores festering in the hot sun.

Suraj will be asleep in the shade of a peepul or banyan tree, a book lying open beside him, his tray a few feet away. Sometimes the crows are fascinated by his many coloured combs, and come down from the trees to inspect them.

At this hour of the day I lie naked on the stone floor of my room, because the floor is the coolest place of all; and as I am too listless to work or sleep, I study my navel, the hair on my belly, the languid aspect of my genitals, and the hair on my legs and thighs. I study my toes, and with the dust that has accumulated on my feet, I trace patterns on the walls and disturb the flaking plaster which in itself has formed a score of patterns—birds and snakes and elephants . . . With a little imagination I can conjure up the entire world of the *Panchatantra* . . .

Of all the joys of the senses, I think it is the sense of touch I relish most—contact of the cool floor on a hot day. That is why I lie naked in my room, so that all my flesh is in touch with the cool stones.

The touch of the earth—soft earth, stony earth, grass, mud. Sometimes the road is so hot that it scorches the most hardened feet; sometimes it is cold and hard and cruel. Grass is good, especially dew-drenched grass; then the feet are stained with juices, and the sap seems to pass into the body. Wet earth is soft and sensuous, and when the mud cakes on one's feet it is interesting to bathe at a tap and watch the muddy water run away. Splashing through puddles and streams . . .

*

There are days and there are nights, and then there are other days and other nights, and all the days and nights in Pipalnagar are the same.

A few things reassure me . . . The desire to love and be loved. The beauty and ugliness of the human body, the intricacy of its design. These things fascinate me. Sometimes I make love as a sort of exploration of all that is physical; falling in love becomes an exploration of the mind.

SIX

It is difficult to fall asleep some nights. Apart from the mosquitoes and the oppressive atmosphere, there are the loudspeakers blaring all over Pipalnagar—at cinemas, marriages and religious gatherings. There is a continuous variety of fare—religious music and film music. I do not care much for either, and yet I am compelled to listen, both repelled and fascinated by the sounds that permeate the midnight air.

Strangely enough, it does not trouble Suraj. He is immune to noise. Once he is asleep, it would take a bomb to disturb him. At the first blare of the loudspeaker, he pulls a pillow or towel over his head, and falls asleep. He has been in Pipalnagar longer than I, and has grown accustomed to living against a background of noise. And yet he is a silent person, silent in his movements and in his moods; and I, who love silence so much—I am clumsy and garrulous.

Suraj does not know if his parents are dead or alive. He lost them, literally, when he was seven.

His father had been a cultivator, a dark unfathomable man, who spoke little, thought perhaps even less, and was vaguely aware that he possessed a son—a weak boy, who resembled his mother to a disconcerting degree in that he not only looked like her but was given to introspection and dawdling at the river-bank when he should have been at work in the fields.

The boy's mother was a subdued, silent woman—frail and, consumptive. Her husband did not expect that she would live long. Perhaps the separation from her son put an end to her interest in life—or perhaps it has urged her to live on somewhere, in the hope that she will find him again.

Suraj lost his parents at Amritsar railway station, where trains coming over the border disgorged themselves of thousands of refugees—or pulled into the station half-empty, drenched with blood and piled with corpses.

Suraj and his parents were lucky to escape the massacre. Had they been able to travel on an earlier train (they had tried desperately to get into one) they might easily have been killed; but circumstances favoured them then, only to trick them later.

Suraj was clinging to his mother's sari, while she kept close to her husband, who was elbowing his way through the frightened, bewildered throng of refugees; looking over his shoulder at a woman sobbing on the ground, Suraj collided with a burly Sikh and lost his grip on his mother's sari.

The Sikh had a long, curved sword at his waist, and Suraj stared up at him in terror and fascination, at his long hair, which had fallen loose, and his wild black beard, and the blood-stains on his white shirt. The Sikh pushed him out of the way, and when Suraj looked round for his mother she was not to be seen.

He could hear her calling to him, 'Suraj, where are you, Suraj?' and he tried to force his way through the crowd, in the direction of her voice, but he was carried the other way.

SEVEN

At a certain age a boy is like young wheat, growing, healthy, on the verge of manhood. His eyes are alive, his mind quick, his gestures confident. You cannot mistake him.

This is the most fascinating age, when a boy becomes a man—it is interesting both physically and mentally: the growth of the boy's hair, the toning of the muscles, the consciousness of growing and changing and maturing—never again will there be so much change and development in so short a period of time. The body exudes virility, is full of currents and counter-currents.

For a girl, puberty is a frightening age when alarming things begin to happen to her body; for a boy it is an age of self-assertion, of a growing confidence in himself and in his attitude to the world. His physical changes are a source of happiness and pride.

*

There were no inhibitions in my friendship with Suraj. We spoke of bodies as we spoke of minds, and discussed the problems of one as we would discuss those of the other, for they are really the same problems.

He was beautiful, with the beauty of the short-lived, a transient, sad beauty. It made me sad even to look at his pale slim limbs. It hurt me to look into his eyes. There was death in his eyes.

He told me that he was afraid of women, that he constantly felt the urge to possess a woman, but that when confronted with one he might just as well have been a eunuch.

I told him that not every woman was made for every man, and that I would bring him a girl with whom he would be happy.

This was Kamla, a very friendly person from the house run by Seth Govind Ram. She was very small, and rather delicate, but more skilled in love-making than any of her colleagues. She was patient, and particularly fond of the young and inexperienced. She was only twenty-three, but had been four years in the profession.

*

Kamla's hands and feet are beautiful. That in itself is satisfying. A beautiful face leaves me cold if the hands and feet are ugly. Perhaps this is some sort of phobia with me.

Kamla first met me when I came up the stairs shortly after I had moved into the room above the bus stop. She was sitting on the steps, eating a melon; and when she saw me, she smiled and held out a slice.

'Will you eat melon, bhai sahib?' She asked, and her voice was so appealing and her eyes so mischievous that I couldn't help taking the melon from her hands.

'Sit down,' she said, patting the step. I had never come across a girl so openly friendly and direct. As I sat down, I discovered the secret of her smile; it lay in the little scar on her right check; when she smiled, the scar turned into a dimple.

'Don't you do any work?' she asked.

'I write stories and things,' I said.

'Is that work?'

'Well, I live by it,'

'Show me,' she demanded.

I brought her a magazine and began turning the pages for her. She could read a little, if the words were simple enough. But she didn't get as far as my story, because her attention was arrested by a picture of a girl with an urchin hair-cut.

'It is a girl?' she asked; and, when I assured her it was: 'But her hair, how is it like that?'

'That's the latest fashion,' I protested. 'Thousands of women keep hair like that. At least they did a year ago,' I added, looking at the date on the magazine.

'Is it easy to make?'

'Yes, you just take a pair of scissors and cut away until it looks untidy enough.'

'I like it. You give it to me. I'll go and get scissors.'

'No, no!' I said. 'You can't do that, your family will be most upset.'

She stamped her bare foot on the step. 'I have no family, silly man! I have a husband who is happy only if I can make myself attractive to others. He is skinny and smells of garlic, and he has given my father five acres of land for the favour of having a wife half his age. But it is Seth Govind Ram who really owns me; my husband is only his servant.'

'Why are you telling me all this?'

'Why shouldn't I tell you?' she said, and gave me a dark, defiant look. 'You like me, do you not?'

'Of course I like you,' I hastened to assure her.

*

I think I hate families. I am jealous of them. Their sense of security, of interdependence, infuriates me. To every family I am an outsider, because I have no family. A man without a family is a social outcast. He has no credentials. A man's credentials are his father and his father's property. His mother is another quantity; it is her family—her father—that matter.

So I am glad that I do not belong to a family, and at the same time sad, because in our country if you do not belong to a family you are a piece of driftwood. And so two pieces of driftwood come together, and finding themselves caught in the same current, move along with it until they are trapped in a counter-current, and dispersed.

And that is the way it is with me. I must cling to someone as long as circumstances will permit it.

*

Having no family of our own, it was odd and even touching that Kamla should have adopted us both as her brothers during the Raksha Bandhan festival.

This is the time of year when sisters tie the sacred thread to the wrists of their brothers. As a token of affection, the brother makes her a small gift of money, and promises her his protection.

It was a change to have Kamla visiting us early in the morning instead of late at night; and we were surprised, and rather disconnected, to be treated as her brothers.

She tied the silver tinsel round our wrists, and I said, 'Kamla, we are proud to be your brothers, and we would like to make you some gift, but at the moment there is no money with us.'

'I want your protection, not your money,' said Kamla. 'I want to feel that I am not alone in the world.'

So that made three of us. But we could hardly call ourselves a family.

*

Kamla visited us about once a week, when she found time to spare from her professional duties.

Though I was the more accomplished lover, I think she preferred Suraj. He was gentle and he was beautiful, and I think she felt, as I did, that he would not live very long. She wanted to give him as much of herself as she could in so short a time.

Suraj was always a bit embarrassed with her. At first I thought it was because of my presence in the room; but when I offered to leave, he protested. He told me that he would have been completely helpless if I was not present all the time. In fact, I think he slept with Kamla only in order to please me.

376

EIGHT

Suraj and I were sitting in the tea-shop one night. Most of the customers were outside on a bench, where they could listen to the shopkeeper, a popular story-teller. Sitting on the ground in front of the shop was a thick-set youth, with a shaved head. He was dumb—they called him Goonga—and the customers often made sport of him, abusing him and clouting him over the head from time to time. The Goonga didn't mind this; he made faces at the others, and chuckled derisively at their remarks. He could say only one word, 'Goo,' and he said it often. This kept the customers in fits of laughter.

'Goo,' he said, when he saw Suraj enter the shop with me. He pointed at us, chuckled, and said, 'Goo.'

Everyone laughed. Someone got up from the bench and, with the flat of his hand, whacked the Goonga over his bald head. The Goonga sprang at the man making queer noises in his throat, and then someone tripped him and sent him sprawling on the ground. There was more laughter.

We were sitting at an inside table, and everyone was drinking tea, except the Goonga.

'Give the Goonga a glass of tea,' I told the shopkeeper. The shopkeeper grinned but complied with the order. The Goonga looked at me and said 'Goo.'

When we left the shop, the full moon floated above us, robbing the stars of their glory. We walked in the direction of the Maidan, towards my room. The bazaar was almost empty, the shops closed, lights showing only from upper windows I became conscious of the sound of soft footfalls behind me and, looking over my shoulder, found that we were being followed by the Goonga.

'Goo,' he said, on being noticed.

'Why did you have to give him tea?' said Suraj. 'Now he

377

probably thinks we are rich, and won't let us out of sight again.'

'He can do no harm,' I said, though I quickened my step. 'We'll pretend we're going to sleep on the Maidan, then he'll change his mind about us.'

'Goo,' said the Goonga from behind, and quickened his step as well.

We turned abruptly down an alley-way, trying to shake him off; but he padded after us, chuckling ghoulishly to himself. We cut back to the main road, but he was behind us at the clock tower. At the edge of the Maidan I turned and said:

'Go away, Goonga. We've got very little, and can't do anything for you. Go away.'

But the youth said 'Goo' and took a step forward, and his shaved head glistened in the moonlight. I shrugged, and led Suraj on to the Maidan. The Goonga stood at the edge of the Maidan, shaking his head and chuckling to himself. His body showed through his rags, and his feet were covered with mud. He watched us as we walked across the grass, watched us until we sat down on a bench; then he shrugged his shoulders and said 'Goo' and went away.

The beggars on the whole are a thriving community, and it came as no surprise to me when the municipality decided to place a tax on begging.

I know that some beggars earned, on an average, more than a chaprasi or a clerk; I knew for certain that the one-legged man, who had been hobbling about town on crutches long before I come to Pipalnagar, sent money-orders home every month. Begging had become a profession, and so perhaps the municipality felt justified in taxing it, and besides, the municipal coffers needed replenishing.

Shaggy old Ganpat Ram, who was bent double and couldn't straighten up, didn't like it at all, and told me so. 'If I had known this was going to happen,' he mumbled, 'I would have chosen some other line of work.'

Ganpat Ram was an aristocrat among beggars. I had heard that he had once been a man of property, with several houses and a European wife; when his wife packed up and returned to Europe, together with all their savings, Ganpat had a nervous breakdown from which he never recovered. His health became steadily worse until he had to hobble about with a stick. He never made a direct request for money, but greeted you politely, commented on the weather or the price of things, and stood significantly beside you.

I suspected his story to be half true because whenever he approached a well-dressed person, he used impeccable English. He had a white beard and twinkling eyes, and was not the sort of beggar who invokes the names of the gods and calls on the mercy of the passer-by. Ganpat would rely more on a good joke. Some said he was a spy or a policeman in disguise, however, devoted to his work, would remain a beggar for five years.

I don't know how blind the blind man was, because he always recognized me in the street, even when he was alone. He would invoke blessings on my head, or curses, as the occasion demanded. I didn't like the blind man, because he made too much capital out of his affliction; there were opportunities for him to work with other blind people, but he found begging more profitable. The boy who sometimes led him around town didn't beg from me, but would ask 'Have you got an anna on you?' as though he were merely borrowing the money, or needed it only for a minute or two. He was quite friendly, and even came up to my room, to see how I was getting on. He was very solicitous about my welfare. If he saw me from a hundred yards down the street, he would run all the way up to enquire about my health, and borrow an anna. He had a crafty, healthy face, and wore a long, dirty cloak draped over his shoulders., and very little else. He didn't care about the tax on begging, that was the blind man's problem.

In fact, the tax didn't affect the boys at all; with them, begging was a pastime and not a profession. They had big watery eyes, and it was difficult to resist their appeal.

'I haven't any small change,' I would say defensively.

'I'll change your note,' offers the boy.

'It's not a note; it's a fifty paise coin.'

'What do you want to change that for? Give me the coin and I won't trouble you for the rest of the week.'

'That's very kind of you.' But even if I gave him the two annas, he would accost me again at the first opportunity and wheedle something more from my pocket. There was a time when beggars asked for one or two pice; but these days, what with the rise in the cost of living, they never ask for anything less than an anna.

Friday is Leper day.

There is a leper colony a little way out of town, on the banks of a muddy, mosquito-ridden ditch, the other side of the railway station. They come into Pipalnagar once a week to beg, and wander through the town in small groups, making for wealthy-looking individuals who give them something if only to avoid being followed down the road. (Of course the danger of contagion is there, but if the municipal authorities do not let the lepers beg, they will have to support them, and that would prove expensive).

Some of the leper girls have good faces, but their hands are withered stumps, or their arms and legs are eaten away: the older ones have lost their ears and noses, and the men shuffle about with one or two limbs missing. Most of the sufferers belong to the hill areas, where it is still widely believed that leprosy is punishment for sins committed in a former life; the victim is ostracized and often driven out by his family; he goes into the towns and, in order to get work, makes a secret of his affliction; it is only when it can no longer be concealed that he goes for treatment, and then it is too late. The few who get into the hospitals are soldiers and policemen, who are looked after by the State, and a few others whose families have not disclaimed responsibility for them.

But the tax didn't affect the boys or the lepers. It was aimed at the professionals, those who had made a business of begging over the past few years. It was rumoured that one beggar, after spending the day on the pavement calling for alms, would have a taxi drawn up beside him in the evening, and would be driven off to his residence outside town. And when, some months back, news got around that the Pipalnagar Bank was ready to crash, one beggar, who had never been seen to stand on his own two feet, leapt from the pavement and sprinted for the Bank. The professionals are usually crippled or maimed in one way or another—many of them have maimed themselves, others have gone through rigorous training schools in their youth, where they are versed in the fine art of begging. A few cases are genuine, and those are not so loud in their demands for charity, with the result that they don't make much. There are some who sing for their money, and I do not class these as beggars unless they sing badly.

Well, when the municipality decided to place a tax on begging, you should have seen the beggars get together; anyone would have thought they had a union. About a hundred of them took a procession down the main road to the municipal offices, shouting slogans and even waving banners to express the injustice felt by the beggar fraternity over this high-handed action of the authorities. They came on sticks and in carts, a dirty, ragged bunch, one or two of them stark naked; and they stood for two hours outside the municipal offices, to the embarrassment of the working staff and anyone who tried to enter the building.

Eventually somebody came out and told them it was all a rumour, and that no such tax had been contemplated; it would be far too impractical, for one thing. The beggars could all go home and hoard their earnings without any fear of official interference.

So the beggars returned jubilant, feeling they had won a moral victory, conscious of the power of group action. They went out of their way to develop their union, and now there is a fully fledged Beggars' Union. Different districts are allotted to different beggars, and woe betide the trespasser! Beggars are becoming more demanding than ever, and it is rumoured that they intend staging demonstrations outside the houses of those who refuse to be charitable!

But my own personal beggars, old Ganpat Ram and the boys, don't take advantage of their growing power; they treat me with due respect and affection; they do not consider me just another member of the public, who has to be blackmailed into charity, but look upon me as a friend who can be counted upon to make them a small loan from time to time, without expecting any immediate return.

NINE

'Should I go to Delhi, Suraj?'

'Why not? You are always talking about it. You should go.' 'I would like you to come with me. Perhaps they can make you better there, even cure you of your fits.'

'Not now. After my examinations.'

'Then I will wait . . .'

'Go now, if there is a chance of making a living in Delhi.'

'There is nothing definite. But I know the chance will not come until I leave this place and make my chances. There are one or two editors who have asked me to look them up. They could give me some work. And if I find an honest publisher I might be encouraged to write an honest book.'

'Write the book, even if you don't find a publisher.'

'I will try.'

We decided to save a little money, from his small earnings and from my occasional erratic payments which came by money order. I would need money for my trip to Delhi; sometimes there were medicines to be paid for; and we had no warm clothes for the cold weather. We managed to put away twenty rupees one week, but withdrew it the next, as Pitamber needed a loan for repairs on his cycle-rickshaw. He returned the money in three instalments and it disappeared in meeting various small bills.

Pitamber and Deep Chand and Ramu and Aziz all had plans for visiting Delhi. Only Kamla could not foresee such a move for herself. She was a woman and she had no man.

Deep Chand dreamt of his barber shop. Pitamber planned to own a scooter-rickshaw, which would involve no physical exertion and bring in more money. Ramu had a hundred-and-one different dreams, all of which featured beautiful women. He was a sweet boy, with little intelligence but much good nature.

Once, when he had his arm gashed by a knife in a street fight, he came to me for treatment. The hospital would have had to report the matter to the police. I washed his wound, poured benzedrine over it to stop the bleeding, and bandaged his arm rather crudely. He was very grateful and rewarded me with the story of his life. It was a chronicle of disappointed females, all of whom had been seduced by Ramu in fantastic circumstances and had been discarded by him after he had slept with each but once. Ramu boasted that he did not go twice to the same woman.

All this was good-natured lying, as it was well-known that a girl-teaser like Ramu had never seen anything more than a well-shaped ankle; but apparently Ramu believed in many of his own adventures, which in his own mind had acquired a legendary aspect.

I did not ask him how he got his arm cut, because I know he would have given me a fantastic explanation involving his honour and a lady's dishonour. Later I discovered that an irate brother had stabbed him for spreading discreditable rumours about his sister.

Ramu slept in my room that night. It was the sweet sleep of childhood. Suraj read his books, and Kamla came and went, while Ramu dreamt—he told us about it in the morning—of a woman with three breasts.

TEN

'Look, Ganpat,' I said one day, 'I've heard a lot of stories about you, and I don't know which is true. How did you get your crooked back?'

'That's a very long story,' he said, flattered by my interest in him. 'And I don't know if you will believe it. Besides, it is not to anyone that I would speak freely.'

He had served his purpose in whetting my appetite. I said, 'I'll give you four annas if you tell me your story. How about that?'

He stroked his beard, considering my offer. 'All right,' he said, squatting down on his haunches in the sunshine, while I pulled myself up on a low wall. 'But it happened more than twenty years ago, and you cannot expect me to remember very clearly.'

In those days (said Ganpat) I was quite a young man, and had just been married. I owned several acres of land and, though we were not rich, we were not very poor. When I took my produce to the market, five miles away, I harnessed the bullocks and drove down the dusty village road. I would return home at night.

Every night, I passed a peepul tree, and it was said this tree was haunted. I had never met the ghost and did not believe in him, but his name, I was told, was Bippin, and long ago he had been hanged on the peepul tree by a band of dacoits. Ever since, his ghost had lived in the tree, and was in the habit of pouncing upon any person who resembled a dacoit, and beating him severely. I suppose I must have looked dishonest, for one night Bippin decided to pounce on me. He leapt out of the tree and stood in the middle of the road, blocking the way.

'You, there!' he shouted. 'Get off your cart. I am going to kill you!'

I was, of course, taken aback, but saw no reason why I should obey.

'I have no intention of being killed,' I said. 'Get on the cart yourself!'

'Spoken like a man!' cried Bippin, and he jumped up on the cart beside me. 'But tell me one good reason why I should not kill you?'

'I am not a dacoit,' I replied.

'But you look one. That is the same thing.'

'You would be sorry for it later, if you killed me. I am a poor man, with a wife to support.'

'You have no reason for being poor,' said Bippin, angrily.

'Well, make me rich if you can.'

'So you think I don't have the power to make you rich? Do you defy me to make you rich?'

'Yes,' I said, 'I defy you to make me rich.'

'Then drive on!' cried Bippin. 'I am coming home with you.' I drove the bullock-cart on to the village, with Bippin sitting beside me.

'I have so arranged it,' he said, 'that no one but you will be able to see me. And another thing. I must sleep beside you every night, and no one must know of it. If you tell anyone about me, I'll kill you immediately!'

'Don't worry,' I said. 'I won't tell anyone.'

'Good. I look forward to living with you. It was getting lonely in that peepul tree.'

So Bippin came to live with me, and he slept beside me every night, and we got on very well together. He was as good as his word, and money began to pour in from every conceivable and inconceivable source, until I was in a position to buy more land and cattle. Nobody knew of our association, though of course my friends and relatives wondered where all the money was coming from. At the same time, my wife was rather upset at my refusing to sleep with her at night. I could not very well keep her in the same bed as a ghost, and Bippin was most particular about sleeping beside me. At first, I had told my wife I wasn't well, that I would sleep on the veranda. Then I told her that there was someone after our cows, and I would have to keep an eye on them at night: Bippin and I slept in the barn.

My wife would often spy on me at night, suspecting infidelity, but she always found me lying alone with the cows. Unable to understand my strange behaviour, she mentioned it to her family. They came to me, demanding an explanation.

At the same time, my own relatives were insisting that I tell them the source of my increasing income. Uncles and aunts and distant cousins all descended on me one day, wanting to know where the money was coming from.

'Do you want me to die?' I said, losing patience with them. 'If I tell you the cause of my wealth, I will surely die.'

But they laughed, taking this for a half-hearted excuse; they suspected I was trying to keep everything for myself. My wife's relatives insisted that I had found another woman. Eventually, I grew so exhausted with their demands that I blurted out the truth.

They didn't believe the truth either (who does?), but it gave them something to think and talk about, and they went away for the time being.

But that night, Bippin didn't come to sleep beside me. I was all alone with the cows. And he didn't come the following night. I had been afraid he would kill me while I slept, but it appeared that he had gone his way and left me to my own devices. I was certain that my good fortune had come to an end, and so I went back to sleeping with my wife.

The next time I was driving back to the village from the market, Bippin leapt out of the peepul tree.

'False friend!' he cried, halting the bullocks. 'I gave you everything you wanted, and still you betrayed me!'

'I'm sorry,' I said. 'You can kill me, if you like.'

'No, I cannot kill you,' he said. 'We have been friends for too long. But I will punish you all the same.'

Picking up a stout stick, he struck me three times across the back, until I was bent up double.

'After that,' Ganpat concluded, 'I could never straighten up again and, for over twenty years, I have been a crooked man. My wife left me and went back to her family, and I could no longer work in the fields. I left my village and wandered from one city to another, begging for a living. That is how I came to Pipalnagar, where I decided to remain. People here seem to be more generous than they are in other towns, perhaps because they haven't got so much.'

He looked up at me with a smile, waiting for me to produce the four annas.

'You can't expect me to believe that story,' I said. 'But it was a good invention, so here is your money.'

'No, no!' said Ganpat, backing away and affecting indignation. 'If you don't believe me, keep the money. I would not lie to you for a mere four annas!'

He permitted me to force the coin into his hand, and then went hobbling away, having first wished me a pleasant afternoon.

I was almost certain he had been telling me a very tall story; but you never can tell. . . . Perhaps he really had met Bippin the ghost. And it was wise to give him the four annas, just in case, after all, he was a CID man.

ELEVEN

Pitamber is a young lion. A shaggy mane of black hair tumbles down the nape of his neck; his body, though, is naked and hairless, burnt a rich chocolate by the summer sun. His only garment is a pair of knickers. When he pedals his cycle-rickshaw through the streets of Pipalnagar, the muscles of his calves and thighs stand out like lumps of grey iron. He has carried in his rickshaw fat baniyas and their fat wives, and this has given him powerful legs, a strong back and hollow cheeks. His thighs are magnificent, solid muscle, not an ounce of surplus flesh. They look as though they have been carved out of teak.

His face, though, is gaunt and hollow, his eyes set deep in their sockets: but there is a burning intensity about his eyes, and sometimes I wonder if he, too, is tubercular, like many in Pipalnagar. You cannot tell just by looking at a person if he is sick. Sometimes the weak will last for years, while the strong will suddenly collapse and die.

Pitamber has a wife and three children in his village five miles from Pipalnagar. They have a few acres of land on which they grow maize and sugar cane. One day he made me sit in his rickshaw, and we cycled out of the town, along the road to Delhi; then we had to get down and push the rickshaw over a rutted cart-track, until we reached his village.

This visit to Pitamber's village had provided me with an escape-route from Pipalnagar. I persuaded Suraj to put aside his tray and his books, and hiring a cycle from a stand near the bus stop (on credit), I seated Suraj in front of me on the cross-bar, and rode out of Pipalnagar.

It was then that I made the amazing discovery that by exerting my legs a little, I could get out of Pipalnagar, and that, except for the cycle-hire, it did not involve any expense or great sacrifice.

It was a hot, sunny morning, and I was perspiring by the time we had gone two miles; but a fresh wind sprang up suddenly, and I could smell rain in the air, though there were no clouds to be seen.

When Suraj began to feel cramped on the saddle-bar, we got down, and walked along the side of the road.

'Let us not go to the village,' said Suraj. 'Let us go where there are no people at all. I am tired of people.'

We pushed the cycle off the road, and took a path through a paddy-field, and then a field of young maize, and in the distance we saw a tree, a crooked tree, growing beside a well.

I do not know the name of that tree. I had never seen one of its kind before. It had a crooked trunk, and crooked branches, and it was clothed in thick, broad crooked leaves, like the leaves on which food is served in the bazaars.

In the trunk of the tree was a hole, and when I set my cycle down with a crash, two green parrots flew out of the hole, and went dipping and swerving across the fields.

There was grass around the well, cropped short by grazing cattle, so we sat in the shade of the crooked tree, and Suraj untied the red cloth in which he had brought our food.

We ate our bread and spiced vegetables, and meanwhile the parrots returned to the tree.

'Let us come here every week,' said Suraj, stretching himself out on the grass and resting his head against my shoulder.

It was a drowsy day, the air humid, and soon Suraj fall asleep. I, too, stretched myself out on the grass, and closed my eyes—but I did not sleep; I was aware instead of a score of different sensations.

I heard a cricket singing in the crooked tree; the cooing of pigeons which dwelt in the walls of the old well; the quiet breathing of Suraj; a rustling in the leaves of the tree; the distant hum of an aeroplane.

I smelt the grass, and the old bricks round the well and the promise of rain.

I felt Suraj's fingers touching my arm, and the sun creeping over my cheek.

I opened my eyes, and I saw the clouds on the horizon, and

Suraj still asleep, his arm thrown across his eyes to keep away the glare.

Being thirsty, I went to the well, and putting my shoulders to it, turned the wheel, walking around the well four times, while cool clean water gushed out over the stones and along the channel to the fields.

I drank from one of the trays and the water was sweet with age.

Suraj was sitting up, looking at the sky.

'It is going to rain,' he said. When he had taken his fill of water we pushed the cycle back to the main road and began cycling homewards, but we were still two miles out of Pipalnagar when it began to rain.

A lashing wind swept the rain across our faces, but we exulted in it, and sang at the tops of our voices until we reached the bus stop.

I left the cycle at the hire-shop. Suraj and I ran up the rickety, swaying steps to my room.

Soon there were puddles on the floor, where we had left our soaking clothes, and Suraj was sitting on the bed, a sheet wrapped round his chest.

He became feverish that evening, and I pulled out an old blanket, and covered him with it. I massaged his scalp with mustard oil, and he fell asleep while I did this.

It was dark by then, and the rain had stopped, and the bazaar was lighting up. I curled up at the foot of the bed, and slept for a little while; but at midnight I was woken by the moon shining full in my face; a full moon, shedding its light exclusively on Pipalnagar and peeping and prying into every room, washing the empty streets, silvering the corrugated tin roof.

People are restless tonight, with the moon shining through their windows. Suraj turns restlessly in his sleep. Kamla, having sent away a drunken customer, will be bathing herself, as she always does before she finally sleeps . . . Deep Chand is tossing on his cot, dreaming of electric razors and a plush hair-cutting saloon in the capital, with the Prime Minister as his client. And Seth Govind Ram, unable to sleep because of the accusing moonlight, paces his veranda, worrying about his rent, counting up his assets, and wondering if he should stand for election to the Legislative Assembly.

In the temple the moonlight rests gently on the generous Ganesh, and in the fields Krishna is playing his flute and Radha is singing. . . . 'I follow you, devoted. . . . How can you deceive me, so tortured by love's fever as I am. . . .'

TWELVE

I n June, the lizards hang listlessly on the walls, scanning their horizon in vain. Insects seldom show up—either the heat has killed them, or they are sleeping and breeding in cracks in the plaster. The lizards wait—and wait . . .

All Pipalnagar is waiting for its release from the oppressive heat of June.

One day clouds loom up on the horizon, growing rapidly into enormous towers. A faint breeze springs up. Soon it is a wind, which brings with it the first raindrops. This is the moment everyone is waiting for. People run out of their chawls and houses to take in the fresh breeze and the scent of those first raindrops on the parched, dusty earth.

Underground, in their cracks and holes, the insects are moving. Termites and white ants, which have been sleeping through the hot season, emerge from their lairs. They have work ahead of them.

Now, on the second or third night of the monsoon, comes the great yearly flight of the insects into the cool brief freedom of the night. Out of every crack, from under the roots of trees, huge winged ants emerge, at first fluttering about heavily, on this the first and last flight of their lives. At night there is only one direction in which they can fly—towards the light; towards the electric bulbs and smoky kerosene lamps that illuminate Pipalnagar.

The street lamp opposite the bus stop, beneath my room, attracts a massive quivering swarm of clumsy termites, which give the impression of one thick, slowly revolving body.

The first frog has arrived and comes hopping on to the balcony to pause beneath the electric bulb. All he has to do is gobble, as the insects fall about him.

This is the hour of the lizards. Now there are rewards for those days of patient waiting. Plying their sticky pink tongues, they devour the insects as fast as they come. For hours they cram their stomachs, knowing that such a feast will not be theirs again for another year. How wasteful nature is . . . Through the whole hot season the insect world prepares for this flight out of darkness into light, and not one of them survives its freedom.

*

As most of my writing is done at night and much of my sleeping by day, it often happens that at about midnight I put down my pen and go out for a walk. In Pipalnagar this is a pleasant time for a walk, provided you are not taken for a burglar. There is the smell of jasmine in the air, the moonlight shining on sandy stretches of wasteland, and a silence broken only by the hideous bellow of the chowkidar, or night-watchman.

This is the person who, employed by the residents of our Mohalla, keeps guard over us at night, and walks the roads calling like a jackal: 'Khabardar!' (Beware) for the benefit of prospective evil-doers. Apart from keeping half the population awake, he is successful in warning thieves of his presence.

The other night, in the course of a midnight stroll I encountered our chowkidar near a dark corner, and wished him a good evening. He leapt into the air like a startled rabbit, and immediately shouted 'Khabardar!' as though this were some magic word that would bring me down on my knees begging for mercy.

'It's quite all right,' I assured him. 'I'm only one of your clients.'

The chowkidar laughed nervously and said he was glad to hear it; he hoped I didn't mind his shouting 'Khabardar' at me, but these were grim times and robbers were on the increase.

He said yes, there were probably quite a few of them at work this very night. Had he ever tried creeping up on them quietly? He might catch a few that way.

But why should he catch them, the chowkidar wanted to know. It was his business to frighten them away. He could do that better by roaring defiantly on the roads than by accosting them on someone's premises—violence must be avoided, if he could help it.

'Besides,' he said, 'the people who live here like me to shout at night. It makes them feel safe, knowing that I am on guard. And if I didn't shout "Khabardar" every few minutes they would think I had fallen asleep, and I would be dismissed.'

This was a logical argument. I asked him what he would do if, by accident, he encountered a gang of thieves. He said he would keep shouting 'Khabardar' until the people came out of their houses to help him. I said I doubted very much if they would come out of their houses, but wished him luck all the same, and continued with my walk.

Every five minutes or so I heard his cry, followed by a 'Khabardar' which grew fainter until the chowkidar had reached the far side of the Mohalla. I thought it would be a good idea to give him a helping hand from my side, so I cupped my hands to my mouth and shouted, 'Khabardar, Khabardar!'

It worked like magic.

Three dark figures scrambled over a neighbouring wall and fled down the empty road. I shouted 'Khabardar' a second time, and they ran faster. Imagine the thieves' confusion when they were met by more 'Khabardars' in front, coming from the chowkidar, and realized that there were now two chowkidars operating in the Mohalla.

*

On those nights when sleep was elusive we left the room and walked for miles around Pipalnagar. It was generally about midnight that we became restless. The walls of the room would give out all the heat they had absorbed during the day, and to lie awake sweating in the dark only gave rise to morbid and depressing thoughts.

In our singlets and pyjamas Suraj and I would walk barefooted through the empty Mohalla, over the cooling brick pavements, until we were out of the bazaar and crossing the Maidan, our feet sinking into the springy dew-fresh grass. The Maidan was broad and spacious, and the star-swept sky seemed to meet each end of the plain.

Then out of the town, through lantana scrub, till we came to the dry river-bed, where we walked amongst rocks and boulders, sitting down occasionally, while great horny lizards watched us from between the stones.

Across the river-bed fields of maize stretched away for a few miles, until there came a dry region, where thorns and a few bent trees grew, the earth splitting up in jagged cracks like a jigsaw puzzle; and where water had been, the skin was peeling off the earth in great flat pancakes. Dotting the landscape were old abandoned brick kilns, and it was said that thieves met there at nights, in the trenches around the kilns; but we never saw any.

When it rained heavily the hollows filled up with water. Suraj and I came to one of these places to bathe and swim. There was an island in the middle of one of the hollows, and on this small mound stood the ruins of a hut, where a night-watchman once lived and looked after the bricks at night.

We swam out to the island, which was only a few yards away. There was a grassy patch in front of the hut, and here we lay and sunned ourselves in the early morning, until it became too hot. We would oil and massage each other's bodies, and wrestle on the grass.

Though I was heavier than Suraj, and my chest was as sound as a new drum, he had a lot of power in his long arms and legs and often pinioned me about the waist with his bony knees or fastened me with his strong fingers.

Once while we wrestled on the new monsoon grass, I felt his body go tense, as I strained to press his back to the ground. He stiffened, his thigh jerked against me, and his legs began to twitch. I knew that he had a fit coming on, but I was unable to extricate myself from his arms, which gripped me more tightly as the fit took possession of him. Instead of struggling, I lay still, and tried desperately to absorb some of his anguish; by embracing him, I felt my own body might draw some of the agitation to itself; it was only a strange fancy, but I felt that it made a difference, that by consciously sharing his unconscious condition I was alleviating it. At other times, I have known this same feeling. When Kamla was burning with a fever, I had thought that by taking her in my arms I could draw the fever from her, absorb the heat of her body, transfer to hers the coolness of my own.

Now I pressed against Suraj, and whispered soothingly and lovingly into his ear, though I knew he had no idea what I could be saying; and then when I noticed his mouth working, I thrust by hand in sideways to prevent him from biting his tongue.

But so violent was the convulsion that his teeth bit into the flesh of my palm and ground against my knuckles. I gasped with pain and tried to jerk my hand away, but it was impossible to loosen the grip of his teeth. So I closed my eyes and counted one, two, three, four, five, six, seven—until I felt his body relax again and his jaws give way slowly.

My hand had blood on it, and was trembling: I bound it in a handkerchief, before Suraj came to himself.

We walked back to the town without talking much. He looked depressed and hopeless, though I knew he would be buoyant again before long. I kept my hand concealed beneath my singlet, and he was too dejected to notice this. It was only at night, when he returned from his classes, that he noticed it was bandaged, and then I told him I had slipped on the road, cutting my hand on some broken glass.

THIRTEEN

Rain upon Pipalnagar: and until the rain stops, Pipalnagar is fresh and clean and alive. The children run out of their houses, glorying in their nakedness. They are innocent and unashamed. Older children, by no means innocent, but by all means unashamed, romp through the town, inviting the shocked disapproval of their elders and, presumably betters.

Before we are ten, we are naked and free and unafraid; after ten, we must cloak our manhood, for we are no longer certain that we are men.

The gutters choke, and the Mohalla becomes a mountain stream, coursing merrily down towards the bus stop. And it is at the bus stop that pandemonium breaks loose; for newly-arrived passengers panic at sight of the sea of mud and rain water that surrounds them on all sides, and about a hundred tongas and cycle-rickshaws try all at once to take care of a score of passengers. Result: only half the passengers find a conveyance, while the other half find themselves knee-deep in Pipalnagar mire.

Pitamber has, of course, succeeded in acquiring as his passenger the most attractive and frightened young woman in the bus, and proceeds to show off his skill and daring by taking her home by the most devious and uncomfortable route, and when she gets her feet covered with mud, wipes them with the seedy red cloth that he ties about his neck.

The rain swirls over the trees and roofs of the town, and the parched earth soaks it up, exuding a fragrance that comes only once in a year, the fragrance of quenched earth, the most exhilarating of all smells.

And in my room, too, I am battling against the elements, for the door will not shut against the breeze, and the rain is sweeping in through the opening and soaking my cot.

When eventually I succeed in barricading the floor, I find the roof leaking, and the water trickling down the walls, obliterating the dusty designs I have made on the plaster with my foot. I place a tin here and a mug there, and then, satisfied that everything is under control, sit on my cot and watch the roof-tops through my window.

But there is a loud banging on the door. It flies open with the pressure, and there is Suraj, standing on the threshold, shaking himself like a wet dog. Coming in, he strips off all his clothes, and then he dries himself with a torn threadbare towel, and sits shivering on the bed while I make frantic efforts to close the door again.

'You are cold, Suraj, I will make you some tea.'

He nods, forgetting to smile for once, and I know his mind is elsewhere, in one of a thousand places and all of them dreams.

When I have got the fire going, and placed the kettle on the red hot coals, I sit down beside Suraj and put my arm around his bony shoulders and dream a little with him.

'One day I will write a book,' I tell him. 'Not a murder story, but a real book, about real people. Perhaps it will be about you and me and Pipalnagar. And then we will break away from Pipalnagar, fly away like eagles, and our troubles will be over and fresh new troubles will begin. I do not mind difficulties, as long as they are new difficulties.'

'First I must pass my exams,' said Suraj. 'Without a certificate one can do nothing, go nowhere.'

'Who taught you such nonsense? While you are preparing for your exams, I will be writing my book. That's it! I will start tonight. It is an auspicious night, the first night of the monsoon. Let us start tonight.'

And by the time we had drunk our tea it was evening and growing dark. The light did not come on; a tree must have fallen across the wires. So I lit a candle and placed it on the window-sill (the rain and wind had ceased), and while the candle spluttered in the steady stillness, Suraj opened his books and with one hand on a book, and the other playing with his toes—this helped him to read—he began his studies.

I took the ink down from the shelf, and finding the bottle empty, added a little rain-water to it from one of the mugs. I sat down beside Suraj and began to write; but the pen was no good, and made blotches all over and I didn't really know what to write about, though I was full of writing just then.

So I began to look at Suraj instead; at his eyes, hidden in the shadows, his hands in the candle light; and felt his breathing and the slight movement of his lips as he read shortly to himself.

*

A gust of wind came through the window, and the candle went out. I swore softly in Punjabi.

'Never mind,' said Suraj, 'I was tired of reading.'

'But I was writing.'

'Your book?'

'No, a letter. . . .'

'I have never known you to write letters, except to publishers asking them for money. To whom were you writing?'

'To you,' I said. 'And I will send you the letter one day, perhaps when we are no longer together.'

'I will wait for it, then. I will not read it now.'

FOURTEEN

At ten o'clock on a wet night Pipalnagar had its first earthquake in thirty years. It lasted exactly five seconds. A low, ominous rumble was followed by a few quick shudders, and the water surahi jumped off the window-ledge and crashed on the floor.

By the time Suraj and I had tumbled out of the room, the shock was over; but panic prevailed, and the entire population of the Mohalla was out in the street. One old man of seventy leapt from a first floor balcony and broke his neck; a large crowd had gathered round his body. Several women had fainted. On the other hand, many were shrieking and running about. Only a few days back astrologers had predicted the end of the world, and everyone was convinced that this was only the first of a series of earthquakes.

At temples and other places of worship prayer meetings were held. People moved about the street, pointing out the cracks that had appeared in their houses. Some of these cracks had, of course, been there for years, and were only now being discovered.

At midnight, men and women were still about; and, as though to justify their prudence, another, milder tremor made itself felt. The roof of an old house, weakened by many heavy monsoons, was encouraged to give way, and fell with a suitably awe-inspiring crash. Fortunately no one was beneath it. Everyone was soaking wet by now, as the rain had come down harder, but no one dared venture indoors, especially after a roof had fallen in.

Worse still, the electricity failed and the entire Mohalla plunged into darkness. People huddled together, fearing the worst, while the rain came down incessantly.

'More people will die of pneumonia than earthquake,' observed Suraj. 'Let's go for a walk, it is better than standing about doing nothing.'

We rolled up our pyjamas and went splashing through the

puddles. On the outskirts of the town we met Pitamber dancing in the middle of the road. He was very merry, and quite drunk.

'Why are you dancing in the road?' I asked.

'Because I am happy, that's why,' said Pitamber.

'And what makes you so happy, my friend?'

'Because I am dancing in the road,' he replied.

We began walking home again. The rain had stopped. There was a break in the clouds and a pale moon appeared. The neem trees gave out a strong, sweet smell.

There were no more tremors that night. When we got back to the Mohalla, the sky was lighter, and people were beginning to move into their houses again.

*

We lay on our island, in the shade of a thorn bush, watching a pair of sarus cranes on the opposite bank prancing and capering around each other; tall, stork-like birds, with naked red heads and long red legs.

'We might be saruses in some future life,' I said.

'I hope so,' said Suraj. 'Even if it means being born on a lower level. I would like to be a beautiful white bird. I am tired of being a man, but I do not want to leave the world altogether. It is very lovely, sometimes.'

'I would like to be a sacred bird,' I said. 'I don't wish to be shot at.'

Aren't saruses sacred? Look how they enjoy themselves.'

'They are making love. That is their principal occupation apart from feeding themselves. And they are so devoted to each other that if one bird is killed the other will haunt the scene for weeks, calling distractedly. They have even been known to pine away and die of grief. That's why they are held in such affection by people in villages.'

'So many birds are sacred.'

We saw a bluejay swoop down from a tree—a flash of blue—and carry off a grasshopper.

401

Both the bluejay and Lord Siva are called Nilkanth. Siva has a blue throat, like the bluejay, because out of compassion for the human race he swallowed a deadly poison which was meant to destroy the world. He kept the poison in his throat and would not let it go any further.'

'Are squirrels sacred?' asked Suraj, curiously watching one fumbling with a piece of bread which we had thrown away.

'Krishna loved them. He would take them in his arms and stroke them with his long, gentle fingers. That is why they have four dark lines down their backs from head to tail. Krishna was very dark-skinned, and the lines are the marks of his fingers.'

'We should be gentle to animals. . . . Why do we kill so many of them?'

'It is not so important that we do not kill them—it is important that we respect them. We must acknowledge their right to live on this earth. Everywhere, birds and animals are finding it more difficult to survive, because we are destroying their homes. They have to keep moving as the trees and the green grass keep disappearing.'

Flowers in Pipalnagar—do they exist?

I have known flowers in poetry, and as a child I knew a garden in Lucknow where there were fields of flowers, and another garden where only roses grew. In the fields round Pipalnagar I have seen dandelions that evaporate when you breathe on them, and sometimes a yellow buttercup nestling among thistles. But in our Mohalla, there are no flowers except one. This is a marigold growing out of a crack in my balcony.

I have removed the plaster from the base of the plant, and filled in a little earth which I water every morning. The plant is healthy, and sometimes it produces a little orange marigold, which I pluck and give away before it dies.

Sometimes Suraj keeps the flower in his tray, among the combs and scent bottles and buttons that he sells. Sometimes he offers the flower to a passing child—to a girl who runs away; or it might be a boy who tears the flower to shreds. Some children keep it; others give flowers to Suraj when he passes their houses.

Suraj has a flute which he plays whenever he is tired of going from house to house.

He will sit beneath a shady banyan or peepul, put his tray aside, and take out his flute. The haunting little notes travel down the road in the afternoon stillness, and children come to sit beside him and listen to the flute music. They are very quiet when he plays, because there is a little sadness about his music, and children especially can sense that sadness.

Suraj has made flutes out of pieces of bamboo; but he never sells them, he gives them away to the children he likes. He will sell anything, but not his flutes.

Sometimes Suraj plays his flutes at night, when I am lying awake on the cot, unable to sleep; and even when I fall asleep, the flute is playing in my dreams. Sometimes he brings it with him to the crooked tree, and plays it for the benefit of the birds; but the parrots only make harsh noises and fly away.

Once, when Suraj was playing his flute to a group of children, he had a fit. The flute fell from his hands, and he began to roll about in the dust on the roadside. The children were frightened and ran away.

But they did not stay away for long. The next time they heard the flute play, they came to listen as usual.

FIFTEEN

As Suraj and I walked over a hill near the limestone quarries, past the shacks of the Rajasthani labourers, we met a funeral procession on its way to the cremation ground. Suraj placed his hand on my arm and asked me to wait until the procession had passed. At the same time a cyclist dismounted and stood at the side of the road. Others hurried on, without glancing at the little procession.

'I was taught to respect the dead in this way,' said Suraj. 'Even if you do not respect a man in life, you should respect him in death. The body is unimportant, but we should honour it out of respect for the man's mind.'

'It is a good custom,' I said.

'It must be difficult to live on after one you have loved has died.'

'I don't know. It has not happened to me. If a love is strong, I cannot see its end. . . . It cannot end in death, I feel. . . . Even physically, you would exist for me somehow.'

*

He was asleep when I returned late at night from a card-game in which I had lost fifty rupees. I was a little drunk, and when I tripped near the door way, he woke up; and though he did not open his eyes, I felt he was looking at me.

I felt very guilty and ashamed, because he had been ill that day, and I had forgotten it. Now there was no point in saying I was sorry. Drunkenness is really a vice, because it degrades a man, and humiliates him.

Prostitution is degrading, but a prostitute can still keep her dignity; thieving is degrading according to the character of the theft; begging is degrading but it is not as undignified as drunkenness. In all our vices we are aware of our degradation; but in drunkenness we lose our pride, our heads, and, above all, our natural dignity. We become so obviously and helplessly 'human', that we lose our glorious animal identity.

I sat down at the side of the bed, and bending over Suraj, whispered, 'I got drunk and lost fifty rupees, what am I to do about it?'

He smiled, but still he didn't open his eyes, and I kicked off my sandals and pulled off my shirt and lay down across the foot of the bed. He was still burning with fever, I could feel it radiating through the sheet.

We were silent for a long time, and I didn't know if he was awake or asleep; so I pressed his foot and said, 'I'm sorry,' but he was asleep now, and did not hear me.

*

Moonlight.

Pipalnagar looks clean in the moonlight, and my thoughts are different from my daytime thoughts.

The streets are empty, and the moon probes the alley-ways, and there is a silver dustbin, and even the slush and the puddles near the bus stop shimmer and glisten.

Kisses in the moonlight. Hungry kisses. The shudder of bodies clinging to each other on the moonswept floor.

A drunken quarrel in the street. Voices rise and fall. The night-watchman waits for the trouble to pass, and then patrols the street once more, banging the lathi on the pavement.

Kamla asleep. She sleeps like an angel. I go downstairs and walk in the moonlight. I met Suraj coming home, his books under his arm; he has been studying late with Aziz, who keeps a junk shop near the station. Their exams are only a month off. I am confident that Suraj will be successful; I am only afraid that he will work himself to a standstill; with his weak chest and the uncertainty of his fits, he should not walk all day and read all night.

When I wake in the early hours of the morning and Kamla stirs beside me in her sleep (her hair so laden with perfume that my own sleep has been fitful and disturbed), Suraj is still squatting on the floor, reading by the light of the kerosene lamp.

And even when he has finished reading he does not sleep, but asks me to walk with him before the sun rises, and, as women were not made to get up before the sun, we leave Kamla stretched out on the cot, relaxed and languid; small breasts and a boy's waist; her hair tumbling about the pillow; her mouth slightly apart, her lips still swollen and bruised with kisses.

I have been seeking through sex something beyond sex—a union with all mankind.

SIXTEEN

It was Lord Krishna's birthday, and the rain came down as heavily as it must have done the day Krishna was born in Brindaban. Krishna is the best beloved of all the gods. Young mothers laugh and weep as they read or hear the pranks of his childhood; young men pray to be as tall and strong as Krishna was when he killed Kamsa's elephant and Kamsa's wrestlers; young girls dream of a lover as daring as Krishna to carry them off like Rukmani in a war chariot; grown up men envy the wisdom and statesmanship with which he managed the affairs of his kingdom.

The rain came suddenly and took everyone by surprise. In a few seconds, people were drenched to the skin, and within ten minutes the mohalla was completely flooded. The temple tank overflowed, the railway lines disappeared, and the old wall near the bus stop shivered and fell silently, the noise of the collapse drowned by the rain.

Those whose beard had not yet appeared enjoyed themselves immensely. Children shrieked with excitement, and five naked young men with a dancing bear cavorted in the middle of the vegetable market.

Wading knee-deep down the road, I saw roadside vendors salvaging what they could. Plastic toys, cabbages and utensils floated away and were seized upon by urchins. The water had risen to the level of the shop-fronts, and the floors were awash. Aziz was afloat in his junk shop. Deep Chand, Ramu and a customer were using buckets to bail the water out of their premises. Pitamber churned through the stream in his cycle-rickshaw, offering free lifts to the women in the bazaar with their saris held high above their knees.

The rain stopped as suddenly as it had begun. The sun came out. The water began to find an outlet, flooding other low-lying areas, and a paper-boat came sailing between my legs.

*

'When did you last go out of Pipalnagar?' I asked Suraj. 'I mean far out, to another part of the country?'

'Not since I came here,' he said. 'I have never had the funds. And you?'

'I don't remember. I have been stagnating in Pipalnagar for five years without a break. I would like to see the hills again. Once, when I was a child, my parents took me to the hills. I remember them vividly—pine trees, the wind at night, men carrying loads of wood up the steep mountain paths—yes, I would like to see the hills again . . .'

'I have never seen them,' said Suraj.

'How strange! I don't think that a man can be complete until he has lived in the hills. Of course we are never complete, but there is something about a mountain that adds a new dimension to life. The change in air and altitude makes one think and feel and act differently. Suraj, we must go to the hills! This is the time to go. Let's get away from this insufferable heat, from these drains and smells and noises—even if it is only for a few days. . .'

'But my exams are only a few weeks off.'

'Good. The change will help. Bring your books along. You will study much better there. You will feel better. I can guarantee that you will not have a single fit all the time we are away!'

I was carried away in a flood of enthusiasm. I waved my arms about and described the splendour of the sun rising—or setting—behind Manda Devi, and talked about the book I could write if I stayed a few weeks in the hills.

'But what about money?' interrupted Suraj, breaking in on my oration. 'How do we go there?'

'Money?' I said contemptuously. 'Money?' I said again, more respectfully. And then doubtfully, 'Money.'

'Yes, money,' I muttered to myself, and sat down on the string cot, suddenly deflated and discouraged.

Suraj burst into laughter.

'What are you laughing about?' I hissed.

'I can't help it,' he said, holding his sides with mirth. 'It's your face. One minute it was broad with smiles, now it is long and mournful, like the face of a horse.'

'We'll get money!' I shouted, springing up again. 'How much do we need—two hundred, five hundred—it's easy! My gold ring can be pawned. On our return we shall retrieve it. The book will see to that.'

I was never to see my ring again, but that did not matter. We managed to raise a hundred rupees, and with it we prepared ourselves feverishly for our journey, afraid that at the last moment something would prevent us from going.

We were to travel by train to the railway terminus, a night's journey, then take the bus. Though we hoped to be away for at least a week, our funds did not in fact last more than four days.

We locked our room, left the key with Kamla, and asked Deep Chand to keep an eye on both her and our things.

In the train that night Suraj had a mild fit. It helped reduce the numbers in our compartment. Some, thinking he suffered from a communicable disease, took themselves and their belongings elsewhere; others, used to living with illness, took no notice. But Suraj was not to have any more fits until we returned to Pipalnagar.

We slept fitfully that night, continually shifting our positions on the hard bench of the third-class compartment; Suraj with his head against my shoulder, I with my feet on my bedding roll. Above us, a Sikh farmer slept vigorously, his healthy snores reverberating through the compartment. A woman with her brood of four or five children occupied the bunk opposite; they had knocked over their earthen surahi, smashing it and flooding the compartment. Two young men in the corner played cards and exchanged lewd jokes. No general companionship was at all evident, but whenever the train drew into a station everyone cooperated in trying to prevent people on the outside from entering the already crowded compartment; and if someone did manage to get in— usually by crawling through a window—he would fall in with the same policy of keeping others out.

We woke in the early hours of the morning and looked out of the window at the changing landscape. It was so long since I had seen trees—not trees singly or in clumps, but forests of trees, thick and dark and broody, commencing at the railway tracks and stretching away to the foot hills. Trees full of birds and monkeys; and in the forest clearing we saw a deer, it's head raised, scenting the wind . . .

SEVENTEEN

There were many small hotels in the little town that straddled two or three hills; but Suraj and I went to a dharamsala where we were given a small room overlooking the valley. We did not spend much time there. There were too many hills and streams and trees inviting us on all sides; it seemed as though they had been waiting all those years for our arrival. Each tree has an individuality of its own—perhaps more individuality than a man—and if you look at a tree with a personal eye, it will give you something of itself, something deep and personal; its smell, its sap, its depth and wisdom.

So we mingled with the trees. We felt and understood the dignity of the pine, the weariness of the willow, the resignation of the oak. The blossoms had fallen from the plum and apricot trees, and the branches were bare, touched with the light green of new foliage. Pine needles made the ground soft and slippery, and we went sliding downhill on our bottoms.

Then we took paper and pencil and some mangoes, and went among some rocks, and there I wrote odd things that came into my head, about the hills and the sounds we heard.

The silence of the mountains was accentuated by the occasional sounds around us—a shepherd boy shouting to his mate, a girl singing to her cattle, the jingle of cow bells, a woman pounding clothes on a flat stone . . . Then, when these sounds stopped, there were quieter, subtler sounds—the singing of crickets, whistling of anonymous birds, the wind soughing in the pine trees . . .

It was hot in the sun, until a cloud came over, and then it was suddenly cool, and our shirts flapped against us in the breeze.

The hills went striding away into the distance. The nearest hill was covered with oak and pine, the next was brown and naked and topped with a white temple, like a candle on a fruit-cake. The furthest hill was a misty blue.

EIGHTEEN

The 'season' as they called it, was just beginning in the hills. Those who had money came to the hill-station for a few weeks, to parade up and down the Mall in a variety of costumes ranging from formal dinner jackets to cowboy jeans. There were the Anglicized élite, models of English gentry, and there was the younger set, imitating western youth as depicted in films and glossy magazines. Suraj and I felt out of place walking down the Mall in kameez and pyjamas; we were foreigners on our own soil. Were these really Indians exhibiting themselves, or were they ghastly caricatures of the West?

The town itself had gone to seed. English houses and cottages, built by unimaginative Victorians to last perhaps fifty years, were now over a hundred years old, all in a state of immediate collapse. No one repaired them, no one tore them down. Some had been built to look like Swiss chateaux, others like *Arabian Nights* castles, most like homely English cottages—all were out of place, incongruous oddities desecrating a majestic mountain.

Though the Sahibs had gone long ago, coolie-drawn rickshaws still plied the steep roads, transporting portly Bombay and Delhi businessmen and their shrill, quarrelsome wives from one end of the hill-station to the other. It was as though a community of wealthy Indians had colonized an abandoned English colony, and had gone native, adopting English clothes and attitudes.

*

A lonely place on a steep slope, hidden by a thicket of oaks through which the sun filtered warmly. We lay on crisp dry oak leaves, while a cool breeze fanned our naked bodies.

I wondered at the frail beauty of Suraj's body, at the transient beauty of all flesh, the vehicle of our consciousness. I thought of Kamla's body—firm, supple, economical, in spite of the indignities to which it had been put; of the body of a child, soft and warm and throbbing with vigour; the bodies of pot-bellied glandular males; and bodies bent and deformed and eaten away. . . . The armours of our consciousness, every hair from the head to the genitals a live and beautiful thing . . .

I believe in the death of flesh, but not in the end of living.

When, at the age of six, I saw my first mountain, it did not astonish me; it was something new and exhilarating, but all the same I felt I had known mountains before. Trees and flowers and rivers were not strange things. I had lived with them, too. In new places, new faces, we see the familiar. Even as children we are old in experience. We are not conscious of a beginning, only of an eternity.

Death must be an interval, a rest for a tired and misused body, which has to be destroyed before it can be renewed. But consciousness is a continuing thing.

Our very thoughts have an existence of their own.

Are we so unimaginative as to presume that life is confined to the shells that are our bodies? Science and religion have not even touched upon the mysteries of our existence.

Let me not confine myself to the few years between this birth and this death—which is, after all, only the period I can remember well . . .

In moments of rare intimacy two people are of one mind and one body, speaking only in thoughts, brilliantly aware of each other.

I have felt this way about Suraj even when he is far away; his thoughts hover about me, as they do now.

He lies beside me with his eyes closed and his head turned away, but all the time we are talking, talking, talking. . . .

*

To a temple on the spur of a hill. Scrambling down a slippery hillside, getting caught in thorny thickets, among sharp rocks; along a dry water-course, where we saw the skeleton of a jungle-cat, its long, sharp teeth still in perfect condition.

A footpath, winding round the hill to the temple; a forest of silver oaks shimmering in the breeze. Cool, sweet water bubbling out of the mountain side, the sweetest, most delicious water I have ever tasted, coming through rocks and ferns and green grasses.

Then up, up, up the steep mountain, where long-fingered cacti point to the sloping sky and pebbles go tumbling into the valley below. A giant langur, with a five-foot long tail, leaps from tree to jutting boulder, anxious lest we invade its domain among the unattended peach trees.

On top of the hill, a little mound of stones and a small cross. I wondered what lonely, romantic foreigner, so different from his countrymen, could have been buried here, where sky and mountain meet . . .

NINETEEN

T hough we had lost weight in the hills, through climbing and riding, the good clean air had sweetened our blood, and we felt like spartans on our return to Pipalnagar.

That Suraj was gaining in strength I know from the way he pinned me down when we wrestled on the sand near the old brickkilns. It was no longer necessary for me to yield a little to him.

Though his fits still occurred from time to time as they would continue to do—the anxiety and the death had gone from his eyes . . .

Suraj passed his examinations. We never doubted that he would. Still, neither of us could sleep the night before the results appeared. We lay together in the dark and spoke of many things— of living and dying, and the reason for all striving—we asked each other the same questions that thousands have asked themselves— and like those thousands, we had no answers, we could not even comfort ourselves with religion, because God eluded us.

Only once had I felt the presence of God. I woke one morning, and finding Suraj asleep beside me, was overcome by a tremendous happiness, and kept saying, 'Thank you, God, thank you for giving me Suraj . . .'

The newspapers came with the first bus, at six in the morning. A small crowd of students had gathered at the bus stop, joking with each other and hiding their nervous excitement with a hearty show of indifference.

There were not many passengers on the first bus, and there was a mad grab for the newspapers as the bundle landed with a thud on the pavement. Within half an hour the newsboy had sold all his copies. It was the only day of the year when he had a really substantial sale.

Suraj did not go down to meet the bus, but I did. I was more nervous than he, I think. And I ran my eye down the long columns of roll numbers so fast that I missed his number the first time. I began again, in a panic, then found it at the top of the list, among the successful ones.

I looked up at Suraj who was standing on the balcony of my room, and he could tell from my face that he had passed, and he smiled down at me. I joined him on the balcony, and we looked down at the other boys comparing newspapers, some of them exultant, some resigned; a few still hopeful, still studying the columns of roll numbers—each number representing a year's concentration on dull, ill-written text books.

Those who had failed had nothing to be ashamed of. They had failed through sheer boredom.

*

I had been called to Delhi for an interview, and I needed a shirt. The few I possessed were either torn at the shoulders or frayed at the collars. I knew writers and artists were not expected to dress very well, but I felt I was not in a position to indulge in eccentricities. Why display my poverty to an editor, of all people....

Where was I to get a shirt? Suraj generally wore an old red-striped T-shirt; he washed it every second evening, and by morning it was dry and ready to wear again; but it was tight even for him. What I needed was something white, something respectable.

I went to Deep Chand. He had a collection of shirts. He was only too glad to lend me one. But they were all brightly coloured things—yellow and purple and pink.... They would not impress an editor. No editor could possibly take a liking to an author who wore a pink shirt. They looked fine on Deep Chand when he was cutting people's hair.

Pitamber was also unproductive; he had only someone's pyjama coat to offer.

In desperation, I went to Kamla.

'A shirt?' she said. 'I'll soon get a shirt for you. Why didn't you ask me before? I'll have it ready for you in the morning.'

And not only did she produce a shirt next morning, but a pair

416

of silver cuff-links as well.

'Whose are these'? I asked.

'One of my visitors',' she replied with a shrug. 'He was about your size. As he was quite drunk when he went home, he did not realize that I had kept his shirt. He had removed it to show me his muscles, as I kept telling him he hadn't any to show. Not where it really mattered.'

I laughed so much that my belly ached (laughing on a half empty stomach is painful) and kissed the palms of Kamla's hands and told her she was wonderful.

*

Freedom.

The moment the bus was out of Pipalnagar, and the fields opened out on all sides, I knew I was free; that I had always been free; held back only by my own weakness, lacking the impulse and the imagination to break away from an existence that had become habitual for years.

And all I had to do was sit in a bus and go somewhere.

It had never occurred to me before. Only by leaving Pipalnagar could I help Suraj. Brooding in my room, I was no good to anyone.

I sat near the open window of the bus and let the cool breeze freshen my face. Herons and snipe waded among the lotus on flat green ponds; bluejays swooped around the telegraph poles; and children jumped naked into the canals that wound through the fields.

Because I was happy, it seemed that everyone else was happy—the driver, the conductor the passengers, the farmers in their fields, on their bullock-carts. When two women began quarrelling over a coat behind me, I intervened, and with tact and sweetness soothed their tempers. Then I took a child on my knee, and pointed out camels and buffaloes and vultures and pariah-dogs.

And six hours later the bus crossed the swollen river Yamuna, passed under the giant red walls of the fort built by Shahjahan, and entered the old city of Delhi.

TWENTY

The editor of the Urdu weekly had written asking me if I would care to be his literary editor; he was familiar with some of my earlier work—poems and stories—and had heard that my circumstances and the quality of my work had deteriorated. Though he did not promise me a job, and did not offer to pay my fare to Delhi, or give me any idea of what my salary might be, there was the offer and there was the chance—an opportunity to escape, to enter the world of the living, to write, to read, to explore . . .

On my second night in Delhi I wrote to Suraj from the station waiting room, resting the pad on my knee as I sat alone with my suitcase in one corner of the crowded room. Women chattered amongst themselves, or slept silently, children wandered about on the platform outside, babies cried or searched for their mothers' breasts . . .

*

Dear Suraj:

It is strange to be in a city again, after so many years of Pipalnagar. It is a little frightening, too. You suffer a loss of identity, as you feel your way through the indifferent crowds in Chandni Chowk late in the evening; you are an alien amongst the Westernized who frequent the restaurants and shops at Connaught Place; a stranger amongst one's fellow refugees who have grown prosperous now and live in the flat treeless colonies that have mushroomed around the city. It is only when I am near an old tomb or in the garden of a long-forgotten king, that I become conscious of my identity again.

I wish you had accompanied me. That would have made this an exciting, not an intimidating experience!

Anyway, I shall see you in a day or two. I think I have the job. I saw my editor this morning. He is from Hyderabad. Just imagine the vastness of our country, that it should take almost half a lifetime for a north Indian to meet a south Indian for the first time in his life.

I don't think my editor is very fond of north Indians, judging from some of his remarks about Punjabi traders and taxi-drivers in Delhi; but he liked what he called my unconventionality (I don't know if he meant my work or myself). I said I thought he was the unconventional one. This always pleases, and he asked me what salary I would expect if he offered me a position on his staff. I said three hundred; he said he might not manage to get me so much, but if they offered me one-fifty, would I accept? I said I would think about it and let him know the next day.

Now I am cursing myself for not having accepted it there and then; but I did not want to appear too eager or desperate, and I must not give the impression that a job is indispensable to me. I told him that I had actually come to Delhi to do some research for a book I intended writing about the city. He asked me the title, and I thought quickly and said, 'Delhi Is Still Far'—Nizamuddin's comment when told that Tughlaq Shah was marching to Delhi—and he was suitably impressed.

Thinking about it now, perhaps it would be a good idea to do a book about Delhi—its cities and kings, poets and musicians. . . . I walked the streets all day, wandering through the bazaars, down the wide shady roads of the capital, resting under the jamun trees near Humayun's tomb, and thinking all the time of what you and I can do here; and while I wander about Delhi, you must

419

be wandering around Pipalnagar, with that wonderful tray of yours . . .

*

Chandni Chowk has not changed in character even if its face has a different look. It is still the heart of Delhi, still throbbing with vitality—more so perhaps, with the advent of the enterprising Punjabi. The old buildings and landmarks are still there, the lanes and alleys are as tortuous and mysterious as ever. Travellers and cloth merchants and sweetmeats-sellers may have changed name and character, but their professions have not given place to new ones. And if on a Sunday the shops must close, they may spill out on the pavement and across the tramlines—toys, silks, cottons, glassware, china, basket-work, furniture, carpets, perfumes—it is as busy as on any market-day and the competition is louder and more fierce.

In front of the Town Hall the statue of Queen Victoria frowns upon the populace, as ugly as all statues, flecked with pigeon droppings. The pigeons, hundreds of them sit on the railings and the telegraph wires, their drowsy murmuring muted by the sounds of the street, the cries of vendors and tonga drivers and the rattle of the tram.

The tram is a museum-piece. I don't think it has been replaced since it was first installed over fifty years ago. It crawls along the crowded thoroughfare, clanging at an impatient five miles an hour, bursting at the seams with its load of people, while urchins hang on by their toes and eyebrows.

An ash-smeared ascetic sits at the side of the road, and cooks himself a meal; a juggler is causing a traffic jam; a man has a lotus tattooed on his forearm. From the balcony of the Sonehri the invader Nadir Shah watched the slaughter of Delhi's citizens. I walked down the Dariba, famed street of the Silversmiths, and find myself at the steps of the Jama Masjid, surrounded by bicycle shops, junk shops, fish shops, bird shops, and fat goats ready for slaughter.

Cities and palaces have risen and fallen on the plains of Delhi, but Chandni Chowk is indestructible, the heart of both old and new . . .

*

All night long I hear the shunting and whistling of engines, and like a child I conjure up visions of places with sweet names like Kumbekonam, Krishnagiri, Mahabalipuram and Polonnarurawa; dreams of palm-fringed beaches and inland lagoons; of the echoing chambers of some deserted city, red sandstone and white marble; of temples in the sun, and elephants crossing wide slow-moving rivers . . .

Ours is a land of many people, many races; their diversity gives it colour and character. For all Indians to be alike would be as dull as for all sexes to be the same, or for all humans to be normal. In Delhi, too, there is a richness of race, though the Punjabi predominates—in shops, taxis, motor workshops and carpenters' sheds. But in the old city there are still many Muslims following traditional trades—bakers, butchers, painters, makers of toys and kites. South Indians have filled our offices; Rajasthanis move dexterously along the scaffolding of new buildings springing up every where; and in the surrounding countryside nomadic Gujjars still graze their cattle, while settled villagers find their lands selected for trails of new tubewells, pumps, fertilizers and ploughs.

*

The city wakes early. The hour before sunrise is the only time when it is possible to exercise. Once the sun is up, people must take refuge beneath fans or in the shade of jamun and neem trees. September in Delhi is sultry and humid, relieved only by an occasional monsoon downpour. In the old city there is always the danger of cholera; in the new capital, people fall ill from sitting too long in air-conditioned cinemas and restaurants.

At noon the streets are almost empty; but early in the morning everyone is about, young and old, shopkeeper and clerk, taxi driver and shoeshine boy, flooding the maidans and open spaces in their vests and underwear. Some sprint around the maidans; some walk briskly down the streets, swinging their arms like soldiers; young men wrestle, or play volley-ball or kabaddi; others squat on their haunches, some stand on their heads; some pray, facing the sun; some study books, mumbling to themselves, or make speeches to vast, invisible audiences; scrub their teeth with neem twigs, bathe at public taps, wash clothes, tie dhotis or turbans and go about their business.

The sun is up, clerks are asleep with their feet up at their desks, government employees drink innumerable cups of tea, and the machinery of bureaucracy and civilization runs on as smoothly as ever.

TWENTY-ONE

S uraj was on the platform when the Pipalnagar Express steamed into the station in the early hours of a warm late September morning. I wanted to shout to him from the carriage window, to tell him that everything was well, that the world was wonderful, and that I loved him and the world and everything in it.

But I couldn't say anything until we had left the station and I was drinking hot tea on the string-bed in our room.

'It is three hundred a month,' I said, 'but we should be able to manage on that, if we are careful. And now that you have done your matriculation, you will be able to join the Polytechnic. So we will-both be busy. And when we are not working, we shall have all Delhi to explore. It will be better in the city. One should live either in a city or in a village. In a village, everyone knows you intimately. In a city, no one has the slightest interest in you. But in a town like Pipalnagar, everyone knows you, nobody loves you; when you die, you are forgotten; while you live, you are only a subject for malicious conversation. Poor Pipalnagar. . . . Will you be sorry to leave the place, Suraj?'

'Yes, I will be sorry. This is where I have lived.

'This is where I've existed. I only began to live when I realized I could leave the place.'

'When we went to the hills?'

'When I met you.'

'How did I change anything? I am still an additional burden.

'You have made me aware of who and what I am.'

'I don't understand.'

'I don't want you to. That would spoil it.'

*

423

There was no rent to be paid before we left, as Seth Govind Ram's Munshi had taken it in advance, and there were five days to go before the end of the month; there was little chance of the balance being returned to us.

Deep Chand was happy to know that we were leaving. 'I shall follow you soon,' he said. 'There is money to be made in Delhi, cutting hair. Why, even girls are beginning to keep short hair. I shall keep a special saloon for ladies, which Ramu can attend. Women feel safe with him, he looks so pretty and innocent.'

Ramu winked at me in the mirror. I could not imagine anyone less innocent. Girls going to school and college still complained that he harassed them and threatened to remove their pigtails with his razor.

The snip of Deep Chand's scissors lulled me to sleep as I sat in his chair; his fingers beat a rhythmic tattoo on my scalp; his razor caressed by cheeks. It was my last shave, and Deep Chand did not charge me anything. I promised to write to him as soon as I had settled down in Delhi.

*

Kamla had gone home for a few days. Her village was about five miles from Pipalnagar in the opposite direction to Pitamber's, among the mustard and wheat fields that sloped down to the banks of the little water-course. I worked my way downstream until I came to the fields.

I waited behind some trees on the outskirts of the village until I saw her playing with a little boy; I whistled and stepped out of the trees, but when she saw me she motioned me back, and took the child into one of the small mud houses.

I waited amongst the sal trees until I heard footsteps a short distance away.

'Where are you?' I called, but received no answer. I walked in the direction of the footsteps, and found a small path going through the trees. After a short distance the path turned to meet a stream, and Kamla was waiting there.

'Why didn't you wait for me?' I asked.

'I wanted to see if you could follow me.'

'Well, I am good at it,' I said, sitting down beside her on the bank of the stream. The water was no more than ankle-deep, cool and clear. I took off my shoes, rolled up my trousers, and put my feet in the water. Kamla was barefooted, and so she had to tuck up her sari a little, before slipping her feet in.

With my feet I churned up the mud at the bottom of the stream. As the mud subsided, I saw her face reflected in the water; and looking up at her again, into her dark eyes, I wanted to care for her and protect her, I wanted to take her away from Pipalnagar; I wanted her to live like other people. Of course, I had forgotten all about my poor finances.

I kissed the tips of her fingers, then her neck. She ran her fingers through my hair. The rain began splatting down and Kamla said, 'Let us go.'

We set off. Soon the rain began pelting down. Kamla shook herself free and we dashed for cover. She was breathing heavily and I kissed her again. Kamla's hair came loose and streamed down her body. We had to hop over pools, and avoid the soft mud. And then I thought she was crying, but I wasn't sure, it might have been the raindrops on her cheeks, and her heavy breathing.

'Come with me,' I said. 'Come away from Pipalnagar.'

She smiled.

'Why can't you come?'

'Because you really do not want me to. For you, a woman would only be a liability. You are free like birds, you and Suraj, you can go where you like and do as you like. I cannot help you in any way. And what use is a woman to a man if she cannot help him? I have helped you to pass your time in Pipalnagar. That is something. I am part of this place. Neither Pipalnagar nor I can change. But you can, simply by going away.'

'Will you come later, once I have started making a living in Delhi?'

'I am married, it is as simple as that . . .'

'If it is that simple, you can come.'

'I have to think of my parents, you know. It would ruin them if I ran away.'

'Yes, but they do not care if they have broken your heart.'

She shrugged and looked away towards the village. 'I am not so unhappy. He is an old fool, my husband, and I get some fun out of teasing him. He will die one day, and so will the Seth, and then I will be free.'

'Will you?'

'Why not? And anyway, you can always come to see me, and nobody will be made unhappy by it.'

I felt sad and frustrated but I couldn't take my frustration out on anyone or anything.

'It was Suraj, not I, who stole your heart,' she said.

She touched my face softly and then abruptly ran towards her little hut. She waved once and then was gone.

TWENTY-TWO

At six every morning the first bus arrives, and the passengers alight, looking sleepy and dishevelled, and rather depressed at the sight of our Mohalla. When they have gone their various ways, the bus is driven into the shed. and the road is left clear for the arrival of the municipal van. The cows congregate at the dustbin, and the pavement dwellers come to life, stretching their dusty limbs on the hard stone steps. I carry the bucket up three steps to my room, and bathe for the last time on the open balcony. Our tin trunks are packed, and Suraj's tray is empty.

At Pitamber's village the buffaloes are wallowing in green ponds, while naked urchins sit astride them, scrubbing their backs, and a crow or water-bird purchases on a glistening neck. The parrots are busy in the crooked tree, and a slim green snake basks in the sun on our island near the brick-kiln. In the hills, the mists have lifted and the distant mountains are covered with snow.

It is autumn, and the rains are over. The earth meets the sky in one broad sweep of the creator's brush.

*

A land of thrusting hills. Terraced hills, wood-covered and windswept. Mountains where the gods speak gently to the lonely heart. Hills of green and grey rock, misty at dawn, hazy at noon, molten at sunset; where fierce fresh torrents rush to the valleys below.

A quiet land of fields and ponds, shaded by ancient trees and ringed with palms, where sacred rivers are touched by temples; where temples are touched by the southern seas.

This is the real land, the land I should write about. My Mohalla is but a sickness, a wasting disease, and I should turn aside from it

427

to sing instead of the splendours of tomorrow. But only yesterdays are splendid. . . . . There are other singers, sweeter than I, to sing of tomorrow. I can only sing of today, of Pipalnagar, where I have lived and loved.

Yesterday I was sad, and tomorrow I may be sad again, but today I know that I am happy. I want to live on and on, delighting like a pagan in all that is physical; and I know that this one lifetime, however long, cannot satisfy my heart.

READ MORE IN PENGUIN

In every corner of the world, on every subject under the sun. Penguin represents quality and variety—the very best in publishing today.

For complete information about books available from Penguin—including Puffin, Penguin Classics and Arkana—and how to order them, write to us at the appropriate address below. Please note that for copyright reasons the selection of books varies from country to country.

In India: Please write to *Penguin Books India Pvt. Ltd. 11, Community Centre, Panchsheel Park, New Delhi, 110017*

In the United Kingdom: Please write to *Dept JC, Penguin Books Ltd. Bath Road, Harmondsworth, West Drayton, Middlesex, UB7 0DA, UK*

In the United States: Please write to *Penguin Putnam Inc., 375 Hudson Street, New York, NY 10014*

In Canada: Please write to *Penguin Books Canada Ltd. 10 Alcorn Avenue, Suite 300; Toronto, Ontario M4V 3B2*

In Australia: Please write to *Penguin Books Australia Ltd. 487, Maroondah Highway, Ring Wood, Victoria 3134*

In New Zealand: Please write to *Penguin Books (NZ) Ltd. Private Bag, Takapuna, Auckland 9*

In the Netherlands: Please write to *Penguin Books Netherlands B.V., Keizersgracht 231 NL-1016 DV Amsterdam*

In Germany: Please write to *Penguin Books Deutschland GmbH, Metzlerstrasse 26, 60595 Frankfurt am Main, Germany*

In Spain: Please write to *Penguin Books S.A., Bravo Murillo, 19-I'B, E-28015 Madrid Spain*

In Italy: Please write to *Penguin Italia s.r.l., Via Felice Casati 20, I-20104 Milano*

In France: Please write to *Penguin France S.A., 17 rue Lejeune, F-31000 Toulouse*

In Japan: Please write to *Penguin Books Japan, Ishikiribashi Building, 2-5-4 Suido, Tokyo 112*

In Greece: Please write to Penguin Hellas Ltd, dimocritou 3, GR-106 71 Athens

In South Africa: Please write to *Longman Penguin Books Southern Africa (Pty) Ltd, Private Bag X08, Bertsham 2013*

ROOM ON THE ROOF
Ruskin Bond

Unhappy with the strict ways of his English
guardian, Rusty runs away from home to live
with Indian friends. Plunging for the first time
into the dream-bright world of the *bazaar*, Hindu
festivals and other aspects of Indian life. Rusty
is enchanted . . . and is lost forever to the prime
proprieties of the European community.

'Has a special magic of its own'
—*Herald Tribune Book Review*

'Considerable charm and spontaneity . . .'
—*San Francisco Chronicle*

'Very engaging . . .
—*The Guardian*

'Moving in its simplicity and underlying
tenderness . . . a novel of marked originality.'
—*The Scotsman*

'Mr Bond is a writer of great gifts . . .'
—*The New Statesman*

OUR TREES STILL GROW IN DEHRA
Ruskin Bond

Semi-autobiographical in nature, these stories span the period from the author's childhood to the present. We are introduced, in a series of beautifully imagined and crafted cameos, to the author's family, friends, and various other people who left a lasting impression on him. In other stories we revisit Bond's beloved Garhwal hills and the small towns and villages that he has returned to time and time again in his fiction.

Together with his well-known novella, *A Flight of Pigeons* (which was made into the film *Junoon*), which also appears in this collection, these stories once again bring Ruskin Bond's India vividly to life.

TIME STOPS AT SHAMLI
Ruskin Bond

Ruskin Bond's characters—who live for the most part in the country's small towns and villages—are not the sort who make the headlines but are, nonetheless, remarkable for their quiet heroism, their grace under pressure and the manner in which they continue to cleave to the old values: honesty, fidelity, a deep-rooted faith in God, family and their neighbour. They do have problems, of course—the sudden death of a loved parent, unfulfilled dreams, natural calamities, ghostly visitations, a respected teacher gone crooked, strangers who make a nuisance of themselves in a town marooned in time—but these are solved with a minimum of fuss and tremendous dignity. Taken together these stories are a magnificent evocation of the real India by one of the country's foremost writers.

'An educative, charming and often memorable onetime read . . . .'

—Sunday Observer

'An enjoyable rustic trip back in time.'

—Straits Times